04

D0611165

The
Responsible Scholar

Ethical Considerations
in the Humanities and Social Sciences

GÉRALD BERTHOUD

and

BEAT SITTER-LIVER

Editors

Watson Publishing International
1996

First published in the United States of America
by Watson Publishing International
Post Office Box 493
Canton, MA 02021

© Watson Publishing International 1996
ISBN 0-88135-165-2

Sole distributor for Europe, excluding Great Britain:
Universitätsverlag Freiburg, Switzerland
ISBN 3-7278-1057-2

Library of Congress Cataloging-in-Publication Data

The responsible scholar : ethical considerations in the humanities and social
sciences / Gérald Berthoud and Beat Sitter-Liver, editors.
    p.   cm.
    Papers from the 2nd Conference of the Swiss Scientific Academies, held
1993 in Aeschi bei Spiez, Switzerland.
    Includes bibliographical references and index.
    ISBN 0-88135-165-2 (hard cover : alk. paper)
    1. Learning and scholarship—Moral and ethical aspects—Congresses.
2. Scholars—Professional ethics—Congresses. 3. Humanities—Moral and
ethical aspects—Congresses. 4. Social sciences—Moral and ethical
aspects—Congresses. 5. Professional ethics—Congresses. I. Berthoud,
Gérald. II. Sitter-Liver, Beat, 1939– III. Conference of the Swiss Scientific
Academies (2nd : 1993 : Aeschi bei Spiez, Switzerland)
AZ101.R47 1996
001.3—dc20   95-53708
                                                          CIP

Designed and Manufactured in the U.S.A.

Contents

MORAL AND SOCIAL LIMITS TO THE MARKET MODEL

THE PRODUCTION OF KNOWLEDGE ETHICALLY CHALLENGED

RESPONSIBLE CHOICE AND USE OF METHODS

EPILOGUE

Published on behalf of the
Conference of the Swiss Scientific Academies
Swiss Academy of Engineering Sciences
Swiss Academy of Humanities and Social Sciences
Swiss Academy of Medical Sciences
Swiss Academy of Sciences

Acknowledgments

In 1988, the Conference of the Swiss Scientific Academies, led by the Swiss Academy of Humanities and Social Sciences, staged an interdisciplinary symposium devoted to the reflection of responsibility in scientific, medical, and technological research. (The results of that conference can be found in *Scientists and Their Responsibility*, ed. by W.R. Shea and B. Sitter-Liver, Canton MA: Watson Publishing International 1989.) Five years later, the Conference furthered its endeavor with a second symposium focusing on ethical aspects of research in the humanities and social sciences.

The editors wish to thank the Conference of the Swiss Scientific Academies (Swiss Academy of Engineering Sciences; Swiss Academy of Humanities and Social Sciences; Swiss Academy of Medical Sciences; Swiss Academy of Sciences) for providing the intellectual and financial support that made the meeting and this book possible. They also wish to acknowledge the editorial assistance provided by Alessandro Lazzari (University of Fribourg, Switzerland), Linda Bolzern (Berne), and Kathrin Pieren and Veronique Ischi (Swiss Academy of Humanities and Social Sciences). Finally, they would like to acknowledge their publisher's patience, understanding, and efficiency in the production of this book.

Abbreviations

NIH	National Institutes of Health (USA)
BIS	Bank for International Settlements
OECD	Organization of Economic Cooperation and Development
NIRA	Japanese Institute for Research Advancement
UNESCO	United Nations Educational, Scientific and Cultural Organization
UNCAST	United Nations Conference on the Application of Science and Technology Development
R&D	Research and Development
APA	American Psychological Association
UN	United Nations
IIPT	International Institute for Peace through Tourism
UNEP	United Nations Environmental Programme
NSDAP	Nationalsozialistische Deutsche Arbeiterpartei
EDA	Exploratory Data Analysis
HUGO	Human Genome Sequencing Project

Foreword

To reflect upon freedom and responsibility in the fragmented world of the humanities and social sciences, or for simplicity's sake "the human sciences"—characterized as they are by disciplinary separation and mutual isolation—is, to say the least, an uneasy task. Raising moral issues within the realm of research and teaching is still widely considered an impossible undertaking, or is simply judged devoid of any importance. Thus it seems almost hopeless to try to reconcile the traditional "subjectivism" of humanities with the overeager and endless quest for objectivism in a predominant part of social sciences. And then, the ethical challenge is often taken simply as a nuisance and a barrier to so-called scientific progress, which is considered an indisputable aim in itself.

However, a growing number of scholars hold it ever more urgent to develop their consciousness as to the limits of scientific freedom, and they admit the growing weight of the various responsibilities they ought to assume as members of a national society. They feel pressed to focus on moral issues raised by the dramatic problems our world is facing.

If we wish to tackle that complex and difficult field of inquiry with some chance of success, we first have to establish a common ground—some sort of a frame to assure our collective endeavor the necessary coherence. Consider, therefore, that freedom and responsibility within the human sciences may be made a topic starting from four particular points of view:

1. To begin with, any specific domain or any particular sphere of organized knowledge may be viewed as an autonomous order. This entails, quite obviously, the demand for self-organization and, as a

consequence, self-regulation—*freedom* as it were. Institutionally, such an order is sometimes seen as a scientific community in which knowledge is shared through an exchange system based on gift. More often, however, the order is interpreted as a scientific market, with scientists as intellectual entrepreneurs. In both cases, the actors either have to collaborate in order to gain intellectual recognition, or they must compete, in a self-interested way, for the truth in their particular area of competence. According to the adopted view the question of responsibility pertains in different ways. There is no doubt that knowledge gained in specialized fields has produced important results, even though methodological and theoretical divergence among representatives of the same field are very often patent. Notwithstanding those divergences, there is always tacit agreement on some basic principles which form the minimal conditions for the definition of a specific research domain.

2. It should, however, be clear that insulating any particular scientific order, or considering it in isolation, is increasingly inadequate. That procedure would result in imprisoning oneself within a self-referential order, which does not lead anywhere. Any particular field, although partially autonomous, is embedded in a broader scientific order. Every responsible scholar must therefore seek out the relations connecting his or her work to other fields within the gamut of human sciences—the encompassing whole. While specific fields of knowledge are but fragments and are, ideally, complementary in the search for truth, they are in fact conceived of by a large majority of specialists as competitive, or placed within a hierarchical order of cognitive and practical hegemony. Scholarly responsibility would demand the abandonment of this pseudo-free way of looking at things and defending one's own socio-intellectual interests, in favor of assuming a more inclusive view.

3. As soon as we consider, apart from any disciplinary reflection, the object on which the various research approaches are focused, questions of objectivity, universality, and truth are inextricably linked with the problem of value. The contention of ethical neutrality must be rejected without exception. The tension between cognitive and normative requirements with scholarly investigation imposes a fundamental interrogation as to the kind of method to be chosen in order to get the most reliable data, while showing the greatest respect for those who are the objects of research. Freedom of research is intensely linked to the responsibility of understanding the involved persons. For a responsible scholar, there is no way to escape the dilemma

between scientific rules and ethical considerations. Any scholar must be fully aware of his or her potential harm-doing capacity. Hence the epistemological imperative and the ethical obligation to thoroughly consider the relationship between the subject and the object constitutive of any research, and to form that relationship in compliance with the principle of human dignity. In contrast with a still commonly accepted disjunction, morality ought to be an integral part of all scientific procedures striving for knowledge. Even though it might sound odd to many ears, a scientist must also be a moralist, without, however, confusing the two roles.

4. Finally, human sciences as a set of quite specialized social activities are inextricably situated within the broader societal context. Although society may grant them relative autonomy, they are, in every one of their particular fields, confronted with various external demands and pressures urging them to contribute to solutions for individual and collective problems. The coercion embodied in the ever-increasing demand for social usefulness does restrict the freedom of action of a great number of scholars; they may even see themselves driven to adjust their research activities to strictly utilitarian objectives. Since public and private grants flow more readily for research activities directed towards such objectives, scholars tend to orient their activities towards the socially and politically imposed directions. This puts the human sciences in front of a heavy scientific as well as ethical responsibility, both on the individual and collective levels. Taken within a pervasive utilitarian culture, they quite spontaneously tend to be in accordance with such cultural rules. But does following this track, even with technical competence, mean that we comply with our moral responsibility? Are we not much more obliged to question the mainstream views, taking into account the actual pressure of financial penury and other threats against freedom of thought throughout the world, considering the danger we face of being even further driven into an unsustainable natural and social environment? Do we not have, at one and the same time, the obligation to make alternative voices heard and to open paths for unorthodox but promising approaches, which are very often simply discarded? These are but a few examples of many new and hitherto unexpected questions which are still considered devoid of any particular relevance by the prevailing research trends.

The objective of this volume, in keeping with the four points raised above, is to defend the view that human sciences are already concerned, but must increasingly deal with the moral dimensions of their activities.

In a quite stimulating and sometimes provocative way, the essays of the book provide various attempts to broaden our consciousness of and deepen our insight into such issues. They try to elaborate ideas and proposals for developing empirical research and teaching based on a number of fundamental moral rules. They shed some light on the responsibilities we must assume as social beings within various collective entities, for example as members of a faculty or as citizens of a state. But they also emphasize our obligations as human beings who ought to be conscious of the unity of the human species, and should therefore participate in a worldwide effort to create and organize what could be labeled, granted the necessary optimism, a truly international community.

While humanities and social sciences have to deal with crucial issues, they must never forget that their normative horizon may extend not only to what is possible for today's humanity, but also to what might be the conditions for a truly humane life in the future.

The Editors

The Focus:
Dignity of Man, Dignity of Creation

Responsibility Towards Creation

PETER SALADIN

INTRODUCTION

It is—or should be—common knowledge that man has learned to harm the dignity of creation on a very large scale and in a radical way. The topic of my paper is the question whether or not the humanities and social sciences have a responsibility in this drama, whether or not they have a duty (and a chance) to fight against such harm-doing, and whether or not they have the appropriate means to do so.

Before entering into this rather ambitious discussion I feel obliged to make three preliminary statements.

1. Freedom and Responsibility of Natural Sciences

In the Gerzensee symposium[1] we discussed mainly the topic of freedom and responsibility of natural sciences—in a broad sense of the term—holding that from such sciences, more than from any others, or more exactly from the application of their results, heavy dangers arise for dignity and survival of creation. In my Gerzensee paper[2] I tried to draw a legal line between freedom of such sciences and their responsibility, calling in particular for legal provisions limiting freedom of research by the "respect of life in dignity of human beings and of animals and plants, in short, of all beings." I still am convinced that such a legal limit should be brought into international, constitutional, or statute law, but I shall not deal with it in my new paper, at least not at great length.

2.   Harm-Doing Capacity of Humanities and of Social Sciences?

The question arises, then, whether or not such provisions should become effective exclusively for natural sciences, or for humanities and for social sciences as well. And, using a broad perspective so as to cover every scientific activity, we should discuss, in the context of our present colloquium, the question of whether humanities and social sciences have any harm-doing capacity at all, or more precisely, if they are in a position to harm dignity of creation.

It would certainly be imprudent to deny such harm-doing capacity categorically. Let me put forward some examples:

- Sociological, ethnological, anthropological theories pretending the superiority of this or that human race can, as we know from terrible experience, lead to suppression or even extinction of human beings;
- Sociological and psychological research can hurt its "objects";[3]
- Empirical social research can damage a person badly by handling him or her in an undignified way or by making his or her name public in a bad context;
- Economic theories may have a very great (indirect) impact on the chances of economic survival, for thousands and even millions of human beings;[4]
- Economic theories can lead as well (indirectly) to the destruction of extra-human nature: of landscapes, of biotopes, of species, of a sound natural environment as a whole. As a matter of fact, a pure and unlimited market economy must lead to such destruction, because those natural goods have no "natural" price and seem therefore to be free for everyone's unlimited consumption or even destruction;[5]
- Historical research can lead to qualifications of persons whose offspring may feel badly hurt in their personal or their family's dignity;
- A certain theological interpretation of the Holy Scriptures (namely: Gen. 1, 28) has had greatest (negative) impact on nature.[6]

These examples show, in my view, quite clearly that research within the frame of humanities and of social sciences is by no means exempt from harm-doing. Of course, it is usually not the result of such research itself which hurts people or nature, but the use made thereof by governments or private powers. However, in natural sciences this is equally true, and it is neither here nor there a strong argument against responsibility of those engaged in scientific activities; this again has been discussed in the Gerzensee symposium. It is probably even not true that the harm-doing capacities of human and social sciences are necessarily narrower than those of natural sciences. Philosophy or theology, taken in its broadest sense, is the source and foundation of every major historical development, be it constructive or destructive. So we have to accept the idea that the legal provisions mentioned above will have to be observed, theoretically and practically, both by natural and by non-natural sciences.

3. Dignity of Man or Dignity of Creation?

You may have noticed that up to now I have spoken of "dignity of creation" and not specifically of "dignity of man." Of course I did so by intention. According to the introductory paper written by Beat Sitter-Liver on behalf of the group that prepared this symposium I have to consider not only dignity of man, but also dignity of other created beings, in short of all earthly creatures, or of the whole creation. This concept may sound to some of you rather revolutionary, and so might my strange habit of avoiding mention specifically of dignity of man. Of course such dignity is included, but this is just the point: it is included in a bigger concept; it does not stand for itself. This way of thinking needs some explanation.

DIGNITY OF CREATION

Dignity of man is an old category, developed in European enlightenment philosophy, particularly by Immanuel Kant, but obviously rooted in much older strata of philosophical and theological history.[7] After the Second World War the concept was revitalized, particularly in Germany, in order to construct a bulwark against atrocities such as had been cruelly experienced in the years before. The new German constitution of 1949 starts, in its first article, with the recognition of undestroyable human dignity.[8] The idea was taken up in international law as well, in the UN Charter and, in 1948, by the Universal Declaration of Human Rights. As a matter of fact, the modern human rights movement—one of the most important achievements in post-war international law—is nothing other than the primary concretization of the principle of human dignity.[9]

In such thinking, human dignity usually appeared as something unique and incomparable; dignity seemed to be a category appropriate exclusively to human beings. In other cultural traditions, however, dignity has been attributed to human beings and to non-human creatures as well. This is true for Indian,[10] and also for some African cultures. But even in the European tradition there were such wider positions taken—let us remember Saint Francis of Assisi, or Albert Schweitzer. In recent times the idea of dignity belonging to all creation of nature, be it human or not, was developed systematically by philosophers like Beat Sitter-Liver and others.[11]

Very recently it was even brought into the Swiss federal constitution, as a principle governing legislation with regard to genetic engineering.[12]

I personally have been convinced by such theories. However, in saying yes to dignity of human and of non-human beings, I stress the fact that such dignity cannot and must not be the same for all its subjects. Human dignity has its specific realm, and its specific weight. It is not identical with the dignity of animals or plants or rivers. But human beings as well as animals and plants have been created by God, thus they are not at the entirely free disposal of any (human) being. They have all (probably) been outfitted with impulses and inclinations—particularly with the impulse to live and to survive—and at least some of them are equipped with a whole range of emotions. Man therefore has to respect his "fellow-beings" as equal in the sense of being equally created by God—and as necessary for his own survival! In fact, man should consider the ensemble of natural creatures as a community in which he has his proper, specific, enhanced position, as a "polis" (Beat Sitter-Liver).[13] Two consequences are to be drawn immediately from such a concept: Man is not allowed to destroy, damage, or make suffer parts of nature except where it is unavoidable for his own survival. And man has no right to leave nature in a worse condition, particularly in lesser variety, than he found it in the moment of his birth.[14]

This is a short résumé of a very complex theory. I shall not elaborate on these subjects any further, and in particular I shall not try to discuss the possibility of avoiding damages to dignity of creation caused in specific humanities or in specific social sciences. I do not have the necessary qualifications to do so, and I must leave such (very important) discussion to the representatives of the disciplines concerned, in fact every single discipline.

In what follows I shall concentrate not on the defensive, but on the constructive aspect of our problem: What can humanities and social sciences contribute to enhance and to strengthen dignity of creation?

HOW CAN HUMANITIES AND SOCIAL SCIENCES CONTRIBUTE TO THE PROMOTION OF DIGNITY?

Research Assessment through Research

As I have mentioned above, research in the field of natural and technical sciences is not necessarily more likely or capable of harming dignity of creation than research in any other field. Thus the question arises if any research with harm-doing potentiality should not be accompanied by a different kind of research bound to assess that potential. This idea has been developed recently by the German philosopher Klaus Meyer-Abich. Meyer-Abich asks for complementary research activities which go far beyond a mere "technology assessment."[15] His goal is a narrow and systematic cooperation between natural and technical scientists prepared to open up new fields of scientific recognition, on the one hand, and researchers in the fields of social sciences and humanities who are to embed those new results in the cultural, political, and socio-economic context on the other. Are possible new research results capable of fitting into such given contexts? In what ways will they probably contribute to change given cultural, political, socio-economic conditions? How should such probable changes be evaluated? Such research work has been done in different countries, of course, with regard to specific technologies, namely the so-called peaceful use of atomic energy, in the context of technology assessment.[16] But such research has covered technologies and not the elaboration of their scientific foundations; thus it has always risked coming too late in the process of research, development, and application, i.e., when the pressure to develop a new technology or its application was already too heavy. The point of Meyer-Abich's suggestion, however, is to call for systematic cooperation from the very beginning of a new research and development strategy in the field of natural and technical sciences. Such cooperation should be—as postulated for technology assessment also by Frieder Naschold[17]—"constructive," i.e., it should include discussions about possible alternatives to specific research plans considered to be too risky. Of course, theoretically the same method of interdisciplinary cooperation should take place if new research strategies implying risks of far-reaching alterations are planned in other fields, e.g., in economics. Meyer-Abich does not see the cooperation which he postulates as a means of systematically controlling natural scientists and technicians. He simply wants natural and social scientists (among others) to consider together systematically the non-scientific implications of planned (and on-going) research and development work. Such cooperation of course needs adequate procedures and organization. "Eine sozial- und geisteswissenschaftliche Begleitforschung in der hier vorgeschlagenen Form ist bisher meines Wissens noch nicht versucht worden. Sie wäre aber notwendig, damit die beiden Wissenschaftsgruppen ihrer Verantwortung für die gesellschaftliche Tragweite von Innovation soweit gerecht werden, wie dies wissenschaftlich möglich ist."[18]

I am personally convinced that major research projects with obvious and considerable harm-doing potential should systematically—which means, among other things, from their very beginning—be accompanied by such assessment research. Unfortunately, this is usually not the case; certainly not in my own country. Let me give you some examples of projects which need, in my opinion, such accompaniment: "Schwerpunktprogramme" (priority programs) of the Swiss National Foundation, and the programs within the

European Cooperation in the Field of Scientific and Technical Research (COST) in which the European Union participates. Such examples show, I hope convincingly, that Meyer-Abich's idea will find a broad and significant field of application.

But I would like to extend his proposition to another dimension. I think that those who are engaged in humanities or in social sciences should try to help natural scientists and technicians in a more general way to recognize the various impacts of new important research and development projects and strategies. They should make clear to them (and first, of course, to themselves) that it cannot make sense, on our present level of civilization and particularly of scientific recognition and technical competence, to realize new important research projects or strategies in an isolated manner, within the hermetic atmosphere of laboratories. Science has changed the world in manifold ways—a very trivial statement. Science will continue to change the world, but it should do so consciously, with open eyes, with the utmost regard to possible consequences for our political, cultural, socio-economic situation. Human and social scientists should—by doing adequate research work, by systematically participating in the training of scientists and technicians, by going public with important insights—help to create an atmosphere of broad, "cultural" consciousness. In such an atmosphere it would be easier to discuss rationally the limits which should be respected by research and development intentions.

Original Contributions

But of course humanities and social sciences should not only contribute to the promotion of dignity by reacting to potentially harmful research projects in other fields. They should rather ask themselves in what ways they can make proper, original contributions on their own initiative in order to lay foundations upon which many other research projects—and many other human activities quite generally—may be based. Here again, I would not dare to establish something like an overall catalogue of corresponding research projects in the whole range of humanities and social sciences. Let me try, however, to present some examples in fields which are more or less familiar to me.

One of the most important fields, in this respect, is of course ethics, either philosophical or theological. However, I will leave it aside because it is, in our context, the most discussed one, and because other participants are in a better position to tackle it.

In my proper discipline, *constitutional* and *administrative law*, there is a major need for research on the very substance of dignity. This is true for the concept of dignity of man—a concept or a principle well-established and recognized in international and national constitutional law but far from being sufficiently clarified.[19] Research on the concept of human dignity requires systematic cooperation with other disciplines—anthropology, ethics (religious and non-religious), sociology, psychology, etc. Even more, the concept of creatural dignity has to be illuminated by multidisciplinary research. In the legal field alone several sub-disciplines must make their contributions: constitutional, private, penal and administrative law, all turning around a new concept of "rights of nature." The results of such research can and shall be the basis (or, to be more modest: a basis) for several kinds of political, administrative, private decisions.

One actual example is that of genetic research on human beings, plants, and animals. The Swiss constitution was complemented, almost one year ago, by an amendment covering the application of medicine of procreation, and of genetic research and engineering. Its second paragraph embraces the following points: the prohibition of interference with the genetic makeup of human gametes and embryos; of the implantation of non-human gametes or genotypes into human ones; of the donation of embryos; of surrogate motherhood; of the trading of gametes or their products; of the examination, registration, or revelation of a person's genotype without her consent or without a basis of a legal order. It also sets rules concerning procedures to enhance reproduction; and finally, it guarantees the right of a person to examine data concerning his or her origin. Its third paragraph reads as follows: "The Federal Government promulgates regulations concerning the handling of gametes and genotypes of animals, plants, and other organisms. These regulations are issued with consideration for the dignity of the creature, the safety of human beings, animals, and the environment, as well as the protection of the genetic varieties of animals and plant forms."[20]

This paragraph will have to be made more concrete and precise by federal legislation. The big question now is of course: What does dignity of creature mean? And what are its impacts on genetic research and engineering? Does it allow us to technically change the genomes of animals?[21] Should such altered animals become the objects of legal patents? If so under what conditions? Does such dignity have any impact at all on genetic alterations of plants—or are plants exempt from dignity?

Let me turn to another discipline: *economics*. It is notorious that modern economics usually does not deal with man in his complexity, but with a model-man, the *homo oeconomicus*, be it in its original or in its modernized version (as "resourceful evaluative maximizing man").[22] Here the question arises if economics could and should contribute to the enhancement of human—and creatural—dignity by tackling not only one side of human beings, but, if possible, man as a whole. How would economics look on such an alternative basis?[23] Furthermore, economics should, to a much greater extent than it has until now, consider nature not only as a pool of resources for human activities, not only as a good in the hands of men, but also and primarily as the *foundation* of economic human activities which must be preserved for living and for future generations.[24] For this reason, economics of environmental protection has to be fully integrated in "mainstream economics"—which is obviously not the case today. As a consequence, economists should concentrate, e.g., in the fields of energy and traffic policies, on possibilities to make use of energy resources in a thoroughly sustainable manner in order to steer the needs and the reality of traffic in such a way that neither human beings nor nature have to suffer from excessively.

Another example, perhaps even more important: The *sciences of education* should turn, in my opinion, in a more radical way to the question of what the system of education, taken in its broadest sense, could and should contribute to the development and realization of human (and non-human) dignity. In fact, I strongly doubt if the present school systems found in industrialized and in other countries are honestly and effectively directed toward such a goal; their aims seem to be rather the adaptation of young people to dominating social, economic, and cultural thought and behavior. Education aimed at the promotion of human dignity would emphasize much more the development of creativity and human responsibility—also in respect to nature.[25]

But the most important, the most basic, and the most general contribution humanities and social sciences can forward are *systematic reflections on the motives, aims, and structures of scientific research*. I am convinced that many scientists—in all disciplines—are frighteningly unaware of their motives or goals, or of the fundaments and structure of their thinking. Many scientists would not admit—and are probably not aware of—the fact that by accumulating knowledge they search for and achieve fame, power, and wealth for themselves or for those on whom they confer their knowledge. And they would not admit either that by dedicating their talents and creativity to science, they often avoid developing their personality as a whole and pull away from the problems as well as the richness of life. Each science carries "den Stempel einer gewissen Lebensferne, weil es im Wesen des logozentrischen Ansatzes liegt, über die lebendigen Gegenstände hinweg zu abstrakten Begriffen zu gelangen oder zu manipulatorischen Formen, die qualitative Gegebenheiten in quantitative Bestimmungsgrössen auflösen."[26] There are some obvious proofs: the maintenance of a concept of "objectivity" and its clear-cut separation from subjectivity, despite the fact that neither in modern philosophy nor in modern science such a concept and separation can be justified; or the limitation of "scientific work" to activities which can be repeated *ad libi-tum*—why should single facts not be an important part of reality or even reality itself (every manifestation of life is a singularity!) and therefore be subject to scientific reflection or even of practical use, e.g., in medicine? Such shortcomings in scientific awareness[27] or self-consciousness have been criticized for some time, in fact as long as the modern concept of science has been developed.[28] But the impact of such criticism has been scarce. I hope that modern feminist theory of science will have greater influence.[29] I shall return to this point—and to its relatedness to dignity of human beings and dignity of nature—at the end of my paper.

ARE HUMANITIES AND SOCIAL SCIENCES UNDER AN OBLIGATION TO FURTHER DIGNITY OF CREATION IN SUCH WAYS?

Up to now I have tried to sketch possibilities of furthering dignity of man and dignity of creation in the realm of humanities and social sciences. But are these sciences free to make use of such possibilities? Are they in fact under an obligation to do so? If so, how could such an obligation be conceived, and upon what should it be based?

This question obviously does not only concern humanities and social sciences, but science as a whole. And here we meet again the problem discussed in the Gerzensee symposium: How far does freedom of research extend? I will not turn back to that discussion. Let me only make this remark: There seems to be a general agreement that freedom of research is a principle well-established in international and national law and neces-sary for creative research work. There is much less agreement on the lim-its of such freedom. And it may (and should) even be disputed whether it is correct to speak of "freedom"—as a principle—and of its "limits"—as an exception. Should we not consider that freedom from the beginning as the freedom to construct, to further, to enhance dignity of men and cre-ation, rather than as a freedom to do "n'importe quoi," to decide arbi-trarily on the topics we want to tackle scientifically, and on the methods to be applied? *Should we not stop, as a consequence, to speak of the observance of such dignity as a limit?* Of course, in proposing such an orientation of freedom, I have to lay bare its grounds.

There is, in some aspects, a legal ground: Every researcher who is employed by government or in a state-financed university has to observe the principles recognized by constitution. The first of these principles is—by a rather common agreement—dignity of man. According to Swiss con-stitutional law, dignity of creature has to be respected as well. But these legal articles are nothing other than ethical principles turned into law. As a matter of fact, I cannot think of any modern ethical concept which would not enclose—or even center on—the principle of human dignity, and I have already pointed out that an increasing number of philosophers and theologians are willing to enlarge that principle to a concept of "dignity of creation." In our present historical situation, this concept even has to be extended in a new direction: As mankind has acquired the capacity to damage or even destroy nature with very long-ranging effects, it has to assume—on the same ethical grounds—the responsibility of making life in dignity possible even for the not-yet-born, for future generations; here again an increasing chorus of voices is speaking out in this sense.

Let us resume, then. Humanities and social sciences are indeed under a legal or at least ethical obligation to further and protect dignity of creation. This of course does not abolish freedom of research. There are a thousand ways to give research that orientation. In many contexts it is hardly possible to imagine the potential of specific basic research for promoting or damaging dignity; such research shall of course not be excluded. On the other hand there are indeed research fields and specific research topics with an obvious and considerable potential for promoting or damaging human or creatural dignity. And each researcher, in choosing his research topic, has to ask himself whether the topic chosen belongs rather to this or to that category, and, if the answer is uncertain, he or she should prefer another topic whose positive potential is less dubious.

STRUCTURAL AND PROCEDURAL CONSEQUENCES

I have already tried in my Gerzensee paper to develop some ideas concerning structures and procedures to set up to bring responsibility of researchers into reality. I shall not come back to those ideas. Let me simply add some propositions dealing more with the constructive than with the defensive aspects of such responsibility which concern all scientific disciplines.

First, in procedures leading to the appointment of a new researcher—in a university or in a government agency—an important criterion should be the candidate's willingness to promote, in his research work, dignity of man and creation. Such willingness can be made out, at least tentatively, on the basis of the candidate's previous research work.

Second, university grants committees, or bodies charged with allocating funds to research, should apply the same criterion in selecting research projects for such funding.

Third, university departments should provide for lecturing programs which are directed towards the promotion of human and creatural dignity. For example, every law school should provide courses on human rights, on environmental protection, and on the legal adaptation of technology assessment results.

Fourth, the bodies responsible for allocating Nobel prizes should not only consider intellectual brilliance or the promotion of this or that scientific progress, but also, again, the impact of a scientist's work on the promotion of such dignity. I am thoroughly convinced that the choice of criteria for distributing Nobel prizes heavily influences the orientation of research in all fields covered by such prizes. Perhaps it would be worthwhile to establish special prizes for such research work—something similar to the already existing Alternative Nobel Prize.

Fifth, reflection on research—its goals, its motives, its methods and its effects—should be furthered and generalized wherever research is being done on a larger scale. It does not make sense, in my eyes, to treat the "science of science" as a scientific discipline among many other disciplines. Every young researcher and every young university teacher should be compelled to make some studies of this kind, in order to broaden his consciousness of what he or she is doing or going to do as a researcher or teacher.

THE REACH OF SCIENTIFIC REFLECTION

Humanities and social sciences participate (at least partly in a specific way) in the general responsibility of sciences—or more exactly: of scientists—for promoting dignity of man and nature. I have tried to show some grounds for and some means of assuming such responsibility.

However, humanities and social sciences—as well as other scientific disciplines—seem to be incapable of fully reaching this goal by themselves. Science, according to its traditional philosophy, is rational, and scientific procedures are rational procedures. Responsibility, on the other hand, is not a thoroughly rational concept.[30] We say: "I feel responsible," which means: I accept this or that ground for my being responsible. Such acceptance, however, is partly an act of belief, not only an act of (rational) recognition. Let me give you an example: I personally feel co-responsible for my posterity's ability to live their life in dignity. I accept such responsibility not only because I know that mankind is going to exhaust natural resources and to destroy nature so as to make future life less rich, less easy, less dignified. In addition to such recognition—which is of course of utmost importance—I believe that I have no right to make future life less rich, less easy, less dignified; I believe that I should—together with my whole generation—leave earth in no worse condition than I found it in the moment of my birth. Such belief may have its roots in religion (as in my case) or in a philosophical *a priori*. But it is never an act of purely rational recognition.

This concept, however, is founded on the assumption that between science and belief there is a "wall of separation," like that between church and state according to the first amendment to the U.S. Constitution. It is founded on the absolute separation between object and subject and between *ratio* and *emotio*. Such separation has been at the base of modern science since the late sixteenth century. But in our time its basic soundness has been relativized in physics[31] and fundamentally questioned in biology[32] and philosophy.[33] "What is required . . . is a paradigm that on the one hand acknowledges the inevitable interaction between knower and known, and on the other hand respects the equally inevitable gap between theory and phenomena."[34] This means a whole, comprehensive program for a new conception of systematic understanding the ensemble of beings and processes.[35] It means, among other things, that subjective "beliefs" (feelings, meanings, convictions, "*a prioris*," in short the whole range of "subjectivity") have to be combined with rational conception, and that rational conception, meaning the conception by human *ratio*, is by necessity more than a series of logical conclusions, the potentiality of human *ratio* embracing more than logical connection.[36] (e.g., circular[37] or associative ones). For such a new concept some humanities (symptomatically called "soft" sciences[38]) seem particularly well prepared, namely—in some schools of thinking at least—philosophy, theology, and jurisprudence. The new concept would mean that sciences would have to give up their claim of being (categorically) "objective." It would mean that a *wholesome* approach to other beings and to ourselves has to be incorporated in scientific procedures (and it would therefore go far beyond the concept of "Wertbindung" in the so-called "Werturteilsstreit"[39]). This would open ways for perceiving living beings—human beings, animals, plants, even microorganisms—and perhaps also non-living beings as entities related to the observer, and furthermore not only as belonging to (artificial) categories, but primarily as complex and "complete" and lastly unique *individual* entities (or ensembles of such entities).[40] In such a way science would arrive at dealing with (interconnected) *life* itself, not only with abstractions of life, on both sides of the scientific interaction.[41] The researcher would not be allowed to limit himself to study what is repeatable.[42] He would have to bring his whole potentiality of knowing, thinking and feeling into the research process, and the research object would have to be considered as a "personality" distinct from, but related to his own personality, and quite certainly not as a thing to be brought—in Bacon's sense—under the researcher's power. The "feeling of responsibility" would then be an integral part of scientific research, and the question of how such feeling can be formed would be a scientific question. It would be a scientific achievement to declare that if I am not willing and capable to realize a fellow man/woman with my love, with all my senses, and with my intellectual apparatus; if I am not willing and capable to realize the beauty of an animal or a plant, by "liking," looking at, listening to, smelling, perhaps touching it, I shall not be able to develop the belief that my fellow man/woman needs respect and love, and that this animal or that plant and nature as a whole needs protection.[43] So we may hope that in such a way science would lose its stigma of having by necessity many effects indifferent or even hostile to life.[44] This again would be a basic condition of fully recognizing creation in its "wholesomeness" (Fülle)[45] and thus the dignity of the "subjects" and of the "objects" of scientific research.

A new conception of this kind would lead to a definite rupture in the history of modern science as initiated in the late sixteenth and mainly in the seventeenth century. Its consequences would have to be studied very carefully and thoroughly.[46] There would be, of course, another way out of the modern dilemma in which the traditional concept of science could be brought by science itself: to acknowledge, clearly and openly, the limits of traditional sciences in perceiving "reality" and the necessity of consociating with other ways of perception. For some sciences, this would be an important step. However, it would hardly do; "for we need to radically question the fundamentals of all our intellectual culture, in the name of humaneness and in the name of life on our earth."[47]

NOTES AND REFERENCES

1. Shea, William R./Sitter-Liver, Beat (eds.) 1989, *Scientists and Their Responsibility*, Canton, MA, Watson Publishing International.
2. Saladin, Peter 1989, "Should Society Make Laws Governing Scientific Research?," in: Shea/Sitter 1989, 220 ff.
3. Cf. Lenk, Hans/Maring, Matthias 1991, "Moralprobleme der Sozialwissenschaftler," in: Lenk, Hans (ed.) 1991, *Wissenschaft und Ethik*, Stuttgart, Reclam; Schuler, Hein 1991, "Ethische Probleme der sozialwissenschaftlichen Forschung," in: Lenk 1991.
4. Strahm, Rudolf H. 1992, *Wirtschaftsbuch Schweiz*, Aarau, Sauerländer (especially chap. 1: Wirtschaftliche Sichtweisen, chap. 2: Kosten des Wirtschaftswachstums).
5. Cf. for example Binswanger, Hans Christoph 1991, *Geld und Natur: Das wirtschaftliche Wachstum im Spannungsfeld zwischen Oekonomie und Oekologie*, Stuttgart-Wien, Braumüller; Gore, Al 1992, Wege zum Gleichgewicht. Ein Marshallplan für die Erde, Frankfurt/M., Fischer, 181 ff. (originally: *Earth in the Balance. Ecology and Human Spirit*, Boston-New York-London 1992).
6. Cf. Liedke, Gerhard 1979, *Im Bauch des Fisches*, Stuttgart-Berlin, Kreuz; Zink, Jörg 1982, *Kostbare Erde*, Stuttgart-Berlin, Kreuz; Moltmann, Jürgen

1985, *Gott in der Schöpfung*, München, Kaiser; Altner, Günter (ed.) 1989, *Ökologische Theologie: Perspektiven zur Orientierung*, Stuttgart-Berlin, Kreuz (especially 149 ff.: Krolzik, Udo 1989, "Die Wirkungsgeschichte von Genesis 1, 28"); Link, Christian 1991, *Schöpfung*, Gütersloh, G. Mohn.

7. Cf. Starck, Christian 1987, Art. "Menschenwürde," in: *Staatslexikon* 1987, Freiburg-Basel-Wien, Herder; Häberle, Peter 1987, "Die Menschenwürde als Grundlage der staatlichen Gemeinschaft," in: Isensee, Josef/Kirchhof, Paul (eds.), *Handbuch des Staatsrechts der Bundesrepublik Deutschland*, Heidelberg, C.F. Müller, 815–861, 834.

8. *Grundgesetz*, Art. 1, Abs. 1: "Die Würde des Menschen ist unantastbar. Sie zu achten und zu schützen, ist Verpflichtung aller staatlichen Gewalt." Cf. Benda, Ernst 1983, in: Benda, Ernst/Maihofer, Werner et al. (eds.) 1983, *Handbuch des Verfassungsrechts der Bundesrepublik Deutschland*, Berlin-New York, De Gruyter, 109.

9. Cf. Luf, Gerhard 1987, Art. "Menschenrechte," in: *Staatslexikon* 1987; Häberle 1987, 843f.

10. Cf. for example Müller, Werner 1981, *Neue Sonne—Neues Licht. Aufsätze zu Geschichte, Kultur und Sprache der Indianer Nordamerikas*, Berlin, D. Reimer, 136 ff.

11. Sitter, Beat 1984, *Plädoyer für das Naturrechtsdenken: Zur Anerkennung von Eigenrechten der Natur*, Basel-Frankfurt/M., Helbing & Lichtenhahn; Sitter, Beat 1984a, "Ueber das Recht der Natur im Naturrecht der Gegenwart," in: Heyen, Erk V. (ed.) 1984, *Vom normativen Wandel des Politischen*, Berlin, Duncker & Humblot, 145–172; Sitter, Beat 1984b, "Aspekte der Menschenwürde. Zur Würde der Natur als Prüfstein der Würde des Menschen," in: *Manuskripte, Zeitschrift für Literatur* 23, 83. Heft, 93–96; Meyer-Abich, Klaus Michael 1984, *Wege zum Frieden mit der Natur*, München-Wien, Hanser.

12. Cf. below note 20.

13. Cf. Meyer-Abich, Klaus Michael 1990, *Aufstand für die Natur*, München-Wien, Hanser, 48 ff.

14. Cf. Leimbacher, Jürg 1988, *Rechte der Natur*, Basel-Frankfurt/M., Helbing & Lichtenhahn.

15. Meyer-Abich, Klaus Michael 1988, *Wissenschaft für die Zukunft*, München, Beck.

16. Meyer-Abich, Klaus Michael/Schefold, Bertram 1986, *Die Grenzen der Atomwirtschaft*, München, Beck; Rossnagel, Alexander 1983, *Bedroht die Kernenergie unsere Freiheit?*, München, Beck; Saladin, Peter 1981, "Kernenergie und schweizerische Staatsordnung," in: *Recht als Prozess und Gefüge. Festschrift für Hans Huber*, Bern, Stämpfli 1981, 297 ff.

17. Naschold, Frieder 1989, *Technikkontrolle und Technikfolgenabschätzung*, St. Gallen, Hochschulverlag, 12, 21.

18. Meyer-Abich 1988, 124; Eberlein, Gerald L. 1991, "Wertbewusste Wissenschaft. Eine pragmatische Alternative zu wertfreier und parteiischer Wissenschaft," in: Lenk 1991, 99ff., 109ff.

19. Starck 1987, 834; Larenz, Karl 1979, *Richtiges Recht. Grundzüge einer Rechtsethik*, München, Beck, 47.

20. Art. 24[novies] Federal Constitution:
2 "Der Bund erlässt Vorschriften über den Umgang mit menschlichem Keim- und Erbgut. Er sorgt dabei für den Schutz der Menschenwürde, der Persönlichkeit und der Familie . . ."
3 "Der Bund erlässt Vorschriften über den Umgang mit Keim- und Erbgut von Tieren, Pflanzen und anderen Organismen. Er trägt dabei der Würde der Kreatur sowie der Sicherheit von Mensch, Tier und Umwelt Rechnung und schützt die genetische Vielfalt der Tier- oder Pflanzenarten." Cf. Praetorius, Ina and Saladin, Peter, Die Würde des Kreatur, Bern, forthcoming; Teutsch, Gotthard M., Die "Würde der Kreatur," Bern-Stuttgart-Wien 1995, Haupt.

21. Cf. Sitter-Liver, Beat 1991, "Transgene Tiere: Skandal oder Chance?," in: *Zeitschrift für Schweizerisches Recht* (ZSR), 301.

22. Ulrich, Peter 1986, *Transformation der ökonomischen Vernunft*, Bern-Stuttgart, Paul Haupt, 195; Ulrich, Peter 1990, "Wirtschaftsethik auf der Suche nach der verlorenen ökonomischen Vernunft," in: Ulrich, Peter (ed.) 1990a, *Auf der Suche nach einer modernen Wirtschaftsethik*, Bern-Stuttgart, Paul Haupt; Daly, Herman E./Cobb, John B. Jr. 1989, *For the Common Good: Redirecting the Economy Toward Community, the Environment, and a Sustainable Future*, Boston, Beacon Press.

23. Cf. the new paradigm of "practical social economics" ("praktische Sozialökonomie") as developed by Ulrich 1986 1990.

24. Cf. Binswanger, Hans Christoph 1984, *Oekologisch orientierte Wirtschaftswissenschaft*, St. Gallen; Binswanger, Hans Christoph 1981, *Wirtschaft und Umwelt*, Stuttgart, Kohlhammer; Binswanger, Hans Christoph 1991a, *Geld und Natur*, Stuttgart, Thienemann.

25. Jegge, Jürg 1987, *Dummheit ist lernbar*, Bern, Zytglogge; Burow, Olaf-Axel/ Scherpp, Karlheinz 1981, *Lernziel: Menschlichkeit*, München, esp. 128ff.; Montessori, Maria 1978, *Kinder sind anders*, Stuttgart, Klett; Gruen, Arno 1992, *Der Verrat am Selbst: Die Angst vor der Autonomie bei Mann und Frau*, München, Causa, 70f., 76.

26. Meier-Seethaler, Carola 1992, *Ursprünge und Befreiungen*, Frankfurt/M., Fischer, 350.

27. Gruen 1992, 52ff.

28. Cf. Pietschmann, Herbert 1983, *Das Ende des naturwissenschaftlichen Zeitalters*, Frankfurt/M.-Berlin; Primas, Hans 1992, "Umdenken in der Naturwissenschaft," in: *Gaia*, 5ff.; Müller, Werner 1976, *Indianische Welterfahrung*, Stuttgart, Klett, 81ff.; Beispiel Meister Eckhart in Gruen 1992, 77.

29. Cf.—besides Meier-Seethaler 1992—Fox Keller 1985 (note 34); Merchant, Carolyn 1987, *Der Tod der Natur*, München, Beck (orig. *The Death of Nature*, San Francisco-New York, Harper & Row 1980).

30. Saladin, Peter 1984, *Verantwortung als Staatsprinzip*, Bern, Paul Haupt, with further indications.

31. Cf. Primas 1992; Heisenberg, Werner/Bohr, Niels 1963, *Die Kopenhagener Deutung der Quantentheorie*, Stuttgart, Battenberg.
32. Maturana, Humberto R./Varela, Francisco J. 1987, *Der Baum der Erkenntnis*, Bern-München-Wien, (orig. *The Tree of Knowledge. The Biological Roots of Human Understanding*, Boston-London, Shambhala).
33. Cf. Krohn, Wolfgang/Kueppers, Günther 1989, *Die Selbstorganisation der Wissenschaft*, Frankfurt/M., Kleine; Watzlawick, Paul (ed.) ⁵1988, *Die erfundene Wirklichkeit*, München-Zürich, Piper (orig. *The Invented Reality*, New York-London, W.W. Norton 1984).
34. Fox Keller, Evelyn 1985 (note 29), *Reflections on Gender and Science*, New Haven-London, Yale University Press, 139.
35. Fox Keller 1985, 87, 117; Harding, Sandra 1986, *The Science Question in Feminism*, Ithaca, N.Y., Cornell University Press, chapter 10.
36. Cf. Primas 1992, 12.
37. Cf. Bateson, Gregory 1979, *Mind and Nature: A Necessary Unity?*, New York, E.P. Dutton, chapter II.
38. Fox Keller 1985, 77.
39. Eberlein 1991; Keuth, Herbert 1991, "Die Abhängigkeit der Wissenschaften von Wertungen und das Problem der Werturteilsfreiheit," in: Lenk 1991, 116ff.
40. Fox Keller 1985, 146; Barbara McClintock in Fox Keller 1985, 163ff.; Eisenhardt, Peter/Kurth, Dan/Stiehl, Horst 1988, *Du steigst nie zweimal in denselben Fluss*, Reinbek bei Hamburg, Rowohlt, 18f.: "Wir zeigen, dass die Geschichte der westlichen Wissenschaft die Geschichte (der) Abstraktion und damit der Verdrängung der Wirklichkeit war," "dass die notwendigen Bedingungen wissenschaftlichen Denkens in Klassifikation, Verallgemeinerung und Reproduktion bestehen."
41. Fox Keller 1985, 139.
42. Cf. Primas 1992, 13.
43. Cf. Fox Keller 1985, 116; cf. the opposite opinion presented by Keuth 1991, 120.
44. Cf. Feyerabend, Paul 1987, *Farewell to Reason*, London, Verso Editions, chapter I.10, chapter II (German: *Irrwege der Vernunft*, Frankfurt/M., Suhrkamp 1989).
45. Cf. Feyerabend 1989, 178: Fast alle Wissenschafter und Philosophen "priesen die Einheit (oder, um ein besseres Wort zu gebrauchen, die Monotonie) und verdammten die Fülle."
46. Cf. Primas 1992, and the results of the study of Eisenhardt/Kurth/Stiehl 1988. What I am suggesting here is more than a "methodological anarchy," more than a simple "anything goes" in Paul Feyerabend's sense (cf. *Against Method. Outlines of an Anarchistic Theory of Knowledge*, London, NLB; Atlantic Highlands, Humanities Press 1975); it is an obligation, not only a permission.
47. "Denn es müssen im Namen der Menschlichkeit und im Namen des Lebens auf unserer Erde die Grundlagen unserer gesamten Geisteskultur radikal in Frage gestellt werden," Meier-Seethaler 1992, 25.

Human Dignity, Nature, and the Sciences of Man

CHARLES WIDMER

QUESTIONS

Discussing the *Moral Issues Concerning the Humanities and Social Sciences*, one is inevitably faced with the notion of human dignity, if only because it is part of any serious reflection on ethics. Of course, this is not sufficient to validate the notion. One can still wonder what exactly is meant by *dignity*. Does the word refer to an observable fact? Does it belong exclusively to the realm of *values*? Pragmatically speaking, is it of any use in contemporary debates, particularly in the making of laws? Does the concept of dignity have any relevance for other beings than man? Is it legitimate to speak of the dignity of nature? Supposing man's dignity is a fact, has it anything to do with his relation to nature?

If one chooses to give weight to these questions, then anthropology[1] has an epistemological duty to tackle them, whether it is to give them sense, or to deny it. The questions doubtless also belong to the province of the humanities. This chapter will however deal with some of their aspects essentially in terms belonging to, or compatible with, the sciences of man. The humanities will not be considered as such.[2]

THE UNIVERSAL DECLARATION OF HUMAN RIGHTS

Dignity was deemed an important notion by those who were put in charge of drafting the 1948 *Universal Declaration of Human Rights*.[3] It appears already in the first paragraph of the Preamble, it is there again in the fifth one, and it is the keyword of Article 1. Its last occurrence is in Article 22.

Why mention the Declaration at the start of this discussion? The reason is this: the Declaration is a major reference in the contemporary world. At the same time as it states rights, it conveys a conception of man which is implicitly presented as true; but it does not provide a demonstration of the validity of that truth. It even goes to the point of making of it (including the dignity of man) an object of *faith*.[4]

If "faith" is conceived in the religious, more particularly Christian, way, then the Declaration cannot claim universality. As the Declaration embraces all mankind, whatever the religions of its members, and whether they are believers or not, "faith" must obviously be taken here in a secular sense. It can be thought of as a strongly motivated postulate that dignity not only *is* a fact, but that it *ought to be* one as well. This postulate acts as a prerequisite for the statement of all human rights: only a being capable of, or characterized by, dignity, can have rights.

Why not keep it at that? Supposing it can be done, what is the use of trying to prove that the Declaration tells the truth about man, particularly when it mentions dignity? Should not the Declaration be seen as law texts generally are, i.e., as a set of juridical conventions the strength of which lies in its acceptance by all concerned?

One of the problems is acceptance itself. Though most countries have subscribed to the Declaration, it is still the object of numerous discussions, not to mention disrespect. These originate, or find their justification, in all sorts of ideological[5] positions, and are sometimes very critical of the universality of at least some of the human rights. Let us recall, just as an example, the Western "neo-conservative" questioning of the validity of social and economic rights, which is an indictment of Article 22.

Moreover, agreement on the Declaration as a set of conventions to be respected, were it secured, would still not be sufficient in the world as it is. For instance, jurists are in need of a substantial definition of dignity when they have to imagine laws in order to regulate practices of the sort made possible by techno-scientific progress.[6] Dignity thought of as a value only is useless in such cases. One has to know what dignity actually is, if one is to make of it a criterion not only of acceptable behavior, but also of behavior to be wished for.

Article 1 of the Declaration first asserts the *principles* of equality in freedom, dignity, and rights; they are not meant as testable facts. But, after committing itself to these principles, Article 1 goes on to acknowledge the actual existence of two mental human traits: reason and conscience. The question of scientific truth is then relevant: is man really, and universally, endowed with critical intelligence and a moral sense? Finally, Article 1 requests us to give expression to our capacity, thought of as a fact again, for "brotherhood," i.e., for sympathy, generosity, solidarity—

let us say: *altruism*. And the question can scientifically be raised again: are we capable of genuine concern for all our fellow men, or is selfishness the hard core of our nature?

Insofar as dignity, though asserted as a principle, comes in Article 1 alongside the testable mental traits of reason, conscience, and altruism, one may think that when we come to the question of providing a substantial definition of dignity, it might prove heuristic not to dissociate it from those traits. What could dignity be without them?

In previously published studies,[7] I took a stand, supported by what I think are scientific arguments, favoring the thesis of the universality, either actual or potential, of intelligence (critical reason), conscience, and altruism. There would be no point in repeating these arguments here. But there might be some sense in furthering this thesis by linking these traits more explicitly with the notion of dignity, and by trying to sketch a more detailed outline of the mental fact denoted by the word *dignity*.

RESPONSIBILITY OF THE SCIENCES OF MAN

Before coming explicitly to this point, the responsibility of the sciences of man in this regard must be stated. Various conceptions of responsibility could be considered. A minimal one will be used here: there is some sort of responsibility when an effect can be attributed to an agent—the agent is then answerable, accountable, for the effect. Such a conception excludes ordinary determinism from its field, of course: an apple cannot be deemed responsible for the fact that it caused a bump to appear on Newton's head when it fell. Responsibility then supposes the capacity in the agent of being aware of the effect of his, or her, action, whether the action was intentional or not.

In that sense, anthropology is not devoid of responsibility, insofar as, being a kind of discourse, it belongs to Karl Popper's World 3, a world of objectivated meanings which have an influence on the minds, and *a fortiori* on the behavior, of individuals. Moreover, as anthropology is produced by scientists, these scientists can in their turn be seen as answerable for the consequences of their statements, whether they intended them or not. As an example, just think of the questionable impact of ethical relativism!

A researcher can, of course, say that he is sorry for the consequences and, at the same time, not feel guilty about them. He might well acknowledge that he is an agent of unforeseen, and occasionally regrettable, effects, but he might at the same time point out that the only way of preventing these effects from emerging would be to stop producing science. Innocence would then be dependent on voluntary ignorance.

The choice of at least temporary ignorance is understandable for sciences which produce trustworthy, i.e. adequate, knowledge of a kind which increases man's power over himself and over nature, and which can be put to detestable use. The example is well-known of the French biologist J. Testart, and of his self-imposed moratorium on research which might eventually prove dangerous for the individual as well as for society.

In this respect, the case of anthropology is quite different. Whereas biology, and more generally all the "hard" sciences, can be said to have reached epistemological adulthood, the sciences of man are in a state of infancy. Even though there are still theoretical disputes among physicists, chemists, and biologists, and even though they remain exposed to the possibility of a change of paradigms in their respective fields, nonetheless the "hard" sciences all enjoy some sort of fundamental agreement on methodology and explanatory principles.[8] Moreover, their trustworthiness is strengthened by the efficiency of techniques which are very much dependent on the knowledge they have elaborated.

The sciences of man are in a very different situation. On the one hand, the question of their *efficiency* cannot be put in the same way as that of the "hard" sciences.[9] On the other hand, specialists must be aware that anthropology is riddled with theoretical divergences which can go to the point of a total absence of agreement on what *the object itself* to be studied actually is. This is what reveals a state of "infancy."

What is meant here is that responsibility in the sciences of man is dependent not only on the effects of discourse, but also on the adequacy of discourse.[10] Physics, chemistry, and biology can have a terrible effect and be scientifically right at the same time. This possibility must also be considered for anthropology, of course. But it might not be very relevant to do so, because there are no instances, as far as I know, of consistent, and well agreed upon, anthropological knowledge bringing out devastating consequences. So, as the sciences of man nevertheless exert an influence, it is worth pondering instead the responsibilities of *questionable theories* concerning man.

Our issue is dignity. At this point, it is assumed that the notion of dignity makes sense only when it is thought of as a distinctive mental trait of the human individual. The concept of the dignity of groups, of nations for instance, is deemed here meaningless, and will not be discussed. The question of the dignity of animals, and more widely of nature, will be dealt with further on in the text. So, if dignity is of the human individual, what do the sciences of man have to say about the individual? What are the possible consequences of what they say on that count?

Quite a number of anthropologists show concern for the individual, and some even go to the point of considering him/her as the ultimate, irreducible, *object* of knowledge. Their researches then often act as bulwarks strengthening, and protecting, the validity of the inseparable notions of dignity and human rights.[11] I share these authors' views, as has already been hinted. Reasons for doing so have been set forth elsewhere.[12] What will briefly retain our attention now, to illustrate the responsibility of the sciences of man, are the instances of a few scientists who support theories which are real threats to the individual, and consequently to dignity.

Psychologist Burrhus F. Skinner, one of the most famous proponents of the behaviorist school, in a book meaningfully entitled *Beyond Freedom and Dignity*, sees man as the product of operant conditioning, and reduces the individual to be "at best a locus in which many lines of development come together in a unique set" (1971, 200).

Writing this, he is, willy-nilly, the objective accomplice of all sorts of possible manipulations, insofar as his theory cannot give any reason why respect should be shown to a being whose identity consists only in the results of external influences.

Anthropologist Clifford Geertz, a well-known cultural holist, states (in Schweder/Robert 1990, 126) that "the Western conception of the person as a bounded, unique, more or less integrated motivational and cognitive universe, a dynamic center of awareness, emotion, judgment, and actions organized into a distinctive whole and set contrastively both against such wholes and against its social and natural background, is, however incorrigible it may seem to us, a rather peculiar idea within the context of the world's cultures."

For Geertz, epistemologically speaking, individuals do not matter; moreover, there is no universally valid definition of what an individual might be. The very idea of the uniqueness of the person is culture-bound, and cultures are the things to be studied. They are thought of as complex wholes explainable only in their own terms. Each of these wholes is deemed to be incomparable: it would be irrelevant to evaluate any of them in universal terms of cognitive and ethical adequacy.

Anthropologist Colin Turnbull, a functionalist, wrote a best-seller (1984) on the terrible fate of a displaced African people, the Ik. According to Turnbull, due to their displacement, the Ik lost all those traits which make social life possible, and were inevitably reduced to a state of complete amorality, i.e., to gross, and exclusive, concern with elementary selfish interests. For Turnbull—and this is coherent with his functionalist theory that *mores* are unavoidable, and unintentional, products adapted to objective circumstances—they had no other possible way of coping with their unbearable environment. Thus he cannot wish them any other future than this (1984, 235):

Luckily the Ik are not numerous—about two thousand—and those two years reduced their numbers greatly. So I am hopeful that their isolation will remain as complete as in the past, until they die out completely.

In all three cases[13]—Skinner's, Geertz's and Turnbull's—epistemological *a priori* lead the scientists to negate the validity of the idea that the individual is the ultimate, and hence irreducible, object of anthropology. In their perspectives, a pan-human definition of dignity would then be irrelevant, of course. None of them would agree, or have agreed, with M. E. Spiro, who said in a discussion on the topic (in Schweder/Robert 1990, 14):

> I think that in all societies you would find that individuals have self-representations and ideal self-representations and that there is always a tension between them. I think, too, that it's that tension that's involved in notions of morality, notions of oughtness, as well as self-deprecation and low self-esteem. All these are functions of the tension between self-representation and the ideal self-representation. Hence, I would guess that the distinction is universal.

HUMAN DIGNITY AS FACT

I agree with Spiro, and have given reasons, which will not be repeated here, for doing so.[14] These reasons can be summed up in this statement that anthropological theories which deny the possibility of a universally valid definition of dignity are scientifically wrong, at the same time as they contribute to bring about ethical, and consequently social, havoc. It has been demonstrated that all over the world, and even though conceptions of it might be partially culture-oriented,[15] individuals have an idea of personal excellence, and mentally suffer from not being adequate to the norms they identify with. This means that they have a sense of dignity. When they are devoid of it, it can be shown that this is explainable by the fact that they are psychological cripples, whose infirmity can be explained, among other causes, by social and/or cultural alienation.

Moreover, and the universal existence of this fact must be insisted upon, whatever the norms a person adheres to, so long as she, or he, has not been deprived of *common* sense, i.e. of *reason*,[16] adherence never goes so far as preventing the individual from the feeling of being unique, from the feeling of *otherness*, i.e., more particularly, from the feeling of *not being totally identifiable* with social habits and cultural norms, however coercive these might be.

The feeling referred to here is both positive and negative. It is positive on the affective side, insofar as one passes through life with an emotionally loaded perception, either dim or acute, of permanent selfhood, i.e., of separate and conscious existence as a personality. It is negative on the cognitive side: no individual can give an explicit description of self in affirmative terms. The only thing she or he can do on that count is refuse exhaustive equivalence between what science knows about the individual, and what she or he actually is. And this holds true for psychology as well as for the other sciences of man.

But denying equivalence does not amount to denying relevance. An informed human being is well aware of the various systems of causes she or he is taken in. Curiously enough, though, awareness, i.e. reflexive consciousness, which is itself homogeneous with mental determinism,[17] puts all determinations at a distance, and thus forbids total identification with them.

This refusal of, and impossibility for, identification with determination is a mental fact. It may legitimately be seen as a consequence of all sorts of bio-psychological causes, some of them known, some of them unknown. However, whatever scientific explanations can be given of reflexive consciousness, which is congruent with self-consciousness, none of them is empowered with the competence of declaring the latter illusory. In this case at least, knowing the causes does not authorize us to ignore the specific actuality of the effect.[18] Selfhood, cognitively speaking, is in the demand of the individual that personal identity not be equated with the identity of others, i.e., with knowledge about man in general. This demand is quite legitimate: the sciences of man cannot—do not have the competence to—dismiss it as inadequate, because *the demand is the fact*; as such, it is irreducible; contrary to the feeling of liberty,[19] there is no difference between what it states and what actually is the case.

Dignity is coextensive with that fact. In Kantian terms, it is the demand on the part of the individual that she or he never be treated simply as a means, as an object, but always considered at the same time as an end.[20] This is consistent with the refusal of reduction of the individual by anthropological explanation to dimensions which are relevant only as long as they are not thought of as expressing the whole person. On both counts, practical and epistemological, what is claimed is respect of irreducibility. And this kind of respect is the condition of dignity.[21]

Moreover, existentially speaking, dignity supposes accepted solitude, by which I do not mean loneliness seen as absence of company, but the impossibility for the individual, due to the fact of self-reflection, to fuse mentally with others, with social functions, with ideology, or positivistic theorization about man (reification). Fusion is sometimes a temptation the individual yields to with apparent success, as in the passion of love, and political, religious, or scientific fervor. But it is not because the individual, in these cases, renounces separateness that it is not there as a constant reminder of irreducibility, which can of course be ignored.

Separateness, negative identity (I *am not* this, or that) is congruent with moral conscience, with ethical awareness: acts, and words, are inevitably experienced as one's own, because the idea, and the feeling, of self are consubstantially linked with them. We cannot avoid *being on our own*, i.e., we cannot avoid a sense of responsibility, of autonomy both as a feeling and as an objective competence. The feeling as a mental fact is obvious. One might of course question its adequacy, as is the case with the feeling of liberty.[22] But numerous reasons can be given to support adequacy. To make things short, let us only refer to those very significant common occurrences of two types: we may psychologically be overwhelmed by circumstances to the point of not being able to resist them; or, on the contrary, we may know of personal situations in which we objectively enjoy the mental power of making decisions. In the first case, there is actual deprivation of autonomy (passion, or depression, took the better of us); in the second case, we experience autonomy as an actual competence. It is part, the "noblest" part, of psychological determination; even when we behave in a cowardly way, this can still be considered in quite a number of instances, as Jean-Paul Sartre has shown, to be an autonomous decision, i.e., an action we are accountable for.[23]

Autonomy as separateness goes along with the necessity of creating moral values, or at least with the inevitable facing of existing values (values present in a given culture) as statements about which one must take a stand. This is not the place to dwell at length on this aspect of the human condition. Suffice it to say that the self is a question as much as it is a demand, and that ethics constitute the field of reflection encompassing the answers to that question. All these answers amount to being conceptions of what we ought to do in order to preserve integrity of self, i.e. dignity.

SELF, DIGNITY, AND THE BODY

Integrity of self implies consideration of one's own nature, a dimension of which is one's own body. All sorts of relations are possible with it. For instance, one may detest it or give it unbridled love. But, between these two forms of excess, there is room for a definition of what being on good terms with one's own body can be.

Dignity of self is conditioned by respect for one's own body, which excludes both self-hatred[24] and narcissism. But respect of one's own being is not enough to secure dignity of self. Self-worth supposes, as will be shown further on, that worth should be acknowledged of all sorts of "others"; and foremost among them, all other human beings, including their bodies. Treating the bodies of others as things, as means exclusively, can hardly be thought compatible with respect for their "essential" selves, whatever is meant by that. The actuality of individuals is incarnate in their spatial, bodily, material, presence.

These considerations could serve as an embryonic argumentation in favor of laws which should forbid use of the human body as a merchandise. Since self is inseparable from the body, misuse of the latter amounts to aggression on the dignity of the former. When a woman rents her womb to bear the child of another woman, she makes of her self a marketable object, reducible to one of its functions. When a man sells one of his organs, he is in the same situation. In both cases, there is loss of dignity, which it is the vocational purpose of the law to protect. It should of course be added that when people are practically driven to such extremities by economic and social distress, it would hardly be appropriate to burden them with supplementary guilt. The loss of dignity is then much more in the buyer of "womb-space," or organs, than in the seller, insofar as we are, among other things, the relationships we have with other people. When I am the agent of loss of dignity in others, then my own worth is questioned.[25]

It is not the object of this chapter to deal specifically with bioethics, either in detail or in general. But bioethics can be seen in the wider perspective of the question of the link between man's dignity and his behavior towards nature. After all, *bio-ethics* has to do with our *mores* concerning *life*, i.e. nature, including our nature, the latter being more particularly the domain of bioethics such as it is conventionally circumscribed nowadays. This being so, the reflection to follow is not foreign to bioethics, even though it will not focus on their issues.

DIGNITY, OR RESPECTABILITY, OF NATURE?

Does ascribing dignity to nature make any sense? Considering what has been said of dignity in this chapter so far, the answer to this question is obviously *no*: practically none of the traits deemed necessary to the constitution of dignity are present in any other species than man.[26] Would it mean, then, that non-human nature is to be seen as a world of worthless things, to be disposed of at will? Less obviously, the answer is also *no*: to deprive nature, and more particularly animals, of dignity does not amount to depriving them of respectability.

Respectability has of course nothing to do in this context with its usual sense of successful social conformity. It is taken as meaning "worthy of respect"; it applies to realities that are such that they make respect of them possible. And it must be added that worth is thought of here as never intrinsic to anybody or anything, never an essential and objective character of whatever, or whoever, is being qualified by it. *Worth* is a value which can be given by man, and by man only, to himself, to others, to nature.[27] The aim of this discussion, then, is not to find reasons which would prove that nature is respectable in itself, but to insist on a few points, most of them well-known, which should convince us that it is worth . . . giving worth to it.

Nature is our partner in life, an imposed partner with which we have to make do, whether it is our own nature, or non-human nature. Some aspects of it are lovable, some are detestable. Even though we might conceive a cognitive passion for it, this does not necessarily bring reconciliation with it, i.e., approval of what it is globally. Charles Darwin is very eloquent on this count when he writes, in a letter to the American naturalist Asa Gray (in Desmond/Moore 1992, 479):

> I cannot persuade myself that a beneficent and omnipotent God would have designedly created the *Ichneumonidae* with the express intention of their feeding within the living bodies of Caterpillars, or that a cat should play with mice.

Charles Darwin loved studying nature, and enjoyed his success in this activity, but this did not lead him to love nature as such, as a whole.

A well-known argument for respecting nature lies in the wish to protect our species: for biological reasons, our survival depends on the preservation of nature. Our motivation is then self-interest, and not the interest of nature. We are not its guardians: it can manage without us, as well as with us. Our presence may degrade it, but it will recover, as it has recovered from numerous, and much more dramatic, catastrophes in the million of years preceding our appearance on earth. So, as S. J. Gould has written (1991, 17), we should abstain from believing "(1) that we live on a fragile planet subject to permanent ruin by human malfeasance; (2) that humans must act as stewards of this fragility in order to save our planet."

This being so, the whole question now is whether respect of nature should confine itself to well-informed carefulness as to what we can do to it without degrading it to the point of endangering our own survival. Such wisdom, which could be called "minimal ecological wisdom," would still leave an open field to all sorts of behaviors which are repugnant to a great number of us. Among numerous others, the two examples of the controlled[28] slaughtering of baby seals and of the breeding of minks in cages are relevant in this context. There is no reason to forbid these practices if survival of our species is the criterion. It could even be pointed out that, with no threat to the environment, they improve, both aesthetically and physically, human comfort, insofar as fur coats are beautiful, and very warm.

But what about our dignity? Is respect of nature dictated by this kind of consideration sufficient to secure it? Is the increase of human comfort irrespective of the suffering it implies for animals compatible with morality? Because of its hedonism, utilitarianism has often been, wrongly, accused of justifying nearly anything so long as it brought about augmented pleasure for man. But read Jeremy Bentham on respect of animals (1948, chapter 17):

> The question is not, Can they reason? nor Can they talk? but Can they suffer?

And John Stuart Mill adds (1962, 263):

> The standard of morality . . . may accordingly be defined, the rules and precepts for human conduct, by the observance of which an existence such as has been described might be, to the greatest extent possible, secured to all mankind; and not to them only, but, so far as the nature of things admits, to the whole sentient creation.

Why extend our concern to that particular "whole"? Commenting on the views of proponents of animal rights such as Peter Singer,[29] Lori Gruen concludes (in Singer, 1991, 351), and this might serve as an answer to the question:

> Feelings of outrage or revulsion, sympathy or compassion are important to the development of complete moral sensibilities. As Mary Midgley has said, "Real scruples, and eventually moral principles, are developed out of this kind of raw material. They would not exist without it."

Here is not the place to argue on the validity of this opinion. It will be admitted as correct. The general idea is that men and women cannot confine their sensitivities within their own species. To do so, they would have to ignore their natural sympathy for (some) animals,[30] which would be a kind of self-mutilation. It must be pointed out that sympathy with animals can even reach the point of a feeling of solidarity because of shared contingency: we are members with them of a common world none of us has chosen, and which is devoid of ultimate accessible meaning. That such could be our feeling towards quite a number of non-human living beings is not indifferent for a definition of man's dignity.

To make the question more precise, three statements can be proposed as criteria of ethically adequate behavior towards nature (more particularly towards animals), i.e., as conditions of preserved human dignity. Once they have been enunciated, reasons will be given to bring added support to the possible validity of these criteria.

The three statements are as follows:

First criterion: there is loss of dignity for man when he is responsible for unnecessary destruction of nature.

Second criterion: even though there is no unnecessary destruction of nature, there is loss of dignity for man when he imposes unnecessary suffering on animals.

Third criterion: even though there is neither unnecessary destruction of nature, nor imposition of unnecessary suffering on animals, there is still loss of dignity for man when he produces unnecessarily, for instance through genetic engineering, types of animals which are degraded to the state of simplified biological machines.

In order to make them practically useful, a detailed analysis should be made of the meaning of the word "unnecessary" for each of the three criteria. We shall have to be content with a few rather general considerations.

Semantically speaking, "unnecessary" is relative to a precise conception of necessity. This notion is not taken here, as one might have guessed, in its metaphysical sense. More prosaically, it refers to different types of observable constraints, which go from the very obvious to the much less evident.

"Obviousness" is in a conception of necessity which refers to what is inevitable if one wants to assure mere survival of the individual and of our species. Necessity, in this case, is material and biological. In a utilitarian perspective, one can hardly question it: preferring death of man to the harming of nature could be motivated only by mystical naturalistic ideology.

The problem is much more tricky when we come to the "less evident": social and cultural necessity. In an ethnological perspective, practices such as hunting for reasons other than mere survival, the slaughtering of animals involving suffering for them, religious sacrifice, and passionately invested traditions such as bullfights, can be seen as parts of cultural and social wholes whose integrity would be threatened if people were forced to abandon them. One might not approve of them, yet at the same time be convinced that they mean so much to the cultures and societies concerned that renouncing them would amount to a destruction of the symbolic cement of these cultures and societies. Utilitarianism would then have to decide the question in the difficult terms of the balance between pleasure and pain, for animals as well as for men. The question is difficult, but it is one well worth asking.

Whatever love or respect we feel for nature, we just cannot completely avoid using it as a means to reach *our* ends. Concerning food, vegetarianism is no solution to the question, because plants are part of life. It seems true that they do not suffer. But animals can be painlessly killed. From this we can conclude that there is no more cruelty in the eating of meat than in the eating of vegetables and, consequently, not more dignity in those addicted to an exclusive vegetarian diet than in omnivorous individuals. This is not the question, then. The question is how legitimate can the use of animals be for other than alimentary, i.e., for cultural and social, ends. A whole book could be written analyzing various relevant customs, and taking into account the meanings they have for the peoples they characterize. A good criterion for declaring some of those customs detestable, and so contrary to dignity, would be in showing their lack of necessity for the preservation of the essential symbolic core and social structures considered. When customs satisfy only base, and not basic instincts, they can be deemed gratuitous, and hence it can be concluded that they should be dispensed with.

MAN AS RELATIONS

Utilitarianism, particularly of the John Stuart Mill variety,[31] is a good reference to treat these questions. But it is not enough, as it does not offer an extensive and substantial conception of man's identity which could make of his relation with nature an essential point. Such an anthropological theory, or at least an inkling of it, can be found in Karl Marx's works, particularly in the earlier ones.[32] He saw both man and nature as uncompleted realities, and conceived of their respective completions as being each the condition of the other, so that he could write, for instance (1971, 141):

> . . . only to social man is nature available as a bond with other men, as the basis of his own existence for others and theirs for him, and as the vital element in human reality; only to social man is nature the foundation of his own human existence. Only as such has his natural existence become a human existence and nature itself become human. Thus society completes the essential unity of man and nature: it is the genuine resurrection of nature, the accomplished naturalism of man and the accomplished humanism of nature.

Quite a number of questions are raised by this quotation. They cannot all be treated here. There would be much to say, for instance, in favor of this idea that we can attain an adequate relation with nature only insofar as we establish social justice at the same time. Except in the very improbable case of totalitarianism exerted by a dominant class which would be ecologically—and ecologically only—"enlightened," we can indeed hardly imagine a society riddled by inequality capable at the same time of securing a balanced integration of nature. In such a society, the protection of nature would very likely be a most secondary concern.

There would also be much to be said against this moving, but rather phantasmic, Marxian idea, of which Ernst Bloch was a superb supporter:[33] that it is the destiny of nature to be borne by man to the point of completion. S. J. Gould's wise pronouncement cited above should be sufficient as an argument contradicting a view which smarts of what could be called materialistic, naturalistic, mysticism.

But, concerning the dignity of man as referred to what he feels for, and does to, nature, Marx's central thesis that man's completion implies active, and respectful, communication with it, can, and must, be retained. As Jean Piaget has shown, personal identity[34] is built through a psychological genesis that consists in a progressive, and ever-widening, relation with things and people. *Things*: that means nature as well as man-made objects. And it would be preposterous to think that the process stops once we have acquired the mental structures which will serve as instruments in our adult lives. It is common psychological knowledge that we never stop relating to things and people, that *being*, for man, amounts to *being related to*: we *are* what we *do*; we are, essentially, the *ways* we act and communicate. And the whole question is whether there is dignity in the particular ways we choose.

K. Marx wrote (1971, 140) that man is able "to produce according to the measure of every species and knows everywhere how to apply its inherent standard to the object; thus man also fashions things according to the laws of beauty."

Commentary on this will unfortunately be brief. What should be emphasized first is our capacity, according to Marx, for understanding the particular characters—the "measure"—of the various species of animals. What should be secondly insisted upon is the fact that Marx mentions beauty right after that, in a rather cryptic formulation, which is in need of interpretation, because the philosopher never bothered to elaborate on it. The risk will then be taken of proposing one, however speculative it is. It might bring some more light on what dignity, relative to nature, consists in.

It just happens that man has a sense of beauty that is not restricted to his own works. It applies, sometimes, and selectively, to nature as well. There is no reason to think that the "object" mentioned by Marx in the quotation above is man's works of art; such a reading would actually be meaningless. The "object" is what exists independently, and is appropriated by man's sense of beauty considered as a faculty to bring out, to reveal, what would remain hidden if it were not for him. The object is nature, or rather aspects of it. They can be shown through the "magics" of art. (In painting, cubism, for instance, tried to do just that quite explicitly.) Relevant aspects of nature can also be thought of as potentialities which can become actual only through horticulture or breeding: there is beauty in thoroughbreds and cultivated roses, and then our humanity (our dignity) is enhanced, because we are adding to nature, instead of diminishing it. But is there any beauty in hornless cows confined in industrial stables, and pitilessly crammed in order to produce the greatest quantity of tasteless meat in the shortest possible time? There is not, and an indication of this is found in the fact that we are not particularly proud of having reduced a rather complex animal to the state of a food-producing machine: we exhibit thoroughbreds and roses, but we do not exhibit industrial stables, because they are a stain on our dignity.

In a well-known meditation (1624), John Donne wrote these famous lines:

> No man is an island, entire of itself; every man is a piece of the continent, a part of the main; if a clod be washed away by the sea, Europe is the less, as well as if a promontory were, as if a manor of thy friend's or of thine own were. Any man's death diminishes me, because I am involved in mankind; and therefore never send to know for whom the bell tolls; it tolls for thee.

Man is involved in nature as well as in mankind. Not only death, but also degradation, should be considered. When he is responsible for either, passively or actively, man is the less, because he has forfeited his dignity.

NOTES

1. *Anthropology* or *sciences of man*, rather than *social sciences*, will be used in this chapter. *Social sciences* is deemed rather inappropriate, because it excludes for example psychology, which is of the utmost importance for the treatment of our question. It is true that man is a social being. But it is also true that what makes him social are a number of mental irreducible traits which, though they belong to all individuals, are nonetheless not "social" for all that.

    Anthropology is a very convenient word when taken in its etymological, and philosophically classical (Kant), sense: science of man. It has the advantage of integrating everything that is known, or supposed to be known, about the specificity of man, whether this knowledge has been elaborated by sociology—which is, of course, a *social* science, by psychology—which is not—or by ethology of man—which is not, either.

2. I must confess to some sort of embarassment in seeing humanities quite often associated with social sciences in academic discussions. This embarassment is particularly due to the fact that, whereas the expression "social sciences" is clear enough, even though one might prefer to substitute another one for it (see note 1), the term "humanities" actually is not.

Conventionally, "humanities" can be understood as pertaining to the study of classical Greek and Roman cultures, and one then does not see why they should be associated with the sciences of man. If one extends the meaning of the term "humanities" to include in its scope all these subjects (theology, philosophy, law, philology, literature . . .) which do not belong to scientific anthropology, but are nevertheless concerned with the same object, i.e., man, his societies, and his cultures, then, of course, association with the sciences of man is legitimate, but up to a point only.

Insofar as anthropology and humanities, though having the same object, can be distinguished on the basis, broadly speaking, of the conception of reason they adhere to (e.g., critical, scientific reason *vs* metaphysical speculation, or hermeneutics), then there is a gap between the two categories of subjects. Epistemological sanity demands that they should not be taken as equally valid where the production of knowledge is concerned. Which is not to say that they cannot have fruitful relationships. But anthropology can be fecundated by the humanities only if their intuitions and theories can be translated into scientific language, i.e., the language of critical reason (see below, notes 17 and 23). In this chapter, I shall try to stick to that language.

3. Henceforth: the Declaration.

4. Declaration, Preamble, paragraph 5: "*Whereas* the peoples of the United Nations have in the Charter reaffirmed their faith in fundamental human rights, in the dignity and worth of the human person . . . ."

5. "Ideological" is not meant here in a derogatory sense. It should be taken as a neutral term referring to a *corpus of ideas*, whether they are philosophical, theological, political, or even scientific.

6. This is the case of biogenetics, of course. See *Widmer* 1993.

7. See *Widmer* 1988 and 1992.

8. Whatever their differences, nearly all biologists agree on the validity of the neo-Darwinian framework. Physicists can do research together in quantum mechanics, whether they adhere to the Copenhagen, or to the Paris, conception of chance.

9. The sciences of man have an influence on the shaping of their object, whereas the "hard" sciences have not. See *Widmer* 1988 and 1992.

10. "Adequacy of discourse" is meant as congruence between facts and theories, i.e. truth. Much has been said on this definition of truth. I adopt on this point Karl Popper's stand: we can never be sure of having reached congruence; we

can pretend at best to approximation, while retaining congruence as an ideal for both the "hard" and "soft" sciences.

11. See, for example, the works of R. Keesing (1976) and C. Kluckhohn (1962).

12. See note 7.

13. Radical negation of the individual can be found in the works of quite a number of sociobiologists (E. O. Wilson, R. Dawkins, Trivers, etc.). It can be shown, and it has been shown, that this negation is founded on a form of biological reductionism which is most questionable.

14. See *Widmer* 1992.

15. See, for example, *Berthoud* 1989, 159.

16. See the Declaration, Article 1.

17. Jean-Paul Sartre would not have agreed with this statement, of course. But equating, as he does, liberty with nothingness (*"le néant"*) does not bring any kind of understanding, and there is no valid reason for tearing reflexive consciousness away from general mental determinism.

18. Knowing the cause of a feeling makes it possible, in some cases, to disqualify the ideological pretension founded on that feeling. For example, Sigmund Freud quite legitimately says that the feeling of liberty does not prove in any way that man is actually free. But it never came to Freud's mind to deny the existence of the feeling itself.

19. See note 18.

20. More precise reference to Kant's idea of *Self* might be relevant here. The problem with Kant's idea is that it is cognitive only, and slightly metaphysical, as it is conceived as an *a priori* transcendental form of pure reason. It makes psychology possible. I would add that it gives sense to respect as well, insofar as it can be taken as the basis of an irrevocable demand for acceptance by others as an end. Psychologically speaking, Kant's categorical imperative depends on that demand, and should be considered as a consequence of it, progressively built during mental genesis.

21. I will show, further on in the text, that this kind of respect makes sense only for human beings. Animals, and more widely nature, can, and sometimes should, be respected without having to be seen as irreducible to scientific explanation.

22. See note 18.

23. I owe much to Jean-Paul Sartre's analysis (see *L'Etre et le Néant*) of the *for-itself* (*"pour-soi"*) as consciousness of incompletion of self, and project of completion, never to be carried out except in death. Much of it can be retained, without following Sartre in his rejection of deterministic language. See *Widmer* 1988, 92–94.

24. Self-hatred is usually detestation of mental facts closely linked with the body: all sorts of needs, desires and impulses. The self hates *it*self inasmuch as the individual evaluates these facts negatively. To do so, the self must put them at a distance, must not identify with them. Ultimate self-hatred would be detestation of the whole of self, i.e., of the evaluator as well as of the evaluated. Systematic pessimism tries to do just that, as is shown in the works of the

French-Rumanian thinker Emile Cioran. But, of course, such a stand is philosophically tenable only as long as one trusts, at least implicitly, the critical
function of reason, which is inseparable from self. This means that self-
hatred is then not complete. The demonstration of accomplished self-hatred
lies in actual suicide. Thinking about killing oneself, recommending it explicitly as a solution, as Cioran does, is not enough. Total self-hatred can reach
coherence only through silence.

25. Actual dignity depends of course on adequate social, economic, and cultural
conditions. When one is an accomplice, through a position of quietly enjoyed
privilege, of gross inequality, or of cultural intolerance, then one's dignity is
shattered. The call for justice on all counts in the Declaration of Human
Rights finds its legitimation in these considerations.

   There is no dignity without self-respect, of which John Rawls writes
(1973, 440): "We may define self-respect (or self-esteem) as having two aspects. First of all . . ., it includes a person's sense of his own value, his secure
conviction that his conception of the good, his plan of life, is worth carrying
out. And second, self-respect implies a confidence in one's ability, so far as it
is within one's power, to fulfill one's intentions. . . . It is clear then why self-
respect is a primary good. Without it nothing may seem worth doing, or if
some things have value for us, we lack the will to strive for them. . . . Therefore the parties in the original position *would wish to avoid at almost any
cost the social conditions that undermine self-respect* [italics mine]."

26. When we speak of a lion's, or any other animal's, dignity, we make an an-
thropomorphic statement through confused identification with the animal.
Nobody would speak of a hen's, or of a pig's, dignity, because identification
with them is not very flattering. It is interesting to note that, most of the time,
dignity is attributed to carnivorous predators.

   As John Stuart Mill wrote (1962, 258), "Human beings have faculties more
elevated than the animal appetites, and when once made conscious of them, do
not regard anything as happiness which does not include their gratification."

27. This statement is, of course, not compatible with the Christian conception,
which is, as Raymond Plant writes (1991, 262), "embedded in the natural
law tradition, which takes the view that individual human beings have an
inherent dignity and worth in the sight of God. . . . I may vehemently dislike
your character and what you do, but I must respect your dignity as a human
being. This dignity does not require me to like you or love you, but it does
require that I respect you and do not infringe on your rights."

28. "Controlled" must be understood as being done in such a way that neither the
preservation of the species concerned, nor the biotopic balance, are in danger.

29. See *Singer* 1975.

30. Sympathy for a mosquito, or a worm, is rather difficult. We are able to feel
sympathy essentially for animals which share with us the capacity of obvious
suffering.

31. See note 26.

32. Reference to Karl Marx's works does not make a Marxist of me. I have quite
a few reservations to make on some important points of the theory. I can sum

them up in stating that I do not agree that economics is the main, if not the only, determination of our societies; I do not see dialectics as the fundamental law of social development; and I refuse the thesis of History conceived as a finalized force.

I could, but I will not, discuss here the problem raised by Louis Althusser of the so-called discontinuity between the younger and the older Marx's works. I believe this discontinuity is a figment of Althusser's imagination: Marx never disowned his earlier concerns; they are present in his later writings at least as motivations.

33. See for instance *Bloch* 1959.
34. It could seem strange to refer to Piaget as a decisive reference when personal identity is the question, insofar as we experience it in affective *tones*, and consequently tend to think of it mainly in affective *terms*. But we should acknowledge that the emotional awareness of identity could not make sense if there was not, as an object for it, and as a source of it, some sort of basic structure which can be conceived of, and hence known, only as the result of a constructive cognitive process. After all, human identity is fundamentally *reflexive*. What would emotions be, if they were not emotions of, and about, someone, something—that is, of, and about, an entity which cannot be reduced to amorphous spendings of mental energy? If Piaget can be reproached for ignoring affectivity, there is much to be said against the silence psychoanalysis provides as an answer when we wonder why there is an *Ego*, and an *Ego* such as it is.

REFERENCES

Bentham, Jeremy 1948 [1789], *The Principles of Morals and Legislation*, New York, Hafner Press.

Berthoud, Gerald 1989, "Droits de l'Homme et Savoirs anthropologiques," in: Sosoe, Lukas K. (ed.), *Identité: Evolution ou Différence?*, Fribourg (CH), Editions Universitaires, 137–166.

Bloch, Ernst 1959, *Das Prinzip Hoffnung*, Frankfurt/M., Suhrkamp.

Desmond, Adrian/Moore, James 1992, *Darwin*, London, Penguin Books.

Donne, John 1624, *Meditation XVII*.

Gould, Stephen Jay 1992, *Bully for Brontosaurus*, London, Penguin Books.

Keesing, Roger 1976, *Cultural Anthropology, a Contemporary Perspective*, New York, Holt, Rinehart and Winston.

Kluckhohn, Clyde 1962, *Culture and Behavior*, New York, The Free Press, Macmillan Company.

Marx, Karl 1971, *The Early Texts* (David McLellan, ed.), Oxford, Oxford University Press.

Mill, John Stuart 1962 [1863], *Utilitarianism*, Glasgow, Fontana Press.

Plant, Raymond 1991, *Modern Political Thought*, Oxford, Basil Blackwell.

Rawls, John 1973, *A Theory of Justice*, Oxford, Oxford University Press.

Schweder, Richard A./Levine, Robert A. (eds.) 1990, *Culture Theory; Essays on Mind, Self and Emotion*, Cambridge, Cambridge University Press.

Singer, Peter 1975, *Animal Liberation*, New York, Random House.
———— 1991, *A Companion to Ethics*, Oxford, Basil Blackwell.
Skinner, Burrhus F. 1971, *Beyond Freedom and Dignity*, New York, Bantam Books.
Turnbull, Colin 1984, *The Mountain People*, London, Triad/Paladin Books.
Widmer, Charles 1988, *Dépossession*, Turin, Albert Meynier.
———— 1992, *Droits de l'Homme et Sciences de l'Homme; pour une Ethique anthropologique*, Genève-Paris, Librairie Droz S.A.
———— 1993, "De l'Ethique des Sciences sociales à l'Ethique anthropologique," in: *Revue européenne des Sciences sociales* 31 (95), 167–180.

Science as a Response to Creation

RUDOLF ZUR LIPPE

RESPONSE, FREEDOM, AND RESPONSIBILITY

Reflections on ethics become quite different from the usual speculation about so called values, and their application, when we go back to the Greek roots of the word. Its double meaning may teach us a lesson about the existential context of the argument for the good, and the fact of living, i.e., the fact of living in a given part of the earth. 'ἤθοσ and ἔθα were the words for the dwelling-place of a particular people, their habitat, and the rules of life not only *in* their country, but of life *with* the particular habits and conditions of it.

Ethical principles, then, were not deduced from some abstract ideas, but rather were abstracted from the experiences of life in sharing ground and heaven, rain and sun, earthly forces, and the protection of gods with all other beings in the very island or limited world between that sea and those mountains. Consequently, the habits or rules of cohabitation between men and women; old and young; people, animals, and plants; and winds and seasons differed from Athens to Ionia, from Euboia to Thebes.

This was an attempt at mutual support for survival. If, for the taste of advanced civilization, its unchangeable code resembled too much the impiteous circles of nature, it nevertheless offered, like nature, limited but favorable conditions for the natural and the historic beings to unfold their proper faculties in mutual respect (provided the reader will accept the mythological fiction of mutuality at least as a significant metaphor).

Expansion replaced cohabitation—law replaced ethos. The circle was cut open to become the line of linear, progressing time, as Jean Gebser has put it, when the mental age of humanity rose in the Western world. The circular interpretation of the relationship between a people and the world around them through myth became obsolete. The self-evidence of the habits in a given cohabitation of human and other beings that had ensured the historical consciousness of the conditions of life in self-sustaining reciprocity was, now, seen more as an irrational limit to expansion. The process of its complete abandonment in the *praxis* of modernity took a long time. The simultaneity of the principle of progress and frontier, together with the practical continuation, at least up to some degree, of part of the ancient attitudes, made the mental concept of a world for societies that replaced the ideology of sustainable cohabitation somehow viable. After a preparatory period of about two millenniums, this balance collapsed abruptly in the last few decades.

The traditional context was broken when various peoples of Greece left their dwelling-places in order to colonize countries in quite different regions of the Mediterranean world, and when the new law of the cities came to replace those self-evident rules that had been guarded by the priests as part of the local cult. Now, judges had to decide about right or wrong, moral or immoral. Orestes, condemned for committing matricide in the traditional order, and pursued by the Erynies, could gain liberty under the rule of modern Athenian right with the protection of Athene.

The new liberty led to expansion in many different respects. The principle consequence that arose was the necessity for decision making in the discursive fashion of argument and counterargument, while the epic period of the dialogue between politics and cosmology, spinning on the wheel of oracles, declined. The problem of responsibility became the counterpart to freedom from the ban of nature. At the same time, societies no longer had to invest so much effort to ban the ban of nature, yet they failed to realize that the spare forces should not only be employed to gain power for expansion but rather to ban, now, the possible unlimitedness of that expansion. Freedom from the too narrow context of nature was not conceived of as a challenge to self-reflection that might have led to freedom with nature as a new context. Even within society, the knowledge of what is due and what is sacrilege was replaced by the idea of right and wrong as fixed by the state. Think of Antigone, the sister, eliminated by Creon, the king.

A PLAY OF RESPONSE AND COUNTERRESPONSE

It is, apparently, only the contemporary vastness of damages which makes us fully aware of the fact that there are limits to the expansion of limits. In this historical moment, when we finally realize that we have left or broken the self-evident relations with nature, some natural scientists provide us with insights into how life lives—with a knowledge that may help us to conceive a paradigm of responsibility which is not just a secondary derivation of some sort of values established through convention.

Looking at relations and processes in nature from a human point of view, we can say that all living beings and all things and events always react. While every change in nature responds to some preceding event like an echo, man can act out of his free will. We can at least try to decide about conditions, inversing the relationship of cause and effect to that of finalization.

But since we are to some extent free from reaction bound circles, how do we have to respond to whatever we encounter: the Other, out of our free will? Even a master in his house has to respect rules of cohabitation with respect to his servants. As a matter of fact, human beings live—whether or not we agree to it and accept that truth as part of our culture—never as masters but in coexistence with a sisterly, brotherly world that bears our existence and challenges our will, that invites our senses and nourishes our awareness, and that guides our imagination. We have to imagine our being here as a mode of corresponding relations. The modern world of industrialized humankind requires a very complex relationship to its world in order to cope with the extreme expansion of limits that has become manifest. But however elaborate the correspondences have to be conceived, the main principle will always be the same basic ground of cohabitation or coexistence. As our expansion actually embraces the whole of the world, we should be ready to love her whole. "Make love not war," taken in a general sense, ought to be our maxim. Love is the right word as long as we do not reduce it to signify a particular emotion or a psychological, physiological expectation. Love as the readiness to meet and to live with the Other, whether next to or farthest from us, and as the sensual in the sense of aesthetic attention to the Other. Far beyond the myths of the mythological age, cosmology will always hold the style of answer required.

This leads us to state that, substantially, aesthetics are the better ethics if we read the concept of relationship in terms of forms of material mediation and of how we live those forms as experiences of our life.

Existence realizes itself *as* exchange and *through* exchange with the world around us, just as human life is constituted through the manifold forms of exchange between body and soul, senses and reason. While it is very difficult to deduce the modes of our organic life from the modes of our reason, reasoning may well be understood as a higher differentiation of, and as an abstraction from, the functioning of the organs of our body. "Mind and nature, a necessary unity" in Gregory Bateson's terms. If we give the term "aesthetics" its full and original meaning, then we might properly translate it by consciousness through the senses. Aesthetical understanding, research, and interpretation of the concrete, materialized world is, consequently, an undeniable ground and an irreplaceable part of our knowledge.

Change is the mode of life, and continuation is its necessary counterpart or complement. Or rather, life is the moving balance between both, against a horizon of differences that present the actual results of histories. If there were no continuation, this would lead to the collapse of the horizon in which every balancing movement is suspended. Balancing presupposes that there are limitations to change. Just where such limits will occur, however, cannot be predicted.

But we do know, if we take the trouble to realize it, that in the histories of species there is a play of change and continuity, i.e., limits to change. The roles are distributed in such a way that the species as a whole goes on for continuity, whereas the individuals may go for change, which is either accepted at the level of the species—the result we call mutation— or not—resulting in the respective individuals dying out. So, the risk is existential by definition; all is at stake. At the same time, there is a rigorous limit to speed, at least on the level of living beings, allowing for the play of a balancing movement between one changing species and the other beings and processes that will eventually be affected. We may call this balancing movement a play of response and counterresponse.

SELF-LIMITATION AND SELF-REFLECTION AS A HUMAN RESPONSE TO THE WORLD

How can we—human beings with a historical free will—search for the variations of that play, given the fact that the distance between us and the rest of nature and the respective distinctions do not allow for a simple imitation?

In the practice of human acting the answer is evident: Self-limitation is the practical reflection springing from human freedom to impose the power of will. The moral or spiritual answer transcends self-limitation to the realm of consciousness, i.e., freedom reflecting itself. The conscious reflection that creates a conscious relationship between the world with us and ourselves. Thus we are transcending the *animal rationale*, the *homo sapiens sapiens* on our way towards our real part in creation: to reply to the world transforming its impressions on us into human images, that world which bears us and which extinguishes us as materialized beings. In the metaphors of the Bible this would be Adam giving names to the animals instead of man forcing the world to his knees. The Jews say that the human beings are there so that God may talk to them and have them talking to him. I take it that not only the language of words is the medium for this relationship;

artistic, ritual, and other creation is probably the main human medium through which to realize that eternal exchange of images.

Whether we choose the word and concept of God or not, this is the only real, concrete context for human responsibility. In contrast, the current use of the term responsibility neither evokes nor allows for a response flowing from human existential freedom. Wherever a particular definition of a given situation, whether in terms of science or technology or ideology, is imposed on people, the claim for individual responsibility becomes a strategy for political manipulation. This does not give us the right or even the ability to refuse to accept those facts which are actually given. It is valuable only in respect to the ideology that is made up in order to prevent us from discussing the definition that guarantees the continuation of the principles and strategies producing these given facts. The actual fashion of ethics is very often part of the scenario of manipulation, providing those who want to avoid discussion of the definition of unlimited action with such amendments that only limit some of the symptoms. No other responsibility should ever be accepted than the elevation of self-limitation to the level of reflection within the play of response and counter-response.

THE VALUE OF VALUES IN THE ETHOS OF WEIGHING

I oppose myself to the deductive style of ethics also for a second reason, implied in what has been said. In the deductive style a general category or paradigm is applied to the example of a given case. This procedure generates the procedure of judgment about right or wrong referring to the authority of the category or paradigm. When we consider life as a delicate and moving equilibrium, the appropriate mode of decision is weighing, not deduction and application. While the latter, scientific mode, refers to abstract knowledge and has concrete consequences in the given situation, the former refers to the concrete context, incorporating general knowledge as the horizon of the arising situation. Within the scientific approach, reality is defined on an abstract level, whereas the first approach is conscious of the fact that every situation has to be existentially lived. This is the aspect of the *conditio humana* which, in Jeanne Hersch's words, subjects all our acts to "incarnation," this term being understood in the purely etymological, not in a theological sense. The values from which a theory of ethics deduces its judgments always have a conventional character, i.e., they correspond to a given choice which itself corresponds to a given historical context. When ethics are referred to as deriving from absolute values, the historical context, which in most cases is quite remote, must be eliminated from the actual consciousness. The whole construction becomes obsolete if those values are regarded as more than just a choice of historical propositions that may help in weighing the actual situation. The responsibility towards the world in terms of the actual relationship between us and the beings and processes at stake cannot be replaced by the claim to those "absolute values." I think that this argument is completely in the line of Karl-Otto Apel's ethical hermeneutics.

The difference between the two approaches becomes evident when we regard the key tool of scientific decision making: the concept of threshold or critical values. We can always manipulate the concrete definition by arguing theoretically and leaving the responsibility to the authority of the paradigm. Yet if we live up to our coexisting with the Other on behalf of which our decision is being made, the Other's response to the impact of our decision requires our counterresponse to the consequences of that response, and that in the existential terms of our lives.

This political aspect is very important. But, and this is even more important, the deductive mode affects the whole of our attitudes towards ourselves, towards other human beings, and towards the rest of creation. This is true owing to the devaluation of the aesthetic, i.e., existential modes of encountering the world and knowing it, and ourselves. Here we are facing a vicious circle, vicious mainly in the sense that one side seems to justify the other while, in reality, it accelerates the devaluation of the senses that indeed become less valuable, because they contribute just as little as our mind is ready to become aware of and to elaborate. This is an inversion of the lively play of response and counterresponse—the play constituting the human being from within and in exchange with the world outside. This play never comes to a complete stand still; that would be the proper definition of death. But a system of thought, action, and evaluation, purely or mainly based on highly abstract ideas and deduction, is, in fact, a way to refuse life. It means to refuse the very conditions of human life, conditions that may be changed and expanded, but never overcome. The deductive mode implies finalization in the sense that decision making and problem solving strategies are mere means to the end of a stable equilibrium which is conceived of as the precondition for life. Yet if striving for a state of equilibrium is not considered to be life,—life will never take place. A life in perfect equilibrium would not be a human life— much rather an angelic life or some other phantasm.

Weighing in the existential context invites us to understand the processes of deciding and acting, and experiencing the play of response and counterresponse as our partaking in life. We then unfold our own part in the play through the search of moving balance. In contrast, the purely deductive attitude, still predominating in the West, makes our faculty to live life depend on a situation of stable equilibrium yet to be established—

and to be established first of all. The steps toward this goal are regarded as a suffering and a loss of opportunity to bloom because every presence, judged in terms of the final goal, appears to be deficient.

We realize that the deductive construction not only negates life as it has to be lived in ever-present steps, it implies a strange, if not contradictory attitude toward values; the principle of finalization leads to an attitude of responsibility in the perspective of a final evolution, and leaves the actual concrete relation within the historically given situation completely vague (that relation being reconstructed only indirectly, as a secondary result deduced from the relation we establish between ourselves and a goal that we believe in and the relation between that goal and the actual concrete situation). If such a construction is the very medium of every reflection in reasoning, it becomes destructive of all existential context of life when not reflected into the practice of weighing, facing the very reality of here and now. Freedom is not the liberty to emigrate, but the unavoidable choice between the possible alternatives of *hic et nunc*, in the horizon of the possible and necessary reflection in the abstract. As long as the existential risk is transposed to a final judgment alone, actual responsibility is suspended until those later days thought of as enabling that final judgment.

Together with the principle of practicability—which is the idea that autonomous men and women may decide what reality should be and know how to realize their decision—this is the reason why the deductive style is so attractive. The deductive reconstruction of the world, of life, of concrete situations, transforms present complexity into distant complication, much too complicated to allow identifying and calculating all the possible consequences, so that actual responsibility may and must be reduced in scale out of pragmatic reasons.

Note that my argument is about the deductive style of decision making as suggested by the tradition of the natural sciences, not about science. Science, like other human faculties, will be allowed to unfold and to play its proper role so much better when treated as just one specific way among others to gain knowledge, and as a major element in the historical process of weighing.

THE HUMAN EXISTENTIAL RISK AND
THE BIOLOGICAL RISK IN NATURE

To make sure that the term "existential" is understood in its full meaning we should emphasize the logic of bio-logics which connect weighing to the fact that the resulting response exposes the responding being to the consequences of the resulting change of further conditions of life for itself as well as for the Other. The human species has the power to expose the Other to a very much reduced risk of consequences for itself, at least of more or less immediate consequences. So the question of ethics is: How can we embrace our liberty from those circuits of nature in order to unfold the freedom for conscious coexistence with the Other? At present, the dominating pattern seems to be that of liberty from limitation by pure or mere reaction, while the free capacities are merely employed to expand the limits of risk-free risk taking. This is a kind of reflection. But it lacks the reflection of reflection that should and may replace the limits of the biological level by existential reflection of freedom for ourselves and the Other: love in the sense of Humberto Maturana's concept of a "biology of love." Surely we have shown that this style of relationship—in Ludwig Fleck's sense of different "styles of thought" in different periods of history—with the world, that attitude toward the Other and ourselves is constituted and developing according to a logics of its own. On our way we have entered the domain of hermeneutics in the radical sense explained by Hans Georg Gadamer. To make things even clearer, I wish to add that Immanuel Kant's idea of freedom as an idea of pure reason definitely requires a complementary idea: the very idea of love as mentioned above.

Life understood in such a way means to struggle for the right response to ever-present actual disequilibrium, guided by the loving awareness of the Other, enjoying the possible encounters with the world and with ourselves through the responses of the world to us.

So far, the greatest danger of misunderstanding lies probably in the use of the term *reaction*. It must be rehabilitated and relieved from the reduction of its meaning to mechanical reflection to a stimulus in the model of stimulus and reflex. Reaction does not just mean an impulse repulsed by another. Reaction is an action in the proper media and patterns, and style of the reacting being. It is an answer to a question rather than an autonomous outburst of an isolated will. The answer of the reacting being realizes its very individuality, and its proper impulse pursues its own particular existence; yet both answer and impulse are molded according to the challenging, inviting situation—much in the sense of the observation, shared by so many, that the style of a letter may tell us even more about the addressee than about the author.

The term reaction, understood in this sense, is based on the observation that even reflection in physics implies change on either side. The ray of sunlight reflected from a mirror changes itself as it becomes somewhat more diffuse and weakened; it leaves the mirror changed since the spot of reflection, after the event, differs from the rest of the mirror, in temperature for instance.

We do not need to investigate further steps to complexity in order to accept the idea that human reflection is a very complex member of one and the same family of relationships, now including the repercussions of reflections of reflections, which finally lead to a consciousness that stands for the faculty of self-reflection.

Thus, human beings do not distinguish themselves from nature because of their capacity to reflect. That would mean total dichotomy. We are different from what we call nature in the order of freedom owing to the possible distance between event and response, and the according faculty to anticipate counterresponse by abstract chains of reflection, i.e., speculative reason. In consequence, ours is the responsibility of reflecting not just on an isolated actual question, but much more on the consequences of the virtual chain of possible counterresponses and counter-counterresponses.

Intellectually, this means "responsibility." Existentially, this means that we have to live within ourselves the imaginary process of that possible chain and, in particular, the virtual part of the Other in the process. In other words, if we act at the level of the expanded limits of our intellectual capacities we are bound to play the eventual experience in our imagination beforehand. Not only do reflections of the discursive order come into account. The existential dimension of the play in nature must equally be brought onto the stage. By ways of imagination, we have to incorporate, to embody the part of the Other—"putting ourselves in the place of the other" as we use to say—so that we reflect on ourselves not just in the mechanical reflection of the reflector, but in the ways in which the other beings and processes live their responses. Here, evidently, is the level where art and science must cooperate and integrate their respective methods of research.

HOW TO CATCH A FLY WHILE FLYING

The model of response and counterresponse has a significant disadvantage in comparison to the simplification of impulse and reflex: The fiction of complete determinism which offered a certain perspective to prediction has been abandoned. The scientific approach to life based on such presumable chains of impulse and reflex as cause and effect allowed for a preconstruction of a development in the future. Response and counterresponse imply many variables and also, what is even more important and of a higher principle complexity, all the interdependent relationships which constitute these variables in a living being, and even in any process of nature. The term "nature" must be taken in its full meaning; it stands for the Other in general, which we do not know deeply enough, and which we even cannot know because of the very condition of human existence. We are part of nature ourselves, that is to say, we exist in the very mode of change. Heraklit's famous statement that we never step into the same river again is rarely reflected upon. And still, it gives only half of the truth. We are never the same beings when we step into this river again. While we try to rely on fixed data for future evolution, things change, and we change ourselves.

The fashion to replace deterministic models by so-called scenarios is patently not a solution to the problem, the problem being the ambition of science to predict future situations with reliable exactness. But a scenario is exactly what the term suggests. It belongs to the world of fiction, not of fact. The difference from a novel is rather a negative one: a writer is supposed to translate his or her subjective awareness of not yet graspable evolutions in a forthcoming history, be it that of a society or that of an individual life. Whereas transposed into scientific standards of objectivity, the attempt of developing scenarios is necessarily reduced to establishing facts. Subjective awareness is replaced by objective data; by that which is graspable: statistics. In order to limit the range of possible error, "future" in this sort of futures research is defined as the next twenty years or less. Change is defined as the extrapolation of pre-existing "trends."

That definition, a problem itself, is part of the general problem—the role of time. Reconstruction or deconstruction are characterized by the absence of time as process. Time cannot just be added as one more factor. It is not a variable like others, but the dimension in which things vary. Time is what the histories of the beings and processes do to one another and how they respond. This we cannot reflect upon only in abstract terms, emiological sequences, for instance. We have to somehow live through these histories in our imagination with the Other opposite us. But not as all other beings. Human beings are given the faculty and virtue to imagine somehow an evolution just in their inner being. Love is not an emotional complement to reasoning but rather a reasonable dimension of human reflection. When we sing to the glory of the creation we express our reflecting response, comparable to the bird singing, in whatever function ethology may identify with its behavior. Georg Picht emphasizes in his *Myth and Art* that in nature the very gesture of life produces itself and displays itself at one and the same time, through the same act: *pro-ductio*, while human beings find it so difficult to bridge producing and displaying.

We have come to consider reasoning, along the logics of cause and effect, as one mode of reflection among others. However, our observations on reflection not only lead us to realize that reasoning in concepts is just one, although in some respect an absolutely privileged sort of reflection. We have also become aware of the necessity to search for possibilities of translating and transforming one mode of reflection into the others, and to compare and mediate one mode of reflection with others.

ART, MYTH, DREAM, AND THE LIKE

There are quite a few of those other modes. Under different perspectives, Theodor W. Adorno and Claude Lévy-Strauss provide us with approaches to myth, although their hermeneutic awareness is still limited by the two different philosophical schools they somehow belong to. The tradition to which Hegel and Marx belonged, in one respect converging with nineteenth century evolutionism, insisted on a finalistic continuity. In that perspective, myth is earlier than logic; it has a preparatory function for a higher order on a scale of more and more enlightened consciousness. Myth is defined therefore as of lower rank. This is the concept and practice of "the one after the other" in linear, historical time. The tradition built by Emile Durkheim and the structuralists established, theoretically, an order of "the one besides the other," thus avoiding hierarchy. But even with them the practical insight of considering the one as a complement to the other is still lacking. Myth is certainly not what we want to go back to, and, anyway, it arises from very different historical constellations. But we might identify some characteristics of myth which we could try to imitate out of our own modern situation, thus looking for corresponding tools of reason enlarged beyond the limits of deterministic reasoning. A myth gives an interpretation of the world, or of one of its particular aspects, by telling a story. But telling alone rather reduces the myth to a sort of fairy tale. Two other elements are of crucial importance. The recounting has to be performed periodically—not only regularly, but in a rhythm corresponding to the significance of the key events told and related again and again. The myth has to be told and listened to, responded to by the whole of the historical community. In ancient Greece the last form of such a ritual was the performance of the tragedy of the year in the symbolic presence of the people of Athens. Ritual has a specific meaning and is essential for the reality of the myth. The recounting is a social act, tying history to the path of eternity.

At least three of these elements are very likely to become integrated, or reintegrated, into the context of modern civilizations. One is the epic mode of expression as a form that implies time as a predominant constitutive factor of its texture. Its steps emerge one out of the understanding of the other, as we open up our readiness to understand step by step, realizing one existential moment after another, with our freedom bound to respond to each time-grasped meaning. A second element is of the same order, transposed onto the level of society. Nils Bohr claimed, in the middle of the twentieth century, that scientific research must be translated into common language in order to become integrated into historical knowledge—into society's cultural consciousness. This would entail an interpretation for the collective mind and in the existential reality of the community, comparable to the effect of the Sophoclesian tragedy in Athens. Comparable, not of course identical. A third element constitutes the significance of such a symbol: We must be conscious to be a part of the whole of Life and we must accept being just a part, a truly particular part. We have to content ourselves with these few examples, although it would be tempting to develop them and bring them from the context of myth to the level of logical forms. Let us add one more characteristic trait of living myths: Any particular myth is present in a particular period. Recalled periodically through the ritual of recounting in the cult, it possibly changes with evolution of the community, varies with the different conditions of the different dwelling places, and thus maintains its identity through specific change with respect to specific places, times, and contexts. Such a change is not arbitrary or contingent, and the respective identity is not simply static.

In order to demonstrate the effort of fruitfully complementing traditional science with other modes of reflection, let me just point to three authors who pursued and are still following the same path. Johann Wolfgang von Goethe provides us with a complementary methodology including science and art. To either of them he assigns a particular mode of research which may contribute both to human knowledge and orientation, and to an interpretation of the world. They are proposed as two modes of research, bound to each other by the common effort towards compatibility of their approaches and results. Goethe bases his concept on the systematic observation that in a work of art, everything is concentrated in the one creative moment which remains present in the finished work, while science finds its mode of existence in the indefinite sequence of particular experiences. We might also recall the famous contention by Gregory Bateson (in *Steps to an Ecology of Mind*): "Reason, unaided by art, myth, dream and the like becomes pathogenic and destructive of life." And J.P.S. Uberoi (in his book *The Other Mind of Europe. Goethe as a Scientist*) gives a very precise idea of the possible actual impact of another science that is experimental, empirical on one side, and existential. It is existential insofar as the attention of the researcher includes the evolution of his own awareness and consciousness on all human levels, together with the progress of knowledge.

REFLECTION IN MIND AND NATURE

Our "tour d'horizon" is liable, I suppose, to free the purely cognitive reasoning from its complex of superiority—from the terrible burden of unique responsibility resulting from the idea of being the absolute focus of all reasonable expectations. Even the striving of New Age tendencies for esoteric religions wants the natural sciences to lead the path (cf. Fritjof Capra's *The Tao of Physics* as one example). In the context that we envisage here, addicts to physics may find it easier to reflect in different modes, to compare the respective results, and thus to resist hasty longings for salvation by the jump of quantums.

A very necessary step of self-reflection would be to reflect on the strange "reality" that results from the concept of deductive explanations of the world. The realm of the senses offers probably one of the best examples to nourish and guide such a reflection. Current and still dominating scientific theories treat, let us say, a perception through the eye as a "sensual impulse" very much along the channel of reflection in physics, just because reflection in physics is the simplest model for the theoretical reconstruction. There is a silent assumption that the most primitive level of organic "functions" should belong to that same logical order. This is not even properly stated as an axiom, but just taken for granted. Consequently, there is no account referring to the omitted existential dimension, even though it is an essential part of perception on whatever level of "evolution." In reality, the so-called impulse or information always expresses the link between one being and all the others that take part in the play of a common existence and mutual relationship, referred to above as coexistence.

Silent, even unconscious assumptions, like the abstraction from the practical and logical impact of coexistence just alluded to, are of crucial importance in the history of science, very much as they are in other styles of reflection. They play a constitutive role in the making of a scientific fact and in the theoretical school that has produced this kind of fact instead of others, as Ludwig Fleck, who was awarded the Nobel Prize for his discovery of the typhus virus, explains. The history of science has to be rewritten, analyzing such different styles and schools and their effect on the "facts" produced by them.

PATTERNS OF CHANGE

Ludwig Fleck's "styles of thought" are but the result of an ensemble of attitudes towards life and the world in a particular period. His model is much more substantial, comprehensive, and integrative than the popular record given by Thomas Kuhn. The analysis of a particular historical attitude must evoke all the levels of anthropological knowledge because change is less a question of positive law and formalized moral rules than a "style of being and thought." Rules and laws may interfere in a problematic way even when employed as tools of change, since they always project formalized structures upon the movements of life. Probably the best cultural protection of nature at hand is the institution of "human rights of nature" as postulated by Beat Sitter-Liver, amongst others, for a decade or two, since this idea urges the ecological discussion into assuming a constructive position. Yet a concept of rights will always remain a projection *ex alio genere* and, in the long run, may do as much harm as it seems to do good in the immediate. It cannot replace self-reflection as the logically and existentially necessary complement to the common reasoning about the world as an object of human domination. Indirectly "human rights of nature" declared by human beings reestablish the fatal concept of *homo mensura mundi*, man as the measure for the world. "Human rights of nature" correspond to the claim for self-limitation. But what we really need is self-limitation out of the joy of the encounter with the other beings and processes of life, a joyful asceticism, a loving exercise with all the discoveries of a life in rich exchange. Imposed discipline may establish the framework for a transitory period, during which a new consciousness must be given the chance to evolve in patterns of thought and feeling different from the predominant attitudes in the modern system of society facing the universe. Coexistence cannot be managed, no more than existence; it has to be lived. This is reality. Unfortunately, in the context of our historical practice, instruments are more easily granted the title of being realistic as they are likely to be destructive—"pathogenic and destructive of life," to quote Gregory Bateson once more.

RESPECT OF THE OTHER IS THE BASIS FOR CHANGE

Love and a joyful exchange can evolve only in the free space of a relationship which respect establishes for interplay. Play, in the sense of interplay, is certainly the key concept. Play is our term for an open context—open in time as an ever-evolving, never deterministic process; open in space as the coherence between the constituting elements allowing for a free room between them. Play is neither deterministic nor indeterministic. Play is the context of the higher logical order in which determinism and indeterminism interact. In the terms of reaction in biological life this is the play of reaction and counterreaction. A relation is only possible when a certain distance, in time or space or both, opens ways for mutual reflection of two or more beings. In the human context that distance can be used arbitrarily, up to a certain degree, offering us an alternative: Either we choose to use the distance for a more unilateral action on our side, or we leave some free space to the Other in order to give way to its specific counterreactions. While the first attitude belongs to the arsenal of practicability (following the maxim "Do everything in your direct interest that you have the means to impose onto the Other"), the second gives evidence of practical respect, precisely in the sense of "Respect for Life" as developed by Albert Schweitzer in his *Ethics*.

Here we are very close to art, again. A work of art exists, essentially, in the immaterial or at least invisible sphere of specific reflections emanating from it, called *aura* by Walter Benjamin. This mode of existence in the order of conscious reflections—of concentration on intellectual, emotional, and physiological awareness—is not only that of the work of art itself, but also that of the artist with respect to the Other that has become the object of the artistic creation. That threefold concentration must reign throughout the whole of the artist's attitudes towards the world and himself or herself in the act of creation, so that awareness is the very mode of existence while a human being lives as an artist. This extremely reactive mode of existence, although never purely reactive, allows for the possibility of counterbalancing the artist's action, since creation unavoidably constitutes the Other as an object. The exemplary intensity of this interplay of reactions and counterreactions can give life to the existence of a work of art that, symbolically, presents us with the whole of the world as the Other. That is true because it is based on an act of essential respect, on active reaction: art.

Science evolves in a different mode of human existence, in different relationships with the Other. Neither the artistic nor the scientific mode (and no more other modes of our existing with the world) has the privilege to encompass the Other as such or to establish "the reality." There are other realities and other approaches which must form our attitude towards the world, and must be reflected upon as complements to our scientific consciousness. Artistic and contemplatory consciousness reflects substantial sides of the Other no less than scientific consciousness. There is no phenomenon that could be reduced to a fact, because it always occurs in an existential exchange determining its very being. Phenomena exist virtually by receiving and producing effects. Again, Gregory Bateson provides us with the most basic formula: A difference is only a difference when it is difference to somebody or something. We could say that the mere fact always reaches us within an envelope: the ongoing history through which it has been shaped, together with the context of its "Other." "Envelope" might be a useful term, replacing the philosophical notion of "aura" for the general aesthetic context of life. It may serve as a counter-notion to vivisection. Science is not neutral with regard to the object under research. This has been known and recognized, in principle, by the modern theory of knowledge. Can a comparison with the procedures of men and women in art help to improve scientific attitudes, not only by means of comparative studies of the Other—which would be extremely interesting, anyway—but directly by a transfer of methodology?

There is a general claim for concentration on awareness, already advanced by Goethe two hundred years ago. The subject in art demands our awareness in the highest concentration possible of all our aesthetic organs. This level of quality can be assigned to the subject of scientific research also. In this context it is useful to remember that concentration on awareness, on all probable levels of the human faculties, means, existentially, living fully the presence—the presence of the one and the Other, and the presence of their encounter. In strict reflection this implies that memories and expectations are not allowed to play a role other than that of the horizon of orientation and comparison. Presence implies also that the relationship between, let us say conventionally, subject and object happens in time, i.e., it must be lived on either side instead of being dealt with in terms of timeless "facts." A major characteristic of science is, however, and must be, fixation. Every measurement results in timeless, fixed data. Data are and must be the very basis of research strategies. So, what can we hope for? The first change in the scientific attitude derives from a full consideration of the limitedness of paradigms that are based on and lead to measurement. Fixation must be understood in its full impact on the situation, the beings and processes implied.

Here, interestingly enough, the history of art can produce a demonstration of exemplary clearness because art, at least in the Renaissance, evolved in close exchange with crafts and with science—particularly natural science, the two sources of experimental natural sciences.

Albrecht Dürer is known as the inventor and promoter of a device in drawing that gives an excellent image of the "vivisectionist" method. The artist provided a setting for the practical realization of the principle of central perspective. It provided a means for systematically designing the world in that specifically human approach, getting ever more important and leading right to the invention of the photographic camera. Dürer's invention may be looked upon as a demonstration of the scientific view: A table is divided into two halves by a vertical frame and grid. Behind the squares of the grid we find the object to be represented; in front of it, seen from an artist, we find a second grid work, reproduced on the table in order to receive the lines representing what is seen through one square or another of the vertical frame. The object is being exposed on the empty table, separated from its living context and meant not to move: fixation. The representation is oriented towards a fictive center, the vanishing point, and allows for only one eye point which is equally fixed. Everything fits Daniel Bell's theories. The resulting portrait of the object could be reproduced indefinitely as the setting remains repeatable. It may be falsified by any other observer entering the same setting. The elements can also be measured in functions of the setting. The representation can be judged right or wrong.

"Draftsman drawing a reclining nude," woodcut from the *Manual of Measurement* (second German edition, Nürnberg 1538) by Albrecht Dürer, courtesy the print collection, ETH, Zürich.

But the notion of truth is excluded, and with it the claim for allegiance to the Other—not as it "really" is, but as it may be. Dürer himself was probably first to falsify not the result of the method, but the application of the method to real life. His portraits do not manifest the fixation imposed by the setting of the table with the grid work net. It may, however, have served for making a first sketch in some cases.

"Vivisection" is not just restricted to cutting into a living body. A body is a body, life is living only in the interplay with the other beings and processes of its world and, what is even more difficult to conceive, in the "aura" of its reflection to the world. A being is always playing, in more than the physical sense. Any living being enjoys exchange with the Other, though it may be unconsciously. Even matter and its processes, such as rhythm and symmetry and the like, exist in such ways. Isolating an object from its very context is "vivisection." If systems theories and the paradigm of resonance have opened up the possibility of scientific sensibility, this possibility is still waiting for further changes in attitude. Sensible approaches have to come as a counterbalance. They may well have to come from the side of the arts, for they have studied the many ways to overcome the method of fictive fixation in their own field.

TWO EXAMPLES OF ENVELOPE

Two examples of the "envelope" that are particularly present to my mind take us to the field of "human ecology." The first one comes from Africa. The black cultures have brought to specific consciousness what otherwise is part of all traditional wisdom. While Westerners claim human rights for the isolated individual, Tschiamalenga Ntumba declares the African primacy of the We before the I. While Westerners plead for a right to privacy, Africans plead for a right to common context; key issues in the life of an individual find their solution exactly by reintegration into an ongoing balance of mutual relations. Men or women, elders or children are not identified with "their problem"; nor do the others solve a "problem" for the person considered out of balance. Much like psychotherapy, Western jurisdiction treats the guilty person in order to make her or him part of social life again. Africans are not so astonished when such a treatment fails; their idea is to heal by addressing the embedding social and cosmic context. They even take it that misbehavior is always owing not only to the misbehaving person but to the community which has, obviously, failed to cultivate the envelope for the individual through whom the lack of social balance becomes manifest.

The second example refers to India. Whenever I think of Bombay I feel very strongly that we owe a very different public consciousness to the people who live almost without any answer to basic needs, sometimes with a square of rotten plastic as a shelter. I do not think, of course, of sociological research into the poverty of the poor, which usually adds the status of victim to the practical suffering and striving. The Western strategy of linguistic emancipation mainly leads to a situation where those who suffer are taught to express their suffering; if this capacity does not open up means for improvement, the doubling of poverty by conscious poverty becomes perfect. In most cases those who suffer undignified circumstances become identified mainly with the lack of dignity around them. What should be present to our mind is the stupendous art of living of tens of thousands in the manner of modern nomads squatting in no-man's-lands in and around capitals. Whereas in other big places of the same subcontinent, people in the same conditions stroll about and constitute a considerable danger to the street life of the city, for the time being, in Bombay, the masses of displaced persons seem to have brought with them the texture of relationships that once constituted their village life. We must learn to know much more about the origin and conditions of these relations—displaced *ethos* in the middle of the worst mess of industrialized urban centers. I am convinced that it is absolutely crucial to recognize in public the dignity of which these people provide such incredible proof. Research is important, not only in order to appreciate the whole reach of human dignity against undignifying circumstances. I hope that we might be able to support the ethic strength of these people if we clearly and concretely knew from which roots their attitudes stemmed and, consequently, which conditions still bear them. Probably, the roots are their former traditional village life.

Certainly, public esteem will be a more urgent support than technical help, which, as an isolated measure, would only destroy surviving relationships. What are these relationships to which we owe the unbelievable peace in the surrounding quarters of Bombay, while other cities with equal gatherings of displaced persons have become very dangerous? Why do we not conceive of traditionally elaborated relationships, among human beings and between human beings and other members of creation, as a national heritage or even a heritage of mankind?

CONCLUSION

Responsibility in science means, as in every other field, first of all that scholars and scientists have to develop their particular activities on the ground of responses to the world. However specifically their work has to be shaped, however isolated the subject of their research has to be, they have to reflect its existential context and their own intervention. Every phenomenon is a member of a whole; every "fact" is a reductionist statement—an obligation to prepare the awareness for the "envelope" that is the sphere of its life and relation. Appropriate approaches include a proper methodology, based on self-reflection and the respect for the Other, gratefulness to the world, and love. Aesthetics, as the art of mindfulness, are a better help to realize such methods than ethics as a theory of abstract values. Logics, along the principle of yes-or-no-decisions, are too primitive and prohibitive of reflection if we think of the high complexity of the world we are inhabiting. We must re-acquire the faculty of considering opposites as polar aspects of a field of tension, and to adapt our consciousness to a manifold world of interacting strata of "reality," a world in which differences and limits express separation as much as they invite exchange, differentiating relationships—including the relations between society and nature insofar as scientific intervention may change these relations.

REFERENCES

Adorno, Theodor W. 1969, *Die Dialektik der Aufklärung*, Frankfurt a. Main.

Apel, Karl-Otto 1988, *Diskurs und Verantwortung*, Frankfurt a. Main.

Bateson, Gregory 1980, *Mind and Nature. A Necessary Unity*, New York/ Toronto.

Bateson, Gregory 1972, *Steps to an Ecology of Mind, Collected Essays in Anthropology, Psychiatry, Evolution and Epistemology*, New York.

Bell, Daniel 1974, *The Coming of Post-Industrial Society. A Venture in Social Forecasting*, London.

Benjamin, Walter 1966, *Angelus Novus*, Frankfurt a. Main.

Bohr, Niels 1985, *Atomphysik und menschliche Erkenntnis*. Aufsätze und Verträge 1930–1961, Braun-Schweig/Wiesbaden.

Capra, Fritjof 1980, *The Tao of Physics*, Fontana Bks.

Dürer, Albrecht 1525, *Underweysung der messung mit dem zirkel und richtscheydt*, Nürnberg.

Durkheim, Emile 1968, *Les formes élémentaires de la vie religieuse*, Paris.

Fleck, Ludwig 1980, *Entstehung und Entwicklung einer wissenschaftlichen Tatsache*, Frankfurt a. Main.

Gadamer, Hans Georg 1960, *Warheit und Methode*, Tübingen.

Gebser, Jean 1949, *Ursprung und Gegenwart*, Stuttgart.

Hersch, Jeanne 1995, *Menschsein Wirklichkeit Sein*, Berlin.

Kant, Immanuel 1879, *Critique of Practical Reason*, translated by T. K. Abbot, London.

Kuhn, Thomas 1977, *The Essential Tension: Selected Studies in Scientific Tradition and Change*, Chicago.

Lévy-Strauss, Claude 1962, *La Pensée sauvage*, Paris.

Maturana, Humberto/ Verden-Zöller, Gerda 1993, *Liebe und Spiel, die vergessenen Ordnungen des Menschseins*, Heidelberg
Picht, Georg 1987, *Kunst und Mythos*, Stuttgart.
Schweitzer, Albert 1923, *Kultur und Ethik*, Bern.
Sitter-Liver, Beat 1984, *Plädoyer für das Naturrechtsdenken. Zur Anerkennung von Eigenrechten der Natur*, Basel.—"In Defense of Non-Anthropocentrism in Environmental Ethics," in: Shea, William R. / Sitter-Liver, Beat (eds.) 1989, *Scientists and Their Responsibility*, Nantucket MA.
Sophocles, *The Theban Plays*, Translated by E. G. Watling, London.
Tschiamalenga, Ntumba 1993, in: *Karl Jaspers on Lectures on Matters of Our Time*, Oldenburg.
Uberoi, J.P.S. 1984, *The Other Mind of Europe. Goethe as a Scientist*, Oxford University Press/New Delhi.

Overcoming
the Situation of
Moral Strangers

Ethical Self-Reflection in the Humanities and Social Sciences:
Facing up to the Postmodernist Challenge

THOMAS J. BOLE, III
H. TRISTRAM ENGELHARDT, JR.

REASON'S INABILITY TO GROUND ETHICAL SELF-REFLECTION

Recent reflections in the philosophy of science, epistemology, and the foundations of philosophical theory support the view that all areas of knowledge are framed from a particular perspective. Reflections upon the controversies surrounding Copernicus and Darwin suggest that choice of metaphors and points of investigation frame the reality disclosed. If this is the case in the physical and biological sciences, it is even more so in the case of social sciences and the humanities, the human sciences. The focus of the physical and the biological sciences is on theoretical values that themselves seem to be less colored by practical perspectives and concerns. Not only is the subject matter of the human sciences more frankly freighted with values and social presuppositions, but these sciences themselves assume the interpretative casts of the particular cultures within which they arise. One does not typically speak of a French physics in contrast to an English physics, but the distinction between German and Anglo-American philosophy has been long recognized and accepted.

The implications for the possibility of making universally valid moral judgments are guarded at best, if matters are as sketched. The humanities and social sciences would not escape the particularity of the perspectives in which they were framed. None could lay intellectual claim to the attention of anyone outside that perspective. The social sciences could not give general reasons for what sorts of methods and experiments on human subjects are morally permissible. If there are numerous perspectives and therefore numerous social sciences and numerous humanities, how does one choose among them and decide which are better or worse and by what standards and for whom?

The difficulty is foundational. It appears in principle impossible simply to think oneself out of the babble of moral and philosophical perspectives. One cannot appeal to the differences in consequences between different approaches in order to choose correctly, because one must first know how to compare consequences. One cannot decide which approach will maximally satisfy preferences unless one knows God's discount rate for time. Nor can one appeal to prisoner-dilemma theoretic approaches, for if any of the players are moved by glory or transcendent goals, there will not be compatible solutions. Worse yet, one cannot appeal to a disinterested observer. If the observer is truly disinterested, the observer will not make any choices. If one is able to choose, it is precisely because one is guided by prior commitments. Which is to say, any useful hypothetical chooser or hypothetical contractor is one who has a moral perspective or moral sense. The difficulty is how to choose among the range of possible moral senses, perspectives, or understandings. Does one regard the world from the perspective of a philosopher raised and at home in Cambridge, Massachusetts, or one raised and at home in Singapore? Does one regard as paradigmatic a liberal democracy with robust civil rights or a dictatorial capitalism with robust guarantees of personal security?

We shall argue that reason alone cannot provide the answer, because the problem is in fact foundational. There are ultimately different insights about how foundational moral and epistemic values are to be compared or ranked. There is no general rational way to show one to be correct and the others incorrect. Though reason cannot provide the answer to foundational controversies, we also argue that reason does disclose a generally justifiable framework for resolving such controversies.

Such a framework provides a solution to the disputes about evaluative standards by distinguishing two levels of dispute. The first is the level on which moral friends argue: within the perspective of shared foundational values (whether epistemic or non-epistemic) and understandings, rather than about these foundations. The second is the level of peaceable interchange between individuals who do not share the same foundational perspectives. Their disagreements are to be resolved in the marketplace of ideas, and in the coin of peaceable negotiations and bargaining between moral strangers. This is to say that there are in the end four ways in which one can resolve moral controversy, or indeed any controversy overlaid by values. First, one can simply appeal to force. Though this will bring closure to debates, it brings no intellectual satisfaction. Second, one can hope that one's interlocutors will convert to one's ideological or religious perspective. Third, one might hope in fact to find the privileged, contentfull, rational perspective that will direct choice, while not being driven by parochial values. As has just been suggested, and as will be shown in greater detail later, this hope is vain. The final solution is to understand the ways in which individuals can agree to collaborate in limited fashions, though they do not share sufficient premises about basic epistemic values, basic non-epistemic values, the deep metaphysical structure of the world, the nature of the correct rules of evidence, or the nature of the correct rules of moral inference, so that their disputes can be settled by sound rational argument. In this circumstance, authority is derived from neither God nor reason, but from common agreement.

In fine, we will argue that the pluralism of post-modernity compels theoreticians in both the humanities and social sciences away from naïvely accepting the structures within which they know and act. They must cease being only dogmatic protagonists of their own ideology or metaphysics-infected viewpoint and become in addition critical negotiators across moral perspectives. If, as we shall argue, there is no way to discover release from the observer biases of culture and circumstance, one must either retreat from peaceable dialogue or embrace the one perspective through which further discussion and negotiation can take place. If one retreats, one has no way to protest when visited by coercion and punitive force. If one enters a dialogue based not on a presumption of an objective truth, but on the authority derived from common consent, one can understand both why those who bargain peaceably must be respected, and why those who refuse need not be. This second understanding implies that, in a world of irresolvably different perspectives where there are no meta-values that are clinchers in disputes, all perspectives within the humanities and social sciences are open to exploration and discussion unless they are directly non-peaceable.

WHAT IS AT ISSUE IN ETHICAL SELF-REFLECTION IN THE HUMAN SCIENCES

The humanities and social sciences (the human sciences, in short) consist of the various fields of knowledge about what is properly human: anthropology, psychology, sociology, economics, and political science; literature and language, history, and philosophy. They claim to constitute what systematic understanding we have of ourselves, individually, communally, and culturally. Part of being human is that we shape ourselves by the values we pursue and eschew. Self-reflection is necessary to focus upon these values because they are not explicit in the sense that objects in the world are. They are often only implicit in our viewpoints. The presuppositions of a culture are often so tacit that they are not noticed until brought into question by contact with individuals from outside that culture who do not share them.

Self-reflection functions not only to bring to consciousness the values that are in fact embodied in the human sciences—it also raises the question of which among them ought to be pursued and in what order. Studies in the social sciences provide bases for public policy. In the humanities a particular society's canons of literary and historical worth both reflect the society's self-image and help shape it. Self-reflection in the human sciences is unavoidably ethical.

From the resurgence of secular learning in the modern, or post-medieval, era, into the present century, the Western tradition has been confident of Plato's rejoinder to the Sophists, that reason can give insight into the good and the true, despite differences in individual and societal perspectives. This view has dominated the modern era. Rationalists such as Descartes and Leibniz held that reason can intuit universal norms of both physical nature and human affairs. Even empiricists such as Locke and Hume argue that astute observation can discern whatever reality or fixed regularities there may be. If Kant argues that moral and political values inhabit a domain different from the subject matter of the empirical sciences, he continues the modern project of endorsing the possibility of discovering a content-full morality that should bind all persons. With Hegel, modernity's ethos reaches its Janus-faced epitome. He recognizes the socio-historically conditioned character of knowledge, but nonetheless holds that philosophical reason can deliver absolute knowledge of the rationality of the real. "All revolutions, whether in the sciences or world history, occur merely because spirit has changed its categories in order to understand and examine what belongs to it, in order to possess and grasp itself in a truer, deeper, more intimate and unified manner."[1] As the course of Western imperialism in the nineteenth century gave way to the devastating wars of the twentieth, Nietzsche's suspicion that the other face is the truer, that the claims made on behalf of philosophy and reason are simply implements of the will to power by the dominant culture, seemed ever more plausible. This suspicion is confirmed, as post-modernists such as Foucault, Lyotard, and Rorty have indicated, insofar as the Platonist ideal is bankrupt and no alternative presents itself.

Before examining the reasons for this bankruptcy, however, it is worthwhile to remind ourselves of what is at stake. Ethical self-reflection in the human sciences raises the question of which values these various fields of knowledge ought to embody. If the evaluative standards of ethical self-reflection cannot themselves be justified in terms of general secular reason, then humanities and social sciences become ideological instruments, masks for the special interests of those who propose and define the content. If ethical self-reflection cannot answer questions about which values these various fields of knowledge ought to embody, then there is no theoretical reason to object to their embodying the values of those particular interests that define them. The humanities and social sciences would then be reduced to being at best culturally parochial, and at worst ideological instruments in the hands of the policymakers that use them.

Moreover, if ethical self-reflection cannot show certain values or moral constraints to be normative, then there are no decisive rational grounds on which we can choose between morally obnoxious and morally acceptable undertakings. One could not show the difference in principle between Nazi experimentation upon unconsenting human subjects, and risky experiments upon subjects both adequately informed and freely consenting. There would be no reason why the humanities and social sciences should not be used as instruments by the most all-encompassing state tyranny. If reason cannot by itself justify a content-full morality, and if in addition it cannot provide the framework for adjudicating possible controversies about which values should be normative, then ethical self-reflection in the humanities and social sciences is reduced to an awareness of the ideology dominant in those fields. We will now move to exploring in greater detail why reason cannot justify a content-full evaluative perspective, ethical or theoretical.

THAT REASON CANNOT JUSTIFY A CONTENT-FULL THEORETICAL EVALUATIVE PERSPECTIVE

Ever since Plato, philosophers have argued that the case against the relativization of truth and rational justification and the case against the relativization of value judgments to pursuits of power have the same premises. These would be standards of truth, rationality, and morality that are decisive in the face of competing claims. Such standards would also make it possible to distinguish claims about values that in fact are dictated by and subservient to special interests, from those in the service of the true and good.[2] But if, as we shall contend, reason cannot give any content to these standards, appeal to them does not effectively help us avoid the suspicion that particular claims about theoretical as well as practical values in the humanities and social sciences are ultimately ideological.

The standard move against the skeptic and relativist accounts of truth and knowledge has been, since Plato's Socrates employed it against Protagoras,[3] to defang it by making it self-referential. If one asserts the dubitable or relative nature of all knowledge, the truth of that assertion is itself dubitable or relative. If one wants to exempt the truth of that assertion from doubtfulness or relativity, one must show why it is absolutely true, and thus undermine the claim that all knowledge is dubitable and relative in trying to justify that claim. The radical skeptic or relativist, it seems, contradicts the content of what is asserted by the assertion that this particular content is true (i.e., the assertion which claims that skepticism or relativism is absolutely true).

The line of reasoning implicit in this move is that truth claims require an indubitable or absolute theoretical justification of why true claims are true, rather than false or undecidable. The truth claim of any assertion of propositional content implies that the claim is justifiable in principle; otherwise, it could not be claimed as true. Since the justification of any proposition's truth can only be made by means of other propositional assertions, and these must in their turn be justified, the logic of any truth claim seems to commit it to a theoretical structure of assertions from which it receives its justification. But the notion of justification seems to require that these assertions also be adequately justified. Justification that is inadequate in principle is not justification. Since adequate justification excludes both an indefinite regress and a dogmatic halt, the theoretical structure must depend upon a first principle that is absolute or self-justifying. In the history of philosophy from Plato through Descartes, Kant, and Hegel, this principle has been sought in the medium of theoretical assertion and justification, namely, thinking or reason.

The problem with this approach, however, is that it cannot be shown that justification requires that truth be explained theoretically rather than pragmatically. We want to indicate why this is so by focusing upon one paradigmatic form of theoretical justification, viz., transcendental argument.[4] This type of argument tries to answer what Kant calls the *quaestio juris*, i.e., to give a cogent explanation of why certain general conceptual principles must be invoked by the knower as objectively valid, i.e., as articulating structures of the real, if propositional claims are to be true.[5] Such an explanation cannot appeal to particular realities, because they cannot reveal why reality must be so structured. Therefore it appeals to what is necessary to know the real, and hence to subjectivity as the ground of knowledge. Such a ground is supposed to show what thought, or theoretical propositions, must be in order to be true, and what the real must be in order to be accessible in true knowledge claims.[6] Pragmatic justification, by contrast, argues that adequate explanation is given by appeal to those parts of the cultural and linguistic web of beliefs that justify the particular proposition asserted. It argues that "is true" and "seems to us to be true" can make sense without the notion that they articulate determinations of, or represent, reality. Or rather, the notions of *representation* and *objective reality* make sense just in terms of our epistemic language, without ultimate reference to non-linguistic items.

At issue is whether there are certain concepts, or propositions, or methods, that must be content-fully true for experience in a way that is not logically dependent upon experience. Such concepts or propositions or methods would typically articulate necessary determinations of truth or rational explanation and rational justification. They would constitute *a priori* knowledge, in Kant's sense of knowledge the truth of which is independent of experience of reality[7] but which is also necessary for understanding experienceable reality.

Our contention is that proponents of neither account can make a conclusive case against the other, at least insofar as they incorporate content-full, canonical accounts of values. The choice of one or the other theory will depend upon *desiderata* that cannot themselves be decided on the bases of the theories. If the contention is correct, reason cannot establish a canonical account even of theoretical values.

Theoretical philosophy has traditionally proceeded by analysis of some domain of reality, e.g., of physical nature, into less and more fundamental items, and analysis of the latter in order to elicit and explicate those principles required to make sense of that given domain.[8] The principles constitute a metalevel with respect to the object level from which they are derived and to which they are fundamental. But this means that they are logically correlative to the given object level. Their normativity is relative to their correlative, with which they constitute a contextual whole. If the object level is sufficiently altered, then the metalevel principles must also be altered, and so are not *a priori* in Kant's sense.

Transcendental arguments are designed to undercut this relativity of principles to a particular framework of objective knowledge, and to show their normativity or *a priori* status in terms of subjectivity as ground of knowledge. Even thus qualified, of course, subjectivity may have any of several senses, prominent among which is the factual center of self-conscious experience that constitutes particular knowledge claims about objects experienced. The sense relevant here, however, cannot be that of the self-consciously experiencing subject, because such a sense is necessarily correlative with the object level experienced. Rather, it must be a sense that considers subjectivity as the ground of the necessary truth of the principles, a conceptual ground designed to explain the general character-istics of the logical note of validity that attaches to theoretical claims about any possible object level. Such a sense is congenial to the notion of the factual center of self-conscious experience, because only self-con-sciously experiencing knowers are capable of conceptual thought. But appeal to what self-consciously experiencing knowers do or constitute does not help explain why every theoretical performance or theoretical claim constituted can be true only upon the logical presupposition of the truth of the categories. Only a theory that explains, and can be justified in terms of, theoretical thought can be designed to explain why, if thought is to be the vehicle of true theoretical claims, it must implicate certain cat-egories as determinations of the real *qua* knowable. Kant does not see this difference, and his transcendental subject combines both the logical and the non-logical, the self-consciously experiencing, phenomenological senses of subjectivity. Its justification of principles cannot be freed from a particular notion of objective experience, and could not justify the prin-ciples if that notion were sufficiently altered.

Experiential knowledge may be viewed as a piece. Certain parts of it may be very central for its coherence, and other parts very peripheral. But it cannot be shown that any particular part is immune from revision. To re-count Quine's arguments against the synthetic-analytic distinction, a state-ment can be held true despite recalcitrant experience by reinterpretation, e.g., claiming that the recalcitrant experience is not objective, or even by amending logical laws. Conversely, even particular pieces of logic, math-ematics, or conceptual analysis would be, insofar as they were held neces-sary to make sense of experience, subject in principle to revision.[9]

We have in fact had to reinterpret Aristotle's law of non-contradic-tion in order to maintain it in our organization of experience.[10] The shift is no different in principle from the shift from Newton's to Einstein's framework for organizing experience of physical objects. Again, if one were to axiomatize some domain of propositions about experience and institute the linguistic conventions that fixed the meanings of the terms so that the axioms are true, that domain would be undermined by the same experiences that would have undermined its unaxiomatized predeces-sor.[11] The test of any conceptualization of experience is how well each organizes experience so as to deal with the questions that gave rise to particular conceptualizations, and other questions about experience that the pertinent community might think relevant.

And we are, it seems, willing to reinterpret laws of logic to help us deal with objective experience "more efficiently." The concepts by which we describe experience and the categories, or concepts crucial to organiz-ing those experiential concepts, cannot be shown to be other than two poles of a continuum; they cannot be shown to differ in principle as *a posteriori* and *a priori* respectively.[12]

PROTAGORAS REDIVIVUS

One may at this point argue that the very fallibility of our various conceptualizations of the world requires that truth and rational justifiability be presupposed as ideals. For the alternative is to say that truth and rational justifiability are to be defined in terms of our society's current conception of truth and reason, and our society's procedures for justifying inquiry. Truth and rationality are relative to what seems to be so to our lights.

Such a view would befit Protagoras, and be liable to a rejoinder analogous to that of Plato's Socrates: that to assert that *x* is true relative to the standards of our culture, or justified because it meets our culture's criteria for justifying assertions of its type in its circumstances, is self-refuting. If the proposition is asserted as absolutely true, then the standards and criteria of the claimant's particular culture are held to be absolutely true, and the claimant's relativism is not universal. Moreover, the implication of the claim is cultural imperialism. The norms of the speaker's communities are those by which statements of individuals from other communities are to be judged. Evaluations across communities would be veiled expressions of the speaker's community's preferences rather than evaluations of statements from other cultures that could claim validity across cultures. In the case of the human sciences the consequences would be particularly dismal, because one could not in principle appreciate the values of other cultures save in terms fundamentally alien to those cultures, nor could one claim that the standards for appreciating them do them justice. (If, on the other hand, the assertion of cultural relativism is itself meant to be relatively true, its meaning becomes hazy.)

On this line of reasoning, it seems that truth and rationality must be presupposed as ideals normative for inquiry, in order to explain the circumstance that various cultures and communities continually accept as true, and as compelling in terms of the criteria of rationality prevailing, that which later has turned out to require revision or replacement. It is not as if the revolutions of sun and earth relative to each other changed when the Ptolemaic view of them was replaced by the Copernican view. Without the notions of truth and rationality as normative ideals distinct from what we take to be true and rational, there would be no basis for distinguishing between fallible particular truth claims and what is true. This is the brief mounted by Hilary Putnam against the pragmatist explanation of truth and rationality of Richard Rorty.[13]

The consistent pragmatist, however, is not appealing to cultural criteria as ultimate epistemic authorities. Rather, the consistent pragmatist is denying that there should be an ultimate set of criteria that can halt inquiry, whether these criteria be from a world as a reality determined in itself apart from what we can make of it and to which our beliefs should conform, from the idealist's conceptual schema in which the world is constituted, or from the criteria of the cultural relativist. The pragmatist is denying that there is any set of independent criteria of appeal for truth or justification that may not itself be called into question in the disputes which they are supposed to resolve. There is only the continual reassessment of beliefs in light of their success in helping us deal with experience. This success is not to be construed primarily in terms of prediction and control, which are indeed paramount interests in the natural sciences. Rather, it is success in dealing with reality in the human and non-human world. In this sense physics would be no better guide to dealing with reality than ethics or literary criticism.[14]

Putnam's specific complaints can be answered, then, by denying that a particular culture's criteria are ultimate epistemic authorities. To the contrary, the pragmatist holds that there is no epistemic authority, only historically constituted and revisable norms, nor are there any aims of inquiry beyond those of historically situated inquirers. Questions arise with respect to any particular set of beliefs for dealing with experience when those beliefs leave interests unmet and particular alternative sets of beliefs are feasible. The notion of an ideal norm outside particular practices of inquiry does not help explain how theoretical alternatives arise, or help decide which particular alternative is better.[15]

On the one hand, then, the Rortian pragmatist's account of truth and rational explanation can be made out in terms immune to the objection from the transcendentalist. Truth for the pragmatist does not explain anything apart from what particular true explanations depict in pragmatic terms. On the other hand, what account transcendental arguments offer regarding truth and rational explanation satisfies non-pragmatic, sheerly theoretical interests. Neither the pragmatist nor the speculative transcendental philosopher can give grounds for his own account that would be cogent within the other's framework. The inability of reason to give a neutral account of theoretical values suggests that there is no neutral way to judge the relative truth values of competing standards of self-reflection.

THAT REASON CANNOT JUSTIFY CONTENT-FULL PRACTICAL VALUES

This suggestion is confirmed by consideration of what ethical reflection involves. Ethical self-reflection is not simply descriptive of the values involved in the various human sciences, but also morally evaluative. Moral evaluations require a standard of right and wrong. This standard must be justifiable; otherwise, evaluations based on it would be ideological, i.e., based on parochial canons that themselves cannot be justified. But there are several reasons for thinking that ethical self-reflection cannot justify a particular canonical account of practical values.

One is that reason, at least in the paradigm of transcendental argument, cannot justify content-full moral values. Kant's *Critique of Practical Reason* correctly observes that, if the unconditionality of moral obligation is to be compatible with free will, the moral law must be understood in terms of the same principle as our freedom, viz., reason as shaping will.[16] To act morally is to act rationally, and to act rationally is to act as if the maxim of the action could hold as a principle establishing universal law.[17] Kant thinks that such a formal maxim gives specific content to the moral law, because to deny that content would be self-contradictory if made a universal law. It is instructive to see why he is wrong. In the *Groundwork of the Metaphysics of Morals* he gives two important glosses to the notion of a maxim adaptable as universal law. First, the maxim is said to be such as could be made a universal law of nature.[18] Second, the maxim dictates the treatment of any person not simply as a means but as an end.[19] A person has reason, which is the principle of moral law, and so can be viewed as a lawgiver for the community of moral agents. Kant thus conflates two notions of universal law: the notion of law as that which governs human nature for morally worthwhile ends, and the notion of law that any rational agent could set for him- or herself (because it does not treat that person as merely a means). Kant's derivation of material content from the formal universalization of the maxim of one's action depends upon this conflation.

As an example of content, Kant gives the strict duty to oneself of not committing suicide. In committing suicide, Kant argues, I would be acting in a way which contradicts the proper purpose of my motive (self-love), which is to foster life, and moreover, I would be treating myself as a means merely.[20] Kant's first reason simply assumes that there is an evident and morally good design in the human and non-human world. The assumption is necessary to give content to the duty.[21] His second reason is unintelligible on its face; if I let myself be treated as a means merely, I have set that as my own end.

Kant gets unjustified content for his maxim from his assumption of non-rational nature as incorporating moral norms that should direct rational agents. In terms of his own transcendental argument, nature simply presents the field for incarnate rational agents to work out ends. Kant's maxim would seem to dictate only that one respect other rational agents, in the sense that they not be touched without their consent. We can then see how Kant's second strict duty, not to lie, for example, in order to obtain a loan, might be defended. But we can also see that his first is quite indefensible. This criticism of Kant is similar to the one mounted by Hegel.[22] One knows that one has a duty to fulfill one's contractual promises, and that one ought to strive after the good. But one does not know which promises to make or whose good to seek apart from the particular situations and communities one finds oneself in. Kant's account of morality will not give a content-full notion of rights, nor a content-full understanding of the good. It is for this reason that Hegel turns from Moralität to Sittlichkeit. He recognizes the necessity of a contingent source for moral values. The difficulty consists in determining which of the many possible contingent sources (and therefore which of the various possible Sittlichkeiten) one ought to endorse.

One may appeal to intuition, arguing that particular contents show themselves as self-evidently right and wrong. Nothing else, it may seem, but this approach can avoid an infinite regress. However, if one appeals to intuition to justify ethical standards, proponents of other standards will do the same. If one attempts to resolve this impasse with appeals to consequences, this will not succeed, either. One must have a standard already in hand by which to order the different values of the consequences. One must, for example, already know the relative ranking of liberty, equality, prosperity, and security, in order to know how to compute or compare liberty consequences, equality consequences, prosperity consequences, and security consequences. That prior knowledge of the ranking cannot itself depend upon consequences, but must presuppose the very canonical account of moral content that consequentialism was supposed to supply. It will also not help to appeal to the satisfaction of subjective preferences unless one knows God's discount rate for time as well as how to compare rational versus impassioned preferences.

One might appeal to the formal character of moral reasoning to discover canons of morally correct and incorrect action. Then anyone who acts in accordance with the prescriptions and proscriptions disclosed would be acting rationally, and anyone acting contrarily would be acting irrationally. They could be dismissed as irrational and in addition visited with coercive force to restore them to their true rational selves. But unless one can import some particular sense of what sort of content is ethically right or wrong, such appeals to the character of moral reasoning will yield no content. As Hume already recognized, reason itself does not provide it.

For similar reasons, appeals to the hypothetical choices of disinterested observers as the standard of what rational individuals should choose (i.e., what anyone ought to choose if acting rationally) fail. If the observer is disinterested in the sense of not being the partisan of a particular moral account, he or she will not be able to discern one set of consequences as morally preferable to another. If the appeal to an impartial observer is meant to show which particular moral canons one ought to choose in the first place, the appeal fails. This point regarding hypothetical choice theories in general applies to hypothetical contractor theories as well. For contractors to endorse a particular contract, they must possess a particular thin theory of the good, a particular view of proper risk aversiveness, etc.

The crucial point is that ethical self-reflection cannot provide standards that can be adequately justified in terms of general secular reason, because any content-full standard has a particular sense of what is content-fully right and wrong built into it. The standard cannot be adequately justified to those who do not share that particular sense. If no adequate justification of standards of ethical self-reflection is available, any appeal to standards becomes a mere means to consolidate prevailing opinion. If this line of analysis is sound, ethical self-reflection loses its point. It is no longer able to provide a grounded evaluation of which values are to be pursued or avoided in the human sciences. They are reduced to reflecting the values endorsed by the prevailing ideology.

WHY JUSTIFICATION OF ETHICAL SELF-REFLECTION IN THE HUMAN SCIENCES IS NECESSARY

One may at this point simply bite the bullet, and give up ethical self-reflection in the traditional philosophical sense. One cannot help being ethnocentric, because the procedures for rationality, normativity, and justification only make sense within a particular community. Consequently, one privileges one's own community. But it just so happens that in our case the ethnos is the community of liberal intellectuals of contemporary secular, pluralist, Western democracies, including its toleration of a diversity of opinion, freedom of research, and undistorted communication.[23] Why not agree with Rorty that, as reflection on post-modernist culture indicates, the traditional philosophical notion of a rationality that is both ahistorical and normative for particular perspectives is itself the mark of a particular historical and cultural epoch? One still has available the post-philosophical pragmatist's justification of toleration of diversity of opinion, freedom of research, and undistorted communication: A society embodying these values is a good thing to try for, because those who have experienced both societies prefer a liberal society.[24] Why is this not sufficient, especially in light of the apparent inability of reason to establish its case for either theoretical or practical norms?

One reason is that the post-philosophical pragmatist's justification seems to be either false or viciously circular. Nietzsche and Pope John Paul II are but two examples of individuals who do not prefer Western secular pluralist democracies to all alternatives. That Rorty does not seriously consider counterinstances to the post-philosophical pragmatist's justification suggests that the only individuals whose preferences are allowed are those who will make the appropriate choice. In fact, one would need to know how well the empirical claim is established regarding such choices between societies. In addition, one would need to know what majority of preferences established what claims and how to regard those who disagreed.

But let us admit that Rorty's pragmatic justification does work for the consensus of individuals who have seriously thought about the alternatives. Secular liberal intellectuals do, by and large, favor, or at least fail to provide a viable theoretical alternative to, Western secular pluralist democracies. What are the consequences for the post-philosophical cultural pragmatist's program of admittedly ethnocentric evaluations of other societies' norms and practices? What, in other words, are the consequences for the human sciences of replacing the attempt to find philosophically justified standards for ethical self-reflection with openly ethnocentric ones?

In a post-philosophical culture one knows better than to claim ahistorical or non-culture-relative norms of rationality to evaluate the attitudes and norms of other cultures. In evaluating and legitimating other cultures' attitudes and norms, one properly proceeds by appeal not to foundational arguments but to the pragmatic means by which Western intellectuals evaluate and legitimate them, at present or in the future. Moreover, one would pragmatically implement those values. But since the ethnocentrism of secular liberal Western intellectuals *de facto* dominates the world of ideas, Rorty's program seems to endorse a *de facto* cultural imperialism in the form of post-philosophical pragmatism.

It is not at once clear what is wrong with such a consequence. Rorty can point out that the particular values embodied in *his* post-philosophical pragmatism specifically prevent one of the things to be feared from cultural imperialism: the use of the human sciences as tools for imposing openly ethnocentric standards on other cultures. The ethnocentricity of post-philosophical pragmatism recognizes that there is no foundational rationale for using the human sciences to impose standards on the subjects studied. It explicitly denies a rationale for using the human sciences as social tools for manipulating unconsenting innocent subjects, and would seem to license only the view that the human sciences broaden the sympathies and sense of human community of those who pursue and use them.

There is, however, a theoretical feature of post-philosophical pragmatism that has as a practical consequence the possible legitimation of the very opposite of the secular democratic values it is claimed to support. Theoretically, Rorty's post-philosophical pragmatism is a genetic account. It justifies the values of liberal Western democracy not by a foundational argument for its validity, but by a narrative of how things have "gotten better" in the last centuries as these values have been institutionalized and spread.[25] It justifies itself by appeal to John Rawls's notion of a "reflective equilibrium" between the moral, social, and political opinions of our secular, pluralist, liberal democracy and the network of beliefs and desires that support them.[26] Since this network itself consists of contingent opinions, the reflective equilibrium boils down to the contingently factual intersubjective consensus of the culture. Rorty agrees with Rawls where he disengages the question of whether we ought to be tolerant and Socratic from the question of whether this strategy will lead to the truth. Rawls and Rorty are content that the Socratic commitment to free exchange of views should lead to whatever intersubjective reflective equilibrium may be obtainable, given the contingent make-up of the subjects in question. Truth, viewed in the Platonic way as the grasp of what Rawls calls "an order antecedent to and given to us," is simply not relevant to democratic politics. So philosophy, as the explanation of the relation between such an order and human nature, is not relevant either. When the two come into conflict, democracy takes precedence over philosophy.[27] The difficulty, however, is that this pragmatic legitimation of democracy is simply factual. Rorty's theory justifies whatever happens to be the intersubjective reflective equilibrium of the affected subjects, even where that equilibrium calls as matter of contingent fact for the repression of democratic values.[28] Force —violence or the threat of violence, or breach of contract, or deception—may be suspect, because by itself it lacks intellectual justification and moral authorization. But is there any good reason to exclude it in cases where there is not sufficient consensus produced by the reflective equilibrium to make agreement possible? Rorty's theory provides none.

The need for one can be made vivid by example. In early 1992 the National Institutes of Health [NIH] funded a $78,000 grant to hold a conference to discuss the ways in which claims in behavioral genetics could be used and abused in the criminal justice system. It was to focus upon the ethical, legal, social, and public policy issues raised by research into the possible connections between genetics and criminality.[29] However, a long-time critic of behavioral psychology objected that the conference was part of a federal research agenda to find genetic explanations of violence.[30] He found allies among some members of the Congressional Black Caucus who were suspicious that the conference was part of a federal initiative to seek to find biological correlates of black male violence. These opponents took the conference to be designed to promote research into genetic explanations of criminal behavior rather than to examine the ethical implications of such behavior. "Following a program on Black Entertainment Television in July [1992] that was critical of the meeting," the NIH froze disbursement of the already-granted funds, citing "'unanticipated sensitivity and validity issues.'"[31]

Before the controversy, the peer review engaged by the NIH had concluded that the conference organizers had done a "superb job of assessing the underlying scientific, legal, ethical, and public policy issues and organizing them in a thoughtful fashion." However, after the controversy arose NIH director Bernadine P. Healy stated that the reviewers' endorsement was not strong enough to justify disbursement of the grant funds in the face of public criticism.[32] The deputy director for NIH intramural research, John Diggs, claimed that the brochure for the conference "diverges radically from that approved by the peer review" in that it states that genetic research offers "the prospect of identifying individuals who may be predisposed" to criminal behavior and of "treating some predispositions with drugs and unintrusive therapies."[33] Conference organizer David Wasserman of the University of Maryland claimed the contrary, that the remarks in the brochure had been contained verbatim in the proposal as approved.[34] Nonetheless, the NIH initially withheld disbursement of the funds pending further revisions of the proposal, and after thereby practically undermining the original conference, officially withdrew the grant in April 1993.[35]

The details of this example are much less important than what it highlights: there is no uniform *consensus gentium*, whether in secular liberal democracies or in the more circumscribed academic societies of those engaged in the human sciences. Where consensus breaks down, accusations of bias are often advanced as an excuse for imposing a particular viewpoint, a more politically correct viewpoint, as if it were canonical. In secular pluralist democratic societies there are often, as with the NIH, rules generally agreed to in order to reach decisions for disbursing society's resources in ways that are, as much as practically possible, sheltered from the influence of pressure groups, where such influence is inappropriate to the decisions to be made. Our objection to post-philosophical pragmatism's reliance upon reflective equilibria is that such reliance cannot distinguish peaceable resolution of controversies from resolution by the tyranny of the majority or of the current political or academic fashion. As our example shows, unless there is a rationally defensible framework for controversy resolution, the only sense of ethical self-reflection in the human sciences will be to become aware of the ideologies being imposed.

ETHICAL SELF-REFLECTION WITHIN THE BOUNDS OF POSTMODERNISM: THE FALLBACK POSITION FOR DEALING WITH THOSE WITH WHOM ONE DOES NOT SHARE BASIC STANDARDS

The argument to this point has been that appeals to reason cannot provide canons of either theoretical or practical values; no non-partisan defense can be given for either truth or goodness. Moreover, appeals to a shared, or intersubjective, reflective equilibrium do not offer a generally justifiable framework for resolving fundamental differences in belief. Our example shows that without such a framework there is no rational court of appeal from the imposition of a dominant ideology, e.g., of political correctness, to censure controversial investigations (e.g., into possible relationships between genetics and criminal behavior, or genetics and intelligence, etc.). Still, Western culture has consistently presumed that reason can resolve intellectual and moral controversies and justify a common intellectual and moral viewpoint. This presumption has guided Western philosophy from Plato and Western law from the Roman Empire. If the presumption is wrong—if there is no non-partisan yet content-full canon of truth or rationality or morality—there would seem to be no set of common norms, no common ideal of humanity, to bind men and women. This not only means abandonment of a central tenet of the human sciences. More directly, it means that there is no rational way of adjudicating controversies about fundamental intellectual or moral values between men and women who hold disparate moral visions, whether among the scholars working in the human sciences or between investigators and their subjects, or scholars and the larger community upon whom they depend for financial and institutional support. The traditional Western intellectual project of providing a generally justifiable framework must be fundamentally reconsidered if it is to be normative even for those who are strangers to each other's basic intellectual and moral values, i.e., even for moral strangers.

Because there is no canonical account, nor a content-uninfected algorithm for coordinating values, one must look to the very notion of resolving controversies between moral strangers with morally binding force. This is the notion of ethics as the commitment to resolving controversies between moral strangers without primary recourse to force but with common moral authority. If individuals are interested in resolving controversies without direct appeal to force, where they have no common vision of the good (e.g., a common faith or moral tradition), then the only way to resolve controversies with common authority will be by agreement. That is, if one is interested in resolving controversies without a foundational recourse to force, one can still participate in a common moral world with moral strangers. But the necessary condition for doing so is the recognition that any moral agent, if innocent and unconsenting, has a right to deny claims of others upon his person and his resources. This is nothing more than the non-use of innocent others without their consent.[36]

Mutual respect in this sense is not itself a value. Rather, it is necessary to the grammar of controversy resolution when neither the facts, nor reason, nor ultimate values provide bases for peaceably resolving a dispute. Moreover, whatever mutual agreement is reached on the basis of mutual respect is a source of a common moral authority that can bind moral strangers without arbitrarily endorsing a particular ranking of values. All other ways have the intellectual cost of being founded upon a particular ranking of values (or on a particular content-laden algorithm for coordinating values, or a particular metaphysical view implying a particular ranking). For a moral framework embracing moral strangers, one need only refrain from using them without their consent and acknowledge them as entities that can agree or refuse to negotiate.[37] Those who do not wish to collaborate should be free to withdraw into their rights of privacy, as long as they do so peaceably.

If one is to draw authority other than through force or through appeal to a shared religious or ideological understanding, and if reason cannot discover a content-full communality of values binding persons as such, then authority can still be drawn from mutual agreement. Insofar as individuals act together, they act with common authority. Insofar as individuals use others without their consent, they set aside the one possibility for resolving moral controversies among moral strangers. They thus become outlaws to the only secular moral bond that can justify a common moral discourse. Such outlaws are left without an intellectual basis for protesting against defensive or punitive force. Those who collaborate through common consent have such a basis for justifying the use of defensive and punitive force as well as a moral perspective within which to understand moral outlaws. Moral strangers can still collaborate through procedural devices that allow for the conveyance of authority for common undertakings. Such conveyances of authority will always be limited. Hence, one must argue in principle for a limited rather than robust democracy and recognize as well the unavoidable secular toleration of numerous visions of the humanities and social sciences.

MORAL STRANGERS AND MORAL FRIENDS: A MULTIPLICITY OF HUMAN SCIENCES

If one cannot discover how one ought to frame or direct the human sciences, one must make do with tolerating numerous interpretations of the humanities and the social sciences. All that one can require is that the human sciences not be involved in using persons without their consent. After all, the only way in which moral strangers can peaceably act together with commonly justified moral authority, despite the differences in their moral visions, is by drawing authority from common agreement, and by not using persons without their consent. This will allow one to endorse certain general principles, such as: (1) eschewing unconsented-to force; (2) eschewing fraud (as a form of unconsented-to force); (3) tolerating values in the human sciences of which one will often not approve, as long as persons are not used without their consent; and (4) avoiding the general imposition in the human sciences of one view or ideology as if it were the canonical understanding. If in post-modernity one can speak about responsibility in the human sciences, it must be within the constraints of limited democracies that lack a canonical understanding of appropriate behavior, and which make room for vast areas of privacy, that is, vast areas where individuals can frame their own understandings of how to study and understand the human condition.

This is all that one can say about freedom and responsibility when one speaks with moral strangers. With moral friends, one will be able to make out much more. For example, within the traditions of the West, one will recognize that at least since Heraclitus the Western tradition has attempted to articulate a perspective that would be general and partisan to none. This sense of the logos is the historical antecedent of the regulative views of truth that must guide even pragmatists in their discussions of the truth, and it underlies the perspective of a dispassionate limited democracy compassing various communities of moral belief and of diverse understandings of the humanities and social sciences. From the perspective of moral strangers, these perspectives are historical accidents and yet unavoidable. One must prescind from their content when one attempts to understand freedom and responsibility within the language of moral strangers.[38]

NOTES

1. Hegel 1970, vol. 1, p. 202, sec. 246 Zusatz. In Hegel's own words: "Alle Revolutionen, in den Wissenschaften nicht weniger, als in der Weltgeschichte, kommen nur daher, daß der Geist jetzt zum Verstehen und Vernehmen seiner, um sich zu besitzen, seine Kategorien geändert hat, sich wahrhafter, tiefer, sich inniger und einiger mit sich erfassend." (Hegel 1986, 20f.)
2. The locus classicus is Plato's *Republic*. A contemporary expression of this point is by A. MacIntyre: "[O]nly in those forms of human relationship in which it is possible to appeal to impersonal standards of judgment, neutral between competing claims and affording the best type of rational justifica-

tion both relevant and available, that the possibility opens up of unmasking and dethroning arbitrary exercises of power, tyrannical power within communities and imperialist power between communities. Plato was once again right: the argument against the tyrant and the argument against relativized predicates of truth and justification require the same premises." MacIntyre 1987, 397–398.

3. Plato 1901b, 170e–171c and 172a. Protagoras proposes a relativism that is moral as well as epistemological, that man is the measure of truth and other values, based upon the relativity of each person's sense perception and the dependence of all knowledge and value claims upon this relativity (cf. Plato 1901, 334ab).

4. We take the broad view of transcendental argument articulated by Klaus Hartmann, an argument designed to answer the *quid juris*, i.e., to justify foundational theoretical or practical norms. Our concern in the text at this stage is simply with theoretical norms; practical or, more specifically, moral norms are handled later. Such norms cannot be adequately justified by appeal to facts, or the referents of the theoretical or practical claims. Rather, they are justified by appeal to some principle of subjectivity, because the subject, whether knowing or acting, is the person whom the norms govern. The paradigms of such arguments are Kantian. For example, the categories are necessary for objects of experience because they are necessary for the theoretical subject to be conscious of the object of consciousness, and the categorical imperative is necessary for the practical subject to understand how his actions are both free and under a categorical imperative to be moral. In a broad sense these arguments occur in much of Fichte, Schelling, Hegel, Marx, the Neo-Kantians, Husserl, Heidegger, Sartre, and philosophical hermeneutics, as well as in language-analytic adaptations of transcendental argumentation. Cf. Hartmann 1966, 223–249, and Hartmann 1984, 17–41, reprinted in Hartmann 1988, 193–219 and (in English) 237–264 respectively.

5. Cf. Kant 1929, A84–87/B116–119, 120–122.

6. Cf. Kant 1929, A158/B197, 194.

7. Cf. Kant 1929, A2/B2 f., 42–43.

8. Cf., e.g., Aristotle 1950, 184a15 ff.

9. Quine 1961, 43.

10. Aristotle thought that the principle of non-contradiction was a principle for the determinacy of being as well as of thought because the universe has unchanging elements in it (1957, 1010a32–34).

11. So Philip Kitcher (1992, 71) summarizing Quine's point in Quine 1966, 94–95.

12. We are indebted for this point, as well as for the more general point about the limitations of what transcendental philosophy can accomplish, to Aschenberg 1990, 439–456.

One might view Hegel's *Logic* as providing such a general truth ground by explaining just what explanatory thought is, such that its principles are also principles of its explanandum, being *qua* intelligible. Such a view, however, would require a very much reconstructed view of parts of the *Logic*, e.g., the treatment of pre-Fregean formal logic. Moreover—and this is Aschenberg's general point, which we find inescapable—even if one allowed the result to be a successful transcendental argument, it would not ground any categories in the philosophy of the real. It would not ground any categories of our particular world of full-bodied human experience, as immune from possible revision, as a perusal of Hegel's *Philosophy of Nature* makes evident. It would at best satisfy sheerly theoretical *desiderata*, the sort that the pragmatist does not think worth trying for.

13. Cf. Putnam 1987, 226–234; representative of Rorty's views is "Solidarity or Objectivity?" in Rorty 1991, 21–34. Our answer is indebted to the defense of Rorty by P.D. Forster in Forster 1992, 585–603.
14. Cf. Rorty 1991b, 9.
15. The pragmatist's point is that one can only justify other interpretative schemes in light of one's own historically and culturally constituted reason. Human reason cannot be utterly disinterested: it must have specific questions, from specific points of departure and within specific frameworks that are assumed beyond question. It is always incarnated within a particular historical and cultural context.
16. Kant 1968a, 47; Kant 1956, 48.
17. Kant 1968a, 30; Kant 1956, 29–30.
18. Kant 1968, 421; Kant 1964, 88.
19. Kant 1968, 428–429; Kant 1964, 96.
20. Kant 1968, 422, 429; Kant 1964, 89, 97.
21. To wit, for Kant it is necessary in order to say that suicide involves self-love in a contradiction with its morally worthwhile purpose.
22. Hegel 1986a, especially §§133–141.
23. Cf. Rorty 1991d, 23, 29.
24. Rorty 1991d, 29: "The pragmatists' justification of toleration, free inquiry, and the quest for undistorted communication can only take the form of a comparison between societies which exemplify these habits and those which do not, leading up to the suggestion that nobody who has experienced both would prefer the latter."
25. Cf. Rotry 1991a.
26. Cf. Rotry 1991c.
27. Cf. Rorty 1991c, 191–192. The work of Rawls to which Rorty is referring are essays written after *A Theory of Justice* (Rawls 1971), such as Rawls 1985. See also Rawls 1993.
28. We are indebted for the point of this paragraph to Aschenberg 1989, 70–71.
29. Telephone conversation of December 16, 1992, with Eric T. Juengst, Chief of the Ethical, Legal, and Social Implications section of the National Center for Human Genome Research at the National Institutes of Health.
30. The conference prospectus noted that, even if genetic markers should be found for tendencies loosely linked to criminal behavior, e.g., impulsivity, they would probably "have little specificity, sensitivity or explanatory power" (New storm brews 1992, C1).
31. U. of Md. conference 1992, A6.

32. U. of Md. conference 1992, A6.
33. "Back to the drawing board" 1992, 1474.
34. "Back to the drawing board" 1992, 1474.
35. "Genetics grant killed" 1993, 9A.: "*Washington*—The National Institutes of Health terminated a $78,000 grant to the University of Maryland for a conference examining whether there is a genetic link to crime. Funds for the conference had been suspended since July because of NIH concerns about the way it was being promoted. Black leaders and others complained that the conference, whatever its findings, might lead to assertions that blacks are predisposed to crime and genetically inferior to whites."
36. With respect to our example of NIH funding, it is worth noting that one can show nothing wrong in a particular community objecting to its resources being used for purposes that it holds to be morally objectionable, whether for ideological reasons as in this example, or for religious reasons as with publicly funded abortions. Indeed, particular communities on our view would have veto power upon how their resources are to be used by governmental bodies for society as a whole. Our objection is to the NIH's imposition of a particular substantive view of the good upon society as a whole.
37. Because a morality for moral strangers is grounded in the decision of individuals to negotiate peaceably, only those entities that can negotiate are persons in the strict sense with an unimpeachable secular moral claim to respect. The authors, as Orthodox Catholics, recognize that more can be known, but not by secular reason.
38. The arguments laid out in sections V, VII, and VIII have been set out more substantially in Engelhardt 1996, 2–4, and Engelhardt 1991, c. 5. In addition, the authors have benefited (perhaps not enough, some would say) from the critical remarks upon an earlier version of this paper by the participants in the March 1993 symposium on Freedom and Responsibility sponsored by the Conference of the Swiss Scientific Academies, and especially by Beat Sitter-Liver and Margaret Somerville.

REFERENCES

After Philosophy, ed. by K. Banes, J. Bohmann, T. McCarthy, 1987. Cambridge (Mass.): The MIT Press.
Aristotle 1950, *Physica* (William D. Ross, ed.), Oxford, Clarendon Press.
———— 1957, *Metaphysica* (Werner Jaeger, ed.), Oxford, Clarendon Press.
Aschenberg, Reinhold 1989, "Vernunftlose. Über Anfänge der Philosophie und zwei ihrer vorerst letzten Enden," in: *Schola Anatolica: Freundesgabe für Hermann Steinthal*, ed. by the Kollegium und Verein der Freunde des Uhland-Gymnasiums Tübingen, Tübingen, Osiander Verlag, 57–79.
———— 1990, "Kategoriale Tranzendentale Philosophie?," in: Koch, D./Bort, K. (eds.) 1990, *Kategorie und Kategorialität: Historisch-systematische Untersuchungen zum Begriff der Kategorie im philosophischen Denken*, Würzburg, Königshausen & Neumann, 439–456.

"Back to the drawing board, says NIH" 1992, in: *Science* 257 (September 11), 1474.

Engelhardt, H. Tristram, Jr. 1996, *The Foundations of Bioethics*, 2nd ed, New York, Oxford University Press.

———— 1991, *Bioethics and Secular Humanism*, London, SCM Press.

Forster, Paul D. 1992, "What is at Stake Between Putnam and Rorty," in: *Philosophy and Phenomenological Research* 52, 585–603.

"Genetics Grant Killed" 1993, in: *Houston Chronicle* (April 23), 9A.

Hartmann, Klaus 1966, "On Taking the Transcendental Turn," in: *Review of Metaphysics* 20, 223–249.

———— 1984, "Transzendental Argumentation. Eine Abwägung der verschiedenen Ansätze," in: Schaper, Eva/Vossenkuhl, Wilhelm (eds.), *Bedingungen der Möglichkeit. "Transcendental Arguments" und transzendentales Denken*, Stuttgart, Klett Cotta, 17–41.

———— 1988, *Studies in Foundational Philosophy*. Amsterdam, Rodopi.

Hegel, Georg Wilhelm Friedrich 1970, *Hegel's Philosophy of Nature*, transl. by Michael J. Petry, London, Routledge & Kegan Paul.

———— 1986 [1817], *Enzyzlopädie der philosophischen Wissenschaften II, Werke 9* , ed. by Eva Moldenhauer and Karl M. Michel, Frankfurt/M., Suhrkamp Taschenbuch Wissenschaft.

———— 1986a [1821], *Grundlinien der Philosophie des Rechts, Werke 7*, ed. by Eva Moldenhauer and Karl M. Michel, Frankfurt/M., Suhrkamp Taschenbuch Wissenschaft.

Kant, Immanuel 1929, *Critique of Pure Reason*, transl. by Norman K. Smith, London, Macmillan.

———— 1956, *Critique of Practical Reason*, transl. by Lewis W. Beck, New York, Bobbs Merrill.

———— 1964, *Groundwork of the Metaphysics of Morals*, transl. and analyzed by Herbert J. Paton, New York, Harper & Row.

———— 1968 [1785], *Grundlegung zur Metaphysik der Sitten*, ed. by Paul Menzer, in: *Kants Werke. Akademie Textausgabe IV*, Berlin, Walter de Gruyter.

———— 1968a [1788], *Kritik der praktischen Vernunft*, ed. by Paul Natorp, in: *Kants Werke. Akademie Textausgabe V*, Berlin, Walter de Gruyter.

———— 1968b [¹1781], Kritik der reinen Vernunft, ed. by Benno Erdmann, in: *Kants Werke. Akademie Textausgabe IV*, Berlin, Walter de Gruyter.

———— 1968c [²1787], Kritik der reinen Vernunft, ed. by Benno Erdmann, in: *Kants Werke. Akademie Textausgabe III*, Berlin, Walter de Gruyter.

Kitcher, Philip 1992, "The Naturalists Return," in *Philosophical Review* 101, 53–114.

MacIntyre, Alasdair 1987, "Relativism, Power, and Philosophy," in: *After Philosophy*, 385–411.

"New storm brews on whether crime has roots in genes" 1992, in: *New York Times* (September 15), 1992, C1.

Plato 1901, *Protagoras*, in: *Platonis Opera. Tomus III*, ed. by John Burnet, Oxford, Clarendon Press.

Plato 1901a, *Respublica*, in: *Platonis Opera. Tomus IV*, ed. by John Burnet, Oxford, Clarendon Press.

Plato 1901b, *Theaetetus*, in: *Platonis Opera. Tomus I*, ed. by John Burnet, Oxford, Clarendon Press.

Putnam, Hilary 1987, "Why Reason Can't Be Naturalized," in: *After Philosophy*, 222–243.

Quine, Willard van Orman 1961, "Two Dogmas of Empiricism," in: Quine, Willard van Orman 1961a, *From a Logical Point of View*, New York, Harper & Row.

—— 1966, "Truth by convention," in: *The Ways of Paradox* , New York, Random House.

Rawls, John 1971, *A Theory of Justice*, Cambridge (Mass.), Harvard University Press.

—— 1985, "Justice as Fairness: Political not Metaphysical," in: *Philosophy and Public Affairs* 14, 223–251.

—— 1993, *Political Liberalism*, New York, Columbia University Press.

Rorty, Richard 1991, *Objectivity, Relativism, and Truth*, Cambridge, Cambridge University Press.

—— 1991a, "Cosmopolitanism without Emancipation," in: Rorty 1991, 211–222.

—— 1991b, "Introduction: Antirepresentationalism, Ethnocentrism, and Liberalism," in: Rorty 1991, 1–20.

—— 1991c, "The Priority of Democracy to Philosophy," in: Rorty 1991, 175–196.

—— 1991d, "Solidarity or Objectivity?," in: Rorty 1991, 21–34.

"U. of Md. Conference that Critics Charge Might Foster Racism Loses NIH Support" 1992, in: *The Chronicle of Higher Education* (September 2), A6.

Skepticism:
A Rescue from the Postmodernist Predicament and a Way to Practical Universals

BEAT SITTER-LIVER

At first glance, the above title sounds paradoxical, if not contradictory. To show how far this appearance is erroneus is the first goal of this paper. The second aim is to demonstrate that there is good hope to reach generalizable ethical rules for the interchange of moral strangers. Even when living as moral strangers, we need certain practical universals in order to survive. They must be looked for in the fact of diverging moral attitudes and beliefs. The third objective concerns the application of the results to the field of the humanities and social sciences (the human sciences). It will be shown that some guiding principles ought to govern all research in human sciences, and that they may serve as general standards for the ethical evaluation of such research. There is but little that separates the views developed by Thomas J. Bole and H. Tristram Engelhardt from my convictions and arguments. I share the principles they put forward. One difference, however, is fundamental: I cherish the belief that we may and must rely on reason in order to identify universals that allow us to get along peaceably with each other. The other important difference lies in the fact that the maxims and rules I design for moral strangers are more numerous than the set Bole and Engelhardt seem to admit.

WHAT IS AT STAKE

The question about freedom and responsibility in the humanities and social sciences (the human sciences) is not self-evident. Until recently it was, if at all, but rarely raised. In the sixties the topic became fashionable as a query about the social relevance of humanistic and social studies. Research and teaching were criticized as being isolated from social and political life, and it was not only for ideological reasons that those active in hermeneutic-historic and empiric-analytical disciplines were requested to put their scientific competence at the service of society at large. Later on, research methods, especially those applied in psychology, gave rise to criticism, since they went against generally shared convictions with regard to individual human dignity. Typical are S. Milgram's investigations of the interrelation between authoritarian influence and obedient behavior, and the fervent debate that followed. A third branch of today's question about freedom and responsibility within the human sciences has been growing since the seventies. It feeds on the predominant tendency to justify scientific research—and its necessary funding—by its importance for economic development and competition. Politicians in the first place, accompanied by civil servants and supported by an important part of the general public, wish to be reassured as to the public utility of the humanities. The respective question put to the social sciences may sound identical; it is, however, mostly driven by another motive, viz., the ambivalent fear that social science research might disclose structures and procedures that may indeed serve existing power patterns, yet, on the other hand, lack democratic legitimation.

This roughly sketched enumeration is not complete. It suffices, however, to make clear that the human sciences have to answer the request of a moral and political legitimation which must not be arbitrary but must meet with the approval of—ideally—all members of a given society. That request cannot be ruled out by simply stating the postmodernist character of—at least Western—societies.

Surely the term "postmodernism"—itself unclear and questionable (cf. Wenzel 1994, 43)—possesses some descriptive value as far as it purports that, as a rule, in today's societies contrasting foundational values and attitudes are defended and lived simultaneously. But the term easily leads astray if understood to imply that in these societies there no longer exist any prevalent value orientations supported by a large majority which are therefore generally binding. Yet even if that were the case, common interests of those adhering to a given society might be found. Survival in peace is one of them. Certainly the argument putting forward a fundamentalist fanatic ready to sacrifice his life and that of many others must not be disregarded in principle. However, it is out of place when presented within the debate about postmodernism. The topic of that discussion is the actual coexistence of divergent fundamental attitudes, and not the possible existence of an extreme position abolishing all foundational differences. Postmodernist theoreticians and practitioners, too, have to deal with the fanatic following rules that do not correspond to their fundamental relativist beliefs. Besides, the fanatic presents an extreme case which is not capable of defeating the intention of postmodernist theoreticians, viz., to make out common means to allow for coexistence within divergence.

This is the very core of the postmodernist challenge: to get hold of the minimal consensus which is a prerequisite to factual divergence. The question, therefore, is not whether such a consensus ought to and could be sought for; it is, rather, how narrow or how large that consensus may be designed. In order to realize such a design, a generally acceptable and binding medium is needed, be it of formal, i.e. procedural, or of content-full nature. We usually call that medium reason. Which is equal to saying that, without reason, we shall not succeed in meeting the postmodernist challenge.

This thesis seems to be in contradiction with one of the main contentions forwarded by Bole and Engelhardt. In fact, it only highlights a slight lack of clarity in their argument. What they are explicitly after is "a rationally defensible framework for controversy resolution" (cf. p. 78). They, too, cannot do without reason. If it may be true that reason does not *resolve* factual foundational controversies by comparing and ranking moral values and systems, then at least reason will *constitute framework conditions* such values and systems must respect in order to be acceptable within a postmodernist society. Which is again equal to saying that, in contrast to what Bole and Engelhardt maintain, "in a world of irresolvably different perspectives" *there are* "meta-values that are clinchers" (cf. p. 65). Without any content-full values, there will be no peaceful interchange among moral strangers. To get hold of a first argument for that contention one has but to look at the authors' own position, i.e., at the fundamental function they attribute to *respect* as the basis of *peaceful* interchange between moral strangers (cf. pp. 79–81). Respect as a general principle[1] cannot be thought of without accepting the idea of intrinsic worth within each human being, and it is only that idea which allows for making *peaceful* dealing with foundational controversies the first and most acceptable measure to be taken within that context (and to exclude the fanatic's solution).

Let us assume that we really live in true postmodernist societies where unreconcilable foundational beliefs, relevant to our practical commerce, are confronted with each other. Suppose we share the will to *peaceably* coexist. It would then be inconsistent not to accept each of the foundational beliefs diverging from our own as a possible alternative, i.e., as an attitude that questions ours. Even while adhering to our own belief, we are not in a position to make it an *absolute* point of reference. The same is true, of course, for all the other attitudes cherished within our society, and even worldwide. In the end, the practical consequence of such a situation would be to assume the skeptic stance (reminding ourselves that the ancient skeptics did not simply dismiss the societal, political, or religious customs and rules prevailing in their respective societies).

My intention is to analyze the skeptic position with a view to showing how far even the skeptic is bound to a set of irrevocable ethical principles. They provide the meta-principles or clinchers without which no postmodernist society could survive. At the same time, they constitute a rationally defensible framework for moral strangers which goes beyond the one Bole and Engelhardt construct, although it is co-governed by the same principle of mutual respect grounded in what is traditionally called human dignity. Complementing Bole and Engelhardt, I shall propose a skeptical reconstruction of the notion of human dignity, thus rendering it applicable without having to rely upon religious or otherwise metaphysical beliefs.

Within the context of our general topic—freedom and responsibility within the humanities and social sciences—it is indeed vital to get hold of some general ethical principles. For as Bole and Engelhardt rightly stress, if no evaluative standards of ethical self-reflection could be "justified in terms of general secular reason, the humanities and social sciences" might "become masks for the special interests of those who propose and define the content" (p. 67). However, the primary task of the human sciences does not consist in propagating a particular set of ethical principles or moral directives. They are not originally designed to serve ideological intentions. If generally justifiable principles must be found, then they must be for the purpose of evaluating the values and procedures the humanities and social sciences follow in the course of their research process. Their *doing* must be justifiable in general terms, not the contents they unveil and analyze. We have to clearly distinguish the research process with its own guiding principles from the results it yields. The specific task of human sciences is to detect, preserve, analyze, interpret, enlighten, and criticize. In so far as they proceed to evaluate the contents they investigate, their respective points of reference are subject to ethical debate, on the object as well as on the meta-levels. In that case they are an object of ordinary moral dispute and ethical critique. But independent of the moral judgments they may convey, their ways of proceeding must satisfy generally acceptable standards. It is these standards—or principles—at which the following investigation of the skeptical position is aimed. Since the principles are meant to be of universal validity, they may, in the second place, become standards for evaluating moral behavior in general. The result of our inquiry, despite the fact that it springs from a particular interest, may thus become relevant for the general debate dealing with the ethical foundation of human practice.

I shall proceed in five steps: *first* I shall take a look at the comprehensive and "furthest thought-out" (Hossenfelder 1985b, 9) exposition of classical skepticism by Sextus Empiricus, which gives an insight into the *primacy of practice in all skepsis.*[2] *Second* I shall take stock of a few traits of our historical situation, which in particular push thinking interested in action orientation in the direction of skepis. *Third* I will present a recollection of the half-heartedness in Descartes' methodic doubt in order to lead us to the *fourth* stage, the terrain of *radical*[3] skepis. In scrutinizing this skepsis we shall *finally* look for practical guidelines, which remain withdrawn from skeptical questioning because, being its prerequisites, they make it at all possible.

OF THE PRIMACY OF PRACTICE IN SKEPTICISM

At the beginning of his collection of Pyrrhonic patterns, Sextus Empiricus defines skepsis as "the art of contrasting in every possible way things appearing and imagined, [the art] from which we proceed first to restraint and then to tranquillity, owing to the equivalence of the opposed things and arguments" (PH I, 8).[4] Suspension of judgment or simply suspense, (ἐποχὴ) is a deliberate act,[5] resulting out of insight into the impossibility of resolving a dispute; ataraxia (tranquillity) is the reward for the "suspension of the understanding" as it were, in which nothing is set nor anything invalidated (PH I, 10); it follows ἐποχὴ "like the shadow follows the body," fortuitously without intervention by the skeptic, as Sextus asserts repeatedly (PH I, 29; 26). The experience of this coincidence makes skepticism an objective (PH I, 25): "The originating cause of scepticism" lies in "the hope of attaining quietude" (PH I, 12). The achievement of this relieves the skeptic of disquiet in dogmatic concerns, shields him from the spiritual torments inevitably oppressing him when, persisting in ignorance, he believes in the existence of a truth or good, or when, in momentary possession of the naturally good, he trembles before the possible loss of it (PH III, 276–278). But where the question is not "of matters of opinion" but rather of evil, which strikes him quite independently of himself, suspense frees him from the idea that evil exists by nature. Unlike the dogmatist he does not despair but suffers only moderately (PH I, 25–28, 30; III, 235–237). In this way he arrives at a position from which action is possible by trusting in life experience, without the uncertainties resulting from a presumed knowledge of good. What was and is valid is enough; struggle and zeal emerge not only as superfluous but purposeless.[6]

The skeptic achieves the modest bliss of those who renounce final happiness, the absolute, and that worth striving after for its own sake (cf.

PH III, 172). Since he cannot be entirely inactive (PH I, 23) he leads "a life conformable to the customs of our country and its laws and institutions, and to our own instinctive feelings" (PH I, 17). These are what is left as normative criterion when there is no prospect of discovering absolute certainty. *The supreme goal of the skeptic is thus to arrive at a practice considered optimal for the finite person.* In other words *practice* which takes its orientation from the natural potentialities and limitations of the human being is the *primary* task of skeptical reflection.[7,8]

Sextus laid down his epitome of Pyrrhonic skepsis at a time when various sense-offerings were competing, though apparently he had no hope of reconciling them. The positions of the Aristotelians, Epicureans, and Stoics seemed ultimately incompatible, inducing the Academicists to *absolute* skepsis, i.e., to an assertion, in itself contradictory, of the unrecognizability of all things, whether of theoretical or practical nature. From the aspect of interest in a reasonable mode of living, and this means in controllable practice too, this situation constitutes a scandal. Yet none of the positions represented have been able to provide remedy in a generally acceptable manner.

In response to the competing viewpoints of the Aristotelians, Epicureans, Stoics, academic Skepticists, and other groups beyond them, the possibility arose of *making the dispute itself the starting point for ordering practice*. It was this approach that Pyrrhonic skepticism adopted. In the first of the five Agrippine tropes this is brought to the point: "The trope from the dispute leads us to find that with regard to the object presented there has arisen both amongst ordinary people and amongst philosophers an interminable conflict because of which we are unable either to choose a thing or reject it, and so fall back on suspension" (PH I, 165). By freeing us from zeal and endeavor, suspension leads to "the repose and oceanic tranquillity of the soul" (PH I, 10), to the bliss which, though not absolute, is accessible to human beings as experience teaches.[9] It allows one to lead one's life with adequate reliability, alone as in a community,[10] remaining within tradition, customs, and accepted practices. In view of the radically changed conditions of life, the guiding motivation for skeptical basic attitudes and approaches must certainly be described differently in contemporary skepticism (cf. Note 6). On the other hand, making the dispute the methodic point of departure for considerations of practical philosophy can be maintained undiminished.

REASONS FOR A RADICALIZATION OF SKEPSIS

A brief look at the situation in which we are searching for meaning and orientation for action will soon convince us that things are far more confused than they might have appeared to Sextus in his own situation. Within philosophy *divergent principles* and methods for practice orientation are being defended. Correspondingly varied are the basic attitudes actually assumed and the practical objectives pursued even *in one and the same social unit*. As before, irreconcilable political interests and convictions collide. However, the innocuousness of the intercultural comparison of manners and values, religious views, and political objectives—which Sextus proposed with theoretical intent for his skeptical case—has turned in various places into real strife, even irreconcilable life-and-death conflicts. The *science theory and criticism* of our century long ago established the insight that theories and methods can claim to be valid only contextually and with regard to pragmatic interests. Nevertheless there is considerable dispute among scientists regarding the proper prerequisites and methodologies. As the sole rational process of understanding and orientation for all domains of life, science is both propagated and attacked simultaneously. Even the very term "science" is disputed within the guild, insofar as the dispute is carried on at all and not broken off, everyone maintaining his position without further discussion. In view of the complexity of the problems which it is proposed to solve by scientific means, the spirit of criticism ideally inherent to science evaporates, giving way to decisionist options betrayed by the exclusion or oversight of obvious problem aspects. Contemporary science criticism and sociology also point out the fact that often not simply methodic but also extra-scientific motives are at work, contaminating the process with individual and group-specific power claims, social prestige, and the desire for material gain. In such a situation it is no longer the quest for truth and for what is right that is the cause of controversy; the invocation of the respective ideals only serves as a pretext—or those ideals are simply declared obsolete and dropped from the agenda with the argument that progress and change as such cannot be resisted.

Meanwhile the chasm separating our age from the second century A.D. has grown much deeper. While *recourse to custom* was in fact still possible for the late skeptic as orientation for action, the long-term nature of developments which would be a prerequisite for this has been lost in the present epoch. Not only has the ground which carries us become very narrow and thin; it is under constant pressure from new problems which arise faster than our ability to adapt. These new problematic states cannot be handled, or at any rate only with difficulty, by traditional orientations. One notorious example is provided by the rapid development of science and technology in sensitive areas like human medicine. One has only to think of reanimation, prenatal diagnostics, and gene therapy. It teaches us forcibly what unusual situations scientific and technological progress is pressing us into all the time. And as if that were not enough, our ever-growing ability to intervene—made possible by the ambivalent technico-scientific process and driven by our efforts to improve our economic conditions—makes us overstretch our capacity to the point where we irreversibly damage or even destroy the basis of all that we take for granted: i.e., the natural foundation of human existence.

Perhaps the most important paradox, driving a new secularization process triggered by the disappointment of the hopes placed in science and technology, is common knowledge. Besides the magnificent achievements which make life easier, under the primacy of economics our industrial civilization with its science and technology causes risks, damage, and destruction. It would be naïve to believe these negative effects could be eliminated by the same means without causing considerable hazards and losses in turn. In such a situation it is of no help when O. Marquard, a skeptic of our time who is otherwise well worth listening to, simply places his trust in custom and points to what is usual as the first decisive counter-authority against the will to envisage and implement far-reaching changes in important aspects of our living together.[11]

In so far as philosophy, guided by interest in action orientation, reflects this situation, it must call into question everything that exists and claims validity. It becomes a radical questioning, more forceful and more doubting than ever Pyrrhonists could have imagined. As *radical skepsis* it draws "everything into the vortex of making questionable," first and foremost the customary and the traditional. "To sustain and endure this radical skepticism is one of the essential human thinking exercises of our time" (Weischedel 1980, 38ff.).[12] It is not only a thinking exercise but, more comprehensively, an existential task.

"PROVISIONAL MORALITY" CALLED INTO QUESTION

If this is so, and I think that intellectual honesty demands our assent, then the Cartesian escape route into provisional morality remains barred to us also (cf. Marquard 1981, 18).

To be sure, Descartes was no radical doubter. He did not even reach the level of the Pyrrhonist skeptic, as that would have meant renouncing the goal he had set himself: to find certainty in the face of all skeptical doubts.[13] Though the Pyrrhonist will not deny the existence of such a foundation, he will not concede it either. On the contrary he will avoid committing himself in this matter too, although not without showing that any commitment is impossible. Descartes did not really face up to this telling objection, much less extricate himself from it. True, through his methodic doubting Descartes was able to demonstrate *that doubt exists,* which the Pyrrhonic skeptic does not deny either, speaking of phenomena (Wild 1980, 39). However, moving on to an assertion of the truth of statements, and with it the laying of a foundation for the system of knowledge, remains questionable.[14]

I shall confine myself to a few remarks on the criterion of certainty as developed and applied by Descartes. It consists of course in the clarity and distinctiveness of a perception: if the clarity and distinctiveness of the perception of an object correspond to the clarity and distinctiveness with which doubt becomes sure of itself, then the object is regarded as beyond doubt and therefore real (Descartes 1954, 59, 61).

Already in the objections to the Meditations it has been argued variously that *clara et distincta perceptio* is no criterion of truth, even if the firm conviction is associated with it that what is perceived to be so clear and distinct must be true. For how shall I ever know whether I am so convinced that I shall never have reason to doubt the content of the conviction, as required by Descartes? I need a *criterion* for assessing the reliability of my conviction—a criterion that Descartes fails to provide. Gassendi was very explicit in this respect: if we perceive something clearly and distinctly, he points out, by which art and method can we recognize "that we have such a clear and distinct insight that there is no possibility of our being mistaken" (Descartes 1954, 292; cf. Wild 1980, 43)? This is the question of the standard for judging the Cartesian truth criterion, which is raised here rightly—in good Pyrrhonic manner incidentally: In his criticism of the φαντασία καταληπτική (the cognizant perception) emphasized by the Stoics, which makes a perception *into this*, Sextus Empiricus objects that no criterion of this kind can be found, or if it is found another criterion will be needed to legitimize it, and so on *ad infinitum* (PH III, 241 et seq.).

But why does the Cartesian expedient of a provisional morality remain barred to the *radical* skeptic? One might think that the theoretical difficulties would present no serious obstacle to satisfying the practical need. That supposition is wrong, however, because the radical skeptic is not in a position to follow Descartes' separation of the theoretical and practical spheres and the (ostensibly temporary) shielding of the latter from methodic doubt. With his procedure Descartes imitates the ancient Skeptics exactly. In his "Discours de la Méthode" he explains that while he rejects all his previous insights and convictions, he still has to exist, and therefore cannot do without certain guidelines for conduct. Though he declares his desire to base morality also on an unshakable foundation, he considers that he can do this only when he has cognition firmly anchored. Now in order not to be without direction, and because human existence is possible only following rules, he opts for a provisional morality ("une morale par provision"). This must correspond to the laws of the land and the views of the wisest; after religion the highest criterion must be given to freedom, in order to leave open the possibilities of correcting and altering rules. Descartes wishes to steer clear of extreme positions, so that in the event of error the failure is kept within limits. Even if values and norms to which he subordinates himself are not strictly demonstrable, once recognized they must rank as certain for him—at any rate until compelling insight demands their revision (Descartes 1960, 36–46).

It is easy to see that this concept corresponds to the principal maxims, to which Sextus Empiricus also subscribes. To the *radical* questioner it must remain suspect, however. If he is consistent, he cannot rely on any guidelines put to him from outside, not even in the sense of a provisional morality. Does he thus plunge into the helplessly unprincipled? Does nihilism lurk at the end of the radical skepticist route, compared to which the Pyrrhonist refusal to commit itself in the slightest by assent or rejection emerges as no more than a meaningless gesture? This conclusion would be premature. The skeptic still has the path of self-reflection. It must be examined therefore, whether directives are to be discerned in the skeptical basic attitude *as such*. If so, they might take over the function of the Cartesian provisional morality: directives in the form of conditions of skepsis as practice. They would thus prove to be a basis for practical philosophy, insofar as this is skeptical.

NORMATIVE BASES OF PRACTICE FROM THE CONDITIONS OF SKEPSIS

Skepsis as review, as a questioning search, as a quest for counter-authorities, as confirmation of an aporia, is an act of distancing. One thereby detaches oneself from the immediate determination by a circumstance, an assertion of truth, or a validity claim—an act imaginable and performable only under the assumption of *freedom*. Obviously freedom is definable more closely as freedom of action, but in addition it must be understood as freedom of the will, because skepsis can be visualized purposefully as the execution of criticism only under the condition that free assent or rejection is possible. The *consistent* skeptic[15] must desire the execution of the skeptical reflection *ceaselessly*; but this implies also that he is essentially interested in maintaining the freedom of will and action. He cannot abandon this objective or even call it into question without himself renouncing the possibility of a skeptical attitude. While he may leave open the question of whether or not he is in fact free, he is incapable of imagining himself as anything other than a freely willing and acting entity.[16] As long as he is a skeptic, he must therefore desire and achieve freedom.

Freedom, understood as freedom of will and action, becomes the *first principle* of his practice. Viewed in this light, there is *no skepsis without principles.*[17]

The skeptic is unthinkable as a solipsist. Indeed it is the contradictions he encounters in his dealings with other people that make him a skeptic. In confronting others he comes up against opinions and attitudes which he may be able to render dubious but not exclude, and which on the other hand call his own position into question. He sees himself forced to grant everyone else the same qualities he claims for himself: aloofness, criticism, and suspense (and to promote these for as many people as possible out of philanthropy; PH III, 280f.). In the first instance he is guided here not by any moral standpoint but rather by his self-understanding, for he cannot afford the pragmatic contradiction without losing his skeptical existence. In himself the skeptic finds no reason for negating conclusively other opinions and attitudes, or for denying others the right to a skeptical attitude. On the contrary, he can only impute to everyone he meets the same interest in freedom of volition and action that moves him, at least contrafactually. According to his own (weak) conviction, the adequacy of the skeptical basic attitude ought to be accessible to every reasonable individual. However, this requires his readiness to make the principle of freedom, by which he orients his own practice, into the *principle of everyone,* and to recognize it as a *general principle. Respect* for all others as possible free agents then becomes the *second principle* of skepticism as critical reflection in a social perspective.

It seems to me that this reasoning can be understood as a skeptical reconstruction of the term *human dignity.* The reconstruction gives this term a precise sense without further metaphysical or theological definitions.

To regard everyone else as a possible free agent in skeptical attitude conforms to a *self-obligation* of the skeptic, arising from the life-form that he has chosen for himself. Accordingly the obligation is rooted in the skeptic himself. It is established by his specific rationality, not by any exchange relationship or distribution process which might have been agreed to previously between individuals. Thus there is no need for obligation to be reconstructed via the traditional or contemporary contract theory.[18] This is not altered by the fact that self-obligation can arise only under the condition of sociality, because only then can differences of opinion and competition for respect arise, hence the need for generally binding and pacifying problem solutions. In contrast to the general principle of freedom as well as to the principle of respect, sociality is not a *transcendental* but an *empirical,* anthropologically authenticated, prerequisite for skeptical existence.

To regard everyone as a possible free agent with a skeptical attitude implies moreover viewing oneself and all others as equals in a fundamental, existential respect. Consequently the rivalry of opinions and validity claims of these equals is to be maintained as *competition*—i.e., for skeptical existence *no* final, strictly exclusive and potentially destructive *partisanship* is allowed. This holds at least so long as other opinions and validity claims do not run counter to the principles of freedom and respect, thereby threatening to render skeptical existence impossible.[19] In this way I think a convincing argument can be made for the *principles of equality and impartiality* as guidelines for the shaping of political, judicial, economic—in short socio-cultural—conditions, in conformity with skepticism. The contention of O. Marquard that skepsis is "not the apotheosis of perplexity" is borne out by this. However, his judgment on skeptical existence, that skepsis means "*taking leave from all principles*," appears short-sighted (17). The skeptics, if they reflect their life-form thoroughly enough, can certainly know principles and even refer to them in logic-analytical as in transcendental reflection.

How Marquard reasons his demand for the dismissal of principles is informative. He allows himself to be guided by the experience of finiteness and the shortness of human life. Because we exist under the pressure of time, he contends that what has proved itself till now enjoys a prerogative. The onus of reasoning lies with those promoting change (16). "Because we die too soon for total changes and total reasoning, we need customs" (17). We refer to them when justifying our decisions and actions. A philosophy that demands justification from principles turns reality inadmissibly into a tribunal—reality which, after all, is the factual, the *a priori* of everything fundamental (17). It should be remembered: "The fundamental is long, life is short. We cannot keep life waiting for fundamental permission to begin it and live it, for death is quicker than the fundamental, and dictates departure from this" (18).

In response to this the following may be said: first the recourse to customs for reasoning assessments and actions demonstrates that customs fulfill just the function that falls to principles as well.[20] The requirement of reference to customs is *a fortiori* of principal nature. It may also be asked how the fundamental character claimed for customs and for the methodological directives related to them can be legitimized. Finally, information may be demanded as to how far customs and methodological direction may enjoy priority before other principles. The imputation that in view of the shortness of our life, all thinking by principles may be dismissed cannot be upheld, at any rate when examined skeptically. It may serve watered down as an admonition, when searching for principles, not to neglect or overlook coping with what is here and now. Viewed in this light, the admonition is certainly justified. However, it does not then depart from principles but distances itself from them at most, which means recognizing them too, in a skeptical manner.

From the platform that we have gained, meanwhile, we are able to provide more ground for basing a normative practical philosophy. What has been said about impartiality may be formulated as an—in turn transcendental—*imperative of tolerance:* the skeptic must accept what accepts him in turn. This precept of tolerance is comprehensive, though not without limit. The limit of tolerance lies where practical convictions, validity claims, and individual or collective behavior resulting from them impair the possibility of tolerance, or freedom, or skepsis as the case may be. The skeptic finds no cause *prima facie* for accepting a curtailment of his freedom just because he cannot accept that the possibility of continuing to examine what purports to be right and true is barred to him (cf. note 19).

It has been said above that the skeptic is *unthinkable* as a solipsist. *In fact* too, he cannot exist like Robinson Crusoe. The experience of belonging to a community, of being dependent on and acting upon it, is existential and as such is not to be denied. This is true of all skepticism, from its beginnings until today. The question: what *truth value* does this experience possess, can be left open for our continued deliberations—as in fact the skeptic himself is often compelled to do. The pure and immediate experience of shared existence—with its inherent oppositions, uncertainties, and situations involving existential danger—is sufficient for the skeptic to take on the level of mere phenomena those actions which appear to assure the *de facto* possibility of skeptical existence. In this he differs from empiricist and philosophical anthropologists in that he claims no truth for the contents of his experiences or his statements about them. In other words, the skeptic will have to deal on the level of phenomena too with those apparently indispensable common provisions which ensure individual self-determination for a coexistence of human beings. Viewed in this light, skepsis and political commitment are not only compatible, skepsis which carefully and comprehensively spies out the circumstances of human living is in fact politically alert and active.[21] Quietism, usually associated with the basic attitude of skepticism, certainly remains a possible escape route but is not an inevitable consequence of skepsis. On the other hand, the skeptic may ask whether political recipes and precautions can ever attain their potential effectiveness as long as they are not conceived and implemented in a state of tranquillity.[22]

At this point a *digression* obtrudes itself: here the argument appears to be begging the question. This could lie in the (unassured) precondition of the *will to survive* on the part of the skeptic. He might put an end to his life in order to evade the demand of assuring *de facto* social existence. But why should the skeptic, tired of the uncertainty of truth and good, not simply depart from this world? Strictly speaking, *suicide* is no option for the *consistent* skeptic. It might make sense (and skeptical action is oriented on sense) for the skeptic to take his life only with the intention of putting an end to his problematic existence. But this intention presupposes that the skeptic knows for certain either that suicide means the complete extinction of his existence, or that leading an existence after suicide is without problems. Of all this he can know nothing, hence he cannot consistently decide in favor of this intention and its execution (analogous to Hossenfelder 1985b, 69). As a consequence, the assurance of skeptical existence with a social perspective becomes a necessary interest for him, Pyrrhonistically speaking: a φύσει πάθοσ, which he cannot oppose. Viewed skeptically, the will to survive is not just a well-proven hypothesis but is demanded by insight, comparable with the ἐποχὴ dictated by insight (PH I, 163; cf. note 15). There can be no question of a *petitio principii*.

Let us return to the necessity reasoned by phenomena for the skeptic to make provisions for *de facto* coexistence in freedom. Here *considerations of contract theory* may now point the way. However, they deviate from the usual pattern (direct recourse to enlightened self-interest) in that the skeptic is never in a position to take his own individual interest into account in isolation. It is always identical with the analogous interest imputed to all others, and can therefore be presented adequately by the collectively existing skeptic only as a general interest. It is not only out of well-considered self-interest that he concedes freedom to others (with an eye to the conditions for the application of justice asserted by Th. Hobbes or H.L.A. Hart for instance), thereby ensuring freedom for himself by renouncing arbitrary self-realization (cf. Höffe 1987, 384f.). On the contrary his status and his self-understanding as a skeptic, i.e., he himself without regard to anybody else, compel him to take all others seriously as potential skeptics. In view of the possibility of skeptical existence demanded *without exception* by Skepticism, the skeptic must *always* understand *his* interest as a *collective interest*. From the outset, therefore, the point for him is not to seek *his* interest but to secure *everyone's* interest in freedom against possible encroachments. The community of interest does not have to be formed first: for the skeptic it is always existent. For this community of interest, agreements do not have *constitutive character* but pursue the purpose of defining those restrictions to freedom necessary to preserve collective individual freedom against dogmatic denials from any quarter. Once this foundation is reached, the process of necessary determinations may be represented as a negative exchange of freedom as O.

Höffe has done. With a view to the conditions governing the application of justice (though interpreted only as phenomena by the skeptic), one may set forth the provisions necessary for preserving the greatest possible freedom for all equals; and finally, one may argue for establishing a judicial system and a state, advocating a quite definite social order armed with mandatory powers (Höffe 1987).[23] If the skeptic is to keep in step with this, he can do so only under quite specific *conditions*.

For the skeptic, none of the normative, organizational, or procedural measures taken are final. True, he recognizes the *possibility* of truth and rightness (cf. Barnes 1990, 138 et seq.), otherwise he would not be conceivable as a radical skeptic. As Zeteticist he even defends this *ideal*, i.e., the formal ideas of truth and rightness as motives governing knowledge and action, even though he employs them only as problematic foils. Nevertheless he will never concede a final status to concrete insights and solutions acquired by coming to terms with truth and rightness. These remain indeterminate phenomena in time, whose status is still problematic with regard to intersubjectivity. Though the skeptic may accept certain solutions for pragmatic, apparently plausible reasons,[24] he insists that these solutions not only further the search for something more adequate but also necessitate this search.

Under both moral and political aspects, orders are legitimate for the skeptic only if they have *process character*, can be called in question at any time, entirely and individually, and are established so that their further development *can really happen*. Unlike the Pyrrhonic skepticism, which repeatedly appears quietist, *radical* reflected skepticism is anything but politically innocuous. Its ethics are quite capable of legitimizing *resistance actions* too (cf. note 19). The skeptic principle, however, which the relevant justification must obey, sets a clearly defined limit to all resistance. As a rule at any rate, rebellion must not reach the state where the *possibility* of skeptical existence is suspended, not even in the case of a tyrannical dogmatist.[25]

SOME CONSEQUENCES OF SCEPTICAL RATIONALITY FOR THE HUMAN SCIENCES

Reassured that the skeptical stance offers a way towards establishing a set of general ethical principles, we may say that the humanities and social sciences are not condemned to remain simply mirrors of the cultural prejudices and the social and political interests of those who engage in them or make use of them. The principles put forward by Bole and Engelhardt can easily be justified by the values and norms controlling the skeptical attitude: mutual respect results in the firm will not to use others without their consent. It entails that controversies over moral values and principles ought to be resolved without primary recourse to force, but with authority resulting from mutual agreement. As corollaries, force that is not based on consent must be eschewed, and so must fraud as a form of such force. In contrast, one is obliged to tolerate values in the human sciences of which one does not approve. Therefore, we must not impose our view or ideology as universal, neither in the human sciences nor in any other context of socially relevant activity.

But more can be said from the skeptical stance, and further maxims or rules may be developed which hold even among moral strangers. I wish to submit some such maxims and rules for discussion, although of course I do not intend to provide a complete account.

To begin with, the two main principles Bole and Engelhardt defend warrant some comment. The principle against using a person without his or her consent stands firm, of course. However, it covers only investigations in which living human beings are objects of research. It thus refers merely to part of what is essential within human studies. Consider the explication and interpretation of texts—of a poem for instance, or an archeological excavation—or rather any historical and hermeneutic activity that does not directly deal with human beings. Here, the principle does not seem to apply. In some cases it might even hinder critical and necessary enlightenment, viz., in a case in which an important public person's activity during the Nazi period should be brought to light. The person, having passed away many years earlier, cannot be asked for consent. But the heirs may not wish to disclose facts and actions despite the fact that the information might prove essential for the self-understanding of a whole nation. The heirs deny consent to the opening of their archives, or they may sue researchers for their way of reconstructing and interpreting historical phenomena. Who is to be asked for consent? The heirs anxious about their ancestor's fame and their own renown within society, or the legitimate representatives of that very society which depends on historical investigation in order to learn about itself and gain its true identity? Are historians in search of truth always dependent on the consent of their society, particularly in cases in which those in power prefer to withhold facts from the majority of the citizens? The answer to these questions is not obvious. It must indeed be given by mutual agreement, yet the consent principle will not lead very far in resolving the controversy.

Again, the principle of moral authority drawn from common agreement is convincing. Yet there are problems within the daily reality of human sciences which transcend its extension. The norms guiding the research process must certainly meet the demands implicit in the principle. But the matter treated in the research process—e.g., normatively relevant phenomena—cannot be subject to the same principle. It may be made the object of forthcoming general debate, critique, and possibly general agreement. In the process of research, however, it should be used like a precious stone the function of which is still unknown. The same goes for moral evaluations researchers put forward in the course of their work. These evaluations must evidently be drawn from investigations that respect the general norms of research in the human sciences, but their outcome may assume any content and form, being again simply material for general and open debate, critique, and possibly mutual agreement. When formulating norms for the human sciences we must carefully distinguish, as has been stressed before, the ways and means applied in the process of investigation from the material dealt with in that very process.

Further principles and rules may be found particularly when we consider objectives and activities of human sciences in the perspective of social ethics.[26] That perspective imposes itself to an unbiased view insofar as any research is realizable only in the framework of a society. It is allowed for by that society, or to be more concrete: by personal renouncement of the taxpayers. Fairness, a corollary to the principle of mutual respect, demands scientists in general to let their society have an appropriate share in the achievements and in the profit (understood in a large, not just economic sense) they produce, as early as possible. This entails, e.g., that researchers engage in letting the society have full, timely, and comprehensible information about the process of research and its outcome. It is not acceptable, either ethically or politically, to withhold scientific findings for personal reasons, for instance out of rivalry or overdone perfectionism. Thus there exists a moral obligation to publish, as soon as possible, the insights gained through publicly supported projects.

Since society does not simply consist of the scientific community, the same train of thought implies the researchers' engagement in public cultural activities of many kinds, public lectures being just an example of what might be appropriate forms of communication and education.

Another obligation, again an offspring of the fairness principle, can be seen in a consideration of the different tasks and needs prominent in a given society when designating research topics and projects to be financed by public funds. Suggestions regarding science policy, participation in the respective discourse, and consideration of practical consequences from results reached by mutual agreement are part of the scholars' and researchers' specific responsibility. Drawing consequences may lead to the renouncement of particular research interests since public funds are not unlimited. Openness to self-restriction thus becomes a general moral obligation.

Yet consideration for cultural, for economic, and for political interests clearly articulated within a given society by no means implies that only such interests should guide research activities. Knowledge, and even more, wisdom, are not just a matter of planning and of political consensus. More often they are a gift within a free—though never unintentful—process. A skeptic must be particularly interested in open research spaces, and he is therefore led to accept the moral obligation of struggling for what is usually called free research within his society. That obligation contradicts, in effect, the one developed in the last paragraph. To responsibly mediate tensions created by each of these obligations remains an unending task for the skeptic scholar and scientist. Thus consideration for societal needs and tasks entails for those active in human sciences participation in the societal discourse about the predominant needs and aims of research. They have to contribute their particular knowledge and competence in order to help shape that discourse and the agreements that follow. The specific role of scholars and social scientists consists in reminding their society of other values and orientations than those primarily, often by nonrational trends, followed. They have to—because they possess the means to—unveil the virtual richness of human existence, thus multiplying the practical, theoretical, aesthetic—in short, the *existential* alternatives open to human choice. This is in perfect harmony with the outlined skeptical attitude.

Even if we share the insight that no research project is free from cultural context and utterly unbiased, we do not need to accept—which is not the same as to approve—any possible research endeavor. Projects that clearly oppose the principles elaborated above ought to be discarded without further hesitation. Such are revisionist projects openly intended to deny well-established historical facts, thereby exonerating criminals and opening the door for further crime. The first example at hand is the scientifically supported endeavor to negate the former existence of Nazi extermination camps, or to relativize or minimize their murderous effects. We may add any project designed to put science at the service of racism. As a matter of fact, any project driven by an intention to blur facts falls under the same category, without regard to the depth of its cultural or political relevance.

We need not be moral friends to stick to the few obligations just sketched out. They follow from the skeptical stance—a rational attitude open to all moral strangers accepting argumentation because they are mutually interested in survival. What we need to do, however, is to dismiss the postmodernist dogma touting the all-determining prevalence of irresolvable differences among human individuals and communities. In order to allow us to live with and to live up to the challenge presented by divergent attitudes, values, and normative standards which indeed exist, we have to concentrate on those common views which apparently transcend differences and support the coexistence of rational human beings. Surely it would be naïve to maintain that the universal capability of rational argument could alone assure peaceful coexistence. It is nonetheless a way we cannot renounce if we wish to strive for that form of life.

NOTES

1. Even if respect is not considered a value itself it depends on an ultimate value: human dignity. Within the context Bole and Engelhardt display it could not be justified otherwise, the religious perspective being excluded.

2. R. Löw recalls rightfully that doubt is not capable of justifying itself, though it can be questioned about its sense. Löw's answer to this question confirms the long-standing primacy of practice: "Through itself doubt is not significant," it's significant because it belongs to an *overall context of successful life* and plays the part of a motor in it, driving thought beyond merely passing on what has been previously accepted or still is (Löw 1989/90, 21; author's emphasis).

3. To counter a current objection (self-contradictoriness of skepsis) here at once, it should be made clear that *radical* and *absolute* skepsis are not to be confused. Whereas the latter categorically denies all final cognition (thus invalidating itself), radical skepsis does not wish to settle with any result reached in the non-concludable process of research and investigation (ζητεῖν); it does so programmatically and consistently. It would, however, never claim that it is entirely impossible (epistemologically as ontologically) for the path of research ever to end in a final goal (PH I 226; cf. *Graeser* 1992, 206).

4. Quotations from the "Outlines of Pyrrhonism" (PH) mostly follow R.G. Bury's translation. Where this is not the case, M. Hossenfelder's German translation was of great help.

5. This is in contrast to *Barnes* 1983, 5 et seq., although he points out that some places imply an "intellectual ought" (6). Cf. regarding rationality of skepsis, note 15 and, critical of Barnes, *Flückiger* 1990 89–92. On the (controversial) question concerning the emergence and the object of skepticism, in particular the relationship between the experience of conflict, suspense, and tranquillity, cf. Bächli 1990, 55 et seq., also *Hossenfelder* 1985a, 151 et seq. Contrariwise also *Hossenfelder* (1985b, 54 et seq.), for whom ἐποχή is the "initial state of the Pyrrhonist." He is said to be "in the situation of Buridan's ass." This interpretation does not seem plausible to me, and I would distinguish between doubt or uncertainty as initial state, in which a decision is still sought (PH I, 12 and 26), and the ἐποχή as result of a rational process of striving for knowledge. Cf. *Graeser* 1992 206, who speaks of the inference of abstention from judgment out of reflection.

6. Cf. *Hossenfelder* 1985b, 32. This element of the skeptical position, if it is correctly reproduced, cannot be maintained after only a superficial glance at the present swift socio-cultural development. Where essentially new conditions and demands arise (one has only to think of our enormously increased

possibilities for action due to the achievements of the natural sciences and technology), what was and still is valid is no longer sufficient. A skeptic conservatism would not be adequate to the conditions of civilizatory development; it would also contradict the genuine skeptical requirement of looking around, verifying (σκοπεῖν), and coming to terms with what is new and unexpected. Skepsis would at best be compatible with conservatism in a static, less complex and manageable culture system. Under present conditions of socio-cultural existence, conservatism becomes a target for justified and effective criticism. "The classical escape to the calmness of skeptical ethics is no longer possible owing to the scale of the threats to man and humanity" (*Löw*, 1989/90, 22). But skepticism by no means needs to be conservative in the backward, even blind sense, not even with Sextus' attitude. Just how much the radical skeptic is open-minded to the experience of new things and ready to go beyond what is usual is shown by the medico-therapeutic practice appended by S.E.; cf. note 8.

7. From its motive, skepticism is genuine practical philosophy, not only when it deals with ethics but also where it turns to theoretical objects, i.e., in the realms of epistemology, logic, physics, general and special metaphysics, and philosophical theory (cf. *Hossenfelder* 1985a, 30 et seq., 34). A. Graeser speaks, in the form of a surmise, of the skeptical attitude as a "way of coping with existence" (1992, 203). Concerning ataraxia as a compulsory goal for the skeptic as such, cf. *Bächli* 1990, 55 et seq., who counters Hossenfelder (1985 1, 155) by asserting that "the sceptic . . . is not free to alter his view in this matter . . . as long as he is a Skeptic" (56).

8. For Sextus the primacy of practice might be explained biographically, too. As an adherent of the Empiricist, or as he calls it, the Methodic doctors' school, in his therapeutic actions he bases himself not on abstract theories of the human being and disease but allows himself to be guided by observations and experience, analyzing the disease phenomena and learning from them objectives and means of treatment. He does not rely on dogmatic theories burdened with prejudices. Thus his therapeutic knowledge and actions are always only provisional and, most importantly, are open to new experiences and measures suited for the individual case, for the benefit of his patient. Without equating Skepticism with the Methodic doctors' school (which would not do for a skeptic who must avoid identity statements), Sextus concedes that there is "a certain relationship" between the two (PH I, 241). For explanation, cf. *Graeser* 1992, 204; *Hossenfelder* 1985b, 84 et seq.

9. "Happy is the man who lives undisturbed (ἀταράχωσ) and enjoys peace and oceanic tranquillity (γαληνότησ)" (M XI, 141; quoted by *Hossenfelder* 1985b, 31).

10. Cf. note 6.

11. *Marquard* 1981, especially in the "autobiographical introduction" on p. 18. Here the position is deliberately drawn hard in the light of the problems touched upon. Differentiations are found and are fruitful; just one example is the passage in which Marquard testifies how much he owes to his teacher

Joachim Ritter (7 et seq.). For analyzing the assertion (obvious only at first sight) that skepsis must depart from all fundamentals (e.g. 18, 19), cf. *Sitter-Liver* 1992.

12. Philosophy as a whole, but especially practical philosophy, must make allowance for "Skepticism as the way of thinking that determines our time, must take upon itself the downfall of all thinking that was considered to be assured, and must therefore be skeptical ethics, ethics out of the spirit of Skepticism" (*Weischedel* 1980, 37).

13. *Descartes* 1960, III, 6. Cf. letter to Chanut dated 1st November 1646: Descartes complains that "he has been accused of Skepticism, despite his refutation of the Skeptics" (*Wild* 1980, 30, note 12; cf. also *Descartes* 1954, 482, 483).

14. Thus Wolfgang Stegmüller has objected that the proof of the existence of the perfect god, which alone eliminates the hypothesis of the *genius malignus* and thereby authenticates the perceptive force of the *clara et distincta perceptio*, depends on *just this clara et distincta perceptio*, i.e. it is circular (Stegmüller ²1969, 13; quoted by *Wild* 1980, 41, note 38).

15. *Regarding the problem of skeptical rationality:* To speak of consistent skeptics might be taken as a contradiction in terms insofar as "consistent" points to *rational behavior* and hence to the effectiveness of rules spared from skeptical suspension. However skepsis by no means disputes rational behavior, but is in fact constituted by such behavior. To the insight into the balanced dispute of the positions *follows* a certain behavior: the ἐποχή. Suspension of judgment is willed consistency, resulting from a judgment of a situation analyzed in a certain way (i.e. oriented in turn on a perception goal) that presupposes logical operations. (Cf. *Graeser* 1992, 206: "According to skeptical view the abstention from judgment may be inferred from reflections (PH I, 34) typified in the form of tropes."). Yet the skeptic is distinguished not only by constructive but by prospective rationality as well: with an eye to a practical goal—ataraxia—he will seize the instruments that allow him to reach the objective set (not for himself alone but for others too: i.e. in therapeutic rationality; cf. *Barnes* 1983, 83, 30 et seq.; PH III, 280 et seq.; I, 165). Everything depends on how the skeptic deals with his instruments: whether he can vouch for their validity or merely accepts them at first glance. Sextus always gives exemplary information where he declares skeptical catchwords as indeterminate and questionable in their abstract (i.e. not examined for their concrete effectiveness) validity (exemplary in PH I, 14 et seq., where S.E. explains that the catchwords are potentially eliminated by themselves). The help of theoretical as well as of practical logic is not refused: this would contradict the principle of skeptical life experience that what has been proven should be followed and applied. Only the skeptic will not aver that following rules leads to *particular* results, though this does not prevent him from shaping his conduct according to proven insights and rules as has been said.

Otherwise isosthenia or conflict cannot be established without the weight or force of two objects or arguments being compared with a third: a yardstick, which in this act does not call itself in question, no more than a balance which indicates identical or different weights in its two pans. Cf. in this connection the reply of S.E. to dogmatic objections. He maintains that thinking and investigating might behove the skeptic very well too (PH II, 1-9, then 10; cf. also *Barnes* 1990, 137 et seq.). But this means that the skeptic as well applies the necessary rules (the consequence rule also) in his theoretical as in his practical activities.

That no inconsistency lies here has been asserted by H. Flückiger against J. Annas and J. Barnes (1985, 90, note 3), successfully as I consider. The dispute as to whether ἐποχή as πάθοσ precludes the ἐποχή out of insight and necessity: ἀνάγκη, is decided by Flückiger who points out that skeptical arguments can be both effective and valid. It is suggested that *consistent thinking* is compatible with a skeptical attitude, always provided that the result of consistent reflection is not claimed as a certainty confirmed for all time: "The sceptic can do without objective validity but not without validity altogether" (*Flückiger* 1990, 91 et seq., 108, 111). Incidentally, on p. 108 Flückiger quotes examples showing that S.E. *implicitly* acknowledges and applies the rules of rational argumentation. On skeptical rationality cf. also *Bächli* 1990, who in the analysis of double ταράχη points out the kind of confusion and disturbance to be eliminated "by rational arguments, by the skeptical logos." What is involved is the form of ταράχη which occurs "owing to the perversion of reason and the foolish opinion" (62 et seq.). This manner of speaking by Sextus is incomprehensible without presupposing an average intelligence with its rules recognized by all in principle: in other words, common sense (cf. *Barnes* 1983, 10; *Flückiger* 1990, 87), which not only allows theoretical and practical conclusions for the skeptic, too, but demands them for everyday living.

16. Cf. *Kant* 1963, 4 (note) 55–59, 113 et seq.

17. Cf. PH I, 5, where Sextus characterizes the general debate on skepsis by presenting the term, *the principles* and the nature of the arguments of skepticism in it. Cf. note 11 to Marquard's definition of skepsis as "unprincipled philosophy." In the same passage Marquard dismisses "the fundamental freedom for human beings," leaving them the realm of "real freedom, or freedoms in the plural." But he is talking about different things here when "the freedoms" arise from the diversity of what is given, out of variety, rivalry, equal disputants, and division of power (19), for possibilities of action are involved here which cannot even be conceived without recourse to the principle of the guiding idea of freedom.

18. The indispensable prerequisites for this approach are avoided or circumvented: no reasons have to be given why a contract procedure has been entered into at all. That can happen only if recognition of the equivalency of all concerned is assumed, i.e. a transcendentally reasoned human dignity. Nor must human dignity be anchored metaphysically or theologically as a supreme orientation point, because the skeptical interpretation of this term is sufficient. *Subsequent* considerations and constructions of contract theory

are enough on this basis. Finally the problem of the will to survive can be resolved skeptically also, as is shown in the fifth part.

19. If such threats are resisted on account of skeptic reasoning, then it is in turn always only in a temporary, never a dogmatic manner. What is at stake in such resistance is the possibility of skeptical existence, of keeping open the zetetic route, but not the assertion of any certainty or, politically speaking, the ultimate establishment of a particular order. The resistance serves solely to ensure freedom as a *form* of living, and has insofar *no material* existential goal as its purpose. This does *not* exclude skeptical resistance being offered firmly, mobilizing all forces.

20. This has already been emphasized by F. Dirlmeier in his comments on Aristotle's Nicomachean Ethics. If the modern reader seeks an ultimate norm in Aristotle, he will not find one. For Aristotle there is no difficulty in this, as "his last norm is the collective wisdom of the race (Sir D. Ross): last realities, or viewed differently, first principles of ethics" (1979, 246). They can be interpreted as customs in the sense of Marquard. An analogous criticism of Marquard by *Höffe* 1990, 543; Bayertz, 19.

21. W. Weischedel underlines the difference between skepticism and conservatism. As potential revolutionary the skeptic goes along more with those aiming to alter the world (1980, 194); he criticizes power and institutions rather than defending them (1980, 201).

22. The question is of course not new. It has always been answered in skeptic terms. One has to recall only three examples: the Taoist teaching, by Juang Dsï for instance, according to which excellent deeds are possible only if performed from *sense* (translation of TAO by R. Wilhelm), i.e. neither assenting nor denying; the Paulist admonition to live and act in this world without belonging to it; and Meister Eckhart's teaching of the righteous: he applies himself to the world in (comprehensive) calm, doing what has to be done in it with commitment.

23. Here I must confine myself to noting that this argumentation is tantamount to advocating the liberal, social, and democratic order.

24. The problem of *how* other solutions arise must be left aside here, as must in particular the question of how far *decisionist* approaches too, such as legitimation by procedure, are admissible by virtue of their compatibility with the skeptic attitude. The relation between decisionism as a political theory and skepticism, which contrasts to the (for the conditions of human existence) adequate mode of life, has still to be examined. The same is true of the relation between skepsis and risk, for which there is only the conjecture that skepsis militates more for the minimization than the practice of risk, which, based on the axiom of the unredeemable uncertainty, advocates noncritical risk-taking or the now much-commended courage to accept risks.

25. The problem of *tyrannicide* (sit venia parti pro toto) touched upon by the demand just raised cannot be discussed here in detail. At least two explanations and a summing-up seem indispensable, however: 1. As a consequence of the previous remarks on skeptical ethics, the killing of a totalitarian or

tyrannical political opponent is fundamentally inadmissible. 2. The skeptic too cannot ignore the experience that the survival of the totalitarian tyrant brings with it profound deterioration, even destruction, affecting not only his own existence but that of third parties as well. This brings even the skeptic into a conflict that allows no mediation. The situation demands from him an existential decision, no longer one that can be kept in skeptical suspense, for the consequences of it are irreversible. The theory of the double effect of an action offers no genuine way out. However, the decision may favor rebellion, aimed at the physical elimination of the tyrant. 3. Summing-up: Though killing remains an evil in itself just from the skeptic-transcendental viewpoint, and so can *never* be allowed, under circumstances it may be *excusable* and insofar justifed in the situation outlined.

26. For the following discussion cf. also *Sitter-Liver* 1986 and 1988.

REFERENCES

Annas, Julian/Barnes, Jonathan 1985, *The Modes of Scepticism: Ancient Texts and Modern Interpretations*, Cambridge, Cambridge University Press.

Barnes, Jonathan 1990, *The Toils of Skepticism*, Cambridge-New York, Cambridge University Press.

—— 1983, "The Beliefs of a Pyrrhonist," in: *Elenchos: Rivista di studi sul pensiero antico* IV (1), 5–43.

Bächli, Andreas 1990, *Untersuchungen zur Pyrrhonischen Skepsis*, Bern-Stuttgart, Paul Haupt.

Bayertz, Kurt 1991, "Praktische Philosophie als angewandte Ethik," in: Bayertz, Kurt (ed.) 1991, *Praktische Philosophie: Grundorientierungen angewandter Ethik*, Reinbek bei Hamburg, Rowohlt Taschenbuchverlag, 7–47.

Descartes, Rene 1954 [1641], *Meditationen über die Grundlagen der Philosophie mit sämtlichen Einwänden und Erwiderungen* (Artur Buchenau, ed. and transl.), Hamburg, Felix Meiner (Philosophische Bibliothek, Vol. 27).

—— 1960 [1637], *Discours de la Méthode* (Lüder Gäbe, ed. and transl.), Hamburg, Felix Meiner (Philosophische Bibliothek, Vol. 261).

Dirlmeier, Franz 1979, *Einleitung zu Aristoteles: Nikomachische Ethik*, Darmstadt, Wissenschaftliche Buchgesellschaft.

Flückiger, Hansueli 1990, *Sextus Empiricus: Grundriss der pyrrhonischen Skepsis. Buch I—Selektiver Kommentar*, Bern-Stuttgart-Wien, Paul Haupt.

Graeser, Andreas 1992, *Sextus Empiricus. Grundriss der pyrrhonischen Skepsis*, in: Graeser, Andreas 1992, *Interpretationen, Hauptwerke der Philosophie. Antike*, Stuttgart, Reclam, 197–222.

Höffe, Otfried 1986, "Entscheidung," in: *Staatslexikon*, ed. by the Görres-Gesellschaft, 7th edition, Vol. 2, Freiburg-Basel-Wien, Herder, 287–290.

—— 1987, *Politische Gerechtigkeit: Grundlegung einer kritischen Philosophie von Recht und Staat*, Frankfurt/M., Suhrkamp.

—— 1990, "Universalistische Ethik und Verallgemeinerung: ein aristotelischer Blick auf Kant," in: *Zeitschrift für philosophische Forschung* 44, 537–563.

Hossenfelder, Malte 1985a, *Die Philosophie der Antike 3: Stoa, Epikureismus und Skepsis: Geschichte der Philosophie*, ed. by Wolfgang Röd, Vol. III, München, Beck.

———— 1985b, *Einleitung zu Sextus Empiricus: Grundriss der pyrrhonischen Skepsis*, Frankfurt/M., Suhrkamp, 9–88.

Kant, Immanuel 1963 [1788], *Kritik der praktischen Vernunft* (Karl Vorländer, ed.), Hamburg, Felix Meiner (Philosophische Bibliothek, Vol. 38).

———— 1966 [1797], *Die Metaphysik der Sitten*, in: *Werke in sechs Bänden* (Wilhelm Weischedel, ed.), Vol. 4, Darmstadt, Wissenschaftliche Buchgesellschaft.

Löw, Reinhard 1989/90, "Skeptisches Denken und Philosophie," in: *Scheidewege* 19, 6–23.

Marquard, Odo 1981, *Abschied vom Prinzipiellen*, Stuttgart, Reclam.

Mau, J. 1954, *Sexti Empirici opera*. Rec. H. Mutschmann, Vol. III *Adversos Mathematicos libros I-VI continens*, Leipzig. (=M)

Pascal, Blaise 1947 [1669], *Pensées* (d'après l'édition de Leon Brunschvicg), London, J.M. Dent & Sons Ltd., Paris, G. Crès et Cie (Collection Gallia).

Sextus Empiricus 1955, *Outlines of Pyrrhonism*. With an English transl. by the Rev. Robert G. Bury, Litt. D., London, William Heinemann, Cambridge (Mass.), Harvard University Press (Loeb Classical Library No. 273). (=PH)

———— 1985, *Grundriss der pyrrhonischen Skepsis*. Intr. and transl. by Malte Hossenfelder, Frankfurt/M., Suhrkamp (stw 499). (=PH)

Sitter-Liver, Beat 1986, "Hat die Ethik in der Wissenschaft nichts zu suchen?," in: Sitter-Liver, Beat (ed.) *Wissenschaft in der Verantwortung*, Bern, Paul Haupt, 37–78.

———— 1988, "Konstruktive und destruktive Wechselwirkungen zwischen Wissenschaft und Ethik," in: *Freiburger Zeitschrift für Philosophie und Theologie* 35, 379–413.

———— 1992, "Macht Klugheit Prinzipien entbehrlich?," in: *Deutsche Zeitschrift für Philosophie* 40 (11), 1313–1332.

Stegmüller, Wolfgang ²1969, *Metaphysik, Skepsis, Wissenschaft*, Berlin-Heidelberg-New York.

Strawson, Peter F. 1987, *Skeptizismus und Naturalismus*, Frankfurt/M., Athenäum (orig.: *Skepticism and Naturalism. Some Varieties*, New York, Columbia University Press 1985).

Weischedel, Wilhelm 1980, *Skeptische Ethik*, Frankfurt/M., Suhrkamp (Suhrkamp Taschenbuch, Vol. 635).

Wenzel, Uwe Justus 1994, "Die Moderne redigieren. Zum 70. Geburtstag von Jean-Francois Lyotard," in: *Neue Zürcher Zeitung* Nr. 184, 10 Aug. 1994, 43.

Wild, Christoph 1980, *Philosophische Skepsis*, Meisenheim, Hain.

The Fusion of Science and Culture:
Key to the Twenty-first Century

MAHDI ELMANDJRA

The symposium which the Conference of the Swiss Scientific Academies organized in 1988 dealt with the ethics of—amongst others—the *exact* sciences, while this one is devoted to the *social* and *human* sciences. The interface of the two raises several ethical issues which we cannot ignore—hence the query about the interrelation between science and culture.

What I appreciated most in this meeting is the concern of some of the Western participants as to the limits of the "traditional Western intellectual project." Thomas J. Bole, III and H. Tristram Engelhardt, Jr. are quite explicit on that issue: "The traditional Western intellectual project of providing a generally justifiable framework must be fundamentally reconsidered if it is to be normative even for those who are strangers to each other's basic intellectual and moral values . . . . This is the notion of ethics as the commitment to resolving controversies between moral strangers without primary recourse to force but with common moral authority" (see p. 79).

This concern raises the problem of socio-cultural values when dealing with any of the sciences, which is not often taken into account and which this meeting seems to underline. Do we use different sets of values when dealing with the exact sciences than those we use with social and human sciences?

Michel Serres emphasizes the split between the scientists and what he calls the literary intellectuals (we might say the social and human scientists) and describes it as a form of hemiplegia:

Beaucoup d'intellectuels d'aujourd'hui sont les héritiers directs de la génération précédente qui a été formée par la linguistique, l'ethnologie, l'anthropologie, etc. C'est-à-dire les sciences humaines ou plus exactement le couple humanité–sciences humaines. C'est une génération à laquelle il faut rendre hommage, bien sûr. Mais en ajoutant qu'elle fut totalement ignorante d'un autre versant de la modernité culturelle, scientifique celle-là: mathématique, thermodynamique, physique, chimie, génétique et ainsi de suite. Par conséquent, la réflexion politique contemporaine est le plus souvent conduite par des gens qui ont une culture hémiplégique . . . La génération précédente a gravement failli sur les problèmes qui relèvent de la liaison science-société.[1]

There is a need to find ways to surmount the new forms of scientific illiteracy within the scientific community so as to overcome the gap which Serres mentions. This is essential to a better understanding of the relations between the sciences and society.

THE NEED FOR SOLIDARITY IN SPACE AND TIME

It is commonly accepted that humanity will survive together or vanish collectively. The question of survival "at what cost?" raises more complex and delicate aspects which have to do with values and hence with culture.

Survival calls for solidarity in space—*participation*—and solidarity in time—*anticipation*. The major obstacles to the satisfaction of these prerequisites are: (1) the great economic disparities to be found within and between countries and the consequent social inequity; (2) the hegemony, over the past 200 years, of the "Western" or "Judeo-Christian" system of sociocultural values; and (3) maladapted learning processes and mental structures for coping with an unprecedented acceleration of historical events and a rapid rate of change, which call for greater foresight and much more balanced cultural communication.

NEW ALLIANCE

The basic assumption of this article is that survival cannot be ensured without a "new alliance" between science and culture to the point of fusion. The industrial revolution perpetuated the vision of a society with "two cultures"—one of science and one of non-science. Post-industrial society will inevitably overcome this dichotomy as we move from a civilization of raw materials, production, and capital to one of knowledge, information, and an "immaterialization" of the economy.

This fusion will raise numerous problems, including the reconsideration of the long-standing credo concerning the universality and neutrality of science. Questioning this dogma is essential to overcoming the equation which implies that *modernization* is synonymous with *Westernization*.

The refutation of this hypothesis is what has led me to concentrate my research efforts on the fields of future studies, advanced technologies and cultural change, and the case of Japan. There has never been validity in the simplistic and culturally ethnocentric interpretations which reduce the whole Japanese economic, scientific, technological, and cultural advances to a mere "imitation" of the West. Today, things have changed, and the development of Japan is more and more understood as an inner process directly linked to specific cultural values.

AGE OF DIVERSE CIVILIZATIONS

No contemporary phenomenon has emphasized the intimate link between science and culture more than the Japanese development model which, as with all authentic development models, is, of course, inimitable. To widen one's understanding of the interfacing of science and culture it is useful to read the Japanese Institute for Research Advancement (NIRA) 1988 study which describes 25 ongoing research projects. Its introduction emphasizes the concept of the "age of diverse civilizations" as the new rationale for post-industrial society:

> It has become necessary to look at the world system differently, to put aside a long sustained view of world order based on stratification under American rule. The new world order may be called the "age of diverse civilizations," based on the emergence of an age with multiple co-existing civilizations . . . Although westernization led to progress on a worldwide basis in terms of material civilization, Japan's modernization served as evidence that modernization is different from westernization . . . In order to accurately ascertain the world system, therefore, it is now necessary to examine closely the inner structure of the multipolarized world . . . The world is perhaps searching for the possibility of developing pluralistic civilizations in a multipolar world . . . to deal with its tasks Japan must expand both the time and space dimensions of the concept of self-interest or self-benefit.[2]

I believe that the above quotation summarizes the basic elements of the twenty-first century problem. It emphasizes a geopolitical rupture with the past and the role of cultural diversity in a pluralistic world where survival calls for the elimination of all forms of hegemony. The only thing it leaves out is the sensitive issue of *distribution*—in the case of a country whose total national assets exceeded those of the USA in 1988 this is a serious omission. The reference to Japanese sources helps to set the context for an examination of the relationship between science and culture on the eve of the twenty-first century. Science and culture have become the main determinants of the international system. An understanding of science and technology is no longer possible without reference to the cultural context, a context which is first and foremost a by-product of cultural values.

UNIVERSAL UNIVERSALITY

The age of "science for science's sake" and of "art for art's sake" is over. The twenty-first century will call for a more socioculturally determined paradigm that can no longer live under the illusion of the "universality" and "neutrality" of science and technology. These concepts need redefinition to take into account a much broader and truly universal connotation of what is "universal."

Ilya Prigogine, in his book *The New Alliance,*[3] elaborated on one of his central theses according to which "problems which mark a culture can have an influence on the content and the development of scientific theories." He goes further and states that, "it is urgent for science to recognize itself as an integral part of the culture within which it develops." Prigogine has the intellectual honesty and humility to emphasize that "science today can no longer claim the right to deny the relevance and interest of other points of view; in particular, it can no longer refuse to listen to the views of the humanities, philosophy, and art."

What better way to illustrate the futility of a "universality" which is ethnocentric and the need to discover a new "universal universality" for science which cannot be attained without proceeding first through culture and cultural values. This is the real price of survival. Prigogine is not the sole protagonist of this approach in the West. Michel Serres has written at length about what he terms the "multiple." In his book, *Genèse*, he makes the following appeal: "Que la dite connaissance scientifique dépouille son arrogance, son drapé magistral, ecclésial, qu'elle délaisse son agressivité martiale, la haineuse prétention d'avoir toujours raison, qu'elle dise vrai, qu'elle descende, pacifiée, vers la connaissance commune."[4]

My personal reading of Michel Serres is that science must make peace with culture and human values. The problem is that arrogance is not in science itself but only in the cultural context which cultivates that science. In fact the problem of arrogance is related to perceptions of time and space. The vision of the world and of its future varies according to the cultural timespan one uses. If one believes that human civilization can be reduced to 200 years for its modern period and to 2000 or 5000 years, at most, for its total history, then one has to live with a myth which generates arrogance through cultural reductionism.

The problem with Western culture is that its cultural timespan is relatively limited and that it unconsciously or consciously attempts to make up for it by underestimating the time and space of other cultures. It is so imbued with itself and its material successes that it has found no place for thinking or feeling how others think and feel. This rupture in cultural communication is aptly illustrated by a dialogue between Tagore and Einstein during a conversation which took place in Berlin on 14 July 1930:

> *TAGORE*: It is difficult to analyse the effect of eastern and western music on our minds. I am deeply moved by the western music; I feel that it is great, that it is vast in its structure and grand in its composition. Our own music touches me more deeply by its fundamental lyrical appeal. European music is epic in character; it has a broad background and is Gothic in structure.
>
> *EINSTEIN*: This is a question we Europeans cannot properly answer, we are so used to our own music. We want to know whether our own music is a convention or a fundamental human feeling, whether to feel consonance and dissonance is natural or a convention we accept.[5]

This kind of exchange is unlikely to occur in the twenty-first century. The frankness of Einstein shows clearly that whereas an Eastern thinker is capable of making the effort of understanding cultural expressions of the West in a comparative manner and with an open referential, the European is incapable of undertaking the same process because he is culturally introverted and incapable of reciprocal cultural understanding. Hence the great problem of cultural communication, which is still dominating the contemporary world of knowledge, science, and aesthetic sensitivity.

Coming generations in the Third World will no longer be interested in one-way cultural communication. They do not have the complexes of previous generations which felt that they could not impose themselves intellectually without first mastering the culture of the "others." This effort has led to various forms of cultural alienation which are one cause of economic and scientific underdevelopment in the Third World. The West can no longer count on a "blank cheque" for cultural communication without a minimal counterpart which calls for nothing less than real change. We might thus be able to reduce what Yujiro Nakamura has called "cultural negativity."[6]

This is why the interfacing of science and culture and the necessity for their fusion has become a condition for communication and survival. This has become a systemic necessity, the more so as, at the end of the twentieth century, over 50% of the manpower with training above Ph.D. level will be of non-Western origin.

This is an irreversible trend due to demographic and other fundamental factors. In the U.S., over half the new entrants to the workforce in 1988 with a training of Ph.D. level or above were non-U.S. born.[7] The basic characteristic of the twenty-first century will simply be the de-Westernization of science and culture starting with the U.S.

CULTURAL BASIS OF SCIENCE

Over 26 years ago, René Maheu, then Director General of UNESCO, on the occasion of the opening of the United Nations Conference on the Application of Science and Technology to Development (UNCAST), made a statement which is even more valid today for the future of science:

> La connaissance n'est scientifique que par l'esprit dont elle est le produit et qui seul lui donne sens pour l'homme et son point d'application dans les choses. La science n'est pas un corps de formules ou de recettes qui, d'elles mêmes, conféreraient à l'homme des pouvoirs gratuits sur les êtres . . . le problème du progrès technologique des régions encore insuffisamment développées ne peut être fondamentalement résolu par l'importation de techniques étrangères ou l'implantation hâtive de sciences appliquées en quelque sorte toutes faites. Il ne peut l'être de manière radicale . . . que par la création et le renforcement, suivant un processus endogène, au coeur même de la réalité humaine des collectivités en question du double fait intellectuel et social de la science.[8]

Science, because it is a by-product of a cultural process, cannot be transferred without underestimating the principle of feedback between culture and science. It is cultural values which determine scientific thought, creativity, and innovation. You cannot buy or transfer such outputs unless there are proper cultural inputs which enable you to understand, digest, and add endogenous values to such transfers. You never buy technology—you only purchase gadgets. This is why the best definition of development is the one provided by Maheu: "Le développement est la science devenue culture." This is what I mean by the fusion of science and culture. Science and technology are not the primordial forces of social change; they are merely the "enzymes" or accelerators of such a change by the "genes" of change, i.e., cultural values.

Cultural values facilitate change through the empowerment of individuals and communities, otherwise science and technology can reinforce inequities within the existing divisions of labor. They can also produce a caste system with both technocrats who know the "what" but ignore the "how" and "what for" and new masses of scientific illiterates incapable of participating democratically in the decision-making processes which govern the development and financing of science and technology. This is already happening.

We no longer have sufficient time or the appropriate pedagogical methods to digest and integrate the advances made by science and technology. Hence the growing gap between the developments of science and technology and the use of the results of this progress in a socially and culturally relevant manner. A good measure of this gap is the rate of scientific and technological change, compared with the inertia of political, economic, and sociocultural institutions in the face of such evolution.

How can we enter the twenty-first century with a political philosophy of the eighteenth century, political institutions of the nineteenth century including the nation state and the myth of sovereignty, and decision-making processes which may appear to be formally democratic but which were designed for a world which no longer exists (except in manuals of constitutional law and international law, not to mention in the Charter of the United Nations)?

These are some causes of the underdevelopment of our mental structures and processes and of our incapacity to face the challenges which have been knocking on our doors for more than one or two decades now with increasing intensity.

CRISIS OF ETHICAL VALUES

A serious preoccupation is that there are two exceptions with respect to the above analysis: the military sector of the superpowers and the transnational firms. The military examines and promotes scientific and technological developments in concrete and operationally destructive terms; it mobilizes and administers the major portion of human and financial resources devoted to science and technology (over 60%).

Thanks to the concept of "national security," and due to its highly sophisticated nature coupled with the scientific illiteracy of most elected decision makers, the military sector of the "big" powers is in fact exempt from any truly democratic control and reliable evaluation. This may be a partial explanation for the creativity and innovation which scientific and technological research within the military sector is capable of promoting, and for the recruitment into this sector of so many scientists who do not find the same freedom, facilities, and financial means within existing academic institutions.

The transnational firms (some of which work closely with the military sector)—fully aware of the importance of research and development for the production and commercialization of goods and the penetration of markets, as well as of the value of well trained and competent human resources—have been able to develop adequate learning processes and managerial methods with minimal intervention from the nation state.

The reference to these two exceptions is a mere observation and not a value judgment. It shows that change and adequate learning are possible, but not in the areas which need it most. It also helps explain the abdication of "authorized" national and international decision makers from tackling the new problem of mankind in a global manner, bearing in mind the well-being of humanity at large.

A problem of cultural values arises when one considers that it is precisely at a time when the world is going through a crisis of governance due to the lack of adequate international norms and standards, in the physical and moral sense, and to the lack of proper systemic regulatory functions with a clear definition of purpose, that deregulation in a neo-liberal fashion is being promoted by the major economic powers and imposed unilaterally by international financial institutions.

My preoccupation with the problem of norms and regulatory functions is conditioned by a concern for the clarification of purpose as to the raison d'être of any system, and by a philosophical and operational concern as to who should be involved in the definition of this purpose and in the supervision and control of the societal system. Anyone obsessed by the values which freedom presupposes cannot remain indifferent to neo-liberal deregulatory processes which endanger that freedom through a deformation of its most elementary concept. How can we attain sustainability of the planet without a consensus about respecting a minimal number of norms and standards? We are dealing here with the "problématique" of a crisis of ethics.

REDEFINING SCIENCE AND TECHNOLOGY

The redefinition of the purpose of science and technology on a planetary scale has become one of the fundamental conditions of the new democracy which is needed to face the challenges of the twenty-first century. The absence of a universal consensus on cultural values, norms, and standards has biased the use of science and technology towards productivity and profit with little concern for the harnessing of these powerful instruments of change in favor of more meaningful and purposive actions. This preoccupation does not seem to figure among the priorities of decision makers in the North or in the South.

Thanks to a manifest lack of foresight, the models of development which are promoted throughout the world, directly and with the help of aid in the case of Third World countries, emphasize growth and productivity. The methods and the means used to attain these objectives disempower the citizens by keeping them out of the equation—an equation which considers them as mere components of a chain of production. The new problem facing science and technology as well as culture is to see how the knowledge at our disposal can be used to empower human beings to combat poverty, misery, social injustice, marginalization, disrespect for human dignity and human rights, and the overuse and abuse of nature and its finite resources.

One of the cultural consequences of scientific development is that it has rendered "disciplines" quite obsolete, especially if we think of the latest theories concerning order and disorder in the physical world, which are leading to a new metadiscipline broadly known as "chaos." This new system has no place for the feudalism and imperialism of academic disciplines that compartmentalize knowledge according to boundaries that have become totally artificial. This is the basis of the epistemological crisis which ought to find workable solutions before we enter the twenty-first century.

We must overcome the nationalistic boundaries between the "hard and fundamental" sciences, on the one hand, and the "soft" social and human sciences. Peace must be made with philosophy, which no longer pretends to be *primus inter pares* in the fields of knowledge. We must attempt to construct a new transdisciplinary approach based on the complementarity of the different realms, consciously and comprehensively to overcome the limits of "rationality" which have imprisoned the human mind within a closed and monolithic system and reduced to a critical point the positive role of cultural diversity.

TOWARDS A CULTURAL PEACE

The problem of diversity that biological and ecological models are currently emphasizing is equally important at the cultural level. It is an essential prerequisite for the attainment of a meaningful universality. This is an eco-ethical problem which affects man, nature, and the "new alliance" between the two which is the most essential condition for survival.

The fusion of science and culture is the only reliable path for dignified survival—and not just survival at any cost which is determined by others. It is the way for rediscovering harmony in order as well as in disorder, in the physical as well as the spiritual realms. It is the key not only to the twenty-first century but also for the peace of humanity with itself as well as with the environment. It is the highway for the expansion of the mind and of the heart; of knowledge and love; and of humility, modesty, and humor which may help prevent us from taking ourselves so seriously as to forget what our purpose is on this planet.

We are indeed still in a phase of "cultural negativity," and this has led me to express myself with constant reference to Western thinkers so as to be understood—even if I am fully aware of limits to my comprehension of the systems of values of cultures other than my own. But I conclude this essay with another quotation from a man who has made an effort to go beyond the limits of narrow cultural boundaries. Ilya Prigogine has outlined a possible and optimistic approach to a more universal cultural unity in the following terms:

> . . . le XXe siècle apporte l'espoir d'une unité culturelle, d'une vision non-réductrice, plus globale. Les sciences ne reflètent pas l'identité statique d'une raison à laquelle il faudrait se soumettre ou résister; elles participent à la création du sens au même titre que l'ensemble des pratiques humaines. Elles ne peuvent nous dire à elles seules ce qu'est l'homme, la nature ou la société. Elles explorent une réalité complexe, qui associe de manière inextricable ce que nous opposons sous les régistres de l'Être et du devoir-être.[9]

In a final appeal here to those who are part of a Western culture that has so greatly contributed to the contemporary positive (as well as negative) developments of science and technology, representing a remarkable historical achievement, I would emphasize that I am part of a Third World species which will soon disappear. This species has always gone out of its way, to the point of taking the risk of losing its own identity and its own cultural code, to understand and communicate with the Western species, but has too rarely received an understandable echo or meaningful feedback.

Forthcoming generations in the Third World are not likely to pursue such a frustrating and often intellectually and spiritually degrading effort, because there are limits to cultural abnegation and to a cultural masochism that can lead to alienation. They no longer have any reason to do it, as their self-confidence is certainly higher than that of the generations which preceded them, and because they already possess a hold on world knowledge and will exponentially increase it. Regardless of their geographical location, they will carry with them consciously or unconsciously a set of cultural values which will inevitably have a determining impact on the development of science and technology in the twenty-first century.

Time is short for the conclusion of a cultural peace with the help of science and technology, and not of scientifically illiterate politicians. Every delay in the conclusion of such a peace will systematically increase the social cost of political, economic, and social change on a planetary scale.[10]

NOTES AND REFERENCES

Editors' note: M. Elmandjra's stirring contribution to the symposium is a fervent plea against the unreflected claim of science born of Western culture to be universal by itself. At the same time, it aptly reminds the reader of the cultural roots of any science. If we wish to master the major problems humanity has already been confronted with, we need to develop a new kind of science and technology for a multicultural world. The key to success, says M. Elmandjra, is the fusion of science and culture. The editors wish to explicitly render some moral consequences for the humanities and the social sciences, consequences that to M. Elmandjra may be so obvious that they need not be mentioned. Humanities and social sciences—the sciences of culture—have to meet a threefold obligation and, therefore, are subjects of a threefold responsibility: (1) They have to point out the various cultures and stress their autonomous value so as to demonstrate and preserve mankind's cultural diversity. (2) They have to work on the platform serving the various cultures as a meeting point and a presupposition of mental understanding and esteem. (3) They must actively take notice of the achievements, methods, and ways of thinking proper to the sciences and to technology in order to help bring about the integration of scientific, humanistic, and humane knowledge, skill, and competence in order to achieve the fusion of science and culture M. Elmandjra is propagating.

1. Serres, Michel 1992, "A mes contemporains, ces hémiplégiques," in: *Le Nouvel Observateur*, Paris.
2. National Institute for Research Advancement, Research Output (ed.) 1988, *Agenda for Japan in the 1990s*, Tokyo, NIRA, 1.
3. Prigogine, Ilya/Stengers, Isabelle 1979, *La nouvelle alliance: métamorphose de la science*, Paris, Gallimard.
4. "Let so-called scientific knowledge cast off its arrogance, its magisterial, ecclesiastical wraps, let it abandon its warlike aggressiveness, its hateful claim always to be right, let it speak truthfully, and descend, appeased, to universal knowledge." (Serres, Michel 1982, *Genèse*, Paris, Grasset)
5. Chakravarty, Amiya (ed.) 1961, *A Tagore Reader*, New York, Macmillan, 102.
6. Nakamura, Yujiro 1989, "Place and Rhythmic Oscillation: A New Perspective on a Common Foundation to Science, Art, and Religion," paper given at

Unesco's symposium on *Science and Culture: Agenda for the 21st Century*, Vancouver, Canada, September 1989.

7. By 1983, 51% of engineers with a Ph.D. who entered the U.S. labor market were non-U.S. born (1226 engineers out of 2391). Cf. Zahlan, Antoine 1985, "Brain drain," London, mimes.

8. "Knowledge is only scientific through the mind of which it is the product, which alone gives it meaning for mankind and application. Science is not a body of formulae or recipes conferring on mankind gratuitous power over other beings . . . the problem of technological progress of those regions that are still insufficiently developed cannot be fundamentally resolved by importing foreign techniques or hastily implanting, as it were, ready-made applied sciences. It can only be resolved in a radical way by creating and strengthening, through an endogenous process taking place at the very heart of the human reality of the communities in question, both the intellectual and social aspects of science." The speech was given in Geneva, 4 February 1963. See Maheu, Rene 1968, *La civilisation de l'universel*, Paris, Laffont, 178f.

9. "The twentieth century brings hope of cultural unity, a non-reductionist, more global vision. Science does not reflect the static identity of reason which we must either submit to or resist; it participates in the creation of meaning in the same way as the whole of human activity. Science alone cannot tell us what humanity, nature or society is. It explores a complex reality, which associates inextricably that which we place in the opposing registers of what is and what should be." Translation by the author; cf. Prigogine Ilya 1989, "L'éloge de l'imparabilité," in: *Libération*, Paris 26 January 1989.

10. For a more comprehensive version of this paper cf. FUTURES, April 1990.

Healing the Cleavage:
Emotional Reason as Source of Universals

CAROLA MEIER-SEETHALER

Mr. Elmandjra's paper and my own reflections upon the necessity of merging science and culture are quite complementary. I fully agree with him on the need for a new alliance between science and culture, and I specifically agree with his statement that the age of "science for science's sake" should be over. I should like to consider the common topic in a somewhat different light. I wish to start by giving two examples which illustrate the different approaches of the so-called "hard" sciences and of the humanities, and illustrate how this difference can turn into a veritable chasm across which it is almost impossible to communicate. This will then lead me to some thoughts on the prejudices of science and on possible ways of overcoming the limitations of pure rationality. And last, but not least, I will reflect upon the way out of cultural one-way communication from North to South and the possibility of universal ethical judgments.

THE CHASM BETWEEN HARD
SCIENCES AND HUMANITIES

My first example deals with the contradictory attitudes of Jürgen Drews, Research Director of the pharmaceutical company Hoffmann-La Roche, and Hans Jonas.[1] Hans Jonas does not need to be introduced. In his well-known book, *The Imperative of Responsibility*, Jonas advocates the imposition of limits on what is technically feasible. He also speaks of the primacy of negative over positive prognoses. According to Jonas, it is intolerable for human existence to be jeopardized in the risky game of technology. Jürgen Drews, on the other hand, is responsible for the research goals of one of the world's leading companies in the field of genetic engineering. In a short essay, "Medicine and Genetic Engineering—Do We Need New Ethics?" Drews explicitly rejects Jonas' call for limits. He prefers unimpeded progress, because to him the freedom of the intellect is the supreme, and hence absolute, value. In his opinion, therefore, a moratorium on research would be a violation of a fundamental human right, even if this moratorium were to be imposed to safeguard human existence. Exaggerating somewhat, one could sum up his position as follows: "*Vivat scientia et pereat mundus*" in reference to the notorious "*Vivat justitia et pereat mundus.*" The burning issue underlying the confrontation of Hans Jonas and Jürgen Drews is, of course, their access to power. While Jonas depends on the persuasive power of his thoughts and words alone, Drews is backed by the worldwide economic and—indirectly— political clout of a powerful company.

The second example contrasts Hans Moravec and Joseph Weizenbaum.[2] Both Moravec and Weizenbaum are internationally renowned computer scientists from U.S. institutions, the Carnegie-Mellon University and the Massachusetts Institute of Technology. But while Moravec is totally centered on his field and has outlined a vision of the future role of the robot, Weizenbaum has raised philosophical issues which go beyond his immediate field of research. In 1990, Weizenbaum gave a lecture in Klagenfurt, Austria, on "Artificial Intelligence as the Final Solution of the Human Question" (the term "Final Solution," "Endlösung," of course refers to the Jewish Holocaust). Weizenbaum described his colleagues' efforts to perfect robots to such a point that they will surpass human intelligence. In Moravec's opinion, it would be a goal of natural evolution to achieve perfect intelligence within the universe. Therefore, the robot would reach the next higher rung on the evolutionary ladder; humans would be rendered obsolete or at least be left behind. Weizenbaum expressed his horror at such scientific goals. Most of all, however, he expressed his feelings of frustration when attempting to explain his horror to his MIT colleagues who are enthusiastic about Moravec's vision of the future.

Something very similar happened to me a year later at a congress at Loccum, Germany. There, sociobiologists upheld the same idea, namely that the human species would likely be overtaken by evolution—like so many other species before it—and that the new, more successful species might be the computer. Regrets? Not in the least. "So what," the sociobiologists' chorus went, "if the human species dies out?" I must admit that I could in no way comprehend such cynicism and finally told a large audience, "Look, I'm sorry, but at this point I have to abandon this discussion; I feel as if I were in a madhouse."

On further, calm reflection, I of course realized that we are confronted here with a clash of two completely incompatible ways of thinking. The scientists researching artificial intelligence and sociobiology merely stand for a strictly mechanistic school of thought, which excludes any notion of value and quality and which is incredibly remote from life. I also very clearly realized, however, that the organ of value perception is not our intellect and its discursive logic, which forms the basis for the "hard" sciences. Rather, in order to recognize any quality of life and any ethically relevant values *feeling* needs to be involved. Jonas, too, speaks of a feeling of responsibility. Likewise, "dignity" is a concept which loses all meaning unless we feel what we mean by the term.

TOWARDS A CRITIQUE OF SCIENTIFIC RATIONALITY

As we are all aware, the mainstream of philosophical research since Descartes has paid little attention to what we might call emotional judgment ("emotionale Urteilskraft") or emotional reason ("emotionale Vernunft"). In my opinion, this is due to two very different reasons: First, emotion is subject-bound; it cannot be measured or quantified, and it therefore seems difficult, if not impossible, to apply any criteria of universal validity. Moreover, feelings or emotions have been excluded from philosophical discourse because the occidental mentality has attributed them to women and has split them off from the male consciousness.

As Evelyn Fox Keller demonstrates,[3] it is only through psychoanalytical reflection that we will be able to fathom this aspect of the problem. Keller has shown us, among other things, that the motivation underlying the "hard" sciences consists not only of the much-quoted intellectual inquisitiveness, but also of irrational anxieties and needs for security. She calls this phenomenon the "emotional substructure" of science. Keller refers to our family structure in which, generally speaking, only the mother cares for the young children. Under these conditions, girls and boys will never have equal psychological opportunities, because the girls will be able to identify with the mother all their lives, although they have to develop their own personality. Boys, however, not only have to become adult, they must also become different adults from their mothers—as the psychoanalyst Dorothy Dinnerstein puts it.[4] For the boy, emancipation from the mother means emancipation from everything that is considered female, such as feelings, warmth, subjectivity; it means establishing male autonomy on the principles of hardness and objectivity. In this context, Keller speaks of objectivism as a forced form of objectivity which can misread reality just as well as mere subjectivity. In other words: The mentality of the male is the antithesis to female socialization.

In my own historical and psychoanalytical study on the creation of patriarchy—*Origins and Emancipations: The Gendered Roots of Culture*[5]—I tried to point out that in the very early times of humankind we find a rather similar social pattern on a collective level. For a very long prehistoric period—as we know from the earliest traces found by archaeologists and historians—motherhood and the female principle as a whole must have been of tremendous influence both in the social group as well as in myths and rites. On the other hand, the male groups initially were of lesser social relevance and had to create their own specific identity. Male activities therefore always were somewhat compensatory in the sense of demonstrating male importance to the whole group. In my opinion, this is the basis of male heroism, ambition, and need for ceaseless success—in warfare as well as in economics or in science. Also, the symbolic structure of patriarchal ideology is based on the dichotomy of the sexes, the opposition of mind and nature, spirit and body, heaven and earth. Identifying themselves with heaven and the mind, delegating irrationality and emotions to the female principle, men claimed authority over women and nature. In our context, we might remember that there is a specific male reluctance to getting involved in emotionally "loaded" situations. This is one reason why male scientists prefer neutral conditions which allow them to hide or even repress their own feelings.

Let me add another point which is independent of gender problems and refers to the dynamic relationship between rationality and feeling. I agree with M. Somerville when she says (cf. p. 251) "decision making is, fundamentally, intuitively and emotionally based, but needs to be safeguarded by cognitive and rational processes, which can be regarded as 'secondary verification mechanisms'." However, I think it describes only one side of the relation, because the reverse is also true: Our rationality is not always a verification mechanism. Very often, it is a mechanism of deception. Psychoanalysis calls this mechanism "rationalization." For example, we often urgently feel that we should help somebody, but then our intellect finds arguments why we cannot reasonably do so. In his *Pensées* Blaise Pascal made some brilliant remarks on this issue, saying that if we were capable of critical self-reflection, the logic of our heart would often be more proper than the unconscious lies of our brain.

EMOTIONAL REASON AS A KEY TO UNIVERSAL ETHICAL JUDGMENTS

With regard to feelings and value judgments, we are obviously faced with two fundamental tasks: First, we must recover the area of feeling from repression; then we can start looking for criteria which determine when emotions are merely the expression of a subjective mood or disposition, and when they are the articulations of a more or less universal human voice. Generally speaking, feeling is referred to in a rather vague and undifferentiated manner; everything is jumbled together, while the area of feeling is actually a vast continent with totally separate and distinguishable zones.

I am currently engaged in research on this continent and in adopting that historical epistemological approach which is concerned with qualitative determinations of values. Two female philosophers have recently published extremely competent works on the theory of feeling. They are Susanne Langer in her books *Philosophy in a New Key* and *Mind: An Essay on Human Feeling*,[6] and Agnes Heller, the critical Marxist, in her less well-known study *Theory of Feeling*.[7]

In fact, any qualitative judgment is essentially and intimately connected with the words in which it is formulated. But we obviously need to address the threat of mental colonization which immediately surfaces whenever one particular culture claims to speak for all of humankind. For the language of emotional reason to function as an instrument for universal judgments, a plethora of languages need to be in harmony; their figures of speech need to complement each other in such a way that essential values can be adequately described. It is important not only to overcome the Eurocentricity of the humanities, but also the monopoly of the so-called "high cultures." It is high time that we also study the languages of smaller ethnic communities and their contributions to emotional reason. The point would not be to distill any abstract concepts from the sum total of all those individual languages. On the contrary, the focus should be on the "idola" so greatly feared by Bacon: on the figures of speech which reflect human emotional experiences.

According to Susanne Langer, the semantics of symbols in myths, rites, and art contain universalia which articulate emotional meaning and which share similar gestalts across vast geographical and temporal distances. Likewise, verbal semantics form a worldwide reservoir of significant images that have not, as yet, been discovered and which could complement each other. And, as such images evoke notions of values, they can be read as a kind of universalia of emotional reason.

It is easy to see that such an approach to language would have to be a major, international research venture. But it would be far less costly than, say, "Project HUGO," which is already under full sail and which aims at a complete mapping of the human genome and its 100,000 genes. Again, the "building blocks" of life are being treated as if they were lifeless elementary particles which can be moved around at will. From the point of view of holistic biology and medicine, this is a highly doubtful approach.

On the other hand, the project of a worldwide study of language as the sustainer of emotional reason would create an entirely different scientific community: The most diverse cultures would be perceived as particular; as individual. Such a project would therefore also be of eminent political significance.

NOTES AND REFERENCES

1. Jonas, Hans 1979, *Das Prinzip Verantwortung*, Frankfurt/M., Insel Verlag; Drews, Jürgen 1990, *Medizin und Gentechnik—Brauchen wir eine neue Ethik?*, Basel, F. Hoffmann-La Roche AG (typescript).
2. Weizenbaum, Joseph 1990, *Künstliche Intelligenz als Endlösung der Menschenfrage*, Klagenfurt, Klagenfurter Beiträge zur Technikdiskussion 32; Moravec, Hans 1988, *Mind Children: The Future of Robot and Human Intelligence*, Cambridge (Mass.), Harvard University Press.
3. Fox Keller, Evelyn 1985, *Reflections on Gender and Science*, New Haven, Yale University Press.
4. Dinnerstein, Dorothy 1976, *The Mermaid and the Minotaur: Sexual Arrangements and Human Malaise*, New York, Harper & Row.
5. Meier-Seethaler, Carola 1988, Ursprünge und Befreiungen: Eine dissidente Kulturtheorie, Zürich, Arche Verlag AG.
6. Langer, Susanne 1942, *Philosophy in a New Key: A Study in the Symbolism of Reason, Rite and Art*, Cambridge (Mass.), Harvard University Press.
    —— 1967, 1972, 1982, *Mind: An Essay on Human Feeling*, Vol. I, II, III, Baltimore, Johns Hopkins University Press.
7. Heller, Agnes 1981, *Theorie der Gefühle*, Hamburg, VSA-Verlag.

MORAL AND SOCIAL LIMITS TO THE MARKET MODEL

Economic Beliefs and Moral Responsibility

GÉRALD BERTHOUD

Social sciences in general, with the notable exception of economics, are often poorly appreciated within the academic world and society at large. Of course, such a judgment could be refuted. However, the cultural and social recognition of social sciences is, to say the least, very ambiguous, compared to humanities on the one hand and natural sciences on the other.

Most of the time, when a representative of "hard" sciences expresses himself publicly on a cultural, social, or political question, his writing or discourse is highly valued because of the scientific legitimacy of its author, and not so much because of the intrinsic quality of his contribution. For social scientists, things are quite different. I think that, as a rule, we are considered in a rather suspicious way. The most radical situations of course are found in those countries with authoritarian and totalitarian political regimes. The first academic victims are quite obviously social sciences.

But today, these sciences are confronted with a problem that could have deleterious effects. Given the triumph of the double idea of market and democracy throughout the world, social sciences are constantly threatened with being subverted, reluctantly or not, by a dominant economic worldview. A "utilitarian culture," to use A. Gouldner's expression (1970), makes it more and more difficult for most scholars to escape the imperative of the so-called direct utility of their knowledge.

Undeniably, the present world is submitted to acute contradictions between both disruptive scientific, technical, and economic universalism, and various reactive forms of national, ethnic, or religious particularisms. Nevertheless, for the West, a broad consensus has been reached to accept the idea that market capitalism is indissociably linked with democracy, and as such is the best possible system for the whole of humanity. In

Eastern Europe, the total failure of centralization has been attributed to the final victory of liberal capitalism. Even now, market principles are viewed as the only way to escape a totalitarian system, and forms of nationalistic and ethnic exclusion. The South itself is taken with this general movement. Most countries have no choice. They have to be more and more included within the constraining system of the world economy. In numerous cases, the so-called structural adjustment, under the rigorous policy of the International Monetary Fund and the World Bank, leads to dramatic consequences for a great number of people, who are literally sacrificed for the economic efficiency.

How could social sciences, with their well-known intrinsic weaknesses, avoid the imposition of such an encompassing ideological and political context? In other terms, in the absence of any viable alternative, how could one escape from the limits of such a cognitive and normative conformity? How is it at all possible to overcome the "sacred" words of a Nobel prize winner for whom "the economic approach is a comprehensive one that is applicable to all human behavior" (Becker 1976, 8)? This quote leads the way to proclaiming the end of social sciences as such and their fusion within the scientific excellence of a "generalized economics" (Berthoud 1994).

To add to this uncertain situation, social sciences are, for the most part, overcrowded fields in numerous universities. A ratio of one professor to more than one hundred students is not uncommon at all. In a way, we could argue that there are two different universities within the same institution. Comparatively, with "hard" sciences and medicine, an elite university is the rule, whereas social sciences belong to what could be termed a mass university. Under increasing economic and political pressure, this major part of the university has to defend the very existence of its fundamental research within a cultural context narrowly defined by a utilitarian principle.

THE HISTORICAL ROOTS

This utilitarian bias is far from new. To follow A. Gouldner, the successful middle classes in the eighteenth century imposed a dominant "utilitarian culture" (1970, 61).Within such a system of ideas and values, money is of course "an all-purpose utility in middle-class society," but "there is one other all-purpose utility . . ., and that is knowledge" (1970, 69). Quite obviously, "in order to appraise consequences one must know them; in order to control consequences one must employ technology and science. Therefore, in a utilitarian culture knowledge and science are shaped by strongly instrumental conceptions" (1970, 69).

The followers of this "bourgeois utilitarianism" were thus convinced that the well-known quest of happiness was only possible through either money or knowledge. Utility appeared as a social norm against the two so-called useless classes: the poor at the lower level, charged with laziness and idleness; and the aristocracy with its ingrained habits of splendor at the higher level. These utilitarians emphasized faith in work, were suspicious of the poor and the beggars, and disapproved of any ostentatious expenditure.

Should we consider today that this cultural heritage is so useful that it should be accepted unconditionally? Of course, it is within such a context that social sciences themselves were instituted and developed. It is with no surprise that we are confronted, right from the beginning, with the basic category of utility. Such a utilitarian representation of human being and society is cautiously attested to by such a fundamental author as Adam Smith, the so-called founding father of economic science. For instance, although there is no doubt for him that "where the necessary assistance is reciprocally afforded from love, from gratitude, from friendship, and esteem, the society flourishes and is happy," he nevertheless admits the possible regulation of society through the principle of utility. Thus "though the necessary assistance should not be afforded from such generous and disinterested motives, though among the different members of the society there should be no mutual love and affection, the society, though less happy and agreeable, will not necessarily be dissolved. Society may subsist among different men, as among different merchants, from a sense of its utility, without any mutual love or affection; and though no man in it should owe any obligation, or be bound in gratitude to any other, it may still be upheld by a mercenary exchange of good offices according to an agreed valuation" (1976a, 85–86). Elsewhere, Smith takes up a quite orthodox utilitarian position when he speaks of "this disposition to admire, and almost to worship, the rich and the powerful, and to despise, or, at least, to neglect persons of poor and mean condition" (1976a, 61).

In a way, the utilitarian culture of the middle class is legitimized by a recognized scientific discourse, which will have crucial effects on the subsequent social sciences. To follow L. Dumont, "for the first time, a particular kind of social phenomena, the economic phenomena, were represented as being separated from society and constituting for themselves a distinct system to which all the rest of the social life should be submitted" (1983, I).

Undoubtedly for us with our autonomic economic order, the idea of market is deeply engraved in our ways of thought. However, to represent any societal organization with the metaphor of an idealized market as the model for any social interaction is much more than just a question of a fashionable vocabulary. It is also much more than pure rhetoric. Within the language of market, human subjects are strictly motivated by self-interest and interact with others only if a profit of some kind can be made. Indeed what is outlined here is that any attitude, action, object, or idea is valued simply for its utility conducive to individual happiness.

This reductive way of representing human action and society as a whole is known as the doctrine of utilitarianism among scholars concerned with theoretical and normative questions. Nevertheless, beyond this scientific and philosophical approach, what is obviously defined here is the wider context of the utilitarian culture, which was popularized and even inculcated on the working-class reader (Sockwell 1994). Social sciences and economics themselves are dominantly embedded within such a meaningful world. In other terms, the scientific contribution of these fields is necessarily enclosed within the normative limits of the utilitarian representation of the human subject.

To accept being confined within these ideological boundaries is at best to act as an expert. On the other hand, to be a scholar or an intellectual is to insist on the complexity of science, to recognize the unavoidable tension between belief and knowledge as such, and to make explicit the irreducible narrative part of any scientific argumentation. But is it so obvious to link cultural values, viewed in the anthropological form of a founding myth or a narrative, and the formalized knowledge of economics?

WHAT TALE DOES ECONOMICS TELL?

At first sight, economics has all the appearances of a pure science, its language being accessible to only a small circle of initiates. This view is encouraged by those who see economics as a form of mathematics applied to human and social action. Without any doubt, all indications point toward the conclusion that economics operates within the strictly delimited domain of rational, abstract thinking.

But, implicitly, economics has other things to tell us. To remain at the level of its explicit scientific goals would be to miss the essential, to let ourselves be drawn in by immediate appearances. Indeed, the entire scientific edifice of economics is stripped of all relevance, all cultural and social significance, if we fail to recognize the existence of a system of ideas, beliefs and values that constitutes what must be called its foundational myth. In other words, the triumphant, even imperialistic, science of economics is not immune to the problems posed by the relation between belief and knowledge.

And yet, myth appears to be an alien element in the context of economics, subject as it is to the rationalist structures of formalization, modeling, and quantification. Economics does not tell stories. It announces functional laws governing the spheres of production and exchange—at least, this is the belief widely held by the scientific community. In fact, scientific discourse about economic phenomena is impossible without a foundational myth which tells us what is, what ought to be, and, at least partially, what should be done. This myth, which forcefully asserts the truth of its vision of man and society, is therefore simultaneously normative and prescriptive. According to an orthodox economist, "the point is that economists are like other human beings in that they both use metaphors and tell stories," or "ninety percent of what economists do is such storytelling" (McCloskey 1990: 7, 9).

The foundational myth is made up of two basic tales which assert two axioms of economic science that go without saying: the individualist nature of man, and the exchangist basis of all social relations. Shoring up the scholarly discourse of economics, from at least the end of the eighteenth century through today, is a constant reference to the emblematic figure of Robinson Crusoe, and to a phantasmagoric encounter between two savages.

Even Marx, for all that he mocks the "Robinsonnades" of classical economics, cannot help but fall back on this famous tale when justifying his own theory of value. At a certain point in his argument, and without explanation, the theory shifts from a discussion of Robinson the individual to the level of "social production" (see, e.g., Baudrillard 1972, 168–171). Undeniably, the figure of Robinson is an irresistible point of communality amidst the diversity of scholarly economic discourses. A simple methodological starting point, some would say. But the evocative force of this adventure story, which has enjoyed remarkable international success, contributes decisively to maintaining the aura of truth and normativity surrounding economics' individualist representation of mankind and society.

Of course, economics appropriates the hero of Daniel Defoe's novel only selectively. For example, the presence of a second party in the person of Friday is simply overlooked; Robinson is pictured in his island solitude as an individual with needs and wants, alone confronting nature. In his victorious battle against the natural elements, he incarnates the rational man *par excellence*, capable of satisfying his needs thanks to the surety of his choices. Such is the scholarly banality of the "lone *homo oeconomicus*," as M. Weber describes him in *The Protestant Ethic and the Spirit of Capitalism* (1905).

The science of economics affirms the logical, and consequently historical, priority of the individual over society. In the beginning, there is the individual, and society is built up from this monad, this "utilitarian atom" in the words of Karl Polanyi (1957, 239). Imbued with this faith, generations of orthodox economists have been incapable of theorizing the collective otherwise than from the premise of the individual, stripped of all *a priori* obligations towards others, by nature asocial. The only conceivable means of existing side-by-side and acting concertedly for these supposedly independent individuals would then be exchange. Which leads us to our second elementary tale.

While the emblematic figure of Robinson Crusoe is a recurrent reference in all of the scholarly economic literature, the same cannot be said for the other elementary tale: that which attributes the birth of society to the meeting of two isolated individuals. Perhaps the notion that all human action is by nature rational requires constant repetition in order to forestall a weakening of the faith. By contrast, if the problem of the formation of society is infrequently posed in the contemporary economic literature, this may be because the "idea of exchange" has long been established as "the fundamental idea of political economy," as E. Halévy asserts in his important work, *The Growth of Philosophical Radicalism* (1901). Or, in the words of the nineteenth century economist Frederic Bastiat, "exchange is society."

In the works of numerous eighteenth century economists, however, we find frequent references to the elementary fable of exchange as the basis for all social relations. There is also no doubt that this tale continues to play a crucial, if unstated, role in grounding contemporary economic discourse. Labeled the "barter fable" by the "unbelievers," this tale comes in a number of versions, all of which fundamentally tell the same story.

Let us take a random example from the writings of Anna-Robert J. Turgot: "In the middle of the northern seas, two savages approach a desert island from opposite sides, one carrying more fish in his canoe than he can consume alone, the other carrying more skins than he alone can use to cover himself and make his tent" (quoted by Larrère 1992, 218–9).

In the same spirit, Adam Smith speaks of barter in *The Wealth of Nations* as "this same trucking disposition which originally gives occasion to the division of labour" (1976b, 27). As an example of this process, he recounts an episode in the imaginary encounter of two savages:

> In a tribe of hunters or shepherds a particular person makes bows and arrows, for example, with more readiness and dexterity than any other. He frequently exchanges them for cattle or for venison with his companions; and he finds at last that he can in this manner get more cattle and venison than if he himself went to the field to catch them. From a regard to his own interest, therefore, the making of bows and arrows grows to be his chief business, and he becomes a sort of armourer. . . . And thus

the certainty of being able to exchange all that surplus part of the produce of his own labour, which is over and above his own consumption,
for such parts of the produce of other men's labour as he may have
occasion for, encourages every man to apply himself to a particular oc-
cupation. (1976b, 27–28)

In the exchangist vision, the formation and regulation of society is
viewed as the result of single individuals entering into calculated relations
with one another, each with the aim of receiving useful goods in return.
Individual self-interest (our scientists appear to disregard the indeterminacy
of this notion) is thus the only motivation which causes men to interact. As
the sole given of human nature, self-interest is then the unique cause of
exchange, itself established as the universal law of all social organization.
Social relations are based on a reciprocity of advantages; they reflect, in E.
Halévy's famous phrase, "the natural harmony of private interests." Under
this conception, all reference to moral obligation becomes meaningless. We
can guarantee the permanence of society by instituting relations of exchange which maintain a certain distance between the individuals exchang-
ing, to the point where members of a society see other members as strangers
whose only *raison d'être* is that of mutual utility.

In this representation of society, individuals, through the making of
free and voluntary choices, are perfectly equal, and thus interchangeable.
The social distance between people has the advantage of dissolving all
obligations and creates the constant possibility of choice in establishing,
or not, one's social relations. In his utility function, every individual is
strictly equivalent to every other. The only thing which matters to each is
his relation to material objects, mediated through exchange. The world of
exchange is, in the most immediate sense, a world of objects which circu-
late. In economic terms, these objects are defined as *goods*. This category
has been extended so as to include all those objects which can serve, ma-
terially or otherwise, the satisfaction of individual interests.

In the exchangist logic, goods themselves are evaluated as utilities, or
use values. They are much like human individuals, self-sufficient entities
that can be isolated from all meaningful context. Put in other terms, in
pure exchange, individuals and objects are desymbolized, depersonalized,
and desocialized. Both are constantly available for free circulation, as required by the logic of exchange. Goods possess individual properties, are
alienable at will, and are therefore capable of constituting commodities
readily available to all so long as the rule of *equivalence* between the
goods exchanged is respected.

From the point of view of the individual, this exchangist "alchemy"
does away with the very notion of interpersonal dependence. Individuals,

armed with their numerous free and voluntary choices, become far more concerned with the world of goods than with other individuals. To be an individual amounts, in effect, to asserting that one has been liberated from the weight of preceding generations and from all forms of personal dependence, such as those found in traditional societies in the form of networks of kin and neighbors. An individual in the full sense of the word must provide alone for the material conditions of his own existence so as to be in the position to maintain his role in the system of exchange. In the never-ending game of equivalencies, being an individual amounts to not owing anything to anybody. In this perspective, the demand for freedom becomes indistinguishable from the supposed right to independence.

As we can see from this brief sketch, the categories of the individual and of exchange are at the basis of orthodox teachings on the economy, and also of the economic representation of man and society which is increasingly imposing itself in all of the social sciences. The two elementary tales that legitimize this reductionist picture of mankind and society can be found, in different form, of course, in the scholarly discourse of economists today.

Let us take the widely read introductory textbook by E. S. Phelps entitled simply *Political Economy* (1985). The author makes reference to Robinson Crusoe at various points when discussing the "isolated individual" engaged in the natural process of *rational choice*, who must, in a sense, exchange one good for another with himself. Based on this notion of the "one-person economy," the author goes on to theorize about "the social economy" without explicit reference to the elementary tale of the two savages; he is forced, however, to refer back to the central notion of *equilibrium* in order to assure collective order. Thus, what is viewed as the "cement of society" is the "mutual advantages of its members" obtained through the generalized practice of exchange.

THE META-NARRATIVE OF "IMPROVEMENT"

The individualist and exchangist representation of man and of society, undergirded by the two foundational fairy tales just examined, constitutes the cornerstone of the meta-narrative that legitimizes and gives meaning to the movement of radical global transformation which we have been undergoing for more than two centuries, propelled by the combined forces of science, technology, and the market. This meta-narrative can be characterized in a number of ways, but we need not look any further than Adam Smith, who spoke of "a natural progress of opulence" (1976b, 376). Even more explicitly, for this author, "the natural effort of every individual to better his own condition, when suffered to exert itself with freedom and security, is so powerful a principle, that it is alone, and without any assistance, not only capable of carrying on the society to wealth and prosperity, but of surmounting a hundred impertinent obstructions with which the folly of human laws too often encumbers its operations; though the effect of these obstructions is always more or less either to encroach upon its freedom, or to diminish its security" (1976b, 540).

In sum, a "central social imaginary meaning" (Castoriadis 1987) structures our belief that the imposition of a global capitalism of knowledge, technology, and possession is both True and Good. It dictates the way in which both human beings and objects must act, and it specifies the nature of the relations between them.

According to the meta-narrative of improvement, once upon a time, as far back as we can go, there lived an individual naturally inclined to make rational choices in all matters. This individual entered into a relation of exchange with another individual. From this first encounter, everything else follows. The individual, over the course of an epic history marked by innumerable cultural, social, and political obstacles, slowly asserted control over his happiness and well-being, thanks to an ever more efficient and advanced division of labor.

This narrative has guaranteed an increasing role for the notion of exchange, to the point where we can now imagine its ultimate end being a society contiguous with the generalized market, due to establish itself at the "end of history" on a world scale. Here again, we are faced with an idea which is in no sense new: at the end of the seventeenth century, for example, Sir Dudley North affirmed with some prescience that "the whole world as to trade, is but as one nation or people" (quoted by Appleby 1978, 277).

The meta-narrative of improvement constitutes, without any doubt, the foundation of our scientific vision of the economy, and lends to the community of economists a coherence unequaled among scholars, assuring a fundamental unanimity despite divergent points of view. It is this shared belief in a better future, and not the rigor of their calculations or the complexity of their models, which galvanizes the community, orients individual and collective action, and makes possible the consensus necessary for the radical transformation of nature, mankind, and society.

We see, then, that scholarly economic discourse and everyday common sense rest on the same foundation of legitimating beliefs. They refer back to the same cognitive and normative matrix. The former, like the latter, props itself up by means of the constitutive ideas and values expressed in the meta-narrative of improvement. The ability of contemporary economic discourse to mobilize the entire world is certainly not based on the abstraction of its pronouncements. Economic formalism is a form of camouflaged empiricism; it proceeds by juxtaposing axioms alongside descriptive data, and as such it barely rises above the most superficial description of human social reality. Put more bluntly, despite its tricks of formalization and modeling, and contrary to its imperialistic ambitions for explaining the totality of social reality, economic science merely repeats obvious popular conclusions and reiterates immediate perceptions.

This tendency to reformulate observations of the simplest common sense works not against but for economics; it takes on the aura of an uncontestable operational form of knowledge, thanks to its mythico-commonsensical references. However, contrary to traditional mythology oriented towards the past, the meta-narrative of improvement guarantees the scientific legitimacy of economics even when, as is often the case, its predictions for the future turn out to be false.

No doubt it will be objected that no one today seriously believes in the promise of abundance, or even in the lesser possibility of improvement. However, a number of indices demonstrate that this is not the case. For the present purposes, it is enough to observe that no obstacle seems capable of shaking the solidity of the faith in improvement, despite the fact that social inequality is increasing dangerously as a result of economic measures taken precisely in conformity with this credo.

To maintain the faith in the meta-narrative, even amongst those who in one way or another pay the costs of the transformations, the recourse to a popularized notion of sacrifice is widely practiced. It is through "sacrifice" that an attempt is made to legitimize the myth of improvement in a context where the distance between its promises and the lived reality of a large number of citizens is becoming increasingly large. "Sacrifice" touches first and foremost the most underprivileged. In the name of the intangible principle of economic efficiency, the product, we are told, of ever increasing marketization, general well-being is assured for the more or less near future. The victims, therefore, will not be sacrificed in vain, as it is their relative deprivation that will make it possible for all of us to get back on the road to abundance, and thus to make up for the temporary loss in social unity.

Paradoxically perhaps, projects for the radical transformation of nature, mankind, and society—in the form of programs for technical development—have never been as present as today, for they continue to be viewed as a great opportunity for the future of mankind. Is it not every man's duty to convince himself that everything that can be made should be made, and is it not therefore legitimate always to desire more? Is not the road to true humanity attained by liberating oneself from nature, from society, and even from others, in order to affirm one's full independence?

This "epic" holds out the wild promise that all of humanity might be liberated from its original condition. This would be to follow John Locke, who stated that "[t]hus in the beginning all the World was *America*" (1960, 319). Our only possible future lies in the infinite production of riches, subject to the mediation of the market. For this, it becomes mandatory that all persons and all objects be susceptible to valuation. The market requirement is undebatable, necessary to allow the greatest number constantly to pursue its private happiness, the goal of the fully human being. The search for this happiness is each individual's responsibility. However, to assure this happiness requires a general transformation of society towards increased marketization. Once again, we find the strong belief in the pacifying virtues of trade.

THE PRICE OF HAPPINESS

Behind this harmonious facade, above and beyond the tranquil vision of everything exchanged amongst everyone, there appears a far harsher reality. In an era in which everything is reduced to its monetary equivalent, the individual himself and even nature enter into the vast sphere of all that is both measurable and calculable. Thus human beings, like objects, have their price—indeed, everything is, in one way or another, reducible to the vast category of goods, and even susceptible to the operations of accounting, the calculation of cost and benefit. This is possible, of course, only by disregarding all those qualities specific to human beings and to objects, or in other words, only by removing all symbolic importance from them, so that they become so many means available to assure the general well-being, itself conceived as a purely private matter. Such well-being presupposes an infinite choice of means as the only way to affirm one's individual independence. In other words, the market is nothing more than the confrontation of the private choices of producers and consumers.

Today, marketization has demonstrated a tendency to accelerate and extend itself, thereby reinforcing the common utilitarian credo by which everything can be bought and sold. However, to wonder whether everything has its price is a normative inquiry, the urgency of which is becoming increasingly obvious in all those areas which touch on ecology and human life.

The tendency to reduce human beings to a productive force that can be bought and sold on the labor market is clearly not new, and is tempered, at least in theory, by laws which limit considerably its grossly mercantile aspects. Recently, however, under the seemingly irresistible pressures of biomedical innovation, parts of the human body have been increasingly submitted to the regime of the market. Economic discourse has no difficulty legitimizing this commercialization of life. To circumvent the moral condemnation of contracts for surrogate motherhood, for example, one may choose between two legitimizing notions. On the one hand, there is the demand for individual liberty on the part of the person who "owns" her own body. On the other hand, there is the utilitarian goal of happiness for the greatest number. Both of these arguments appear to justify, for many, the increased use of this and other forms of commercialization of the human body.

In these two arguments, despite their obvious differences, we find the entire set of beliefs about the nature of human beings and social action which make up the meta-narrative of improvement. The credo of individual interest seems thus to mandate the desacralization of life by viewing it in simple material terms as an object at the disposal of science and the biomedical power structure; any other view is taken as pure superstition. To achieve the total abstraction and decontextualization of the human body it would be necessary, of course, to free ourselves entirely from the feeling of sacredness which surrounds death by denouncing, in the name of materialism, sentiments which could be qualified as the last holdover of a superstitious worldview. Eliminating this barrier would at the same time make each of us into a potential reservoir of organs for general use.

In sum, to assure the individual's ever increasing liberty, the human body, alive or dead, is trapped in the infernal momentum of instrumentalization, management, and commercialization. The range of possibilities, constantly enlarged by biotechnological innovation, creates the illusion that the market can satisfy all desires. At the same time, we all become both subjects and objects of economic practices. We must submit ourselves to the requirements of the market, particularly to the one by which scarcity increases with increase in demand, expressed and justified through the legal language of subjective rights. The individual, isolated in his happiness as in his sorrow, is thus subject to the laws of competition, to the fluctuations of supply and demand.

In the case of the natural environment the same dynamic is at work. When economic discourse takes ecological factors into consideration—a situation which, incidentally, cuts against its own traditions—it can only do so by attributing a price to nature's various elements. These simultaneously enter the universe of scarcity produced by unrestrained exploitation of the environment. Water and air, gifts of nature constantly replenished, become commodities, a logical transformation when the market worldview orients individual and collective action. This move is even seen as imperative, the precondition to imposing rational conduct on economic actors in their use of both the means of production and their products. In short, we seem incapable of thinking about ecological threats in any other terms than those supplied by the limits of market logic. The very concern for ecology contributes thereby to strengthening the market perspective and its principle of generalized equivalence.

Must we conclude from all that has preceded that the figure of the market has become the only possible model for imagining and regulating society? There is no doubt that today, as in the 1920s, the market is conceived as a natural order, realizing itself gradually over the course of history despite the many obstacles which have been put in its way. To escape the clutches of this naturalizing representation of the market, we must ask ourselves what is hidden by economic discourse. In other words, only a thorough-going critique of this discourse will allow us to shed light on the relations of power which constitute the economic arena.

What is hidden, for example, behind the popular assertion, emanating from the world's privileged few, that the sharing of human, social, and cultural costs is the necessary price for recovering our general well-being, momentarily threatened? Should we not see in this language an *ad hoc* ideological veil, designed to hide the secondary effects of individualism and exchangism (founded on the notions of free and voluntary relations) by promoting values like consensus and the sentiment of social belonging?

Even when inequalities become too obvious to be easily masked, and when the risks of material and social deprivation touch an ever growing number of people, the scholarly discourse of economics maintains all of its legitimacy. The different seats of power, national and international, share the task of maintaining the faith in the True and the Good; indeed, when necessary, they do not hesitate to impose it on skeptics and recalcitrants. The meta-narrative of improvement is therefore in no way threatened, even when the distance between its vision and reality grows. Rather, it takes on all of the properties of an incantation.

This discourse has told and retold us, for over two centuries now, what it means to be human. The "humanity" of man, reduced to its mere individualistic and exchangist components, then forms the basis for discriminations between people, groups, and nations. The relative non-humanity of the poor and the deprived is illustrated, more or less clearly, through such examples as welfare in England during the early part of the nineteenth century, or the policies of "development" today. In both cases, a widely held view associates poverty with laziness, thereby justifying the contempt which is expressed, often quite overtly, for the "victims of progress" both in the North and in the South. The considerable effort spent throughout the world to extract these "victims" from the vicious circle of poverty and to insert them in the fully human universe of the independent individual serves, despite evident and repeated failures, as logical and sufficient proof of the truth of the economic way.

Perhaps, within an obvious normative view, the economic representation of the world could be considered as "the mathematically most advanced social science," but simultaneously as the "socially and humanly most backward one," because "it has been abstracted from social, historical, political, psychological, ecological conditions," which should be viewed as "inseparable from economic activities" (Morin 1993,181).

HOW TO BE RESPONSIBLE?

Nevertheless, for a great number of social scientists, the way is rather clear. They have to remain confined within the cognitive and normative limits imposed by the "utilitarian culture." Undoubtedly, it is a very comfortable position, defined by a widespread scientific conformism. Social sciences are thus divided into fragmented fields more and more specialized. What is at stake is the question of competence. With such a fragmentation, crucial problems of our time can only be tackled in a functional and technical way with an obvious limited responsibility.

It thus remains for us to signal very briefly, by way of conclusion, a possible alternative; an escape from the clutches of these imaginary visions of the economy. Indeed, we must not hesitate for a moment. We must focus our attention on the irreducible complexity of human existence, an existence which cannot be summed up in the economism of individual interests, no matter how broadly these interests are construed. In this way, the value of human beings would no longer be confused with that of objects; the social status of man would no longer be reduced to his mere economic status; and mankind would no longer be subjected to the imperatives of market pricing.

Only a generalized science of society, opposed to the disciplinary compartmentalization of today, could be capable of embracing within a single scholarly vision the totality of human action and the complexity of mankind's social and political systems.

Moreover, a relevant approach has to address more and more critical societal issues, which cannot be successfully investigated within the narrow limits of a particular discipline. The very acceptance of increasing overlap among social sciences to tackle society's problems seems to be a basic condition to avoid being a victim of the political pressure for "useful" research.

More than that, social scientists should prevent any misunderstanding of what is expected from them. To let people believe that social problems can be directly solved by scientific research is not a responsible attitude, although it may be a convincing one—if not the *only* one in the present situation—to get money for what should be viewed as applied research. Within such a utilitarian movement, social sciences could readily be transformed into a very poor expertise. The danger, however, of this search for professional standards is to be unable to avoid an ideological conformism, to the point of producing a pure tautological knowledge. Social sciences are constantly in danger of repeating, in an apparent scientific language, the evidences of the pervasive utilitarian culture, or of contributing to the "definitive" truth of the "great epic" of capitalism. Taken within this conformist imperative, numerous representatives of social sciences attempt in fact to exhibit their competence. Confined within a narrow utilitarian circle, they hope to be recognized as qualified experts and specialists. Consequently, they may claim to be responsible scholars. But they have to act *as if* they could solve, in a quite concrete and well-defined way, societal problems, and *as if* they could be social engineers. One possible effect of this claim to expertise is to transform social sciences into meaningless discourses.

If, on the other hand, we wish to overcome such drastic limits, we would have to fully reorganize the division of work between what is supposed to be scientific and what is reputed to be philosophical. To transcend this obvious dichotomy would require the practice of what could be labeled, at least for the present time, "social sciences-cum-philosophy," as a way to oppose the radical distinction between "value-free" social sciences and a narrowly defined philosophy. This wide domain of knowledge about human beings and society should take on the form of reflexive knowledge; i.e., knowledge which includes a clear statement of the values on which anthropological and social theories are founded.

More particularly, social scientists have to be fully conscious of the compelling effect of modern ideology on their scientific views. Therefore, "responsibility" for relevant social sciences implies a consideration of the conditions under which knowledge about human beings and society is possible. On this basis, a scientific and moral responsibility would mean, for instance, to follow L. Dumont, when he states: "to isolate our ideology is a *sine qua non* condition to transcend it, for it is the spontaneous vehicle of our thought, and we are confined in it as long as we do not take it as an object of our reflection" (1977, 36). The lesson should be clear. Social sciences are constantly in danger of confusing encompassing cultural meanings with knowledge.

Similarly but in a more direct way, I. Wallerstein, speaking about economic historians, states that they "have built their work around organizing myths" viewed each as "a tale" or a "metahistory" (1991, 51). He thus argues that "it is metahistory which determines our collection of data . . . It is our metahistory which channels our formulation of the hypotheses . . . It is our metahistory which, above all, legitimates our analyses of the data. It is our grand interpretation of history which renders our smaller interpretations credible. The justification, therefore, of our metahistory comes neither from the data it generates nor from the null hypotheses it supports nor from the analyses it provokes. Its justification derives from its ability to respond comprehensively to the existing, continuing real social puzzles that people encounter and of which they have become conscious. It is in fact precisely the reality of the ever-increasing historical disparities of development that has called into question the old organizing myths . . ., and which has therefore been pushing world scholarship to the construction of an alternative metahistory" (1991, 60).

In an even more crucial way, the basic preconditions for competent and responsible social sciences lead us to a few vital questions. For instance, the question of how to preserve what is properly human in each of us, when we are more and more subject to the impelling effects of new technologies and of a globalizing market. Or the question of how to avoid being transformed into pure means in a system which should be the expression of our own collective desires and ambitions.

Indeed, such questions are relevant only for those who consider that knowledge about human beings and society is simultaneously and inevitably an inquiry into "what is" and "what ought to be." This constitutes a very controversial assertion for those who are convinced that social sciences have to be entrenched within a narrowly defined scientific field. But to think about final values is perhaps the ultimate justification for the very existence of social sciences. At least what is to be questioned is the ultimate objective of a pure operational knowledge. The expert with a responsibility confined to the narrow limits of his domain of competence should not be in any way the ideal figure of the social scientist. Moreover, the only responsibility related to economic expertise lies within the range of private interests. Such an orthodox worldview will never meet what we might call social reality.

As opposed to it, a scholarly approach in social sciences cannot equate responsibility to technical competence. Surely research and teaching have to be of high quality, and relevant to societal issues; yet a scholar should be scientifically as well as morally responsible. Beyond their positive and critical competence, social scientists should seriously contribute to the general discussion of what could be a "good" or a "desirable" society. Why should not the project of a sustainable society, free of any form of capitalistic, ethnic, or religious exclusion, be viewed as the main object of moral obligation for social sciences in general?

REFERENCES

Appleby, Joyce O. 1978, *Economic Thought and Ideology in Seventeenth-Century England*, Princeton, Princeton University Press.

Baudrillard, Jean 1972, *Pour une critique de l'économie politique du signe*, Paris, Gallimard.

Becker, Gary S. 1976, *The Economic Approach to Human Behavior*, Chicago, The University of Chicago Press.

Berthoud, Gerald 1994, "L'économie, un ordre généralisé? Les ambitions d'un prix Nobel," in: *Pour une autre économie*, Paris, La Découverte, 42–59 (Revue du MAUSS no 3).

Castoriadis, Cornelius 1987, *The Imaginary Institution of Society*, Oxford, Polity Press (first publication in French 1975).

Dumont, Louis 1977, *Homo aequalis: Genèse et épanouissement de l'idéologie économique*, Paris, Gallimard.

—— 1983, "Préface," in: Polanyi, Karl 1983, *La Grande Transformation: Aux origines politiques et économiques de notre temps*, Paris, Gallimard.

Gouldner, Alvin W. 1970, *The Coming Crisis of Western Sociology*, New York, Basic Books.

Halévy, Elie 1949 [1901], *The Growth of Philosophical Radicalism*, New York, August M. Kelley Publishers.

Larrère, Catherine 1992, *L'invention de l'économie au XVIIIe siècle. Du droit naturel à la physiocratie*, Paris, Presses Universitaires de France.

Locke, John 1960 [1690], *Two Treatises of Government*, (P. Laslett, ed.), Cambridge, Cambridge University Press.

McCloskey, Donald N. 1990, "Storytelling in Economics," in: Nash, Christopher (ed.), *Narrative in Culture: The Uses of Storytelling in the Sciences, Philosophy, and Literature*, London, Routledge, 5–22.

Morin, Edgar 1993, *Terre-Patrie*, Paris, Seuil.

Phelps, Edmund S. 1985, *Political Economy. An Introductory Text*, New York, W.W. Norton & Co.

Polanyi, Karl/Arensberg, Conrad W./Pearson, Harry W. (eds.) 1957, *Trade and Market in the Early Empires*, New York, Free Press.

Smith, Adam 1976a [1759], *The Theory of Moral Sentiments* (D.D. Raphael/A.L. Macfie, eds.), Oxford, Clarendon Press.

—— 1976b [1776], *An Inquiry into the Nature and Causes of the Wealth of Nations* (R.H. Campbell/A.S. Skinner, eds.), Oxford, Clarendon Press.

Sockwell, W.D. 1994, *Popularizing Classical Economics*, London, Macmillan.

Wallerstein, Immanuel 1991, *Unthinking Social Science: The Limits of Nineteenth-Century Paradigms*, Cambridge, Polity Press.

Weber, Max 1952 [1905], *The Protestant Ethic and the Spirit of Capitalism*, New York, Charles Scribner's Sons.

The Social Construction
of the Market

BEAT BÜRGENMEIER

This paper offers some thoughts on the ethical foundations of the market. In order to understand the normative aspects of the economy, one needs to recognize that economic policy recommendations derived from "pure" models must adapt to existing social institutions.

The ideas set out here follow from ones already presented in various earlier publications (Bürgenmeier 1991, 1993). This time, the focus will be on society's perception of the norms and values underlying an economic approach which is increasingly seen to be intruding into the field of social sciences (Swedberg 1990). Economic theory claims that society should be regulated solely by competitive markets, and frequently contrasts direct controls with incentive measures. Such contrasts conceal more fundamental differences of opinion about the role and function of the state within the economy—i.e., where to draw the boundary not only between the private and public spheres, but also between individual and collective interests. What criteria does society use to draw these boundaries and to justify the regulation of society? And what norms and values does it adopt to justify these criteria? In asking these questions, I intend to make it clear that the market includes a moral dimension (Etzioni 1988). The market is simply one of a number of collective decision-making mechanisms, and fits into an institutional context which is codified by laws and regulations. This institutional context is evidence of the normative foundations of the market, on which economic policy recommendations are based. My aim is thus to launch a debate on the values that underlie all efforts to regulate society. Such values cannot be purely economic—instead, they are derived from an ethical frame of reference which needs to be made explicit.

This paper is divided into two parts. The first part discusses the market as a self-regulating entity which disregards all institutional interactions. It reviews the main stages in the development of the economic thinking which has culminated in the notion of a self-regulating mechanism. This mechanism has created much controversy in the field of social sciences with regard to the interaction between institutions and human behavior. Furthermore, it appears to duck the whole issue of values. That being the case, only an interdisciplinary approach can add a moral dimension to economics and alter its ideas on the regulation of society.

The second part discusses the market as regulated by norms, customs, and laws. It focuses on the market as a social construction which is subject to institutional changes brought about by the deliberate actions of the individuals that make up society.

THE SELF-REGULATING MARKET

Defined in objective terms of action, economic theory concludes that:

> Piece meal welfare economics is often based on the belief that a study of the *necessary* conditions for a Paretian welfare optimum may lead to the discovery of *sufficient* conditions for an increase in welfare (Lipsey and Lancaster 1956, 17).

All that has to be done is to make the market work under conditions of perfect competition. The self-regulated market is guided by an "invisible hand." (Smith 1776)

This "hand" has had a more profound influence than any other metaphor on society's understanding of its own workings. Few authors are aware that Adam Smith's "hand" was conceived as a moral imperative in response to arbitrary feudal power (Bridel 1988), rather than as a justification for laissez-faire policies. To quote Walras: "*Laissez-faire . . .* is an economic policy which could be taught to a parrot in a single morning with the help of a few lumps of sugar" (Jaffé 1965, Letter No. 311, 433–444, Léon Walras to Vito Cusumano). Such rote-learning suggests the existence of a natural law that appears to govern the economy and absolve us from all ethical considerations regarding the way in which markets actually operate. This sharp division between the scientific and normative aspects of the economy raises some serious problems of methodology (Bürgenmeier 1994).

The metaphor of the invisible hand is a tautology. If economic agents are rational, they know what is in their best interests. When faced with conflicts of individual interest, they learn to accept the law of supply and demand in determining the exchange value which will settle their differences. The market is thus the logical outcome of human relationships and the only possible method of organizing society, provided that economic agents are fully exposed to competition. Market theory is thus based on a presupposition about human behavior. According to Kristol (1984), man has a natural and incorrigible interest in improving his material living conditions; this interest can only be accommodated by free trade, which generates economic growth and thereby improves material conditions, however great the initial inequality between individuals. Even now, society's perception of how the economy works is based on this presupposition, which underestimates the role of culture and institutions (Hannan 1981) and—for better or worse—ignores the emotional dimension of human behavior. It focuses entirely on the factors which determine a country's overall long-term supply, assuming the full use of all available productive resources based on a technological relationship between labor and capital, i.e., between the working population and the productive apparatus. This model is self-regulating in the sense that market equilibrium is achieved through price flexibility which, in relative terms, leads to substitutions between factors of production. By constantly creating new combinations of technologies, this model supposedly generates maximum economic growth, which innovation may cause to go off at surprising, unpredictable tangents. Variations in relative prices thus ensure that this explanation of the economic workings of society can survive almost *ad infinitum*. All one has to do is combine man's supposedly rational behavior with the unlimited potential of technological development. At the same time, increasingly sophisticated mathematical models (Gleick 1992) are being used in an attempt to provide formal evidence of the relevance of this deterministic view of the economy. By implication, provided enough mathematical formulae are marshalled in defense of this model, its normative content can be safely ignored. However, this disregards both the controversy over methodology which has helped bring about the fragmentation of economic theory (Hausmann 1984) and what Albert Hirschman (1989) calls the "counter-effect."

As regards methodology (Granger 1960), it must be acknowledged that there is no consensus, although it does appear to be accepted that a model cannot be compared with any other unless the results of both, derived from deductive reasoning, are subjected to empirical verification (Popper 1968). Economics is thus considered both an exact science, since it uses deductive reasoning to establish causal links between the variables concerned, and an inexact science, owing to the numerous factors it must disregard. The inevitable proviso "all other things being equal" precludes empirical falsification of the theory. All that then remains is its pretension—despite the uniqueness of the historical events on which economic observations are based—to have created a generally applicable theory which is independent of time and place.

As for the "counter-effect," this supposedly scientific pretension is inevitably ideological, serving the interests of a given minority at a given time. This, at least, is Hirschman's view. Those who oppose all active intervention by the state in the workings of the economy tend to argue that "such intervention will lead, through a combination of unwanted effects, to the exact opposite of what was intended" (Hirschman 1989, 71). This counter-effect is thus a product of the supposedly self-regulating economy. Yet, if the operation of the latter is considered an evolutionary process marked by institutional changes in society that reflect changes in values (Polanyi 1944), the increasingly active role of the state can be seen as a consequence of market failure, rather than a cause that limits the effects of the self-regulating market. Indeed, the liberal ideas originally expressed by John Locke, Adam Smith, and John Stuart Mill were never intended to discredit the state. The "counter-effect" only makes sense with reference to a supposedly immutable social order (Boudon 1977) based on economic laws that are independent of time and place. In practice, however, the role of the state and its institutional arrangements change over time and from society to society, raising questions as to the aspirations of a society that seeks to fulfill ethical criteria.

THE DEVELOPMENT OF ECONOMIC LIBERALISM

In referring to various authors who played a key role in developing the model of the self-regulating market, I wish to emphasize that this model originally included a moral dimension that disappeared only when economics sought to become more rigorous. This rigorousness was achieved by economics growing more abstract and contemptuously relegating its normative aspects to the supposedly less scientific social sciences. Yet one of the first liberal thinkers, John Locke (1721), for all his concern with the individual and the protection of individual life, liberty, and property, never advocated a weak, passive state (Roll 1973); on the contrary, he considered that supremacy of the state over the individual was necessary in order to enable each individual to fulfill himself. However, in concluding that man's principal concern was not to be dispossessed, he reduced the political content of society to a purely economic dimension. It is therefore not surprising that social struggles have revolved around the redistribution of income and wealth, an issue disregarded by this initial liberal vision of the economy. Yet these same liberal ideas led to an affirmation of at least the principles of human rights, which shows that liberalism never considered the economic and social spheres in isolation. They always formed a whole, subject to ethical rules.

As prosperity grew in the eighteenth century, Adam Smith identified the acquisition of wealth as the individual's primary motive. Here liberalism considered the individual as being separate from the state, and required the state to give priority to the accumulation of wealth, particularly by facilitating trade, maintaining law and order, and protecting property.

Not until the nineteenth century was the social dimension introduced into liberal doctrine, by John Stuart Mill, who can thus be seen as the most humanistic of the classical theorists. He saw society as the sum total of subjective individuals under the authority of the state. One of his most noteworthy statements was that it was up to each individual to look after himself, while taking on a certain proportion of public duties. Society consisted of individuals pursuing their own interests, and was accordingly organized in such a way that only individual interests were expressed by the state. The idea of a social contract was thus rejected, since society did not exist as a separate entity. The role of the state was purely representative. In order that such a society should not be destroyed by all-pervading selfishness, Mill relied on education to develop altruistic, as opposed to utilitarian, behavior.

In practice, this liberal view has gradually adjusted to the needs of a society that has grown more and more complex in the wake of increasing industrialization. Sismondi (Waeber 1991), who foresaw this adjustment, can thus be seen as the most realistic economist of his time. Successive adjustments to the growing needs of a highly organized society—specifically including the need for state intervention in social affairs—have led further and further away from the original ideas expressed by Locke, Smith, and Mill. In fact, a truly liberal society has never existed; economic organization has always had to strike a balance between individual subjectivity and social objectivity. The state has always existed in its own right and, as such, has influenced individual behavior. It has never simply been the sum total of individuals single-mindedly pursuing their own interests. The existence of the state in its own right has caused society to evolve into a community, which is necessarily more than just the sum total of private interests. The notion of a community specifically refers to a set of moral values shared by all its members (Tönnies 1935).

The survival of liberalism despite this historically manifest contradiction can, I believe, be attributed to two factors: the history of economic policy in the capitalist countries, and the rise of the socialist countries.

As industrial society grew more and more specialized, it was also exposed to social criticism based on both Christian morality and Marxist philosophy. The pragmatic adjustment of liberalism to these social changes resulted in a reorganization of the state which failed to eliminate the inequalities which existed. On the contrary, large-scale intervention by the state created new inequalities. The civil service, for example, developed a self-preserving strategy of its own. The effectiveness of social policies was often curtailed by bureaucracy, which in turn gave rise to pernicious new kinds of behavior: instead of helping the underprivileged to become independent by freeing them from material constraints, such policies often created what was to be known as a welfare-state mentality and led voters to regroup accordingly.

The alternative path proposed by Marxist thinkers had its origins in the Russian Revolution, whose call for social objectivity to prevail over individual subjectivity culminated in totalitarianism and was ultimately bound to fail. With hindsight, the fall of the Berlin Wall in 1989 can be seen as symbolizing the logical outcome of such a system.

However, during the cold war period 1945–1989, liberalism was forced to adapt to two trends: the partial socialization of the Western democracies and the establishment of collectivism in the socialist countries. It is only recently that a simplistic version of liberal thinking has turned its back on more than a century of economic and social history and attempted to erase all memory of the struggles for social justice that have played such an important part in the development of Western society. Such an approach is only possible if society is viewed in purely theoretical terms. The ground for this return to classical theory was prepared by Friedrich von Hayek (1944), who always distrusted state control of society, preferring self-regulating forces which could only operate in totally unrestricted markets. He therefore called for a social order which trusted individuals and did not restrict their freedom of maneuver, since each individual was the best judge of his own interests. As with the classical liberals, the common interest was thus simply the sum total of individual interests. The notion of society as a community was utopian, and had already led John Stuart Mill to reject the idea of the social contract. Refusing to consider the state as an entity in its own right, Hayek saw democracy as the only available mechanism for settling conflicts of individual interest. The hierarchical nature of this democratic mechanism and the frequent absence of competition from economic transactions did not strike Hayek as sufficient reason to accept institutional intervention in the market by the state. As he saw it (Hayek 1944), man was faced with a simple choice between collectivism and liberalism. In practice, however, this choice is by no means so clear-cut. Indeed, the liberal view that only market forces can solve society's problems leads to a new form of alienation: an individualistic society which denies all notion of community and leaves the individual isolated within his own set of constraints. As Ferdinand Tönnies realized back in 1887 (Tönnies 1935), a society which is simply the sum total of individuals acting in their own interests is not yet a community. A purely monetary society cannot be an end in itself, but can only be a means of approaching the ideal of a civic society in which individuals identify with the common good and so create a community.

Since the market is merely one of a number of social decision-making mechanisms and the economy merely one part of the social sphere, economic theory needs to take a broader view.

This can be illustrated by an example taken from the history of economic thought, regarding conditions of production. Once again, the thinker in question was John Stuart Mill. In his day, production was largely agricultural, but was already exposed to the influence of industrialization. This process could be seen simply as a mechanism whereby one factor of production was substituted for another. Yet Mill challenged the idea that the conversion of cultivated land into pasture was simply a matter of substituting capital for labor. He also dismissed the idea that mechanization would lead to the reabsorption of redundant manpower when demand rose following a fall in the price of goods. A fall in prices did not automatically lead to higher investment. In other words, increased demand for goods did not necessarily stimulate employment (Blaug 1986).

The advantage of increased demand for goods needed to be set against the disadvantage of a fall in the purchasing power of workers made redundant by mechanization. Even though in the long term mechanization led to a fall in prices, stimulating production and thus absorbing the unemployment, in the short term the workers clearly suffered. Moreover, prices would only fall if there were perfect competition. If mechanization occurred under monopolistic conditions, prices could remain unchanged and monopolistic profit would increase. This increase in profits had two effects: it led to an even more unequal distribution of income, to the detriment of the workers, and it stimulated demand through the spending of the extra profit, without any need for a fall in prices. Production increased to meet the additional demand, and ultimately the redundant worker was taken on again.

Mill's liberal position led to the realization that a problem of short-term adjustment might arise, and that economic changes had a social cost. There was therefore a need for policies to adjust production structures, the payment of unemployment benefits during the transitional period, and the retraining of redundant workers. In response to increasingly rapid economic changes, the state would tend to intervene to a greater and greater extent in a market which could not remain unregulated.

This historical debate, which was first triggered by the Industrial

Revolution, regularly recurs in response to technical progress, most recently with regard to electronics and computer science. The high unemployment rate in the industrialized countries in 1991 (BIS 1992) needs to be seen in this light. The resulting social unrest is less serious than in the nineteenth century, thanks to the state's role in providing unemployment insurance and retraining. Public intervention in response to economic change is thus a reflection of society's changing perception of social justice. As will be seen below, there can be no economic change without a corresponding change in society's perception of the economy.

THE MARKET AND THE INDUSTRIAL REVOLUTION

In the nineteenth century, the social friction caused by increasing industrialization and the advent of mechanization was aggravated by the appalling conditions that prevailed in the manufacturing industry. The privately-owned factories did not guarantee the most basic standards of health and safety. Child labor was widespread and, to take one example, the life expectancy of Swiss metalworkers in the mid-nineteenth century was just 35 years (Bergier 1983). It was such conditions that brought the economic and social spheres into conflict, with supposedly natural laws on the one hand and normative moral judgments on the other.

Classical economists were by no means in agreement that the state should intervene, and a consensus only began to emerge towards the middle of the nineteenth century. Britain's first Factory Act, which dates from 1833, was mainly intended to regulate child labor. The central argument was that children lacked the discernment to make their own decisions about how they were employed. This was based on a normative assessment of the age of discernment, without reference to criteria of social justice. Non-interventionists based their views on the liberal doctrine that an individual with responsibility for his or her own choices was the best judge of economic conditions. While action clearly had to be taken to protect children, economists were highly apprehensive about state intervention on behalf of adults. There were those who felt that a reduction in working hours without a corresponding reduction in wages would simply put firms out of business. Others were afraid that the working class would become work-shy. Few economists saw such measures as a means of increasing productivity; the majority thought that wages would fall and that emigration would increase. Mill, for example, was afraid that the brunt of any reduction in working hours would be borne by the weakest categories of workers and that unemployment would increase, especially among women. Ultimately, state intervention in the running of firms would only add to the difficulties of those it was intended to protect—the famous "counter-effect." However, Mill did acknowledge the need to protect individuals, not so much to supplant their own judgment as to enable them to use it.

In short, none of these economists used arguments explicitly based on moral values. They criticized state intervention on two grounds. The first was that a decrease in working hours would lead to economic ruin unless accompanied by a decrease in nominal wages. The second concerned freedom of contract between individuals capable of discernment. However, one cannot help being struck by the fact that the age of discernment varied considerably, and increased not in accordance with the immutable principles of liberal theory, but as a result of social pressure which grew as economic performance improved. Society's perception of the economy thus changed in response to changes in production structures.

Today, when faced with the need for more flexible organization of the labor market (particularly with regard to part-time work, job-sharing and other kinds of active participation), economic theory still insists that the reward to labor must be entirely based on marginal productivity. In continuing to emphasize monocausal relationships, it fails to take account of major normative changes in society, which is now demanding reorganization of the institutional aspects of the labor market. Such demands are an expression of the moral dimension of economics, which adapts its organization to social changes. This process has been going on for a long time. New, more participatory and more motivational forms of organization have been introduced and are continuing to be devised. In response to such developments, the science of economics is increasingly making way for a wide range of diverse theories on the organization of firms (Busino 1993). This trend shows that the market responds to constantly changing institutional arrangements, and hence that it is highly regulated.

THE REGULATED MARKET

If the market is analyzed as a social construction, the link between the state and the economy reveals a coalition of interests between the state and private enterprise, which competitive markets frequently fail to take into account. This suggests that organizational models may be better than market models at explaining the economic sphere. Organizational models certainly take fuller account of the normative dimension of the economy and make explicit reference to power structures. An organizational approach thus sheds light on at least two areas which are neglected in pure market models: the behavior of economic agents, and the evolution of institutions (Granovetter 1991). These can best be examined from the point of view of economic sociology (Smelser and Swedberg 1994).

THE BEHAVIOR OF ECONOMIC AGENTS

The notion of the market as a social construction, which emerges from an organizational approach to society, raises the issue of collective decision-making mechanisms. Who is in charge of the organization, and who holds decision-making power? The behavioral hypothesis that underlies the notion of the self-regulating market must therefore include power motivations. Two different attempts have been made to grasp these motivations; although conflicting, both are in line with economic logic. One extends economic rationality to the political sphere, while the other sets limits to man's rationality.

The first approach has led to public choice theory, which simply applies the neoclassical model to politics, relying entirely on competition and privatization of public activities to regulate society. This is once again based on the idea that the self-regulating market is superior to all other collective decision-making mechanisms used to regulate society. The institutions whose public actions bring about change thus supposedly have no influence on agents, whose behavior is deemed to be immutable.

The second approach sets out from the principle that economic rationality is limited, or "bounded," by lack of information. Market agents are thus restricted in their ability to act, and seek to become more organized in order to protect their interests. This means that profit and utility maximization strategies are better served by coalitions of interest groups than by perfect competition (Simon 1947). It should be noted that the hypothesis of bounded rationality follows logically from neoclassical models, and therefore clashes with sociological theories which emphasize the interdependence of social institutions and individual behavior. Should individual behavior prove to be shaped by social (or indeed psychological) constraints, this would mean that individuals—supposedly the best judges of their own interests—are in fact influenced by institutions when exercising their free choice.

The notion of the market as a social construction thus demands a more complex analysis of individual behavior than the hypothesis of economic rationality will allow. In order to operate properly, the market requires actors whose behavior has been totally permeated by the existing institutions. Market-makers (merchants, stockbrokers, lawyers, etc.) all display a particular kind of mentality which appears to be a prerequisite for economic functioning of any kind. Markets can only emerge spontaneously from specific social conditions; they depend on a mentality which has been shaped by previous institutional developments. This is undoubtedly one of the lessons to be learned from the transformation process currently taking place in Eastern Europe (Matzner 1992).

According to economic theory, market-makers are entirely rational in their behavior. This conflicts with models of human behavior that refer to moral values. Yet it is clear that markets can only operate with reference to such values, for instance those implicit in the legal principle *pacta servanda sunt* (contracts must be performed). Even if economic rationality is in some way the expression of "modernity" in the broadest sense of the term, it still includes an ethical dimension. However, it has evolved in the course of time. The hypothesis of economic rationality has become instrumentalized, and is now considered by many to be the only behavioral hypothesis capable of successfully analyzing human economic and social behavior. Such behavior, which appears to be universal and independent of time and place, is presented as ahistorical and acultural. Unthinking application of this hypothesis in areas beyond the original model disguises the fact that such behavior is not real, but merely an abstraction. One can, of course, object that we only perceive reality through our own conception of it, and that a model is thus merely a simplified attempt to conceive of reality. In any case, the hypothesis of rationality is an essential tool when exploring economic models, as it helps overcome the intrinsic obstacle to empirical verification which is posed by the uniqueness of historical events (Moessinger 1993). Three main conclusions can be drawn from this:

First, as regards methodology, there are no criteria to determine which type of scientific analysis can best explain the regulation of society. Plurality of approach thus becomes a methodological requirement.

Second, economists are trapped within the logic of a model-making system which is cut off from social reality. Deductive models scarcely lend themselves to confrontation with empirical observations. The proviso "all other things being equal" precludes falsification. Many econometric studies based solely on quantitative data are presented *ad hoc*, without any theoretical basis, while certain theoretical models are so highly abstract that they bear little relation to observable social practice.

Third, the notion that self-regulating markets based on economic rationality are superior to all other methods of regulating society has no scientific foundation whatsoever. It is based on a normative presumption that private businesses should be independent of the state.

THE EVOLUTION OF INSTITUTIONS

If individuals' economic behavior depends on institutions, the role of the State becomes active in the sense that it brings about changes by adopting laws and regulations through a collective decision-making mechanism governed by the democratic principle. The State is no longer exogenous to the workings of the market, but is an integral part of the economic sphere which cannot be separated from the political sphere. This aspect is reinforced by the fact that the market generates transaction costs and thus suffers from friction (Coase 1988). Laws which change in response to changing political majorities provide the basic conditions for the market, which is hence defined as a contractual domain. Not only can the market not operate without friction, but its operation must be guaranteed by a number of rules, ranging from freedom of contract to compliance with moral principles. The institutional organization of the market is shaped by an unending sequence of historical changes brought about by the behavior of economic agents. Hence the notion that markets and the State are in conflict is a fiction. The idea that only firms are capable of creating wealth and that the state is unproductive, turns out to be an ideological construction which has shaped our understanding of how society operates. Once again, economic rationality can be seen as a theoretical construction designed to support the thesis that the economic sphere is independent of the social sphere.

If we accept that the market is a social construction, then the State is an endogenous variable in the economic sphere. This justifies an active economic policy. Yet not only does such an interpretation mean emphasizing the organizational aspects of the economic sphere rather than those strictly connected with trade, but—a more fundamental point—it also means abandoning the hypothesis of economic rationality as the sole behavioral hypothesis. What is involved here is nothing more or less than the reconciliation of differing methods and approaches in the field of social sciences. However, such attempts at reconciliation may lead to a new battle of methods (Swedberg 1990), and they do not take sufficient account of the failures that can be observed in the political sphere. According to the theory of the second best, state intervention in the economic sphere is only justified in the event of market failure (Lipsey and Lancaster 1956). The cost of such intervention is then measured in economic terms, while the benefits are appreciated normatively in the political sphere. Once it also becomes necessary to take account of government failures, economic policies must be assessed in a more normative context than economic theory will allow. A telling example of this is provided by state intervention in the transport sector, whose prices are too low when compared with a monetary valuation of not only the economic but also the social costs (OECD 1992). Such undervaluation has given rise to considerable mobility which, though seemingly a step in the direction of the self-regulating market, in fact merely distorts the optimum allocation of factors of production. Government failures thus also call for an analysis of power structures, which are the basis for the legal arrangements for state intervention.

Market and government failures may explain why so many economic decisions are delegated to the administrative and legal sphere, reflecting the breakdown of the current method of regulating society.

CONCLUSION

These thoughts on the theoretical basis of model-making as used in mainstream economic theory raise questions as to the ultimate purpose of the economy. They also raise questions of methodology. To what extent does such model-making result in circular arguments? Is our approach simply the logical consequence of our own particular conception of how the economy works?

The methodological requirement that economic theory should be systematically confronted with observable reality cannot be satisfied by a purely deductive approach. Similarly, a purely inductive approach can link up empirical observations in any order whatsoever. Only economic research based on several empirically verified sub-models can satisfy this methodological requirement. Such models are necessarily "false" in that they fail to grasp social reality in its entirety (Feldstein 1982). Empirical verification cannot be solely based on quantitative methods, but must also take into account qualitative data produced by research in other fields. Such experimental studies show human behavior to be in conflict with the hypothesis of economic rationality, and call for multidisciplinary analysis.

Instead, economic theory has chosen to grow more and more specialized. This may explain why it now seems incapable of offering workable policy recommendations. This can be seen in practically every area of economic policy. Even though it is based on coherent theoretical reasoning, almost insurmountable problems arise when it comes to be applied. A recent example is the tax on CO_2 emissions, which, despite its theoretical credentials, has run into opposition from economic circles.

Should we conclude that State intervention has failed, and return to the perfect-market model advocated by nineteenth century liberalism? Although the State is nowadays involved in practically all economic decisions, this does not mean that it is strong. Instead, it appears to reflect the balance of power between the various organized interest groups. One result of this is that traditional collective decision-making mechanisms have been weakened and that public and private bureaucracies have been growing more powerful. This trend reflects the high degree of organization of society, which can now be seen as a network of relationships rather than of economic transactions. This trend is not confined to government, but is equally inherent in private firms. Returning to a self-regulating market mechanism will not cure the institutional paralysis brought about by an admittedly all-pervasive but nevertheless weak state. Economic theory, which is entirely based on rational individual behavior, continues to sustain an ideology in which an "unproductive" state is in permanent conflict with "productive" markets.

Any analysis wishing to take account of complex human motivations must set out from actual social practice, in which the individual is not simply a rational economic agent, but is also capable of emotions which lead him to perform actions inspired by a sense of ethics inherent in human nature. Such an analysis would necessarily give greater emphasis to non-monetary values, and would therefore consider the goal not to be economic growth, but sustainable development, which involves taking account of the environmental and social dimensions of the economy. Such a change in approach would profoundly modify the symbols which society has chosen to express its goals.

The environmental debate is an attempt to bring about such a change. Indeed, it is a good example of the kind of dead end that a purely economic approach can lead to. In leaving the task of environmental protection up to economists and technologists, society is attempting to avoid a debate on values. Ironically, this serves to confirm the two main criticisms of civilization in the environmental debate (Lascoumes 1994). To what extent can a society which defines itself solely in economic and technological terms be considered a sustainable society? The environment reminds us that there are intrinsic values which lie beyond monetary assessment. How can we acknowledge the importance of such non-monetary values if we view environmental protection simply as a process of converting nature into an economic good? The absence of ethical values from this economic model and the pursuit of economic growth prevent us from explicitly defining our actions in terms of social responsibility towards nature. Such responsibility also extends to relationships between the members of a single generation, as well as to future generations.

In the words of Hans Jonas, "Act so that the effects of your action are compatible with the survival of authentically human life on earth" (Jonas 1990, 30). In its efforts to defend individual freedom, economic theory has become an inappropriate tool for analyzing such a principle of responsibility. In defining the State as being in conflict with the market economy, it has encouraged us to perceive social problems in purely economic terms. Yet, if we go beyond the purely economic dimension, we must begin to discuss the purposes of our actions. Instead of the myth of immutable human behavior shaped by economic rationality, we are dealing with institutions which develop in accordance with man's expectations of them. They thus reflect changes in economic and social values, and in turn shape the human behavior which gave rise to them in the first place. It is time for individuals to realize this and cease confining themselves to a deterministic view. Society's changing perception of nature is changing its perception of the economy. This may explain why issues of economic ethics have recently become so popular.

REFERENCES

Bergier, J.F. 1983, *Histoire économique de la Suisse*, Lausanne, Payot.

BIS 1992, *62nd Annual Report*, Basle, June.

Blaug, M. 1986, *Economic Theory in Retrospect*, Cambridge, Cambridge University Press (4th edition).

Boudon, R. 1977, *Effets pervers et ordre social*, Paris, Presses Universitaires de France.

Bridel, P. 1988, Quelques réflexions sur l'idée de "main invisible," dans "Revue européenne des sciences sociales," No 82.

Bürgenmeier, B.

——— 1992, *Socio-Economics: An Interdisciplinary Approach: Ethics, Institutions, and Markets*, Boston-Dordrecht-London, Kluwer Academic Publishers.

——— 1993, Der Markt: "Selbstregulierung versus institutionelle Veränderungen," in A. Biesecker, K. Grenzdörffer (eds.), *Ökonomie als Raum sozialen Handelns*, Donat Verlag, Bremen.

——— 1994, The Misperception of Walras, in *The American Economic Review* Vol 84, No 1.

Busino, G. 1993, *Les théories de la bureaucratie*, Paris, Presses Universitaires de France.

Coase, R.H. 1988, *The Firms, the Market, and the Law*, Chicago, University of Chicago Press.

Etzioni, A. 1988, *The Moral Dimension: Toward a New Economics*, New York, The Free Press.

Feldstein, M. 1982, "Inflation, Tax, Rules, and Investment: Some Economic Evidence," in: *Econometrica 50*.

Gleick, J. 1992, *Chaos*, New York, The Viking Press.

Granger, G.G. 1960, *Pensée formelle et sciences de l'homme*, Paris, Aubier.

Granovetter, M. 1991, "The Social Construction of Economic Institutions," in: Etzioni, A./Lawrence, P. R. (eds.) 1991, *Socio-Economics. Toward a New Synthesis*, Amonk, M.E. Sharpe Inc.

Hannan, M.T. 1981, "Families, Market, and Social Structures," in: *Journal of Economic Literature*, 20 (1), March.

Hausmann, D. 1984, *The Philosophy of Economics: An Anthology*, Cambridge University Press, Cambridge.

Hayek, F.A. von 1944, *The Road to Serfdom*, London-Henley, Routledge & Kegan Paul.

Hirschman, A. 1989, "Deux cents ans de rhétorique réactionnaire: le cas de l'effet pervers," in: *Annales ESC*, January-February, 67–86.

Jaffé, W. (ed.) 1965, *Correspondence of Léon Walras and Related Papers*, 3 vols., Amsterdam, North-Holland Publishing Company.

Jonas, H. 1990, *Le principe "responsabilité"*, Paris, Cerf.

Kristol, I. 1984, "Der Rationalismus in der Wirtschaftstheorie," in: Bell, D./ Kristol, I. (eds.), *Die Krise in der Wirtschaftstheorie*, Berlin, Springer-Verlag.

Lascoumes, P. 1994, *L'éco-pouvoir: Environnements et politiques*, Paris, Editions La Découverte.

Lipsey, R.G./Lancaster, K. 1956, "On the General Theory of the Second Best," in: *Review of Economic Studies*, 11–32.

Locke, J. 1721, *An Essay Concerning Human Understanding*, London, S. Birt, D. Browne, etc.

Matzner, E. (ed.) 1992, *The Market Shock: An Agenda for the Economic and Social Reconstruction of Central and Eastern Europe*, Vienna, Austrian Academy of Sciences.

Moessinger, P. 1993, *Homo psychologicus—Homo oeconomicus*, mimeograph, University of Fribourg, Switzerland.

OECD 1992, *Market and Government Failures Applied to the Transport Sector*, Paris.

Polanyi, K. 1944, *The Great Transformation*, New York-Toronto, Rinehart.

Popper, K.R. 1968, *The Logic of Scientific Discovery*, (revised edition), London, Hutchinson.

Roll, E. 1973, *A History of Economic Thought*, London, Faber and Faber Ltd.

Simon, H. A. 1947, *Administrative Behavior*, New York, Macmillan.

Smelser, N.J./Swedberg, R. 1994, *The Handbook of Economic Sociology*, Princeton N.J., Princeton University Press, New York, Russell Sage Foundation.

Smith, A. 1976 [1776], *An Inquiry into the Nature and Causes of the Wealth of Nations*, Chicago, The University of Chicago Press.

Swedberg, R. 1990, "The New Battle of Methods," in: *Challenge*, January-February, 33–38.

Tönnies, F. [3]1991 [1887], *Gemeinschaft und Gesellschaft*, Darmstadt, Wissenschaftliche Buchgesellschaft, 3rd reprint of the 8th edition 1935.

Waeber, P. 1991, *Sismondi: une bibliographie*, vol. 1., Genève, Editions Slatkine.

THE PRODUCTION
OF KNOWLEDGE
ETHICALLY
CHALLENGED

The Ethical Paths of Knowledge in the Social Sciences

GABRIEL GOSSELIN

"Freedom and responsibility in the social sciences—what sense does a moral and ethical reflection introduce into these disciplines?" This demand for an ethic, which we analyzed with G. Balandier in 1990,[1] has now won over the analysts themselves and I am delighted that the conference is carrying out pioneering work in this area. It is true that for the last fifteen years or so, the sociology of ethics has been analyzing the consequences of the difficult management of the progress and implications arising from the crisis in many social relations. It has been led in doing this to put into perspective and question the ethics practiced by a given category of decision-makers and by a given social group. The ambition today is different. I should like to take advantage of the opportunity given to us to turn around and have a good look at sociology and anthropology, these social sciences we practice, and to take time for *reflection*. To question them, as we do other social practices, on their ethics.

AN EXAMPLE

The example of the path I have followed in my own research will serve to clarify my point. For ten years or so after the African countries gained their independence in the 1960s, I spent several periods of time carrying out research in country districts of tropical Africa. In Central Africa, in Burkina Faso (Upper Volta) in particular, I studied rural work. I was therefore well placed to understand the relative unsuitability of much development policy, whether local, national, or international.

For this reason the International Labour Office in Geneva and the United Nations High Commission for Refugees—among others—asked me to carry out research and make recommendations covering the relationship between development and tradition in this part of Africa. I had the opportunity in my reports to analyze policies and sometimes stigmatize practices.

But when we were students at the end of the 1950s wondering about the possibility of carrying out sociological or anthropological work in Algeria, for example, which was then at war, it was not only a question, as far as we were concerned, of economic and material *practicability*, of political-cum-military constraints or of ideological or cultural confrontations. It was a question of the legitimacy of scientific work in this context, for the purposes of analyzing what P. Bourdieu called "the revolution in the revolution." It is from the same point of view that G. Balandier's undertaking—to decolonize sociology; to make a sociology out of decolonization—attracted those of us who chose to carry out their sociological or anthropological work in the Southern Sahara. Later, others, sometimes the same people, were confronted in the same way with the legitimacy and ethical limits of their investigations in unusual contexts. What about what the Marxists called "democratic prejudice" in the construction of new states or the place of "traditions" in development[2]? Don't questions concerning the practicability and legitimacy of research arise in the same way in South Africa, Lebanon, and Yugoslavia today?

The question has forced itself so strongly on a whole generation of sociologists and anthropologists—namely, mine—that African managers and research workers have been trained and expatriates have returned to France. The result has been a crisis in ethnology which is not yet over. Like many colleagues, I have concentrated on studying realities closer to my university: on my students . . . and on sources of finance.

But are we not seeing another return as well? Those of us who thought that the crisis in our disciplines would be solved by their repatriation (as if these disciplines had had the same difficulties as we had in submitting to the common law, to its financing, and to its competition) have now realized that "the worm was in the fruit." In reality, we were slow to come back to our disciplines, and the end of the privilege of colonial exteriority has only served to emphasize this fault.

Is it not in fact in France, as previously outside France, that the question arises of the legitimacy and ethical limits of surveys on immigration, on national or religious minorities, on racism, on all the aspects of our multi-cultural societies? Do not surveys of the circumcision of young African girls in France, for example, tell us that anthropology and sociology are directly implicated, just as the women themselves are?[3] Is there not a halfway point between a rejection of the values which lead to protests by humanitarian associations or militant women and the condemnation of these practices in the name of French law or of the Rights of Man (in this case Woman)?

Trained in the comparative analysis of traditions and modern customs, of movements of counter-modernity and forms of a new or third modernity,[4] the anthropological "detour" analyzed by G. Balandier[5] led me therefore, in a third stage, to take a step back, a deliberately reflective one this time, to examine the practices and presuppositions of our social sciences. I am convinced that the explanation of ethical assumptions includes an affirmation of epistemological presuppositions. Both lead me to follow the tradition of a comprehensive sociology and an interactionist anthropology, which I would call interpretative socio-anthropology.[6]

SPECIFIC NATURE OF THE ACTION

An ambiguity should be eliminated right away. The reflection which I am proposing does not, I must emphasize, cover the use or usages, the "applications," or the reception in a given context by a given institution or social group, of the methods, techniques, or results of the social sciences. My reflection is not related to the "consumption" of our disciplines but, rather, to their *production*.

What in fact would be an ethic of the usages of these sciences? If it was not, again, and in a roundabout way, a sociology of these applications which takes into account the ethic practiced by their agents, it would be an ethical reflection in which I, as a specialist, would have no greater right to express myself than any other citizen. If Oppenheimer thought his opinion about the atomic bomb counted more than that of other citizens, it was because he was one of its fathers. History has dealt with this illusion.

The real power of the scientist is not over the uses made of what he creates: it is in the creation itself. So it is there, in the activity itself, that it is necessary to apply the ethical injunction. The spectacular developments in biotechnology are a good illustration of this essential place in the ethical debate: they also show the difficulties involved, as scientists are not used to being questioned about the outcome, because they are too confident in the absolutely positive nature of "scientific progress," and they are accustomed to shifting the responsibility onto the "users" and "politicians." The controversy among German historians about the "singularity" of the extermination of the Jews by the Nazi regime, arising on the 40th anniversary of the 1945 armistice and during the visit of the American president to the military cemetery of Bitburg, has shown that scientists are like other people when it comes to talking about ethics in a *historical* debate which is not simply a discussion between *historians* establishing facts and their possible interpretations.

To these remarks I would, however, add a word of explanation and a nuance. The explanation is as follows: If the sociologist, like any scientist, asks himself about his scientific *production* and not only about its applications, the question will lead him to meet the citizen, not only in the city but also in himself. If the urgency challenges him personally, it is the limit between the "scientist" and the "politician," to use the words of Max Weber, which takes priority in himself. We shall come back to this. The nuance here is: In debates on the applications or the uses of his work, the scientist is not altogether a citizen like any other. He is the only one in fact able to assess in advance the *scientific* relevance of the questions which the general public asks itself. If, as I believe, a thing that has no scientific basis—for example the belief in race—consequently has no ethical relevance either, the scientist will see himself *collectively* invested with the dangerous power of deciding what is scientific and what is not. I say "collectively" because it is only on the strength of a debate within the scientific "community," or of a more or less wide and more or less tacit consensus within it, that one of its members can speak authoritatively on science in a public debate. It is the absence of such a common scientific opinion that has made the German historians' controversy about the extermination of the Jews so acute. Truth in the sciences is always provisional, and always to some extent influenced by the scale of an event (while waiting, of course, for a new minority and contested paradigm, as Thomas Kuhn has noted).

An ethical reflection on the social sciences therefore involves taking an unusual step. Since they cut their links with philosophy, they have developed to the precise extent that they have forgotten their presuppositions. (In doing this, they are only servilely imitating their seniors.) But when you think about it, there is no inevitability about this double movement of progress and forgetting. There is only a double temptation: that of knowledge for the sake of knowledge and knowledge for power. This is where the basic ethical question is located.

In view of the aforementioned, it has to be concluded that the research scientist does not have a monopoly on examining the morality of his research. If the sociologist and the anthropologist sometimes have more to say in the debate, it is through knowledge of the mysteries of their products; but this is only a *de facto* privilege, connected with the power arising from special training and information. It is not legitimacy that comes from a *de jure* exclusivity. Their only specific character, as we have just seen, lies in their power and their duty to say what would be a false debate.

Furthermore, it is necessary to emphasize the unusual nature of this step. Here I can only put forward my ethic of the social sciences, of which I have some experience. Departing from the *we* of scientific majesty, the affirmation in the first person singular shows not ostentatiousness but modesty. It is only me who is speaking, but I am wholly committed in what I say: such are the limits and the importance of this speech *which is not primarily scientific*. An unusual situation gives it its special character: It is not possible here to do without the word, because I myself am the subject.

I can analyze a morality (Puritan or Naturalist, Catholic or Greek) but an ethical *debate*, in my view, calls for the detour and hence the slowness and patience of singular affirmations. Even less can I lay down the law in matters of deontology. Who am I, alone facing my blank page, to offer a speech that only holds up because it is the product of a professional community? To carry out an ethical and deontological reflection, I would therefore emphasize the necessity *and* at the same time the insufficiency of the solution offered by using the first person. This is why I welcome and salute the initiative which brings us together today: It is the condition and the augury of this *debate* which can alone give legitimacy to the adoption, however provisional, of ethical and deontological conclusions for our social sciences.

MAN, OBJECT AND SUBJECT OF HIS KNOWLEDGE

Let us move now to the debate which appears to me central. What is mainly involved in our social sciences, in my opinion, is more an ethic of research itself than a questioning of the ways and means of mastering its applications. It is a specific and general question, both singular and urgent, which addresses the ethical question of the very existence of science.

Artificial intelligence develops, it is said, like a brain outside the skull or like an ovocyte outside the uterus. That is to say, the processes of exteriorization, of objectivization, take on new dimensions. Far from being a creation whose intrinsic norms guide us, the world increasingly becomes an objective manifestation of the human mind. So we are sent back to ourselves, *with an added sense of responsibility*. Man is no longer a spectator or guardian of the world: He is both the subject and the object of knowledge, of *his* knowledge. Will the social sciences, which are so familiar with this problem (at least a certain school of thought amongst them) be left behind the "hard" sciences in drawing conclusions from a transformation which does not exist for them? Man "would not recognize himself as an object without being a subject: the two words only make sense together . . . The more I proclaim myself an object, the more symmetrically my position as a subject arises, fortified by the remarkable performance of scientific knowledge."[7] Our ethical choices consequently become more cultural than ever: far from any natural model certainly, but also increasingly invited to make the jump between "micro" and "macro," particularly at a scientific level. It is a *public* morality in research that we need.

Here the adjective *cultural* has a certain ambiguity which needs to be removed. The ethic concerned is not "cultural" in the sense of being subject to the cultural relativity dear to a number of anthropologists. I have examined the limits to this cultural relativism and found that it is relative itself.

Let us repeat here that ethical activity presupposes a universalism that confronts the relativity of customs and practices. But the fields of *application* of these judgments of universality remain limited. Because scientific research, even if it is that of the relativity of cultures, rests on an assumption of *rational* universality, the ethic of research appears to me a privileged field of application for such judgments of ethical universality.

This remark applies both to the private ethic of the research scientist and to the public ethic of research. But while I wish to place greater emphasis on the latter, it seems weaker and more faltering than the former. There is no need here to recall the celebrated lecture given by Max Weber on the scientist's profession and vocation.[8] To strengthen public morality, it is not enough to draw a distinction between morality of the person and morality of the truth as we have done. This would be to place morality *in* research and morality *of* research in opposition to one another. The former, private morality, would be that of the scientist, of people involved in his research, and of their relationships with each other. As H. Becker says, it is a question here of "the point of view which the research scientist should adopt towards the subject of his research, the judgment which he should make about what is conventionally considered to be evil and the feelings which he has for a given category."[9] The latter would be the "simple" search for the truth, the "application" of this research being handed back to the politicians and their own morality—if they have one. So this would end up in the form of a new dichotomy between the morality of science and the morality of politics (including scientific politics), conceived as the "application" of the discoveries of another order. "Our question," Arthur Kriegel says, "is to know if scientific research raises a specific problem, i.e., if the discovery of a truth can be evil because of the perverse applications that may result from it."[10]

Talking about the public morality of research is a way to avoid presenting the problem in these terms. Nor does it mean considering that the application of research depends on it like the research itself. It is not a question of classifying the application under politics or science. The question, if one presents the problem in our terms, concerns the very *production* of science. Thus morality ceases to be the "cream on the cake of science" of which J. Testart speaks.[11] It is only finally a question of taking C. Bernard seriously. His *Introduction to the Study of Experimental*

Medicine shows the intertwined development of therapeutic research and experimental therapies and raises the question for us of transforming the "experimented" subject into an ethical subject.[12]

Talking about public ethics in the production of science also means understanding that you cannot directly infer any ethic from science any more than you can from politics. Nor can you directly deduce any kind of scientific or political orientation from an ethic. Reintroducing man as the subject, and at the same time as the object, of knowledge, offers the possibility of an ethic for a science of complexity, which certainly clarifies the choice of its finalities. But while a more complex science can clarify our ethical choices, the basis of an ethic of this complexity is elsewhere.

Finally, talking about the ethics *of* knowledge involves integrating the ethical approach into the knowledge approach—which E. Morin connects in passing to this "paradigm of complexity."[13] In "non-modern" societies, L. Dumont recalls, ideas and values are not separate—"the real relation between the thought and the act" is not yet destroyed by an "intellectualist or positivist analysis."[14] It is the nature of our modern and scientific culture to have thus burned the bridges between facts and values, to have constituted individuals, and to have limited morality to private life. However, since Kant, there have been many attempts to remedy this, particularly by the German Romantics.[15] Obviously there is no question of favoring a return to pre-modernity, nor of rejecting the science of Descartes or Galileo. It is a question, in a world marked with the seal of a new or third modernity, in which one wonders if it is necessary for science to take into account a new paradigm of complexity, to reconsider this classic disjunction in order to establish a new and specific link—belonging to the period and to its scientific developments—between morality and knowledge.

This new link to be established seems to me to be the reintegration of morality *in* knowledge, which goes together with that of the subject in its observation. This reintegration leads one directly and fundamentally to ask oneself about the powers in the name of which and on which this knowledge grows. A questioning of this kind of the *bases* of knowledge is in opposition, as we have just seen, to simple, traditional, and inoperative questioning regarding the *applications* of knowledge. It is external to that debate, about which popular opinion periodically oscillates between cynicism and idealism without ever laying the foundations for realistic processes and procedures.

Sometimes it is a question of respecting the exclusive responsibility of politicians. At other times, however, it is a question of constituting an independent scientific power: an enlightened despotism of the scientific community. But science and its technical applications always develop according to their own logic, imperturbable and finally uncontrollable by anyone. The example of the now old debates about energy and atomic weapons, initiated by J.R. Oppenheimer, finds its most up-to-date echo in the debates already mentioned on the subject of bio-medical research. And everything always continues as if nothing had happened . . .

The problem is really elsewhere: it concerns the powers on which the very processes and procedures of knowledge are founded. Which is not to say that this ethical questioning of the bases excludes the relative but certain autonomy of these processes and procedures of rationality in finality—to sound like Weber, or of calculating thought—to sound like Heidegger.

To think of the ethics of science as being a search for truth is to deny that science, too, is going through a crisis.[16] It is, however, no longer the "Solution Science" of the end of the last century, neither is it the "lighthouse" nor the "absolute." It has become the "Problem Science." For the last century the frameworks of a narrow rationality have buckled, in the course of what E. Morin calls "the adventures of rationality in the unknown and obscure lands of the real."[17] One of the important aspects of this transformation is in fact the change in the relationship between science and truth. "The greatest source of error resides in the idea of truth," E. Morin adds. Is it not a basic error to imagine that one can have *the* truth, even if it is scientific? We have learned to understand that truth in science is very relative. We know that K. Popper makes falsifiability the criterion for truth in scientific theories.[18] The truth in science, E. Morin concludes, resides "in the rules of the game of truth and error." While "hard" and "soft" sciences exist, it is not that the rigor of one group is superior to the rigor of the other, but that this game of error and truth "is rigorous in the hard sciences and not rigorous in the soft sciences."[19]

Poincaré's separation between "the indicative" and "the imperative" is questioned everywhere. Nobody, said the mathematician, can draw an imperative precept from knowledge which explains or describes, and therefore is written in the indicative. "This wall, separating the moralist or the lawyer from the scientist, has not moved since it was built. It is cracking this morning," as M. Serres noted.[20] For a long time, however, science has talked to us about unreal beings. Bio-medical research now talks to us about potential beings. Here we are in the conditional, which brings us back to the imperative. "The wall is coming down and we, scientists and philosophers, are meeting for the first time." For the potential being to become real, such requirements *are necessary*: "an imperative is arising and announcing a morality . . . The scientists are waking up moralists."

The ethic of knowledge is in fact invited: "To predict in the sciences, where time is reduced to a movement, leaves the world where you predict unchanged," M. Serres also said. "Predicting in the sciences, where time makes the very being of the object described and of the process in which the prediction takes place, does not leave the world unchanged."[21] Are not all the sciences of man concerned here? Is not the sociologist aware that to know is already to intervene, if only because a survey changes "the object" that it studies? "The ethic of knowledge is born and at once morality no longer depends on the applications of science, but accompanies it in each of its gestures . . . in its speculative conduct," the philosopher concludes. The biologist and the doctor become moralists when knowing means choosing amongst the world of possibles. The sociologist and the anthropologist become moralists when their speech becomes performative, when to know is to change the world.

If the research scientist does not want to be considered a sorcerer's apprentice or an irresponsible technician, he should stop being the "monomaniac mole" to which Einstein referred. "When full vigilance is at the service of a project," J. Testart said, "there is no longer room for questioning the project itself . . ."[22] The Chicago sociologists saw the problem clearly. H. Becker emphasizes that the main difficulty comes from the ambiguity in the notion of axiological neutrality, dear to Max Weber.[23] "Moral questions become more acute if we pass from the technical notion of ethical neutrality to the choice of problems and the ways of presenting them . . ."[24] Considering science as "independent of values," we are led to the distinction which Becker judges impossible to maintain in practice, between the sociologist as a scientist and the sociologist as a citizen.[25] As A. Edel has shown, it is above all difficult to clearly separate the establishment of facts and the construction of theories from ethical judgments.[26]

It is true that our discipline continually raises ethical questions and our research is continually oriented by our ethical interest. "We do not want our values to get in the way of an assessment of the validity of our statements regarding social life, but we cannot prevent them from influencing the choice of our subjects and hypotheses. At the same time, we cannot prevent our ethical judgments from being influenced by the deepening of the knowledge with which our scientific work confronts them."[27] It is in this double sense that science and ethics penetrate one another. One only has to think of G. Balandier's study of the colonial situation, or the one on the "nobility of state" of the "Grandes Ecoles" by P. Bourdieu to have clear illustrations of this relationship.

Should this co-mingling surprise or worry us? Why deny it? On the contrary, to accept it would mean to risk a return of the unconscious. This often manifests itself by camouflaging ethical choices under the cover of science. It is one of the manifestations of ambient scientism: You can sense the advantage to be gained "in the present period," as Becker says, "from claiming to set forth a scientific discovery rather than admitting that you are expressing a moral judgment."[28] But it is then that the mixture of genres should lead to a fear of this return of the unconscious.

Shortly after the Second World War, a meeting of scientists who were anxious not to forget the anti-Semitic persecutions of the Hitler regime adopted a proclamation which stated that, in the current state of scientific knowledge, nothing justified racial discrimination. Leading members of the Jewish community were upset by this. "Justifiably so, in my view," R. Caillois commented during his debate with C. Levi-Strauss. "They did not accept that their destiny was in any way dependent on the experts' opinion. They considered that it was wrong to persecute them, even though science, whose verdicts are unforeseeable, might one day appear to justify their elimination. This is a moral problem, and not at all a question of scientific truth or error."[29] If it is dangerous to connect the two, to provide an ethical position with the support of research, it is because by doing this one is admitting that the strength of an ethical judgment depends on the state of science, which can change.

I would therefore support the view of H. Becker when he writes: "I suggest to the left, whose opinions I share, that we should directly and openly attack injustice and oppression, rather than claim to deduce the judgment which condemns them from the basic principles of sociology, or claim to base it only on empirical results."[30]

QUESTIONS OF METHOD AND TECHNIQUE

Can one go further and establish a link between this research ethic and this epistemology of the subject, in what I have called elsewhere a science of the event and the unusual, with considerations of method or even of research technique?

I will base a hypothesis on this, naturally limiting myself to a few first reflections concerning sociology and anthropology.

In 1985, in Berkeley, the synthetic results of a vast survey of American values conducted under the direction of Robert N. Bellah appeared.[31] The appendix to the book is by no means the least interesting part: "Social science as public philosophy" is in fact a whole orientation of our disciplines put into words.

The American sociologists also give an explanation of their research methods and techniques. "The interview as we employed it was active, Socratic."[32] S. Tipton gives an example of an interview of this kind, covering the feeling of responsibility towards others. A. Swidler gives another, which covers the basis of moral judgments, especially on lying. Is not the research scientist led in this way to involve himself in his research, to show himself as a research worker without trying to hide himself totally behind his research? He will therefore try to make the people concerned react by presenting the ethical and scientific *a priori* of the survey and of his whole research project. Without, I would repeat, confusing the roles of researcher and citizen, but with the knowledge that it is the same individual who is both, and that he is asking someone else to be so bold as to take a step in which each belongs, although differently, to the reality studied. This is a Socratic attitude in fact, linked to techniques—for example, interview—which can be tilted towards maieutics.

But trying to achieve mutual understanding in its strongest sense in the course and as a result of an interview does not mean looking for a common point of view. It is a type of *debate* in which the sociologist too can be led to questioning his investigation—both it and himself.

Clearly not all subjects are as significant in this way as a study of national values. But do not our assumptions also involve the choice of subject? This means therefore that not all subjects of research are as interesting from this point of view.

It is clear that "active" and "Socratic" interviews of this kind, like all in-depth interviews, are not suitable for the same treatment and exploitation as more or less closed questionnaires, designed for statistical processing. The difficulty is of course in finding the techniques which correspond to the original intent of the project, and, in fact, many can be used successively—whether they are qualitative or quantitative—during the same survey.

It remains that a certain number of epistemological and ethical assumptions are present when using the techniques. In particular, these are assumptions having to do with the very nature of the social reality that is researched and therefore postulated. This as we know is the subject of an old and wide debate in our disciplines. It is still current: does not our interpretation of the nature of groups have important ethical implications?

The Americans say that they have only used the survey questionnaire in a secondary fashion, although it contributes useful data. Opinion polls based on representative samples, with their closed and fixed questions that fail to allow for any conversation or provide any opportunity for personalized *feedback*, give results which run the risk of appearing to be "natural" and intangible facts—even if you use successive series of questionnaires to identify temporary trends. But even if the questions are open, they do not allow for a dialogue between the interviewer and the interviewee. The authors add that this poll data is in fact the sum of the private and original opinions of thousands of different people.

"Active" interviews, on the other hand, offer the possibility of a "public conversation." When the data from them is well presented, it encourages specialists and readers—apart from those surveyed, to whom their survey will have been returned—to argue and join in a *debate*. Once again we find this eminently ethical dimension which appears to us so decisive for all the human sciences. Discussions like these stimulate something resembling a really *public* opinion, tested in the field of open discussion. Therefore, there is a paradox: Are not public opinion polls really private opinion polls?[33]

To say that research should be "public" in this sense is to explain, in terms of techniques and methods, the epistemological postulate of an interpretative sociology for which any significant action takes into account that of others in a *Lebenswelt* "for us all." This in turn supposes the necessary ethical transition from the private to the public, from the "micro" to the "macro."

To initiate a "public" dialogue and launch a "public" debate does not mean, for R. Bellah and his colleagues, capturing beliefs and practices like entomologists, without the authors of the research having made their point of view clear. It does not mean taking as an ideal a scientific version of the "hidden camera." It means the reverse: putting one's preconceptions and one's questions on the table. Explaining one's own assumptions in order to try to bring out those of the interviewees is totally different from imposing a "ready-made" survey in which boxes simply have to be filled in as if the interviewees were illiterate. Is not going from the implicit to the explicit a maieutic step for everyone?

This is why our sociologists look for their replies not only in language but also in the very life of the people surveyed. As a result, in their study there is a share of the participating observation which anthropologists know well. Because anthropologists are confronted more than other people by this need for a "public" dialogue and exchange in which they involve themselves—and their culture with them—it is generally impossible for them to resort to other techniques.

Not limiting oneself to interview situations or field surveys is simply acting in accordance with the wish to capture people in their true life in order to "relativize" the explicit character of the least directive interview. To resist putting all one's faith in technical specialization and performance is to go further, challenging the classic scenario: to isolate variables by abstraction and, on the model of the exact sciences, see their influence "other things being equal." In reality, variables can rarely be isolated, therefore the predictive value of such studies is not great.[34] The most interesting data can only be gathered by overall action within situations which are also made up of possibilities and limitations, aspirations and fears . . . Who does not see the epistemological limits of the action and the ethical risks of the situations?

It would certainly be worthwhile to pursue this difficult question concerning the presuppositions of methods and techniques. It leads us to questions that are absolutely basic and insufficiently explored. Amongst sociologists and anthropologists, what is the relation between ethical conviction (religious, moral) and scientific orientation (theoretical, methodological)? How is a subject for research chosen, if there is a choice, and how is the link made, if there is one, with research policies and institutional programs? Why do researchers go in for one type of sociology or one type of anthropology rather than another? And finally, back to Weber, does not the researcher come to ask himself about the purpose of his activity?[35]

FOR DISCUSSION

I am afraid that sociological and anthropological research is very behind in its ethical reflection in comparison with bio-medical research, psychoanalysis, and even history. Economic science is perhaps approaching it faster[36]—and not only as a result of the fashion for *business ethics*.[37] However, political science seems to me to be just as backward as anthropology and sociology, at least in the way it carries out surveys.

Is it therefore out of place or premature to dare situate oneself, *whether one is a specialist or not*, as an expert on the ethics of these disciplines? Are there not useful and perhaps necessary discussions which should be held between specialists? Should they be limited to specialists?

When speaking about an ethic of the social sciences, I have primarily evoked a scientific tradition that is comprehensive, interactionist, and interpretative. I have noted the links between ethics and epistemology. It would also be useful for discussions to take place between scientific traditions, if only to check whether or not they correspond to different schools of thought. Is it possible to conduct a discussion simultaneously on these two levels, between specialists and within traditions which are not only scientific? It should be possible to find or institute a place for confrontations of this kind in a journal, foundation, or scientific society, or perhaps a university or "pure" research organization.

I do not believe that it is necessary to begin with deontological discussions. Because deontology is the fruit of ethical discussion, it is the meeting point of their professional involvement. Our disciplines are really situated at the moment of a reflective transition which leads them from science to ethics and first of all to this first ethic of human rights. They are not so much at a transition from ethics to law on which a deontological discussion should more logically be based. Could one at least conduct these two types of debate at the same time? More generally, in relation to our disciplines, can one already conduct public debates?

I tend to think that the traditional separations between our disciplines and our specializations, which have their own logic, will not always stand up to epistemological and ethical confrontations. "From the 'micro' to the 'macro'" implies that it is a problem of our disciplines that is concerned and that is transversal in relation to these institutional cleavages. On these questions, is it therefore necessary to pursue separate discussions, for example between sociologists and between anthropologists? Besides, is our society sufficiently "tolerant and democratic" to seek a consensus of minimal requirements—and find it—between the ethical implications of our scientific differences?

ETHICAL QUESTIONS FOR ANTHROPOLOGY

At such a general level, and speaking personally, I can hardly not ask questions. However, if I take a particular discipline, the discussion becomes concrete and clear. I have claimed that the social sciences "have so far only reached human rights," which is nevertheless not negligible. Here anthropology is at the forefront.

Its situation relative to the legal implications of its ethical presuppositions is, however, paradoxical. In one sense, it is further away: Confronted by cultural differences, it challenges the very culture from which it comes. But in doing this, it uncovers the branch on which it is sitting: A universality in value underlies its analyses and takes it to its limits. It is this assumption which lays the foundation for an anthropology of human rights, by defining the limit to acceptable differences in the name of this universality which constitutes both the discipline and the humanity of man.

It is even more necessary to recall the implications of such a postulate, in the Europe of 1992, now that the difference is on our doorstep. The immigrants' situation, the statute of cultural and religious minorities, the trials for female circumcision, remind us every day of the need for this universality of human rights in order to create a citizenship pact between us all. The upheavals in Eastern Europe and the great European market of 1993 are only going to exacerbate the disquiet and demands of regional and national cultures queried by the European identity. At all levels "multi-cultural society" raises more and more acute questions, which demand the affirmation of ethical principles and their translation into rules of law to institute citizenships.

Always and everywhere, but more still in this context, racism threatens. The racist, as I have noted elsewhere, is a person who believes in race. Doubt must be cast on this concept, which only exists in the mind of the racist, whose imaginary conscience takes itself for a perceptive conscience. The countering of this false evidence comes by affirming the uni-

versality in value of the humanity of man, which is translated by a universality *in law* of real men. Fortunately there is steady progress with legislation in this respect.[38]

Anthropology has largely contributed to developing this problem beyond "free and equal" individuals, but the importance of the questions
raised, in the framework of a state ruled by law, by "the right to survival,
to land and to self-determination of minority ethnic groups"—in the
words of the president of the association *Survival International
France*[39]—has perhaps not yet been measured.

It is not enough to place yourself on the level of a "moral" requirement to state what goes without saying (but goes even better if it is repeated), as regards the "commitment . . . which links the ethnologist to
his field": "Who, working in distant fields, among minority ethnic
groups, has not witnessed numerous violations of their rights? The invasion of indigenous territories, the forced removal of populations, uncon-
trolled epidemics, deliberate decisions on the part of the state or religious
organizations to destroy traditional cultures, racism and exploitation, the
massive destruction of the environment, abuses of all kinds."[40] Clearly
these situations cannot escape "the professional observer." Should he
adopt "scientific neutrality" and take refuge behind "non-participating
observation" or the duty not to commit himself if he is a civil servant?
Can he not also, without abdicating his scientific requirements, and even
by using them for support, "play the part of a privileged witness"? But
what is the effectiveness of this moral position, our author asks himself. It
is a heavy responsibility for the ethnologist, he adds, speaking of the importance of the "anthropological testimony" and of the "amplification"
that an organization like *Survival International* can give him, "with its
know-how, its networks and its credibility."[41] Certainly scientific journals can echo these testimonies. C. Gros quotes the example of the *Journal of the Society of Americanists* which has created a section on the
question of the Amerindian people. "This backing by the scientific *establishment* is by no means negligible," he adds, emphasizing the usefulness
of also having a journal, *Ethnies*, whose sub-title ("Human rights and
indigenous people") makes its intentions clear, and which brings together
articles by research scientists and analyses by representatives of the ethnic
minorities themselves.[42]

I do not of course disagree about the bond which links the anthropologist to the people he studies, about his role as a privileged witness,
nor about his responsibility because of this.[43] The concept of "anthropological testimony" seems to me to be somewhat more ambiguous, and the
ambiguity increases in my opinion, not as regards the usefulness of having
solid scientific information in order to carry on a battle of this kind, but

as regards the role of explicit guarantor that anthropologists are expected to play. I also question the mixture of two approaches, militant and scientific, in the same journal.

I have incidentally considered this question particularly in relation to female circumcision. I first of all recalled that it was not necessary to go into the whole question of the "commitment" of the social sciences again, nor to reconsider the distinction between "scientist" and "politician." I then formulated an answer by talking of a two-sided limit. On the side of knowledge, relativism comes up against membership in a common humanity. Taking this into account, I added, straddles a wall. I climb over it, as a sociologist, but I come down the other side as a citizen responding to an emergency or distress. It is the same person who carries out the two movements in the name of the same values, but he carries out each one in order, at two different times. The ethical consideration of a common humanity enables me to analyze racism or exploitation, to realize what is involved in this analysis, and to make a critical judgment. But this leads me to the other side of the wall to respond to practical requirements, in the very name of my analysis and its ethical presuppositions. Quite simply I no longer act as an anthropologist, but as a citizen.

This is why I do not agree with C. Gros's conclusion. "Anthropology and its knowledge," he writes, "can no longer limit themselves to a scientific role. The interest of the general public on the one hand and that of the ethnic minorities on the other, combine to demand the dissemination of the knowledge acquired, which allows for a better knowledge of the other, his needs and his rights."[44] There is a confusion here. How could a science be legitimate if it is no longer located on the scientific terrain? Furthermore, how can the dissemination of scientific knowledge make it easier to better understand needs and, even more, rights? It is not enough to say that "knowledge is no longer anyone's monopoly"; that "the happy time of the tête-à-tête between western anthropologists and indigenous people is over"; that "the stage is gradually filling up with new actors: professionals in local anthropology, groups specialized in the defence of human rights, indigenist organizations, churches, local NGOs, etc."[45] I agree. But this does not, yet again, say what an anthropo*logy* would be which no longer confined itself to its "scientific" role: it is in fact the anthropo*logist* who must be reminded that he is *also* a citizen, and that the values of the latter are linked to those which motivate and inspire the work of the former. The situation is not unique to "minority ethnic groups." Nor is it new: the ethnologist met it in colonial times, with the difference that made his tasks more obviously legitimate and more surely risky: He was a citizen of the same country or of the same empire.

This reminder puts us back into the framework at which I wanted to arrive: that of the law-based state. By removing the ambiguities which I have emphasized and by presenting the question more rigorously, the position of the president of SI-France would continue to present the major problem of the "multi-cultural" society: How is it possible to guarantee the rights and be sure of the duties of people, cultures, and minority groups in a law-based state? Does this not presuppose individuals who are free and equal? Can one have co-existing different rules of consanguinity, marriage, education, and relations between the sexes, between generations, between employers and employees, etc.? How far is not too far? To affirm the right of ethnic minorities—apart from the fact that I do not like the word "ethnic"—seems to me to be an ambiguous begging of the question. The whole question is that of the concrete limits which should be fixed, by a legitimate jurisdiction, in precise times and places, between the right of individuals and that of the groups to which they belong or refer.[46]

ETHICAL QUESTIONS FOR SOCIOLOGY

A new paradox: Sociology is perhaps even less accustomed than anthropology to raising problems of law. As we have seen, sociology hardly ever raises problems which are, strictly speaking, ethical—although its activity is carried on in countries that were always, more or less, law-based states. Unless it can be said: *because* it is carried on in these states. As we know, the totalitarian countries have never liked sociologists; neither Stalin's USSR, nor Pinochet's Chile, putting it bluntly. Nevertheless, it is difficult to see why in democratic countries, sociology should spare itself ethical questioning and legal questions when other disciplines do not study them. It appears that this discipline has suffered from significant shortsightedness.

The need for ethical discussion mainly arises from progress in its mastery. It has to be accepted that, in this respect, sociology is not the most advanced of the social sciences. It would only be necessary to regret this poor practical effectiveness of our disciplines if areas for discussion were instituted leading in the long-term to considerations of law. However, such opportunities hardly exist.

The powers of sociology, when they exist, come primarily from the quantifications that it operates with the double risk of a reduction in interpretation and a temptation to manipulate in proportion to this reduction. This is to be seen for example in opinion polls during election periods, or in the use of opinion surveys or statistical processing for commercial purposes. A start has been made in recent years on regulating election polls in France. Magazines and consumer associations are succeeding in obtaining legal guarantees (by making the appropriate governmental department aware of the problem) or even financial compensation through the courts. But we are far from the real counter-weight sometimes exercised by such associations in the USA, and the manipulation of public opinion outside electoral periods rarely gives rise to serious debate.

LIMITS IN THE SOCIAL SCIENCES

The figure of Antigone reveals the basic ethical question to us: What limit should be instituted to the power of man over man? It also shows us that any transgression puts us into an emergency situation: Beyond this limit, no delay can be tolerated.

The ethic therefore defines frontiers that it formulates in prohibitions. It is in no way a question of restricting freedom to insure order. The limit is set as a barrier against what is irreparable: It guarantees the humanity of man, within relations which constitute it, in a world that is fit to live in. Beyond the frontier zone there is no discussion. The imperative becomes unconditional and the requirement immediate.

Revealing the ethical presuppositions of our scientific actions in this sense gives us the conditions for the feasibility of an operational science which is not a power of domination. To question the human sciences on the limit and urgency applying to them is to look for the areas and criteria of their operationality.

A lawyer admits: ". . . the rights of man are mainly a question of limits. Considered in terms of absolute protection, the rights of man sometimes contradict one another (equality and freedom, private life and health . . .). On the other hand, they become operational when they are interpreted in terms of limits, derogations, exceptions, and restrictions."[47]

The anthropologist, as an analyst of cultural relativity, comes up against a limit: that of unacceptable differences in the very name of the universality in constitutive value of his discipline and citizenship. I mean here the conviction of a closeness between people with different traditions that is more fundamental than their dissimilarities. This is why we can communicate and have the ambition to practice anthropology. This is also why there is a limit to the non-involvement of the research scientist in the "subjects-objects" of his research. Not that science "leads" him to commit himself. But when the analysis meets the universality of the other, my *alter ego*, I find myself involved in the name of this proximity, imperatively and without delay. Involved as a citizen of the home country of human rights, not as an anthropologist.

What would become of this value of universality if, in order not to give in to the temptation of barbarity, I recognized the right of others to be barbarians? The equality of cultures thus leads to aporia. To escape from this, it is necessary to go from criticism of superiority to superiority of criticism. Facing traditionalisms and fanaticisms, the anthropologist must state the superiority of analysis and self-criticism. What L. Kolakowski calls "the spirit of incompletion of Europe"[48] is a universalizable value, and should be so peacefully. The anthropologist cannot ignore the frontier where he becomes a citizen again, the moment at which, very urgently, he must refuse final solutions of land and blood.

A whole sociological tradition challenges the actor and his action. But these in their turn challenge another scientific tradition, as they do hyper-rationalist historians or hyper-relativist anthropologists. Quantification gives power to the sociologist. Power linked to forecasting and anticipation which the law of large numbers allows: storage of "sensitive" data, performative effect of political opinion surveys, commercial manipulations . . . But from the point of view of the subject, any death remains an accident and any meeting an event. The sociologist must therefore also apply a science of the unusual, which takes into account the "actor-subject," the sense of what he does, of what he thinks, of what he says or writes, of the things which happen to him.

The sociologist's limit is therefore that of the reduction of the singularities implied by the standardization of behavior and opinions; that of the arbitrary nature of categories constituted of variables; that of the problematical relationship between real behavior and opinions expressed for the survey.[49] This triple limit is however imposed by the quantification needed for forecasting. The sociologist's limit is also, complementarily, the hypothesis that, in the end, institutions—from the smallest group to the state, from social classes to societies—have only an appearance of objectivity. They are really only collections of foreseeable courses of action assignable to employees.[50] P. Ricoeur particularly emphasizes the second limit. As a result of their statistical regularity, certain social relations behave as if they were things, or a written text which escapes its author. To reify this probabilitarian character in a collective entity is to overstep this limit beyond which we can no longer return the text of the action to its authors or the meaning of their acts to the subjects.[51] The frontier is therefore that of this alienation which dispossesses us of our actions and causes them to have repercussions on us, like things.

If sociology is less conscious than other human sciences of the ethical stakes for which it is responsible, it is in my opinion because it has not sufficiently analyzed its limits, or has underestimated the urgency and importance of doing so. This is doubtless not because of a failure to analyze totalitarianism for example, but owing to not having made a connection between these analyses, their ethical importance, and their epistemological implications. Moreover, if you abandon an analysis in terms of actions identifiable by projects, intentions and the motives of agents who impute their acts to themselves, you hypostasize social relations in terms of collective identities. You raise power to heaven and you tremble before the state.[52] In short, you let yourself become fascinated by "the order of things." What is urgent is then the refusal of all destinies and protest against all the distortions of communication.

An ethical clarification like this does not imply opposing, in sociology, quantitative and qualitative methods, nor even explanation and understanding. Formulated in this way, the debate would be simplistic. Here again I would follow P. Ricoeur, when he prefers to talk of an "interpretative arc" which moves from naive comprehension to scientific comprehension, by means of explanation. He adds that in a process of this kind, explanation alone is truly systematic, but that comprehension, a non-systematic moment, includes explanation, as one analytically develops the other. The moment of comprehension is required by the fact that the analyst belongs to the world which he studies, just as the moment of explanation is implied by the need for an alienation that puts this relationship of belonging into the position of an object.[53]

IN CONCLUSION, URGENCY

Beyond the analysis that can be made for each individual science, what conclusion can be drawn, from a global analysis, that applies to each? I would say that in our "post-secular" society which functions in a religious way—but does not know it or denies it—we experience an uncompleted desacralization which leads to transfers of what is sacred. In this context, in which scientific research is an essential route to knowledge and access to considerable technological powers, the limit that we have crossed (without knowing it) is general submission, unreasoned as well as undiscussed, to the desire made sacred for knowledge in order to dominate. Babel appears to me to be the symbol for this *hubris* which the ancient Greeks feared above all else: an exaggeration sufficient to make the gods jealous, belonging to a civilization which refuses to submit its scientific initiative to the ethical question: to an interrogation on the nature of the power it develops and on which it is based. A scientific Babel where we ceaselessly vaunt the force of our ambitions and deplore the atomization of our relationships, without ever accepting the idea of linking the two. Is it not our demiurgic pretention which causes these distortions and breakdowns in communication that we continually complain about?

It is because our knowledge has crossed this invisible limit that it sometimes has a death-dealing character. We continue to be willing to submit "the application" of our scientific discoveries to the ethical question—without great success, however—but we consider it to be a crime against research to submit the research process itself to such a question. In reality we do quite the reverse. We submit the ethic to science and we name this substitute "ethic of knowledge." The name is no less deceitful than the procedure is perverse. In fact what we are naming is the determination to know for knowledge's sake, and to know at any price. Is this really *reasonable*? Are we not *subjected*, as E. Morin says? Remember the "logic of the slaughterhouse," which he makes the paradigm of this subjection. The subject always believes he is working for his own ends, without suspecting that he is working for the ends of an unknown master. The ram thinks he is commanding the flock, whereas in fact it obeys the dog, and the dog obeys the shepherd, and all three obey the logic of the slaughterhouse.[54] To what power are we subjected, when no one masters certain "advances" of science, of which one sometimes wonders whom it is working for?

What I wish to say is that destructive and manipulative potential is no longer limited to the forces of the political game or of social exploitation, external to research. It is now also being produced by the development of scientific knowledge. What would it mean to return within this limit that we should not have crossed? Speaking just of social sciences, I would say that it would mean taking into account, beyond cultural and social differences, a fundamental closeness between the researcher and the people he studies. When the requirements of this proximity become stronger than those of objectivity and difference, scientific work loses its relevance, and the duties of citizenship take over. Criticism and action will no doubt be carried out "in the name of" research because it is the same person, in the same world, who carries out his work as researcher and involves his responsibility as a citizen in the name of the same values. But a frontier has been crossed beyond which taking into account the requirements of proximity very often means hearing the imperative urgency of a call for fraternity.

NOTES AND REFERENCES

1. Cf. *La demande d'éthique*, special issue of *Cahiers Internationaux de Sociologie* (Paris, under the direction of Georges Balandier and Gabriel Gosselin), vol. LXXXVIII, 1990.
2. Cf. Gosselin, Gabriel 1970, *Développement et traditions dans les sociétés rurales africaines*, Geneva, I.L.O.
3. Cf. Raulin, Anne 1987, *Femme en cause: Mutilations sexuelles des fillettes africaines en France aujourd'hui*, Paris, F.E.N.

4. Cf. Gosselin, Gabriel 1979, *Changer le progrès*, Paris, Seuil, chapters 2,3,4,5.
5. Balandier, Georges 1985, *Le détour*, Paris, Fayard.
6. C. Geertz is one of the leading figures of this new approach. Cf. in particular *The Interpretation of Cultures*, New York, Basic Books 1973.
7. Quéré, France 1988, "L'homme, objet et sujet de sa connaissance," in: INSERM (ed.) 1988, *Ethique médicale et droits de l'Homme*, Arles, Actes-Sud and INSERM, 197 and 199.
8. Weber, Max 1959 [1919], "Le métier de savant," in: Weber, Max, *Le savant et le politique*, Paris, UGE, 53–98.
9. Becker, Howard S. 1985, *Outsiders*, Paris, Métailié, 194.
10. Kriegel, Arthur 1989, "Science et conscience en médecine," in: *Revue de Métaphysique et de Morale* 3, 424.
11. Testart, Jacques 1986, *L'oeuf transparent*, Paris, Champs Flammarion, 165.
12. The concept is used by Fagot-Largeault, Anne 1985, *L'homme bioéthique*, Paris, Maloine, 102.
13. Cf. Morin, Edgar 1982, *Science avec conscience*, Paris, Fayard, and the four volumes of Morin, Edgar 1977–1991, *La Méthode*, Paris, Seuil.
14. Dumont, Louis 1983, *Essais sur l'individualisme*, Paris, Seuil, 221.
15. Cf. Dumont 1983, 233 f.
16. Crisis in science connected with a more general crisis of reason: cf. Gosselin, Gabriel 1987, "Le complexe de la raison close," in: *Revue Européenne des Sciences Sociales* XXV, 75, 105–132.
17. Morin 1982, 263 f. (where this "new scientific course" is summarized).
18. At least, I would add, in the context of "normal" science, within what T. Kuhn calls the same paradigm.
19. Morin 1982, 241 f., 245 f., and 22.
20. Serres, Michel 1986, Preface to Testart 1986, 15.
21. Serres 1986, 17.
22. Testart 1986, 92.
23. Weber, Max 1965 [1917], "Essai sur le sens de la "Neutralité axiologique" dans les sciences sociologiques et économiques," in: Weber, Max 1965a, *Essais sur la théorie des la science*, Paris, Plon, 399–477.
24. Becker 1985, 223 f.
25. I shall show further on that this distinction is nevertheless important, that sociology has everything to gain in specifying this, and that sociology *can* and *should* maintain it.
26. Edel, Abraham 1955, *Ethical Judgement: The Use of Science in Ethics*, New York, The Free Press of Glencoe.
27. Becker 1985, 225.
28. Becker 1985, 227.
29. Caillois, R. 1954, "Illusions à rebours," *La Nouvelle Revue Française* 24, 1018.
30. Becker 1985, 227 f.
31. Bellah, Robert N./Madsen, Richard/Sullivan, William M./Swidler, Arlene/Tipton, Steven M. 1980, *Habits of the Heart. Individualism and Commitment in American Life*, New York, Harper and Row.

32. Bellah/Madsen e.a. 1980, 304 (and more generally 304–307).
33. The Americans rediscover in this way—and paradoxically—the original sense of the adjective "public," at the end of the eighteenth century. P. Champagne correctly remarks that at that time "public" was less the reverse of "private" than of "secret," or "hidden," in the context of a parliamentary (public) objection to royal absolutism. "Public" opinion is therefore not popular opinion or the opinion of everyone, but that—which is "made public"—of an enlightened social élite (Champagne, Patrick 1990, *Faire l'opinion*, Paris, Minuit, 45 f.).
34. Cf. Levy Strauss, Claude/Eribon, Didier 1988, *De près et de loin*, Paris, O. Jacob, 146: "With us (in the human sciences) there are too many variables, the observer is inextricably involved with the subject he observes and the intellectual means at his disposal, having the same level of complexity as the phenomena studied, can never transcend them."
35. Cf. for example Wacquant, Loïc J.D. 1990, "Parole(s) de sociologues," in: *Cahiers internationaux de sociologie* LXXXIX, 421–424 (on the subject of the book by Berger, Bennett M. (ed.) 1990, *Authors of Their Own Lives, Intellectual Autobiographies by Twenty American Sociologists*, Berkeley, University of California Press).
36. Cf. in particular Puel, Hugues 1989, *L'économie au défi de l'éthique*, Paris, Cerf.
37. A "socio-economist" movement, which condemns the imperialism of economic reasoning in intellectual life and the teaching of the business schools, has grown rapidly in recent times under the aegis of the sociologist A. Etzioni (cf. his book: *The Moral Dimension. Toward a New Economy*, New York, The Free Press 1989).
38. A summary comparing European anti-racist laws will be found in *Le Monde*, 5 Dec. 1990.
39. Gros, Christophe 1989, "Diffusion du savoir anthropologique et action humanitaire," in: *Bulletin de l'Association Française des Anthropologues* 37–38, 97–107.
40. Gros 1989, 99.
41. Gros 1989, 102.
42. Gros 1989, 104.
43. Far in advance of the French debates, a code of ethics was adopted by the XVIth general assembly of the Brazilian Society of Anthropology, in Campinas (Sao Paulo) on 30 March 1988. It covers the rights of researchers and the people they study, and the responsibilities of anthropologists. A number of meetings were held on these questions in 1990, 1991, and 1992. Notably a seminar at UNICAMP (S.P.) on 5 and 6 April 1990. A recent visit which I paid to the University of Manaus (Amazon) in November 1991 showed me the importance of these concerns when they involve the Amerindians.
44. Gros 1989, 107.
45. Gros 1989, 106.
46. This is exactly why our Brazilian colleagues defend the Indian reserves, arguing that purely and simply inserting the Indian people and their cultures into Brazilian society would ruin them.

47. Delmas-Marty, Mireille 1989, "L'homme des droits de l'homme n'est pas celui du biologiste," in: *Esprit*, 11 Nov. 1989, 117.
48. Kolakowski, Leszek 1979, "Le village introuvable," in: Kolakowski, Leszek 1986, *Le village introuvable*, Brussels, Ed. Complexe, 7–21.
49. Blumer, Herbert 1986, *Symbolic Interactionism: Perspective and Method*, Berkeley, University of California Press (1969).
50. Weber, Max 1971 [1922], *Economie et Société*, Paris, Plon, 24–26.
51. Cf. Ricoeur, Paul 1986, *Du texte à l'action: Essais d'herméneutique II*, Paris, Seuil, 298 f.
52. Ricoeur 1986, 300 ff.
53. Ricoeur 1986, 167 and 181 f.
54. Morin 1982, 70.

Elements of Ethics
for the Researcher

REGINALD FRASER AMONOO

INTRODUCTION

"Freedom and Responsibility of the Humanities and Social Sciences" is a challenging and opportune theme for discussion in our time. We all appreciate the aspiration to freedom of thought for intellectuals, but at the same time we would like to see more of the sense of responsibility to society, to the state, and to our fellow men. Intellectual freedom and social responsibility may appear to be concerns in opposite directions, but ideally, and ultimately, they should be seen as complementary. Gabriel Gosselin's paper on "The Ethical Paths of Knowledge in the Social Sciences," well researched and well argued, focuses our attention on a relatively new aspect: the moral responsibility of the social scientist, in particular the anthropologist and the sociologist, in the *course* of their work or production as researchers, as opposed to the ethics of the *use* of the results of their research endeavors. Discussion on ethics for scientists has largely dwelt upon the moral responsibilities of those who make use of scientific discoveries, e.g., the scientists who used nuclear fission to produce the atom and hydrogen bombs, or those who apply biotechnology to genetic engineering. Social sciences have dealt with racism, which results in a lack of appreciation for the practices of ethnic groups and minorities, the extreme consequences of which can be found in Nazi war crimes such as the use of gas chambers directed against Jews. Some Western historians have dismissed African history based on oral traditions as unworthy of serious academic research. Such pronouncements coming from respected senior academics, who may be biased and narrow-minded, can influence decision makers in certain countries, even though there may not be an admission of prejudice. It is the responsibility of the entire society in any given country, responding, one hopes, to warnings expressed by the scientific community, to avoid the misuse of research findings or the exploitation of the perceived gap between the developed and the developing worlds.

THE ETHICS OF INTELLECTUAL PROFESSIONS

But we are going to focus on ethics for scientists themselves—on the internal discipline—rather than on the morality of the users. Each profession and discipline has evolved mechanisms for maintaining standards of competence in performance and a code of conduct to safeguard the standing in society. These measures are intended to protect the interests of the corporate body, the user agencies, and the general public. Doctors, lawyers, engineers, and the like, have their strict codes of ethics the infringement of which attracts disciplinary measures including, in the last resort, expulsion from the ranks. There are also guidelines and rules governing the conduct of teachers in their behavior towards pupils during the course of their teaching and examining duties. It is generally agreed that a certain kind of conduct is to be expected of a worthy scientist while he is striving for the prestige of making far-reaching discoveries. The goal is to be recognized by the intellectual community—the academies, universities, and research organizations—thus winning distinctions, the most prestigious of which is the Nobel prize. It would appear that there is an expectation that scientific behavior, traditionally, should have a great measure of the following ingredients:

1. *The search for Truth, or more modestly, the search for truth, exactitude in facts, relationships, and theories.* Admittedly in our post-Nietzschean era of skepticism, this might appear to be a futile enterprise. Edgard Morin, cited by G. Gosselin, has postulated that science-solution has now become science-problem.[1] While I concede that science has not solved all the mysteries of life, and that there are even difficulties as to notions of knowing, I am aware that there is less uncertainty about certain natural phenomena than was previously the case, and consequently metaphysics is losing ground to physics. Thus the quest for provisionally accurate knowledge is still valid.

2. *Recourse to rigorous methodology with the foundation of rational logic.* This will enable other researchers to follow the reasoning, to verify the way in which the results were achieved, to rectify problems, and to improve upon the knowledge. Here again I concede that there has been a questioning of the faculties of reasoning and of rational logic.[2] Other additional modes of knowing, such as "intuition"[3] and

"examined emotions"[4] are coming back into favor in certain quarters.[5] Whatever the means adopted to achieve results, there should be sufficient transparency to enable others to participate in the intellectual process. Otherwise we would have regressed to the dark days of dogma and unverifiable "truths" handed down.

3. *A quest to achieve objectivity, as far as it is practicable, and therefore to apply honesty and sincerity in presenting results of intellectual inquiry.* Objectivity may appear to be illusory, conditioned as it is by history and culture, just as reasoning is. Certain topics and themes readily stir up emotions, with the likelihood of subjectivity coloring our judgment, e.g., immigration from less prestigious areas to developed countries or the death penalty as a deterrent. But objectivity, however problematic, must remain a goal.

4. *Exhaustive and thorough investigation and research before making pronouncements and proclaiming results.* In the conduct of research, where appropriate, inter-disciplinary approaches will be encouraged. It would be an advantage to have the ability to engage in teamwork, cooperating with other researchers in the same and in cognate fields. The general aim should be to present an all-around picture of man.

5. *Finally, an extension role in society.* Scientists have an obligation to give the best advice to society, furnishing the decision makers with all the alternatives and relevant data.

These five ingredients, in various guises and formulations, constitute a basis for discussion which could lead to a general code of ethics for scientists and researchers in all areas of intellectual endeavor. Furthermore, each discipline would have to examine the particular ethical issues facing its practitioners.

PERSONAL EXPERIENCE OF
CONFLICTUAL SITUATIONS

G. Gosselin's paper explores the difficulties facing anthropologists and sociologists, beginning with his own personal experience of research in conflictual and delicate situations. As a social anthropologist researching in Africa, on consultancies for the United Nations High Commission for Refugees and the International Labour Organization, he was able to comment on the inadequacies of development plans in some African countries. But as a French citizen, he had problems with the legitimacy of the scientific approach when confronted with the Algerian situation during the late 1950s. It would appear that nationalism, not necessarily his own, could be at variance with attempts at objectivity. It would have been interesting to know if, in the event, G. Gosselin took a stand on the Algerian problem and, if so, what were the consequences. For example, an inquiry into the recourse to counter-revolutionary methods used by the French would have engendered political controversy; the line separating research and political activity could be blurred. At the present moment any social scientist working in places like South Africa, Lebanon, or Yugoslavia is likely to face similar dilemmas. In Europe, research into immigration, racism, and ethnic practices of immigrant groups living in Europe, e.g., the circumcision of young African girls, can stir up a hornet's nest. Respect for others' cultural traditions may be at loggerheads with concern for civilized behavior as one knows it. Should researching be interventionist, with the acquiescence of the researched group? G. Gosselin's reflections on his experiences led him to propose as a working framework "comprehensive sociology" and "interactionist anthropology," which he later synthesized as "interpretative socio-anthropology," underlining the involvement and sympathy of the social scientist, going beyond detached objectivity. My own personal view is that perhaps there needs to be another word added to this last formula, for example "active," to underscore the interventionist and interactive nature of the new kind of researcher G. Gosselin has in mind, as indeed expressed later on in his paper.

METHODS AND TECHNIQUES OF THE MORALLY-CONSCIOUS SOCIAL STUDIES RESEARCHER

The emphasis being on the desirability of moral consciousness in the very process of creation, the methods and techniques adopted in research should reflect the new awareness. G. Gosselin rightly maintains that the scientist has to meet the citizen in society, and more importantly *be* a citizen in himself. It is easy to see that the citizen in the researcher would influence the choice of research topics, with a bias towards applied research rather than pure research. The double temptation of "knowledge for the sake of knowledge" and "knowledge for power" can be overcome by the sense of civic responsibility of the academic. Obviously the researcher-citizen having the advantage of prior and better knowledge of the scientific processes leading to the results, will give the best possible advice to the community, as well as to his peers and other research workers.[6] The acquisition of knowledge should ideally be used to better the world. The UNESCO Symposium in Beijing in 1989 on education to prepare for the twenty-first century highlighted the imperative that education should make for caring citizens. Montaigne had long ago asserted that the fruit of education should be to make us better,[7] but dwelling on this advisory aspect could sidetrack us into reflecting on the ethics of the use of research findings.

In utilizing the various research techniques, G. Gosselin recommends essentially the human touch: researchers being encouraged to remember to consider the human being as the subject and object of sociological and anthropological research. Hence the importance given to "active and Socratic interviews," looking for responses not only in the language but in the life of the researched individuals, and to the exhaustive survey of countless individual views in order to arrive at general trends. While these humanizing methods have been practiced by many social scientists, the new emphasis on the human aspect is refreshingly welcome at a time when research methods in the social sciences are being drawn towards the methods of the exact sciences, with much recourse to statistics and the use of computers and other gadgets.[8] The humane dimension has been stressed several times during the symposium, especially in M. Schaffner's contribution on "Research and its Objects: The Case for the Ethics of Dialogue."[9] There is always room for the researcher to ask himself what is the aim of his activity. Research for advancement in one's career? Research in order to solve a vital problem for the good of the community? Commissioned research?

MAN, THE OBJECT AND SUBJECT OF KNOWLEDGE ABOUT MAN

This section of G. Gosselin's paper incorporates many of his main ideas and suggestions, which are developed elsewhere. Some of these ideas are familiar, but there is a new emphasis, and there are nuances worthy of comment.

It is interesting to note that G. Gosselin makes a plea for "a public morality in research." Individual ideas on the ethics of production, which is a relatively new concept, should be discussed in debates in order to arrive at generally acceptable broad principles. The discussions should start with specialists in specific disciplines before involving others across the disciplines, to avoid wooliness. While ideally ethics should be internalized, some stimulus and encouragement towards an awareness of the need for ethics could be derived from confronting experiences in different fields.

Concern about ethics for social scientists raises the issue of the criteria for appreciating the behavior of societies other than one's own. Are there universal values? "Ethical activity presupposes a universalism which confronts the relativity of customs and practices," says G. Gosselin. The debate as to whether it is valid to postulate universal values is open. I am inclined to think that the noticeable differences between men: race, color, social set-up, etc., often detract from the appreciation of human qualities which are more fundamental and general. The belief in the basic humanity of all mankind, from whatever standpoint (e.g., as part of creation, cf. another justification of the humane approach in Peter Saladin's paper, "Responsibility Towards Creation"), can motivate a reassessment of the status of the object of study. "The transformation of the 'experimented' subject into an ethical subject," as G. Gosselin puts it.

Where there are complexes of superiority and, conversely, of inferiority, these could diminish or disappear altogether with experience and reflection on the part of social scientists. It is necessary to remind ourselves, especially the inhabitants of the so-called Third World countries which are technologically and, supposedly, intellectually outdistanced by the Western world, that we all belong to the same species of mankind, the *Homo sapiens*, and that education and the environment, in the broadest sense of the word, can encourage us to achieve the levels of proficiency and competence of the West, in all spheres. Therefore if the present imbalance between North and South is creating problems of achieving recognition for some Third World intellectuals, they should not forget that, taking a long-term view of things, ancient civilizations, some non-Western, have made a greater impact on mankind than the present Western one.[10] In the long run, no civilization is permanent, and just as the great civilizations of the past have had their moments of glory and decline, the present-day civilizations may disappear one day and be replaced by others.[11] For the present, social scientists from the Third World could perform the useful tasks of setting the records straight in, say, African history and explaining the rationale behind certain African customs. This would be useful because scholarship of high caliber and the spirit of tolerance manifested by Africans should make a greater impact on the international academic community than the aggressive defense of African cultural values and contributions to universal knowledge.

Turning now to another aspect of ethical behavior in this section of G. Gosselin's paper, I could not agree more with the assertion that the finality of the study of man by man must surely be the improvement of man. To seek to know—to investigate—is therefore to choose and to influence. "The sociologist and the anthropologist become moralists when their speech becomes performative, when to know is to change the world," says G. Gosselin. This is a philosophic ideal cherished by many. But there is the question of how to decide upon what is best for the community. Should, for instance, a team of European sociologists researching polygamy in a West African traditional set-up work towards bringing about a change to monogamy through a comparative study? It would be better to leave the choice to the traditional set-up. Within a homogeneous society, seeking a consensus, as argued above,[12] seems to be the only safe way to proceed, thus involving a broad spectrum of the scientific community and society at large.

Allowing scientific thinking to contribute to the ethics of scientists appears to be a reasonable course. But G. Gosselin sounds a note of caution, using the example of the proclamation of scientists to the effect that there is no scientific basis justifying the persecution of Jews. "If it is dangerous to connect the two (scientific inquiry and behavior towards Jews) it is because by doing this one is admitting that the strength of an ethical judgment can depend on the state of science, which changes." My reaction is that, if science is not to be used as one of the bases of ethics, then we are left with the traditional sources, religion and civic codes. It seems to me that there is need to examine more exhaustively the ways in which scientific thinking, in the broadest sense, can contribute to the ethics of scientists in their work, and also to ethics for the generality of citizens, in our scientific and technological age.

AWARENESS OF ETHICAL PROBLEMS

In the section devoted to specific questions addressed to anthropologists and to sociologists, G. Gosselin raises the issue of ethical awareness and he decides in favor of anthropologists. I am not sure that there will be a great measure of agreement over this judgment, especially as sociology is such a wide area with so many different practitioners exhibiting various degrees of ethical awareness. In any case there is some overlap between the two disciplines. For example, immigration, minority groups, and racism can be researched by anthropologists and sociologists alike, from their respective viewpoints. They all have to face the dilemma of the conflicting demands of scientific scholarship, on the one hand, and of concerned citizenship and sympathetic fraternity, on the other hand. Individuals may have to make provisional *ad hoc* decisions in certain exceptional situations, e.g., researching under a military dictatorship, where one's sense of fair play may be at variance with the prudence required for survival. On humanitarian grounds alone, we all wish there was greater courage in fighting against injustice. For the scientist, while functioning as a scientist, is a human being with a conscience, and a citizen.

Anthropologists, working on peoples and cultures far removed from their own, are probably more likely to reexamine their own cultures through contact with other cultures and, one hopes, to end up by discovering *universals* in cultures. Thus they themselves would gain as human beings by helping the researched groups. However, sociologists studying organized societies should also be able to benefit from confronting cultures other than their own. Even within one's own society, there are differences in outlook which should provide material for contrasting analyses.

This brings me to one of the strong points about sociology advocated in G. Gosselin's paper: the superiority of analysis, or criticism—especially of self-criticism—as one of the criteria for judging cultures. I do subscribe to the importance of using rational methods, despite the reservations made earlier in this paper, but I wonder whether we are not in danger of applying a set of Western criteria too generally. While we are on the subject of criteria for judging cultures, should we not emphasize humaneness especially in respect to the weaker and less privileged, in a spirit of reciprocity, and with aspirations to ideals beyond material existence?

CONCLUSION

I have no doubt that scientists will continue to be tempted by the pitfalls of "knowledge for knowledge" and "knowledge for power." The incomprehensions produced by the scientific Tower of Babel will also continue to exasperate members of the intellectual community. The suggestions put forward by G. Gosselin and others concerning ethics for scientists in their work as researchers would certainly contribute to further humanizing research, for the benefit of the researcher and the researched group. It is a new and a worthwhile ideal to establish and to maintain "a fundamental closeness between the researcher and the people he studies," a fraternal sympathy between the researcher and the researched group, especially if there is an apparent disparity between them. There is of course the possibility of the loss of scientific "objectivity," with too much sympathy being brought into play, resulting in conflicting and ambivalent pulls. However, since intellectual rigor should characterize all research enterprises, for the reasons stated in my remarks on the ethics of intellectual professions, it is as well for us to emphasize the humane aspects of research. It will be up to each area of specialization to work out, from the general suggestions made, how to set about arriving at a suitable code of ethics.

Ethics for the humanities and social sciences is a relatively new field and G. Gosselin has done well to adopt a cautious approach, presenting his suggestions tentatively and requesting a debate on the various aspects in the hope of arriving at a consensus. G. Gosselin deserves our congratulations for stimulating us all to reflect on the possibilities of further humanizing research in our specialized fields of endeavor in the humanities and social sciences.

NOTES

1. G. Gosselin cites Morin, E. 1982, *Science avec conscience,* Paris, Fayard, and, 1977–1991, *La méthode,* Paris, Le Seuil.
2. I found the paper by Thomas J. Bole, III, and H. Tristram Engelhardt, Jr. "Ethical Self-Reflection in the Humanities and Social Sciences: Facing up to the Postmodernist Challenge" very thought-provoking. I am with them in their conclusions, making a rational use of reasoning to arrive at tentative solutions.
3. Intuition was considerably rehabilitated by Henri Bergson in his writings beginning with his thesis, 1888, *Essai sur les données immédiates de la conscience.* Cf. a modern edition, e.g., Paris, Presses Universitaires de France, 1980.
4. The term was used by Margaret Somerville in her paper, "Transdisciplinarity..." I was reminded of Wordsworth's "emotions recollected in tranquillity" as a source of poetry, which is sometimes knowledge.
5. European rationalism peaked with the Encyclopédistes of the Age of Enlightenment. But then Jean-Jacques Rousseau gave a powerful impetus to instinctiveness and to nature. Ideally rationalism and other forms of knowing should complement each other. Cf. Margaret Somerville's paper cited above.
6. See point 5 of "The ethics of intellectual professions."
7. Montaigne, *Essais,* "Le guain de nostre estude, c'est en estre devenu meilleur et plus sage." Livre I, ch. XXVI, "De L'institution des Enfants," Livre premier, deuxième tome, Paris, Société Les Belles Lettres, 1960, 17.
8. By all means let us use the newest instruments of precision for our research, but we must use them judiciously, making them serve the ultimate human purpose. Cf. Hanspeter Kriesi's paper on "Enticement by Methods."
9. See especially the section on "Oral History" of M. Schaffner's paper.
10. Cf. Mahdi Elmandjra's paper on "Fusion of Science and Culture: Key to the 21st Century."
11. A well-known text by Paul Valéry comes to mind. "Nous autres, civilisations, nous savons maintenant que nous sommes mortelles ..." *La crise de l'esprit,* 1919, in *Variété, Oeuvres,* tome I, Paris, Gallimard, Bibliothèque de la Pléiade, 1962, 988.
12. See point 4 under "The ethics of intellectual professions," and par. 2 of the section "Man, the object and subject of knowledge about man." Cf. the conclusions of the paper by T. Bole and H. Engelhardt.

Research and Its Objects:
The Case for an Ethics of Dialogue

MARTIN SCHAFFNER

The central element in any basic consideration of the sciences is the question of the relationship between researchers and the objects of their scientific curiosity. Deliberations on the normative aspects of this relationship in particular hit a sensitive nerve of scientific activity. For even the generally-accepted approach of contrasting, and thus objectifying, researcher and scientific object disguises the fact that problems are at play here which touch the very core of scientific understanding and thus the habitus of the researcher.[1] The way in which this relationship is perceived, reflected upon, and structured has far-reaching consequences for the research process, for academic activity, and for our further dealings with knowledge. This is a sore point in respect to the problems of methodology and research not merely in the natural sciences but also in the humanities and social sciences.

A well-known anecdote, told by Socrates in his "Theaetetus" dialogue, vividly expresses the difficulties of researchers in the face of the objects of their research:

> "The story is that he was doing astronomy and looking upwards, when he fell into a pit; and a Thracian servant, a girl of some wit and humor, made fun of him, because, as she said, he was eager to know the contents of heaven, but did not notice what was in front of him, under his feet."[2]

This anecdote, which has accompanied the history of philosophy from its beginnings, is generally used to point out the contrast between philosophy and the real world. But it can be understood just as well as an image for what can happen to the scientist who is so fixated upon the objects of his knowledge that he loses his distance to them and thus fails to reconcile scientific interest and the real world.

In this article, I am dealing with this relationship by looking for basic principles by means of which the concrete structure of the relationship existing between researchers and the objects of their interest can be assessed and examined. I have no intention, however, of attempting to formulate and canonize abstract principles that in any way lay claim to general validity. The purpose of my search lies in the self-examination of the sciences. This represents the true aim of basic ethical reflection—a *movement* to thought; an encouragement of contemplation—which repeatedly draws our eyes towards our feet and thus prevents our falling into holes like the mathematician from Asia Minor. I draw here on experience from the field of historical study, in which I am active, but would suggest that similar problems occur equally in other areas of the humanities and social sciences.

Within the framework of a project investigating the lives of mentally-ill people at the end of the nineteenth century, I requested permission some time ago to use the archives of a psychiatric clinic. The government authorities responsible gave me their permission subject to certain conditions (principally that I should keep all personal data anonymous). The director of the clinic, however, with the support of his legal advisor, maintained that he alone was authorized to make decisions concerning access to the archives. He granted me only limited access to individual patient records and refused me admittance to the archives themselves, with the result that the scope of my project had to be severely reduced. Of interest here are the reasons that led him and his staff to refuse a historian access to the medical records of patients who had been inmates of the clinic a century earlier. They maintained that, firstly, the files were the property of the clinic and thus subject solely to their authority; secondly, only qualified psychiatrists had the necessary knowledge to evaluate the material; thirdly, they claimed that the files must remain closed on principle so that the therapeutic work of today, the relationship of trust between doctor and patient, should not be impaired. Without attempting to examine the legal problems inherent in this argumentation or to investigate the question of whose interests the clinic was in fact trying to protect, the following does strike me as interesting: (1.) Rights are posited to scientific objects; (2.) The holders of these rights are assigned unlimited freedom to dispose of these objects; (3.) On a higher level, general interests (the therapeutic relationship between doctor and patient) are introduced into the argument which are ethically justified on their part. Also of interest, however, is what questions are excluded from the argumentation of the clinic administration: Do people (as scientific objects) have no rights on their part even after their deaths? and: By what superior standards can such rights be justified?

Questions of this nature occupied Swiss courts during the 1980s.[3] In a major trial in 1989, seventy-five historians had to answer charges of defamation and libel. At the center of this and other similar cases was the protection of the individual as an object of contemporary research. At the time, Swiss courts tightened up their practice by extensively defining individual rights and reinforcing the posthumous protection of the individual. In the controversial relationship between freedom of research and personal rights, jurisprudence tipped the balance in favor of data protection and personal rights. It tightened up the researcher's obligation to due diligence and laid down conditions which disproportionately narrowed the scope of contemporary research. When seventy-five academic and media personalities protested against this tendency in an open declaration, they found themselves unexpectedly in court facing a charge of violation of privacy. It struck them as questionable that when the public benefit of freedom of research was weighed against that of personal rights, freedom of research came off second best. This "attack by judicial-legalistic logic on autonomous scientific discussion" must, in their opinion, inevitably weaken and block contemporary research.[4] At a time when the study of history in Switzerland was increasingly distancing itself from the authority of the state and conventional historical myths, this practice of the courts could not but appear repressive.

The cases that were heard by Swiss courts at that time were concerned with a different problem from the dispute surrounding the opening of clinic records. The clinic dispute focused on the right to case material, the object of scientific research, and the restrictive delineation of the group of persons who could lay claim to these rights, while the rights of the object were not further discussed (with implicit appeal to internal professional regulations). In the cases before the Swiss courts, on the other hand, rights asserted on the part of the objects were so extensive as to represent a serious hindrance to scientific activity.

The fact that the relationship between researchers and the objects in which they are interested contains dimensions that are not covered by the various legal categories is most clearly shown where scholars obtain their information in the course of their research through direct contact with people. In the framework of historical study, this concerns the area of oral history, where historians obtain their data by the direct questioning of their contemporaries. In this respect, they act basically no differently from members of other disciplines in the humanities or social sciences who carry out interviews. There are a variety of experiments from the field of oral history which attempt to formulate and implement an ethical code of behavior. Although legal principles play a certain role here, the real problems occur at another level. They concern the relationships of the persons questioned in the oral history interview and the interpretation of this interview by those involved. The oral history discussion cannot count on a clear framework; the rules to which it is subject are not clear. It concerns neither a therapeutic discussion nor the questioning of experts. These uncertainties surrounding the setting intensify the imbalance between interviewers and interviewees even further to the disadvantage of the latter. For this reason, questions such as: How is it possible to avoid the parties to an interview falling victim to manipulative questioning strategies (even if these are unconscious) so that they divulge information they wish to keep to themselves? How is it possible to avoid interviewees being steered by the direction of the questioning into saying things that contradict their convictions? The ethical guidelines mentioned aim to provide a firm basis for the oral history interview by informing the interviewees fully as to research objectives and the structure of the project. Similar questions are raised by the processing of the material obtained in oral history interviews. These concern, for instance, respecting the content of the statements made, that is to say dealing scrupulously with the testimony given by the witnesses. Here, however, it is less a question of specific problems of oral history than of the principles that should govern the evaluation of historical sources. The assumption on which the ethical guidelines are based is oriented towards the idea of oral history research as a cooperative, communicative process in which the interviewees become the researchers' partners; the hierarchical differences between subject and object in the research are removed.

My examples from the field of practical historical research show how complex the relationships between researchers and research objects are. At the *legal* level, it is a question, on the one hand, of the right to scientific access to the object of the research in the name of scientific freedom, and, on the other hand, of protecting the objects of scientific research from just such access in the name of personal rights. As the resulting tension is in principle insoluble, it is essential to weigh up arguments carefully when seeking solutions for concrete projects in specific social situations: use of psychiatric case material yes, but not unrestricted use; protection of the privacy of the living and recently deceased yes, but not unlimited protection. Deciding the extent of these restrictions should neither be subject solely to a ruling that pleads the inner autonomy of the sciences, nor solely to a standardization which bases its authority on a catalogue of fundamental rights. The precise, situation-oriented formulation of appropriate rules of procedure and behavior should first be oriented to the current legal norms and should be implemented within the framework of the institutions responsible for ruling on the conflicts of interests arising here; it is embedded in a legal-ethical discourse. But by pleading freedom of research, the researchers involved bring a dimension other than the legal into play. For freedom of research cannot be conceived in isolation from certain scientific ideals and prevailing research practice. These comprise—to maintain the image—the weight that is added to the scales when the benefits are weighed up. It is precisely the example of oral history that demonstrates that the relationships between research subject and object of inquiry represent a central element in scientific understanding. For this reason, it is necessary to enter the field of scientific discourse and to examine this dichotomy in greater detail.

The historian can approach the question of what is meant by the opposition of "subject" and "object" when speaking of the research process in no other way than with the means at his disposal in his own discipline. For however valuable philosophical or linguistic analysis might be, the inescapable task of the historian is to insist that habits of thought and speech are historically conditioned. In the face of the structuralist or structural-functional temptations to which many of my professional colleagues fall prey, I consider it by no means superfluous to draw attention to this banal but essential task. Even the contrasting relationship of research subject and research object cannot simply be taken for granted as an immutable construct. Instead it originates from specific circumstances and concrete conditions. On my way into the past, which is not a detour since it makes the crux of the problem visible, I would like to touch on three points. I am not aiming, therefore, at sketching an overview of the history of scientific understanding. Historical survey never features unbroken reconstruction among its objectives. On the contrary, its real purpose lies in making a rigorous selection from a conceivable continuum of events, occurrences, and developments whose criteria and results are only to be measured in terms of how far they provide necessary clarifications for the present.

We often use the expression "empirical reality" to describe the objects of research, the object matter of the sciences. Through its Greek roots, this term calls to mind the idea of "experience" and thus leads us into a dimension that is not contained in the talk of "object." "Experience" means a process in which a researcher and an object enter a relationship to each other, a process in which the researcher acquires "reality" and thus constitutes knowledge. Empirical reality should not therefore be equated with "reality proper," instead it represents a reconstruction that reflects the sense of what appears to be given. The reason for this lies in the structure of consciousness itself: "Consciousness is always intentional. It always intends or is directed towards objects."

This quotation is from one of the basic texts of phenomenological sociology, the work by Berger and Luckmann on the social construction of reality.[5] My aim is to clearly present the historicity of our idea of empirical reality or object matter. Anyone who appeals so consistently to sense as a constitutive element of all cognition and action as Berger and Luckmann (and A. Schütz before them) argues in favor of a rigorously social and thus historical view of the subject-object relationship. To quote Berger/Luckmann again: "I experience the reality of the everyday world as a system of reality. The reality of the everyday world already appears objectified, i.e. constituted by means of an organization of the objects that had already been declared objects long before I appeared on the scene."[6]

The idea of what is accepted as "real" or "empirical" is thus linked to social factors and is subject to historical change. This is not only true of the reality of the everyday world mentioned in the quotation, but also—and very much so—of the reality, empirical reality, with whose research science is concerned. For the specific forms of institutionalization which science exhibits (constitution and administration of secure stocks of knowledge, development and differentiation of a methodological canon, the emergence of a scientific community) separates it from the everyday world and makes it more visibly subject to historical change than this. A historical survey thus shows what at various times was taken to be empirical reality, as scientific object matter. This is also true for the natural sciences, in whose history a variety of different concepts of reality held sway at different times. It is sufficient to recall here the empirical understanding of Aristotelian and Copernican science in order to demonstrate this historical variability. In modern natural sciences, a certain idea of empirical reality found acceptance during the emergence of their paradigmatic structure.[7] It is worthwhile recalling the constitutive features of these ideas of reality since they have also influenced the humanities and social sciences. During the second half of the eighteenth century scientific rationality began to assert itself outside mathematical physics, in which it had scored its triumphs. Society and politics were declared object matter that was subject to the same logic with which the inquiry into inanimate nature had been advanced.

No one embodies the endeavor to spread scientific calculation into the realms of the economy and politics better than the mathematician and secretary of the Parisian Académie des Sciences, Pierre Condorcet, who, in his "Tableau des progrès de l'esprit humain" of 1794, placed mathematical-physical and socio-political science on the same level.[8] He was the most outstanding among an entire group of scholars, knowledgeable and enthusiastic disciples of mathematics and physics who, as political arithmeticians in absolutist France, attempted to modernize the study of political economy and sociology. Carrying mathematical-physical models and processes over into the economic, political, and social spheres implied an understanding of reality that was modeled on the empirical reality of natural science. This was intended to be subject-independent, substantialist, and asocial; a structure that could be registered by the use of objectifiable, that is to say measurable, features; a causality that could be explained as the function of individually ascertainable factors. The search for causalities, which became the goal of all research strategies, was served by the experiment by means of which empirical reality was modified and manipulated.

In his illuminating investigation "Die Einübung des Tatsachenblicks," Wolfgang Bonss describes how "this scientific model was taken over" by the social sciences and interprets the "way in which factual reality asserted itself as paradigmatic change."[9] In fact, a corresponding empirical and methodological understanding can be found both in the social investigations of English commissions of inquiry during the 1830s, with their elaborately polished questionnaires, and in the voluminous works of social statisticians, such as the Belgian Quetelet who, with his "Physique sociale," attempted to justify a social science based on statistics. In any case the disciplines categorized as the "humanities," "liberal arts," "Geisteswissenschaften," and "lettres" continued to plead epistemological independence and successfully prevented the monopolizing of scientific understanding by the natural sciences.

It is indicative that their independence was at times curtailed in polemic disputes on the lack of real object matter with their being seen as "not empirical."[10] In the social sciences, too, alongside the scientific paradigm that has marked its development from the first half of the nineteenth century to today, that other tradition of thought remained alive which was adopted and developed further by G.H. Mead, A. Schütz and P.L. Berger/T. Luckmann. The social realities that constituted these sciences as empirical reality come into being in communicative processes, are conveyed symbolically, and in this sense represent a construct.

The search for a starting point for a careful investigation of the questions formulated in the problem outline leads via scientific-historical survey to the dichotomy of subject and object. The turning point of the ethical considerations with which we are concerned here lies in this structure and the order that gives it reason, or to put it more precisely: in the ideas that we have concerning this relationship and in the language of the symbols by means of which we communicate within the scientific community (and beyond its confines). The contrast of researchers and their objects goes back to a model from the physical sciences and establishes a firm hierarchy: the researchers—who give social legitimacy to their re-

search on the basis of their academic competence and general interests—
are superordinate to empirical reality, to the objects of the research.

Traces of this scientific attitude are to be found in practice in all
branches of the humanities.[11] A well-known example is the case of L.
Humphrey's investigations into the sexual practices of homosexuals in
the U.S.[12] Humphrey utilized methods of concealed investigation that
were based on deceiving the men whose behavior he was investigating. In
the controversy surrounding his procedures, he defended himself by citing his results, which he argued were in the higher interests of the objects
of the investigation since they weakened stereotypes. But even a historian
concerned with people from an age long past in a village in the fourteenth
century is not immune to the danger of peering through a distorting lens
that falsifies the image he makes for himself of the peasants in his village.
E. LeRoyLadurie, who used the protocols of the Inquisition as a direct
route to peasant realities, failed to reflect the situation of the interrogation in which the information he evaluated had been obtained.[13] In a similar fashion, the anthropologist Evans-Pritchard failed to show the
political context in which he worked when engaged in fieldwork with the
Nuer: an Englishman under the protection of colonial rule.[14] In a certain
way, both LeRoyLadurie and Evans-Pritchard reproduced in their works
on peasants in a Southern French village and in the valley of the Upper
Nile an authority which they had borrowed from the rulers in the societies they were investigating. They illustrate in a particularly drastic way
the imbalance between researchers and the people in whom they are interested within the framework of a scientific practice that still orients itself
to thought patterns from the seventeenth century.

It is hard to imagine a more rigorous criticism of discursive practices
in the humanities than that voiced by Michel Foucault, particularly in
"Les mots et les choses."[15] His investigation of discursive systems whose
constitutive element he saw in the dichotomy of subject and object is
aimed at the consistent deconstruction of the subject and conveys,
through this, far-reaching impulses for the process of decentralization of
knowledge and cognition, which in the humanities was inspired primarily
by linguistics. Can the criticism of the subject by Foucault and others be
useful for ethical reflection on the relationship of researchers to the objects of their interests?

If we discard the view that contrasts researchers as subjects with their
research material as objects—that emphasizes the division between the
two and defines the described hierarchy between them—there emerge
other possible ways of understanding the research process. The most important element in an alternative understanding of research in the humanities and social sciences consists in the idea of reciprocity between the

parties involved in the cognitive process. By "involved" I mean here not only those persons directly involved and still alive today, but also people to whom we have access only via textual records or other artifacts. They become "involved" through our interest in them; this makes them participants in the research process. I understand reciprocity in this sense as a "dialogical relationship." "Dialogue" in this connection should be understood metaphorically. The image contains the idea of two sides that face each other on equal terms.[16] In addition, the metaphor conveys the idea of a basic openness. In a dialogue, the result of the discussion is not predetermined from the outset, it is far more a matter of mutual concern to the participants, the result of which is not necessarily predictable in advance. This is the premise under which a dialogue exists.

Moreover, the "dialogue" is subject to certain socials norms and rules; this means neither everyday conversation nor theatrical production. Which rules then apply to the "scientific dialogue" I have postulated? When looking for answers, we should avoid the risk of being tugged into the maelstrom of the discourse that Foucault has subjected to such critical investigation. At this point, I do not wish to devise any rules of this kind, instead I would like to limit myself to the formulation of criteria which could be used to examine such rules. These include the principle, clothed in the formula of equality, whose consequence for practical research lies in the fundamental renunciation of manipulative strategies of investigation. At the level of text production, this includes the requirement not to fit observations into a coherent context at any price, i.e., not eliminating or compensating for contradictions in the empirical evidence at all costs.

A second basic principle for assessing the rules for this "dialogue"—that is, for procedures in the humanities and social sciences—I see in the recognition that the points of view held by researchers are fundamentally open to change. When a scientific investigation presupposes the dialogical understanding for which I here put the case, it must not merely recognize that its starting point can be revised, but—on the contrary—it must accept this as the actual "raison d'etre" of its work. I use the term "position" consciously rather than "hypothesis," whose critical examination has long been postulated in Popper's logic of research. "Position" means more and includes the questioning and the cognitive interest that supports it.

The dialogue metaphor includes ideas towards which procedures in the humanities and social sciences can be oriented. While in the traditional scientific model, the researcher's activity is contrasted with the passivity of the object of his research, dialogue postulates a relationship that can be described metaphorically as interaction or communication between the two. "Metaphorically" because in practical research in the humanities and social sciences the researcher and the object under investigation often do not confront each other directly, since these disciplines generally deal with textual sources. Dialogues in the literal sense do not occur. Between those "involved" there is a principal imbalance, reciprocity is excluded, consensus is not the goal. The space measured out in Habermas's ethics of discourse is missing.[17] For this reason, it is necessary at least to touch on what "dialogue" can mean in practical relation to texts. For this purpose, I would like to return to the beginning of my deliberations and again look at the psychiatric case with which I started, this time in order to reflect upon the questions that arise and their possible answers by means of a concrete example from a project of my own.

At the center of my research project is the life story of a man born in 1856, a hairdresser who on account of his mental disturbance was institutionalized on several occasions. His story is unusual because it has survived in the material of informative records. Not only is his case extensively documented in files from the judicial administration and the hospital, he also wrote about his illness himself and described his systemized delusions in a text that still exists in manuscript form. What does it mean to speak of "holding a dialogue" with this man? And in what way should this proceed? "Entering into a dialogue" with him first requires the acceptance of a premise which *a priori* concedes sense to the statements made by the patient, i.e., which circumvents categories of justice and psychiatry through which the case was at the time constituted. Anyone reading the contemporary text material, in particular the writings of the man himself, with this attitude accepts that the sentences put down on paper at the time by the sick man contain messages to his environment; that it is possible to decipher his statements and their meaning; that this can only occur as attribution, as an approximation, without aiming to produce logical coherence in the confusion of writing at any price. Secondly, a reading oriented towards these principles requires a carefully thought-out research methodology, e.g., reflected reading strategies (for example, such that are directed towards syntactical and grammatical patterns and divergences from these). If we read the writings of the sick man by deciphering the messages contained in them and thus circumventing the categories of psychiatry, a life story appears that points beyond its own horizons and which brings social realities into view that were missed by other contemporaries and not treated in their discourses.

Thus the researcher's starting point shifts: new insights and problems come into his horizon. Here an important element of the research process becomes visible as dialogue: third-person description becomes self-examination. The gap between science and everyday life which caused the Thracian maid to shake her head is for once bridged.

NOTES

1. On the concept of *habitus* cf. Bourdieu 1980, 90–92.
2. Plato 1973, 174a. The translation is from John McDowell, Plato, *Theaetetus* (Oxford 1973), 50–51.
3. Cf. regarding the following: Tanner 1991.
4. Tanner 1991, 253.
5. Berger/Luckmann 1966, 20.
6. Berger/Luckmann 1966, 24.
7. Kuhn [2]1970, 23–34.
8. Lüthy 1973, 16–19.
9. Bonss 1982, 48, 77.
10. Bonss 1982, 41.
11. Elias 1987, 24, 31 ff.
12. Beauchamp/Faden/Wallace/Walters 1982, 11–14.
13. Rosaldo 1986, 77–87.
14. Rosaldo 1986, 77–87.
15. Foucault 1966. Cf. also Deleuze 1986 and Dreyfus/Rabinow 1987.
16. Crapanzano 1990.
17. Ferrara 1990.

Translated by Robert Bannister, Basel.

REFERENCES

Beauchamp, Tom L./Faden, Ruth R./Wallace, R. Jay/Walters, LeRoy (eds.) 1982, *Ethical Issues in Social Science Research*, Baltimore-London, The Johns Hopkins University Press.

Berger, Peter L./Luckmann, Thomas 1966, *The Social Construction of Reality: A Treatise in the Sociology of Knowledge*, New York, Doubleday.

Bonss, Wolfgang 1982, *Die Einübung des Tatsachenblicks: Zur Struktur und Veränderung empirischer Sozialforschung*. Frankfurt/M., Suhrkamp.

Bourdieu, Pierre 1980, *Le sens pratique*, Paris, Editions de Minuit.

Cavarero, Adriana 1992, *Platon zum Trotz: Weibliche Gestalten der antiken Philosophie*, Berlin, Rotbuch.

Clifford, James/Marcus, George E. (eds.) 1986, *Writing Culture: The Poetics and Politics of Ethnography*, Berkeley, University of California Press.

Crapanzano, Vincent 1990, "On Dialogue," in: Maranhao 1990, 269–291.

Deleuze, Gilles 1986, *Foucault*, Paris, Minuit.

Dreyfus, Hubert L./Rabinow, P. 1987, *Michel Foucault: Jenseits von Strukturalismus und Heumaneutik*, Frankfurt/M., Suhrkamp.

Elias, Norbert 1987, *Engagement und Distanzierung: Arbeiten zur Wissenssoziologie I*, Frankfurt/M., Suhrkamp.

Ferrara, Alessandro 1990, "A Critique of Habermas' Diskursethik," in: Maranhao 1990, 303–337.

Foucault, Michel 1966, *Les mots et les choses*, Paris, Gallimard.

Holzhey, Helmut/Jauch, Ursula P./Würgler, Hans (eds.) 1991, *Forschungsfreiheit*.

Ein ethisches und politisches Problem der modernen Wissenschaft, Zürich, Verlag der Fachvereine.

Kuhn, Thomas S. ²1970, *The Structure of Scientific Revolutions*, Chicago, University of Chicago Press.

Lüthy, Herbert 1973, *Der entgleiste Fortschritt*, Zürich, Arche.

Maranhao, Tullio (ed.) 1990, *The Interpretation of Dialogue*, Chicago, University of Chicago Press.

Plato 1973, *Theaetetus* (John McDowell, ed.), Oxford, Clarendon Press.

Rosaldo, Renato 1986, "From the Door of His Tent: The Fieldworker and the Inquisitor," in: Clifford/Marcus 1986, 77–87.

Tanner, Jakob 1991, "Datenschutz als Schutz historischer Mythen? Die Geschichtswissenschaft im Spannungsfeld von Persönlichkeitsrechten und Forschungsfreiheit," in: Holzhey/Jauch/Würgler 1991, 251–268.

On the Need for Humane Dialogue: From Authoritarian Monologue to Dialogue
A Comment from the South

GRACIELA ARROYO PICHARDO

Professor Schaffner considers research work in the social sciences as a dialogue between two parties, rather than a monologue of the researcher about the research object, be it persons, phenomena, or processes. According to him this type of relationship requires not only certain ethics, which are the fulfillment of rules or requirements dictated by the research work itself, but also respect due to the other party, namely the research "object," and, in the case of people, the acknowledgment of their rights. I fully agree yet should like to complement Professor Schaffner's enlightening and important reflections.

DIALOGUE IN THE SOCIAL SCIENCES

In the social sciences, dialogue between the researcher and the object is a type of conversation. Here questions are posed by the researcher, but they can also be asked by the informant, or information can be retrieved from records or files. For this information to be useful, it must be grounded within the time and place where it was gathered, and it must be acknowledged that the researcher's personality and background influence not only the results, but also the data itself.

Thus the dialogue between the researcher and informant, as a tool or means for scientific activity, poses, together with ethical issues, epistemological and philosophical problems. The construction or reconstruction of knowledge requires attention to meaning, conditions of truth, degree of objectivity, and the researcher's scientific attitude in general.

The ethical requirements are undoubtedly a contribution to research work in the social and human sciences. However, a brief bibliographical search shows that there are few authors, methodologists, or epistemologists who are concerned with this point. Recommendations of most specialists in the field have to do with scientific attitude and methods, rather than with ethical questions.[1]

The process that leads to the construction of knowledge is, according to Jean Piaget, an expression of the relationship between the subject and the object when the former develops a cognitive activity regarding the latter.[2] Then the need to determine other boundaries appears between ethics and epistemology, between epistemology and methodology, between methodology and logic, and between logic and philosophy. Piaget partially addresses this problem when he states that methodology has no precise boundaries nor organic unity,[3] but the problem is not solved. On the contrary, within Piaget's reasoning, it is more difficult to understand a research problem, since epistemology deals with the nature of relationships between the object and the subject. In such a relationship, he says, there are other knowledge structures involved, such as language and logic, and certain psychological and biological conditions.[4] Thus, boundaries of ethics in a research dialogue where, besides the issues mentioned above, surrounding social conditions are involved, cannot have an exclusively normative character.

In the fields of sociology and history, the social conditions of research are never the same. This makes similar problems seen by different people yield different conclusions. This conflict is evident, for example, in the study of history common to two or more countries; different view points on demographic problems such as the need for family planning; border conflicts as seen from the two different sides of the border; etc. Regarding history Karl Mannheim points out that the study of the past is always based on the present: a present which is also subject to different social conditions that influence the researcher. These conditions change individuals' ideas on social problems.[5] This has considerable implications for claims to objectivity and validity in social and historical research.

This situation becomes more complex with the realization that social reality constitutes the subject as well as the condition of social knowledge. As Sergio Bagú says: social reality and knowledge are two poles of the same process.[6]

SOCIAL SCIENCES AND NON-EUROPEAN SOCIETIES

Another paradox which has dramatically marked the path and the problems of social knowledge is the fact that social sciences originated in Europe. Analytical methodologies and categories appropriate for Western Europe have been applied unsuccessfully to the non-European world.[7]

Immanuel Wallerstein is even more radical when he states that certain social sciences such as Economics, Political Science, and Sociology which examine traditional levels of social activity (i.e. the market, political institutions, society, and culture) were inspired by the European reality of the nineteenth century and particularly for the use of the nation-state.[8] Knowledge furnished by European social science does not take into account the historical and social processes and conditions of other realities. Nor does the social knowledge generated in the Europe of the nineteenth century continue to correspond to European and world conditions at the end of the twentieth century.

From the beginning, social sciences were in the service of power. Economics served industrialization, finance, and the development of capitalism; sociology the needs of management and government bodies; political science the study of the mechanisms and dynamics of politics; and anthropology and ethnology served imperialism.[9]

Currently, Social Sciences are on hold, due to the following reasons:

- The boundaries which had previously defined different disciplines have become vague, while the different disciplines have at the same time become more complex, creating a need for new areas of study and, correspondingly, a new theoretical and methodological basis.
- Institutions and specialists entrenched in their antiquated theories and methodologies are hostile to new ways of thinking, and are opposed to the creation of social knowledge based on new foundations and "new" study objects.
- The impact of mankind on the ecosystem demands a reevaluation of the relationship between society and nature.
- The transformation of economic and political structures in Central and Eastern Europe requires a revamping of the prognostic theories in social science, which failed abysmally to explain such changes and their impact.
- There is no global perspective that enables us to understand the dynamics of the world system as a whole and that of its different parts and processes, including individuals with their rights and duties.
- In a new field of social research, the subject-object relationship becomes at the same time single- as well as multi-dimensional. The dia-

logue has to become a conversation. "New" social research teams are
required to tackle such a varied, complex, and versatile research task.

- The growth of information fostered by the techno-electronic revolution makes it difficult to introduce ethical principles in social sciences.
- This information revolution also increases the cognitive complexity
  of the object of study.
- Social sciences are in danger of becoming new tools of manipulation,
  which alter and endanger the dialogue.

As new paradigms appear and a new science develops, the social reality of our time is more naked than ever before. Violence, conflict, poverty,
illness, ignorance, fanaticism, crime, and racism multiply in the midst of
indifference and a sense of "no future"—the dark side of rationality.

After two centuries of social science, it is necessary to examine the
fulfillment of its objectives. As to solving the problems of mankind, its
success has been minimal. According to Robert Cohen[10] this goes hand in
hand with the failure of education as a humanist solution to social problems, and except for a few cases, scientific and technologic elites have not
been able to transcend their social origins and have failed to identify the
elements controlling ideology within the sciences.[11]

It must be recognized that the opposing currents within the social
sciences support solutions in the political arena according to their own
interests. For example, within Latin American sociology the debate on the
need to build concepts and categories to describe and explain the characteristics of "late and dependent" industrialization processes of Latin
American countries is of utmost importance. The difference in circumstances and historical processes of the region have made the categories
formerly developed to explain the social development in Eastern Europe
inappropriate. However, for a long period of time the "ideological,
sociocentric conception of dominant societies"[12] was taken as a model for
Latin America as well as for Eastern Europe, just as the development and
underdevelopment categories were considered valid before the acceptance of the globalization theory.

Historical and cultural differences, as well as unforeseen changes
such as the ones currently taking place in Eastern Europe, manifest the
inadequacy of such so-called universal categories as development,
progress, modernization, and democracy. Thus, general concepts and
theories are inadequate to define concrete societies. The object under
study does not correspond to theory, the word does not reflect the fact,
and the dialogue becomes a monologue. Is then social science "neutral"?
No, because in its cognitive structures, criteria that represent certain interests are included. Social sciences study the structures and processes

that in the history of mankind have produced differences and antagonisms. This has been analyzed from different perspectives. Rationalism and materialism have traditionally defined the theoretical content of social sciences. Neither the idea of the "end of ideologies" nor the mediation of a single thought have been able to disintegrate this duality.

Before recent global changes, economic determinism created a new cultural determinism. However, problems cannot be solved as long as the traditional model of social sciences continues to consider only aspects of a cognitive disintegrated reality.

The current world is interconnected by hundreds of information routes that enable the inhabitants of the antipodes to experience what is happening on either end of the planet and be capable of receiving information from anywhere in the world at the speed of light. Social philosophers of our time cling to the inherited habits of almost two centuries of social sciences that now, paradoxically, seem to reinforce their dominion.

Peruvian writer César Vallejo (1882–1938) was convinced that the scientific rationalism of the Western world did not enable him to transmit in his pain the image of a far away reality, historically prosecuted, badly understood, and unjustly exploited.[13] He decided to translate his philosophical and legal reflections into poetry. Since his experience of that paradoxical situation and his way of trying to overcome it might serve as a useful piece of instruction—or admonition—in view of an all-too-hasty application of methodological universals in social sciences, I wish to conclude my comment by citing one of his poems:

"Oración para el camino

Ni sé para quién es esta armagura!
Oh, sol llévala tú que estás muriendo,
y cuelga, como un Cristo ensangrentado,
mi bohemio dolor sobre su pecho.
       El valle es de oro amargo;
       y el viaje es triste, es largo.
Oyes? regaña una guitarra. Calla!
Es tu raza, la pobre viejecita
que el saber que eres huesped y que te odian,
se hinca la faz con una roncha lila.
       El valle es de oro amargo,
       y el trago es largo... largo...

Azulea el camino; ladra el rio...
baja esa frente sudorosa y fria,

fiera y deforme. Cáe el pomo roto
de una espada humanicida!
Y en el mómico valle de oro santo,
la braza de sudor se apaga en llanto!

Queda un olor de tiempo abonado de versos,
para brotes de mármoles consagrados que hereden la aurifera canción
de la alondra que se pudre en mi corazón!"[14]

NOTES AND REFERENCES

1. Young, Pauline 1960, *Metodos cientificos de investigacion social*, México, Instituto de Investigaciones Sociales, UNAM, 143 a 1488 y Bunge, Mario 1989, *Treatise on Basic Philosophy*, U.S.A. D. Reidel Publishing Company, 255.
2. Piaget, Jean 1970, *Naturaleza y metodos de la epistemologia*, Buenos Aires, Ed. Proteo, 15.
3. Piaget 1970, 17 y 19.
4. Piaget 1970, 17 y 19.
5. Schaff, Adam 1994, *Historia y verdad*, Argentina, Ed. Planeta' Agostini, 165 a 167.
6. Bagú, Sergio 1970, *Tiempo, realidad social y conocimento*, México, Siglo XXI, 11.
7. Bagú 1970, 11 a 16.
8. Wallerstein, Immanuel 1988, "¿Hay que impensar las ciencias sociales del siglo XIX?," in: *Revista internacional de ciencias sociales*, No. 118. Paris, UNESCO, 551 a 554.
9. Bagú 1970, 16 a 20.
10. Cohen, Robert S. 1982, "La ciencia y la tecnología en una perspectiva global," in: *Revista internacional de ciencias sociales*, No. 91. Paris, UNESCO, 72.
11. Cohen 1982, 73.
12. De Riz, Liliana 1979, "Algunos problemas teórico metodológicos en el análisis sociologico y político de América Latina," in: *Ideologia y ciencias sociales* (Colectivo), México, UNAM, 80.
13. Canabal-Torres, Evelyn 1933, "La Tradición Filosófica Occidental en César Vallejo," in: *Revista Topodrilo* No. 27, Paradigmas del fin del Milenio, México, UAM Iztapalapa, 83 a 87.
14. Vallejo, César 1990, *Los heraldos negros*, Buenos Aires, Ed. Losada, 53–54. Note: There is an English version in: Vallejo, César 1990, *The Black Heraldics*, Latinoamerican Literary Review Press.

RESPONSIBLE CHOICE AND USE OF METHODS

Enticement by Methods

HANSPETER KRIESI

INTRODUCTION

The question to be discussed in this paper is what the use of quantitative methods does to the practice of social science. Put bluntly, the question is whether quantitative methods are an easy way to incompetence, and, if so, what should be done about it. Discussing this question allows me to reflect on my own practice as a social science researcher who frequently uses quantitative methodology. I shall do so with the guidance of other, more experienced social scientists who have previously reflected on their own research practices. Let me announce my point of view right from the start: my position in this matter is a pragmatic one, which tries to steer a line in the middle of the road. It is the position of a practitioner of empirical political science. While agreeing with the idea that there are many ways in which enticement by methods can contribute to incompetence by technical oversophistication, I would like to suggest that there is also the opposite problem of a lack of methodological sophistication which stems from an aversion to methods. Moreover, I believe that there is an additional trap to avoid, that of overconscientiousness which always lurks around the corner in discussions of methodological issues. As Galtung (1970, 1) has written in the preface to his introduction to *Theory and Methods in Social Research* many years ago, there are in fact two types of oversophistication with respect to the application of quantitative methods in the social sciences: one is of a technical type, which applies a quantitative statistical apparatus simply because it exists, independently of the question whether it makes any sense to apply these techniques. The other concerns what he calls the "conscientious philosophical scrutiny of the foundations of social research." However laudable such efforts may be, according to Galtung, they may easily lead "to sterile debates where the plain fact that quite a lot of contemporary sociology simply *works* (italics in the original) is lost in efforts to apply philosophical categories developed by people who often are unacquainted with contemporary sociology and have little or nothing constructive to offer." The position that I will try to defend is that we need these methods, and that, if applied properly, they are indispensable tools for progress in the social sciences.

All I shall have to say concerns quantitative methods, but I think the quantitative aspect is not essential to the argument. The argument I put forward can be formulated more sharply with respect to quantitative methodology, but it also applies to qualitative approaches. Thus, I do not think we should be making too much of the quantitative/qualitative distinction in this context. My perspective is limited in another respect, too. I focus my discussion on the analysis of data, and I shall have little to say about the equally burning question of data collection, i.e., the research phase where the researcher meets his "object." It is not that I do not regard this phase of the research process as crucial from an ethical point of view—I have addressed some of the problems involved in that phase in another context (Kriesi 1992, see also Punch 1986). But, as will become apparent in what follows, the process of data analysis is in its own way particularly susceptible to the "enticement by methods." My perspective, finally, is a rather modest one. I shall not deal at all with the great questions concerning the ethical aims of the social sciences (Bellah 1983). I am discussing a minimal standard: the responsible use of the methods we have at our disposal. Even if we restrict our point of view to the discussion of this minimal standard, it will become evident that, as Robert Bellah suggests, social inquiry is indelibly linked to ethical reflection. But then, I submit, this is not a peculiarity of social inquiry. It applies to any kind of research.

TECHNICAL OVERSOPHISTICATION

A former colleague of mine at the University of Amsterdam, Johan Goudsblom (1979), has written an interesting introduction to sociology in which he starts by assessing the state of the art in the discipline. While sociology has made considerable advances with respect to the provision of a wealth of exact and reliable data and a series of systematic theories, he deplores a loss of range and relevance of sociological knowledge. According to his view, having become ever more precise and systematic in the details, the discipline has tended to lose sight of the interrelatedness of the different events that bear different labels or happen at different moments in time. Empirical research, he suggests, is ever more specialized and tends to be myopic with respect to larger structures and larger questions.

This global assessment can be corroborated by more detailed evaluations of the development in particular fields of the social sciences. Thus, van Deth (1986), who takes a closer look at the development of the field of voting research over the past thirty years, comes to an even more serious conclusion. He takes as his standard of comparison the classic American voting studies of the fifties. These studies are famous examples of large scale survey research. Van Deth concludes that there are "no important substantive differences between modern voting research and that undertaken more than twenty-five years ago in Michigan." He even finds that the practice of voting research seems to have suffered from a theoretical impoverishment. However, running parallel to this substantive impoverishment, he notes an astonishing development of techniques: while the classic studies of voting research used elementary techniques of data analysis, more recent studies in the field use highly sophisticated techniques, which have made large areas of the field inaccessible for nonspecialists. In his view (190), these "technical developments are far ahead of the state of theorizing in this field and have hardly contributed to our understanding of voting behavior. The only gain seems to be that today, nonrecursive and time-lagged models can be tested more directly than in the past. However, the bottleneck in theoretically relevant research has never been the lack of adequate estimation techniques but the scarcity of insightful ideas." He diagnoses "a coup d'état by the technicians" and characterizes modern voting research as "no-risk political science, typified by intellectual laziness and the exchange of substance for technique," obstructing further development of the field (196).

Van Deth is, of course, a polemical man, who, in his assessment of the state of the art in his discipline, conveniently neglects the fact that important voting studies have been published since the great American classics in several European countries. But these may be the exceptions which prove the validity of his general point. In my own quite limited experience, I have also found his point to have some truth. Recently, for example, I was asked to review a paper of two young Swiss political scientists for a social science journal. The two authors pretended to test the relative merits of three theories of voting behavior on the basis of data about voting in the Swiss direct democracy. They first provided caricatural sketches of the three theories, which did not give the impression that they had really understood the general thrust, let alone the intricacies of any one of them. Then, they proceeded to operationalize the various concepts of the three theoretical approaches in a haphazard way, ignoring completely the problematic character of much of the data, which they had not collected themselves, but taken over from the work of other researchers. As the paper approached its climax, they embarked on a highly complex statistical analysis of the data.

The methods chosen for this purpose—log-linear analyses—however, did not allow them to compare the three theories in a rigorous manner. Being aware of their inability to draw any rigorous conclusions on the basis of their analyses, they closed the paper by attributing this lack of closure to the "variable rigor with respect to the development of hypotheses" of the three theories compared!

The exchange of substance for technique has, of course, many facets. I would only mention one more aspect which constitutes a pervasive element in the everyday practice of social scientists: the way statistical tests are used. As is observed by McCloskey (1985, 156) in his discussion of the rhetoric of economics—a science which I conveniently include among the social sciences for the present purposes—the abuse of the word "significant" in connection with statistical arguments is universal: "Statistical significance seems to give a criterion by which to judge whether a hypothesis is true or false. The criterion seems to be independent of any tiresome consideration of how true a hypothesis must be to be true enough." But, as he points out, the statistical criterion of significance cannot do as a replacement of any substantive criterion for evaluating the significance of an empirical result. The world does not serve up free intellectual lunches. The only thing statistical tests of significance do is tell the intrepid investigator what the probability is that, because of the small sample he faces, he will make a mistake of excessive gullibility in accepting a false statistical proposition. It protects the investigator from an error that comes from having too small a random sample. That is all. "The procedure keeps one from being made to look a certain, narrow kind of fool" (160). The error one is protected against is comparable to the error of a judge who convicts an innocent man. However, the statistical test does not prevent one from making the other possible error of the judge, which is to acquit a guilty man. Thus, it does not prevent us from overlooking theoretically relevant alternatives. Moreover, the procedure does not protect us against misspecifications, i.e., using entirely wrong variables in one's regression equations; or even using a single wrong variable, which is sometimes enough to make one look foolish indeed. And a statistical test of significance does not answer the question: How large is large?

McCloskey's point is that the limited functions fulfilled by statistical tests of significance are typically overlooked by practitioners of econometrics, and, one might add, of any other social science. Typically, he suggests, practitioners of this discipline let the statistical test decide about the substantive significance of a research finding. He bases his conclusion on a probability sample of ten papers drawn from the 1981, 1982, 1983 volumes of the *American Economic Review*. Even among this sample representing the best work economists do, he found an overuse of statistical significance testing, which is to say that a majority of these papers used the test for purposes other than what they were designed to do.

Why this enticement by methods? Where does this tendency to neglect substance and to overuse techniques come from? The first answer to this question simply refers to the availability of ever more statistical tools. Give a little boy a hammer, and he will think that everything he encounters needs to be pounded. Statistical packages have become readily available for social scientists since the early seventies. Moreover, the revolution of the micro-computer has enormously facilitated access to these packages since the early eighties. But this does not seem to be the only answer. The enticement by methods also has something to do with the organization of the teaching and research in the social sciences. Consider the curriculum of any of the social sciences in any country in the world today, and you will most likely find some introductory courses in statistics figuring prominently in the early coursework a student has to do. These courses more likely than not serve an important selective function, since the results obtained in such courses are easily quantifiable in objective terms (Bürgenmeier 1990, 45). The social sciences, in other words, are increasingly populated by practitioners who have been able to pass the initiation rites of statistics courses. This does not necessarily qualify them to apply quantitative methods sensibly in the course of their later career, but it at least prevents those least likely to apply such methods from continuing their studies in the discipline. Moreover, it attributes a special prestige to those who have passed these rites successfully. A second reason why method is so central to social science research has to do with the lack of any other agreed upon criteria for evaluating the work of those within the social science disciplines. As Phillips (1973, 154) pointed out, by "placing a heavy emphasis on correct method, all members of a scientific community are assured a kind of collective protection: madmen, charlatans, fakers, and sophists are hopefully excluded from the ranks." As a consequence the representatives of quantitative methods enjoy a lot of prestige within the disciplines and get a considerable amount of influence as gatekeepers in the production of research—as experts in scientific foundations and on boards of prestigious journals. Third, the reliance on quantitative methods also serves to legitimize the social sciences for a larger public that is otherwise often not very favorably disposed to these disciplines (Kriesi 1980). Fourth, and related to this point, certain methodologically highly sophisticated branches of social science research, notably public opinion research, public policy analysis, and public choice, have become servants of the bureaucratized state (Lowi 1992), and, one might add, of marketing departments of private firms as well. That is, they have proven their social or at least political and economic usefulness.

Methodological prowess has become a marketable skill allowing its practitioners to make a career.

Finally, and maybe most important, the enticement by methods has a
more substantive reason, too. It is related to the problem of how to cope
with the enormous amount of information about an ever more complex
world. This problem is particularly acute in social science research. This
research is mainly non-experimental research, since it takes place in a
"natural setting." In the social sciences, we often lack the possibility of
controlling the impact of important variables by an appropriate design of
our research. There are exceptions (especially in social psychology), and,
it is true, we should think more frequently of possibilities to introduce
(quasi-)experimental designs (Berk 1988). But, as far as I can see, there
are inherent limits to the availability of such an option. In other words, to
test our theories, in the phase of data analysis we have to control a large
number of variables which, in addition to the variables of interest to our
theories, might possibly have an influence on the dependent variables,
too. In order to control such a larger number of variables, however, we
need large numbers of cases, an elaborate statistical apparatus, and powerful computers.

LACK OF TECHNICAL SOPHISTICATION

The invasion of quantitative methods into the social sciences has, however, not only given rise to their oversophisticated application by those
who came under their spell. The enticement by methods has its limits, a
fact quite apparent from a quick glance at the reactions of many of our
students to the statistics courses which they are required to take at the
beginning of their studies. Most of the students we get in the social sciences are not the mathematical types. This implies that the ordeal of the
initiation rite of statistics courses assumes for them all the more serious
proportions, with the effect that many of them actively reject any consideration of a quantitative kind of research for the rest of their careers.
Moreover, there still exist a considerable number of practitioners in our
disciplines who were trained before the mid-seventies, i.e., before the
great development of quantitative methods and before the introduction of
micro-computers. Given the highly selective attraction of the quantitative
types to certain specialties in our disciplines, there are a number of fields
of research in the social sciences where the enticement by quantitative
methods is far from dominant.

Having done much of my own research in the field of collective action, and being at the same time not averse to quantitative methods, I
have recently had some pertinent personal experiences. The first experi-

ence I would like to relate concerns a paper that I wrote for a book on comparative applications of contemporary social movement theory, edited by three leading American scholars. In my contribution to the volume I had used a causal model which I had estimated with the computer program LISREL, one of the standard programs for this kind of analysis. The editors asked me, however, to either drop or explain the LISREL analysis in more detail, since we could not expect many of our readers to be intimately familiar with LISREL; my truncated description of it, its results, and what they meant was likely to baffle most of them. Since I was at the same time urged to cut down on the number of pages in my contribution, I preferred to abandon the causal model, resorting instead to a qualitative summary of what I had found. This summary could, of course, no longer be checked by an inspection of the results by those who would have been able to do so.

Another experience concerns a paper on collective action, which essentially contained a discussion and estimation of a complex causal model for the mobilization of environmental protest, that I had submitted to a most prestigious American journal. The paper has been rejected for the second time, after I was first given a chance to resubmit. What struck me most in the cumbersome process of modifying, resubmitting, and finally being rejected is that one of the referees who had originally been quite critical about the paper—among other things on methodological grounds, since he worried about "measurement contamination"—had later on urged the editor to discount his comments because of lack of methodological competence. After having been rejected in the U.S., I then submitted the paper to a European journal. The two reviewers of this journal both heavily criticized the paper and asked for modifications on methodological grounds. Since the number of specialists in the field of research on social movements in Europe is not very large, I quickly found out about the identity of the reviewers. While both are well-known specialists on social movements, neither of them has ever used any quantitative methods in his research. After I had modified the paper, they finally accepted it. The modifications I introduced were quite substantial and consisted essentially in presenting the paper in what I would call a more "pedagogical" way. You might say that in both cases, the review process served an important function, since it has forced me to adapt my message to a presumably technically unsophisticated public. However, my point in the present context is that these examples indicate to what extent even a professional public remains technically unsophisticated in the disciplines of the social sciences.

In earlier times, the lack of technical sophistication has in part been overcome by a division of labor between the theoretical social scientists, on the one hand, and the statistical and methodological specialists, on the other hand. This division of labor often took the character of a master-servant relationship, with the theoretician—typically the holder of a chair—being in the role of the master, and the statistician or methodologist playing the part of the servant. Conceptual mastery was considered to be essential; technical matters could be delegated to lesser academic figures. It was also quite generally understood that the contribution of the technical specialists was not important enough to justify the mentioning of their names on the cover of the publications which resulted from the joint efforts. While it overcame some of the technical undersophistication, this means of dividing up the tasks of social research was still rather deficient from the point of view of the development of such research. On the one hand, technical specialists often lacked sufficient insight into the theoretical problems, and, on the other hand, theoretical specialists typically were unable to grasp the possibilities of one or the other technical development, which could have been usefully applied to the theoretical problem at hand. As a result of its inefficiencies and as a consequence of the growing prestige of the technical specialists in the social sciences, this type of division of labor is, as far as I can see, rapidly disappearing from our disciplines. But it still flourishes in other disciplines, such as the various medical specialties, where the quantitative social scientists often find positions as servants of the representatives of the more prestigious medical science.

We find technical undersophistication, of course, also at the origin of a most serious phenomenon in the social sciences: technical errors. Given the prestige enjoyed by quantitative methods, even those who are not particularly inclined to use them may be induced or forced to resort to them. To legitimate their research results in the scientific community or in a larger public; to get ahead in their academic career; or simply to try to make sense out of the wealth of data they have amassed in an early stage of their research, even those social scientists not very convinced by, or even quite averse to, quantitative methods may resort to their use. This particular form of enticement by methods is facilitated by their general accessibility in standard statistical packages, which makes it very easy for them to be applied even by the uninitiated. As Duncan (1984, 226) observes, coupled with downright incompetence in statistics, paradoxically, we often find the syndrome that he has come to call "statisticism": "the notion that computing is synonymous with doing research, the naive faith that statistics is a complete or sufficient basis for scientific methodology, the superstition that statistical formulas exist for evaluating such things as the relative merits of different substantive theories or the 'importance' of the causes of a 'dependent variable'; and the delusion that decomposing the covariations of some arbitrary and haphazardly assembled collection of variables can somehow justify not only a 'causal model' but also, praise the mark, a 'measurement model'." Duncan goes on to castigate the present state of the art in social science research. He points out that there is no clearly identifiable sector of social science research wherein such fallacies are clearly recognized and emphatically out of bounds: "Individual articles of exemplary quality are published cheek-by-jowl with transparent exercises in statistical numerology. If the muck were ankle deep, we could wade through it. When it is at hip level, our most adroit and most fastidious workers can hardly avoid getting some of it on their product."

In exceptional cases, it is easy to discover an error—if one pays sufficient attention to the details of the argument (which is a condition that more often than not is not fulfilled). In my capacity as editor of the Swiss Yearbook of political science, I have, for example, received an article applying multiple regression to the evaluation of a public policy. The choice of the method of multiple regression was quite adequate, the analysis seemed to have been performed correctly, but the author had apparently not understood the precise meaning of regression coefficients. That is why he interpreted his results incorrectly and proceeded to make a policy recommendation which was completely unjustified by his results. However, lack of technical sophistication takes such enormous proportions because it is typically rather difficult to detect. The uninitiated user of sophisticated methods can count on the lack of sophistication on the part not only of the lay, but also of the academic audience, and even of judges of major journals (see above).

Moreover, the lack of replication in many fields of the social sciences allows most of the errors to go undetected. In some rare instances of redesigned replications it has been possible to detect errors of previous research. Thus, several studies pretended that there exists a close connection between the percentage of unemployed and that of people voting for the NSDAP in Germany during the period from 1928 to 1933. This result seemed plausible: the increasing number of unemployed apparently had voted for the Nazis, thus assuring their legal coming to power. As is pointed out by Falter et al. (1983), however, all of these studies suffered from some methodological deficiencies, although not all of them of the same type. One of the methodologically more careful studies, had, for example, only measured the two characteristics in question on the level of the 13 Länder, i.e., at a highly aggregate level. In fact, Falter et al., who took the pains to collect data on the more disaggregate level of the Kreise, found exactly the opposite, i.e., a negative correlation between the two percentages. In other words, the higher the unemployment in a Kreis, the less the people of the Kreis were inclined to vote for the Nazis. They also provided an explanation of this correlation pointing out that it is not unemployment which makes people go over to the extreme right, but above all the fear of getting unemployed.

Unfortunately, reanalysis does not always clarify the situation. There are instances where it leaves the reader even more perplexed than s/he was at the outset. A most famous example concerns the research done for the report on Equality of Educational Opportunity published in the United States in 1966. The best known finding of the Report is that quantity and quality of school inputs (facilities, curriculum, and personnel) have little or no bearing on achievement; home environment and the student's peers are what really count. Obviously, such a finding has far-reaching implications for educational policy. At the very least, it raises serious questions about the efficacy of the billions of dollars now spent on public education. A reanalysis of the results by Hanushek and Kain (1972) has raised serious doubts about this and several other findings attributed to the Report. These doubts result both from a critique of the methods used by the empirical analysis of the Report, and from their interpretation. However, another extended reanalysis by a team led by Jencks (1973) has more or less confirmed the results of the original Report with respect to the impact of schools on achievement. Who is to be believed?

WHAT TO DO?

Some draw radical conclusions from the problems which I have tried to sketch. Thus, Feyerabend (1970) has advocated a methodological permissiveness, the major principle of his "anarchistic" methodology being that "anything goes." Others such as Phillips (1973) have gone as far as to suggest that we should abandon methods altogether. He proposes a playful stance to free ourselves from the dogmatism of method: "Play may not only give free rein to imagination, intuition, and creative urges, but may help us see more clearly" (163). He suggests that a playful attitude is a necessary precondition for "experiencing" the world. In his view, curiosity and play are "not subject to method, but rather to thought" (165). His alternative to method and demonstration is to employ and rely on reasoning and argumentation (169). What is needed is, he suggests, "not statistics or empirical research, but a better interpretation" (175). In other words, he wants us to do better on conceptualization and theorizing. But he tends to throw out the baby with the bathwater. While I heartily agree with his stress on reasoning, argumentation, and interpretation, it seems to me that returning to "armchair reasoning" does not constitute a sufficient recipe for good work in social research.

The opposite reaction consists in accepting that there are a large number of tools available to assist researchers trying to do quantitative non-experimental research, which can be quite helpful in coping with the wealth of information in the context of non-experimental research. Taking this point of view, one tries to distinguish between proper and improper practice, and insists on the upgrading of the current practices. The question then becomes one of how to improve these practices without falling into the trap of methodological overconscientiousness.

Some do so by taking what I would call a dogmatic position. They pretend that there is only one way to do proper social science research. Consider the example of the type of coefficients—standardized or unstandardized—one should use in regression analysis. In an article that tries to teach the practitioners in political science "how not to lie with statistics," King (1986) ridicules the use of standardized regression coefficients and admonishes his audience to use non-standardized coefficients only. He argues that standardized coefficients are in general: (1) more difficult to interpret; (2) do not add any information that may help to compare effects from different explanatory variables; and (3) may add seriously misleading information. Compare this advice to the summary of the discussion on this point in a popular computer program manual (Nie et al., 1975, 397): "To summarize, if one is interested in the relative amount of variance explained in Y (the dependent variable, H.K.) for a given sample or population by various independent variables, the standardized coefficients are appropriate. If the independent variables are measured in different units and the main interest is in assessing the overall effect of one variable over another variable in the same sample or population, the standardized coefficients will be more intelligible. However, if one is interested in finding causal laws or causal processes, and/or in comparing parameters of one population to those of another, the unstandardized coefficients should be preferred." Note that the authors of the manual concede that, under some—important—circumstances, unstandardized coefficients are the appropriate ones. Contrary to King, however, they insist on the fact that standardized coefficients are easier to interpret than their unstandardized counterparts. From a practitioner's point of view, I certainly agree with the manual. Typically the number of variables used in explanatory models in social science research is large, because, as a substitute for experimental control, the social science researcher is obligated to include in his regression equations all variables that might have an important effect. Moreover, the units of measurement of the different variables are typically quite different from one another. This means that the effects of the different explanatory variables are difficult to compare. Standardization facilitates these comparisons among effects of the different explanatory variables. The drawback is that standardized coefficients are not comparable across populations. That is, they cannot be used to generalize the findings to other populations, because they depend on the specific characteristics of the sample that has been used to estimate them. But the practitioner may be primarily interested in understanding what is going on in the population at hand, before s/he wants to or is able to compare results across different populations.

An undogmatic position relative to the predicament of social science research is exemplified by Leamer (1983), who discusses the situation of econometrics in particular. He is very critical of what he calls the "sad and decidedly unscientific state of affairs" econometricians find themselves in. And he cites a joke (37): "There are two things you are better off not watching in the making: sausages and econometric estimates." In fact, the econometric art as it is practiced at the computer terminal does not at all correspond to the textbook prescriptions. It involves fitting many, perhaps thousands, of statistical models. One or several that the researcher finds pleasing are selected for reporting purposes. As Leamer notes, this searching for a model is often well-intentioned, but there can be no doubt that such a specification search invalidates the traditional theories of inference. As a result of the practices used by applied econometricians, hardly anyone takes data analyses seriously—or perhaps more accurately, as Leamer suggests—hardly anyone takes anyone else's data analyses seriously. In order to get out of this state of affairs, he proposes that the econometricians ought to discard first the counterproductive goal of objective inference, which they have been taught by their textbooks. They ought to acknowledge the whimsical character of statistical inference; they ought to admit that subjective opinions play a crucial role in their analyses. As he sees it (38), "the fundamental problem facing econometrics is how adequately to control the whimsical character of inference, how sensibly to base inferences on opinions when facts are unavailable."

As he points out, at least a partial solution to this problem has already been found by practicing econometricians, who have started to report inferences implied by alternative sets of assumptions. It is, for example, shown, how an inference changes as variables are added to or deleted from the regression equation. What Leamer proposes to do is to pursue systematically this type of sensitivity analyses to indicate the extent to which the results obtained are fragile. In other words, an inference is not believable if it is fragile—if it can be reversed by minor changes in the assumptions. A researcher, he suggests, should be less concerned with convincing himself, and more concerned with anticipating objections of the consuming public with respect to the weaknesses in his inferences. S/he should, in other words, be more skeptical, or, more critical of him- or herself. Leamer then illustrates his general argument with an example. He studies the question of whether or not capital punishment has a deterrent effect. On the basis of data on the situation in the different states in the U.S., he runs regressions making different assumptions about the kind of variables that ought to be included in the analysis. His point of departure is that individuals with different political views about capital punishment will have different ideas about the kind of variables that play a role in explaining the crime rate in a given state, and will, therefore, arrive at different specifications of the causal model. His analyses indicate that, indeed, a right winger will always find that capital punishment has a deterrent effect, whereas people of a left wing persuasion may, on the basis of the same data, find that execution actually encourages murder. Leamer concludes from his analyses that any inference from the data at his disposal about the deterrent effect of capital punishment is too fragile to be believed.

This conclusion is quite frustrating for the analyst, who would like to draw conclusions for public policy. But, apart from the fact that it teaches us to be prudent with respect to our methods, this example has the advantage of pointing out to what extent good practice precludes thoughtless application of methodological recipes. The point I wish to make is that Leamer's proposed sensitivity analysis has a lot do with the playful character that research is supposed to have according to Phillips. There is only one difference: curiosity and play in this case are subject to method; to systematic doubt. Contrary to Phillips, who thinks of playing without rules, playful exploration of the type proposed by Leamer is rule-bound. In other words, playful exploration does not imply that one abandons method altogether. As a matter of fact, new advances in exploratory data analysis (Tukey 1977) and in computer programming implementing these advances for the social scientists (Horber 1991; Tierney 1990; Velleman 1989) allow for an increasingly playful approach to the analysis of data without giving up the rigor of classical statistics. It is in this direction rather than in a roundabout attack on methods that we should continue to improve our practices.

THE PREDICAMENT OF THE PRACTITIONER

But even such a playful approach makes a lot of assumptions which the practitioner should be aware of if s/he is not to draw erroneous conclusions from his or her data. Applying the statistical models to social science data is not like picking up a telephone. You can make a phone call without knowing anything about the technical side of telecommunication. By contrast, in order to apply statistical models in the social sciences, you need to know something about the assumptions underlying these models. Doing quantitative data analysis is not quite like driving a car either. Driving implies more practical knowledge than making a phone call. You do not have to know how the car's engine works, but you have to have an intuitive notion of certain physical laws. For example, you have to know that if you enter into a curve of a given radius at a certain speed, you will be unable to keep your vehicle on the road. In the case of driving, you will immediately notice if you violate the physical laws. In the case of data analysis, however, the difficulty is that you may violate the assumptions of the models you apply without noticing it. It is true that, sometimes, the computer programs will be able to warn you if assumptions are violated. A program may, for example, draw the user's attention to an identification problem. However, more likely than not, violations of assumptions go unnoticed. In other words, the social scientist may be quite unaware of the fact that s/he has long been ejected from the road and has landed in the mud.

Consider the covariance structure model (Schoenberg 1989). Over the last twenty years, since the LISREL model has been introduced, the covariance structure model has gained considerable popularity among serious researchers in many fields of social research. This has happened for three reasons. First, covariance structure models depict in a natural way the "causal" models researchers have in mind when thinking about the processes they are looking at. They can be represented by intuitive path diagrams that do not require math courses to understand. They incite the researcher to think in terms of more or less elaborate theoretical models. Second, computer software has simplified the estimation of the parameters of covariance structure models, making it possible to estimate large, sometimes intricate, models using an easy syntax. The coefficients generated by the computer software have the advantage of being directly analogous to regression coefficients in multiple regression and have identical substantive interpretations. Third, the model is especially attractive for its unified treatment of what were once several complex problems for the researcher. However, the model makes quite restrictive assumptions with respect to the quality of the data, assumptions which the data social scientists work with typically do not meet. Thus, the model requires variables with "metric" measurement (i.e., continuous over the real line), while the data used in social science research are most commonly comprised of categorical or ordinal variables. Moreover, there is rarely any theoretical justification for the assumption that the data possess a multivariate normal distribution, as is required by the procedure used to estimate the model. An acute awareness of these problems among statisticians has prompted a number of them who are specialized in the development of covariance structure models to generalize the model and enhance its features so that it becomes applicable to categorical and non-normal variables. But these developments are not likely to satisfy the critics, since at the root of their criticism lies the claim that the application of this type of model to real data is inherently ad hoc. That is, according to its critics, in no case is the investigator able to generate a fundamental theory that justifies all of the required assumptions. Moreover, there doesn't seem to be any likely future prospect of supporting the claim of a multinormal distribution that is required by the estimation procedure. Therefore, covariance structure analysis will always remain an ad hoc approximation according to some critics who therefore urge the abandonment of its use.

In reaction to these arguments, one of the defenders of the model (Schoenberg 1989) has pointed out that, for many researchers, an ad hoc approximation will do quite well. He also points out that parameter estimates of variables that are not at all measured on a "metric" scale are still consistent, although not efficient. In his view, the key issue in structural modeling is not estimation—since asymptotic consistency will withstand a lot of misspecification—but rather statistical inference and the testing of models. He also notes that progress is being made in this respect, and he comes to the conclusion that the problem of the treatment of non-metric data in the covariance structure model may finally be solved by the statisticians working on them.

What is a practitioner to do in a case like this? Suppose s/he is aware of the assumptions of the model and the discussion among statisticians? Whom is s/he to believe? How much statistical knowledge is s/he supposed to have to be able to decide the matter? Or, conversely, how much ignorance in statistics is compatible with its responsible use? The practitioner will try to keep informed about progress made in the development of the statistical model in order to be able to get the latest versions of computer programs which allow him or her to profit from them. But what if these developments are not progressing fast enough, or if the researcher does not have access to the information about these developments, because, after all, s/he is not a professional statistician? Being pragmatic and attracted to the model's elegant features, s/he will be inclined to continue to use it, even if his or her data do not exactly meet its assumptions. Since violations of the assumptions are a matter of degree, the question then becomes to what extent s/he may transgress the requirements. Just how pragmatic may one be? Under certain circumstances, the social scientist could make an additional effort with respect to the measurement of data. Increasing the quality of the measurement may be one way out of the dilemma. But often this is not possible, since the variables involved are inherently non-metric. Consider, for example, the participation in a vote (one participates or abstains) and the vote one casts (one votes for or against a given project or a given candidate). These are very important variables in political science, which a researcher might want to explain, but they are dichotomous and, therefore, do not fulfill the assumptions of the LISREL model—particularly not if they are used as dependent variables in the model. Should s/he renounce using the model? S/he may be inclined to do so, if there exist viable alternatives, of which s/he is aware, to which s/he has access (via statistical software packages), and which s/he is able to handle. But, as in the case of LISREL, there may be no equally attractive alternatives available. Logistic regressions do not allow for complex modeling such as LISREL. Log-linear procedures, while allowing for such modeling may get very cumbersome if the model includes more than a very few variables.

CONCLUSION

These are some of the dilemmas a conscientious social scientist using quantitative methods is facing in practical data analysis today. While trying to live up to the standards of proper practice, s/he is constantly aware of the deficiency of his or her statistical competence and often uncertain about whether or not s/he has gotten off the safe road of proper practice. Nevertheless, s/he is likely to be avid about the tools statisticians and computer scientists develop, since only these tools allow one to cope with the complexity of the large amount of data, which form the indispensable basis for the test of social science theory, and with the elements of variability and chance (errors of measurement, errors in sampling, and random behavior) that are inherently present in the non-experimental research designs that dominate in the social sciences. If responsible use of the methods at one's disposal is a minimum standard for the social scientist, it constitutes, as I have tried to indicate, a standard which is not as easy to meet as it might have first appeared.

REFERENCES

Bellah, Robert N. 1983, "The Ethical Aims of Social Inquiry," in: Haan, Norma et al. (eds.), *Social Science as Moral Inquiry*, New York, Columbia University Press.

Berk, Richard A. 1988, "Causal Inference for Sociological Data," in: Smelser, Neil (ed.), *Handbook of Sociology*, London, Sage.

Bürgenmeier, Beat 1990, *Plaidoyer pour une économie sociale*, Paris, Economica.

Deth, Jan W. van 1986, "Political Science as a No-Risk Policy: The American Voter and Contemporary Voting Research," in *Acta politica* XXI (2), 185–199.

Duncan, Otis Dudley 1984, *Notes on Social Measurement*, New York, Russell Sage Foundation.

Falter, Jürgen W. et al. 1983, "Arbeitslosigkeit und Nationalsozialismus," in *Kölner Zeitschrift für Soziologie und Sozialpsychologie* 35, 505–524.

Feyerabend, Paul 1970, *Wider den Methodenzwang*, Frankfurt, Suhrkamp.

Galtung, Johan 1970, *Theory and Methods of Social Research*, London, George Allen and Unwin.

Goudsblom, Johan 1979, *Soziologie auf der Waagschale*, Frankfurt/M., Suhrkamp.

Hanushek, Eric A./Kain, John F. 1972, "On the Value of Equality of Educational Opportunity as a Guide to Public Policy," in: Mosteller, F./Moynihan, D.P. (eds.), *On Equality of Educational Opportunity*, New York, Vintage Books, 116–145.

Horber, Eugene 1991, *EDA User's Manual*, Université de Genève.

Jencks, Christopher 1973, *Chancengleichheit*, Reinbek, Rowohlt. (original: 1972, *Inequality—A Reassessment of the Effect of Family and Schooling in America*, N.Y., Basic Books).

King, Gary 1986, "How Not to Lie With Statistics: Avoiding Common Mistakes in Quantitative Political Science," in: *American Journal of Political Science* 30 (3), 666–687.

Kriesi, Hanspeter 1980, "Methode zur Legitimation soziologischer Praxis," in: *Schweizerische Zeitschrift für Soziologie* 5, 383–388.

———— 1992, "The Rebellion of the Research 'Objects'," in: Diani, Mario/ Eyerman, Ron (eds.), *Studying Collective Action*, London, Sage, 194–216.

Leamer, Edward E. 1983, "Let's Take the Con out of Econometrics," in: *The American Economic Review* 73 (1), 31–43.

Lowi, Theodore J. 1992, "The State in Political Science: How We Become What We Study," in: *American Political Science Review* 86 (1), 1–7.

McCloskey, Donald N. 1985, *The Rhetoric of Economics*, Madison, The University of Wisconsin Press.

Nie, Norman H. et al. 1975, *SPSS-Statistical Package for the Social Sciences*, Second Edition, New York, McGraw-Hill.

Phillips, Derek L. 1973, *Abandoning Method*, San Francisco, Jossey-Bass.

Punch, Maurice 1986, *The Politics and Ethics of Fieldwork*, London, Sage.

Schoenberg, Ronald 1989, "Covariance Structure Models," in: *Annual Review of Sociology* 15, 425–440.

Tierney, Luke 1990, *LISP-STAT: An Object-Oriented Environment for Statistical Computing and Dynamic Graphics*, New York, Wiley.

Tukey, John W. 1977, *Exploratory Data Analysis (EDA)*, Reading, MA, Addison-Wesley.

Velleman, Paul F. 1989, *Learning Data Analysis with DATA DESK*, New York, W. H. Freeman.

Transdisciplinarity:
A Response to "Enticement by Methods" by Hanspeter Kriesi

MARGARET A. SOMERVILLE

I wish to respond through some "free associations" that were stimulated by reading and listening to the excellent paper of Professor Hanspeter Kriesi. These associations relate to issues we have confronted or structures, concepts, and approaches we have evolved in the area in which I work, that of "medicine, ethics and law."

The potential range of free associations and insights that could be raised by Professor Kriesi's paper is very broad. For example, one of his opening statements: "put bluntly, the question is whether quantitative methods are an easy way to incompetence, and, if so, what should we do about it,"[1] goes to the heart of our modern academic dilemma. This dilemma is connected with the dramatic increase in the speed and spread of communications technology, and the concomitant explosion of information and textual materials. The enormous amount of information that has been generated, the human limits on converting this information to knowledge, and the even more stringent constraints on converting such knowledge to wisdom (which may be less, rather than more, abundant than previously) are central issues in this dilemma. As well there are two other phenomena which characterize the "academic dilemma." First, "the more that we know, the more that we know that we do not know." Second, we have a much greater ability now than in the past to identify risk, in particular, risk that our academic contributions may be judged, or worse, proven to be, scientifically valueless. In combination, these factors have caused a major increase in feelings of uncertainty and accompanying anxiety, which in turn have given rise to a dubious search for certainty as a means to reduce the anxiety. This search is often manifested as an unusually diligent seeking of consensus. It has recently been proposed that seeking consensus on fundamental values can be a "terror-reduction mechanism."[2] Could we be terrified not only about the amount of information that we need to handle in the social sciences ("information anxiety"), but also about the authenticity of our knowledge in these areas? Could the use of quantitative methods (in particular, statistics) seem to be an appropriate and palatable antidote to this terror, or some form of talisman that offers protection?

One way to respond to complex situations that raise such deep anxieties is to find a "marker event," a single point, usually on a continuum of factors, that is taken to indicate that those who are on one side of the marker are the initiated or "the blessed," and those on the other side, the uninitiated or "the damned." This means that the way in which we treat persons in the latter group need not set a precedent for how we do or must treat those in the former group, which will usually include "us." It could well be that our use of quantitative methods (or more accurately, the ability to pass an examination in statistics) is playing the role of marker event in relation to admission to, or recognition and success in, the social sciences. The perceived need for such a marker event would not be surprising in view of the fact that the social sciences have multiplied in this century, extending the range and depth of the knowledge base they have produced and must deal with, to a point unthinkable a hundred years ago. It is also interesting to note that, if demonstration of an ability to handle statistics is functioning as a marker event, and all the social sciences require this, the marker event indicating eligibility for entry into all social sciences would be identical. This would give some common measure of competence or badge of authenticity across the social sciences.

In addition there is no doubt that the extraordinary developments that have occurred in the physical and life sciences, and the wide recognition that these sciences have received, may have induced social scientists to feel that their credibility and recognition depended on emulating these "hard" sciences. In this case, an ability to function through quantitative methods could be seen as a common denominator across all of the sciences, both "hard" and "soft," serving to identify and "glue" the social sciences with the other sciences. In other words, it could be that "passing a statistics examination" has been chosen as the "initiation rite"[3] for all the sciences.

Professor Kriesi's statement that a "quantitative statistical apparatus [is used] simply because it exists, independently of the question whether it makes any sense to apply these techniques"[4] brings to mind the concept of the "technological imperative"—the pressure to use technology simply because it exists. We have learned much about this imperative in medicine, and how to guard against it, particularly through analysis in medical ethics. There is now a concept, not simply of wrongful underuse of medical technology but also, of its wrongful overuse, both of which can be compared with appropriate use.[5] The same "imperative response" would also appear to be likely to occur with respect to the use of intellectual technologies, such as statistics and other quantitative methods, which is the point made by Professor Kriesi.

Professor Kriesi's paper also brings to mind the need to utilize "other ways of knowing" (which include intuition and "examined emotions"), in addition to logical, cognitive, rational ways of knowing that are identified with production of "hard" scientific data, especially in the recognized disciplines. Moreover, these two kinds of knowing need to be integrated with each other. In short, some of our traditional approaches may be necessary, but not sufficient, for "the kind of knowing" that we need in certain areas, particularly the social sciences.

It may also be that we have been operating on a binary model, which in fact consists of operating at either pole of a continuum with "hard" science at one end, and so-called "soft" science, at the other. What we need, particularly in terms of the social sciences, is a midway approach on the continuum that connects these poles: one which would accommodate what we may presently regard as impossible combinations of values, perceptions, methodologies, knowledge, events, or even persons. I have referred, elsewhere, to efforts to establish this middle position, as "the search for the purple-pink middle."[6] It is proposed that we should change the colors of the poles from black and white, which are necessarily seen as in opposition to each other, to red and blue, which are more complementary to each other, and which, in combination, give a purple-pink middle, rather than a grey one, and in doing so display the color of creativity and imagination, rather than that of depression.

I would now like to comment on the first section of Professor Kriesi's paper.

Professor Kriesi notes increasing specialization and focus on narrow questions, and the resulting tendency "to be myopic with respect to larger structures and larger questions."[7] This is to raise the need for transdisciplinarity, a term used to describe a nascent proposal for the development of new collaborative research methodologies. Within the theory of transdisciplinarity, as that term is used here, we would envisage a three-level structure for the development of knowledge, and, for instance, for use within our universities. The first level is represented by the "renaissance person" who in modern times is personified in the undergraduate student who has completed a good general liberal arts or general science education. The second level can be seen in our current disciplinary specializations, which will become increasingly necessary and almost certainly narrower, with our rapidly expanding information base. The disciplinary division and disciplinary level both need to be maintained and strengthened, which is not to say that this level is static. "Old" disciplines may disintegrate and "new" ones appear. But, as well, a new and third level now needs to be added—the transdisciplinary level—in which persons from the various disciplines can interact in a structured, systematized manner to produce "integrated knowledge." It merits noting that we envisage transdisciplinarity as involving "something more" than consciously undertaken parallel disciplinary activity, which has been relatively common in recent times. What the "something more" is remains to be articulated through research on transdisciplinary research, itself. In short, it is proposed that it may only be through consistently applying articulated methodologies which allow systematically organized collaborative research to be carried out, that we will be able to obtain an adequate perspective on "larger structures and larger questions."

Professor Kriesi notes that form has replaced substance. While attention to form is essential (as lawyers say, "form is no mere formality"), there is a danger in this respect in developing and applying transdisciplinarity methodologies because they will largely emphasize process, although the concept entails that the aim of this process is to create "space(s)" for substance from a wide variety of disciplines and perspectives. It is important, therefore, in developing transdisciplinary methodologies, to ensure that process does not replace substance. Consequently, there will need to be conscious articulation, within the concepts that set up transdisciplinarity, that these are methodologies, forms, and procedures for the development of knowledge and, one hopes, wisdom, and not their substitutes. In short, these procedural instruments should give us better access to knowledge and lead to theoretical enrichment of our knowledge, not "theoretical impoverishment,"[8] which Professor Kriesi notes is a risk taken when emphasizing process at the expense of, or as a replacement for, substance.

One of the problems has been that information is replacing knowledge (rather than vice versa, as should and needs to be the case) because without knowledge, wisdom cannot be an outcome. The aim in transdisciplinarity, then, is to establish a structure that will enable us to develop wisdom, if we have the capacity for it both as individuals and collectives. A further problem at present is that individuals and collectives may have this capacity and accompanying potential for wisdom, but it is not realized because the structures which are needed for it to develop do not exist, or, even worse, the structures that do exist inhibit its development. We need to take an unbiased, disinterested, detached look at our university structures and research funding "mechanisms" with such concerns in mind. One can be an "academic star" only as an individual, and this is essential to tenure and promotion and obtaining research funding. Our structures may well be strongly antithetical to the development of wisdom. Professor Kriesi states this in a much more succinct way when he notes that there has been a "scarcity of insightful ideas,"[9] that is, information has not developed to knowledge, and then to wisdom.

It may also be that our information explosion and our relatively easy and complete access, through communications technology, to all information on a given subject, has interfered with the development of wisdom in another way. When we recognized, as was usually the case, that we did not have all the information that existed regarding a certain issue, we had a "fact gap," which could be filled by the exercise of discretion—often a basis for wisdom. The closing of this gap or space may have eliminated opportunities for the exercise of discretion and hence the development of wisdom. This does not leave us with a choice of either accepting this situation or intentionally refraining from accessing the full range of information available. The other alternative is expressly building into the structures we use for decision making a space for the exercise of discretion.

In developing transdisciplinarity we must keep clearly in mind not only our own needs, but also the needs of the next generation: our students, who link us to future generations. In fact, the three-tiered structure proposed for transdisciplinarity may correspond to provision of information at the primary level (undergraduate education), generation of knowledge at the second, disciplinary, level (disciplinary specialization in post-graduate study), and potential for wisdom[10] at the third, transdisciplinary, level. If we accept such a structure, transdisciplinarity could be viewed as the tertiary level of tertiary education. Just as, until recent times, university (tertiary) education was not universal (when more than 30% of an age cohort in a population attend university, access to such education can be classified as "universal"[11]), participation at a transdisciplinary level is not likely to be universal. Most persons with disciplinary training will live their professional lives in their disciplines. But some intellectual adventurers need to be able to undertake their explorations in the outer space of transdisciplinarity. They will, like astronauts, be both self-selected and other-selected.

The three-tiered structure described may also reflect the stages of development of knowledge. The first level represents "true simplicity" when often we do not know a great deal. The second level is often experienced as chaos—we know or are discovering much, but have not yet structured and organized our knowledge. The third level can be called that of "apparent simplicity." It may often look very similar to the first level, but it is based on the knowledge of the second level, which has now been structured and incorporated. It is interesting to contemplate at which of these levels the social sciences are operating, with respect to the various activities undertaken within them.

Transdisciplinarity is also very likely to cause us to realize that we must have a very intimate link between practice and theory, and that these two modes of interacting are feedback mechanisms for each other and must take place concurrently. There has been a tendency in academia to divide the world, including the academic world, into practitioners and theoreticians, and for each to decry the limitations of the other. There is a need for some of us, at least, to be both theoretician and practitioner, and to integrate the different kinds of knowledge and, one hopes, wisdom, that are gained from each of these types of activity. Again, medical ethics, especially the development of clinical ethics, provides a strong example. In clinical or "applied ethics," ethics—which has tended until very recently to be more or less limited to theory—has become an important area of professional practice in the health care context.

We also need to consider the use of "exclusion mechanisms." The requirement that one pass an examination in statistics in order to be permitted to engage in the study of social sciences may be such a mechanism. First, in practice it excludes those who are unable to pass the examination, regardless of whether or not ability to do statistics is relevant to being a practitioner in the social sciences in general, or in a particular social science. Second, it gives an aura of "hard" science credibility to the would-be social scientists who pass, in that they are identified as being able to pass a "hard" science examination. Third, we often use exclusion mechanisms when we are worried about our own authenticity or credibility, or even integrity. In relation to the social sciences there may be concerns of this sort in relation to the "discipline" of social science itself, and possibly some of its individual practitioners. Fourth, as has been noted already, when we are doubtful even of our own or our discipline's authenticity, we need stronger affirmation that there is consensus on shared values than when we are not doubtful. There may *not* be a large area of shared values and, therefore, consensus within the social sciences. Recognition of the need for statistics and the special place given to this skill may provide such a point of consensus. Finally, we sometimes exclude people for the purposes of engaging in an "isolation ritual." This is not aimed primarily at eliminating the persons who are excluded, but seeks to bond the persons who remain, the theory being that they bond through shared guilt for having excluded others, in a situation in which they personally would feel very harmed by being excluded.[12] In short, this shared guilt provides a very strong bonding mechanism for the persons who remain in the group. Could examinations in statistics be fulfilling such a function? In particular, do persons in the social sciences feel a need to bond strongly, internally, in order to feel that their discipline's existence is justified?

We also need to ask why we choose to rely on "hard" data, especially statistics, in situations where there is a choice between using this basis and other bases for our propositions and arguments. A good example of persons who in particular rely on statistics (usually with only the vaguest understanding of what the data mean) is politicians. Dr. Anna Howe has suggested that often politicians choose to use statistics in order to reduce uncertainty, establish apparent certainty, and base arguments on "hard facts" which cannot be disputed or defeated.[13] In other words, politicians feel much more secure and certain—much less able to be challenged—arguing on the basis of statistics than when they argue on other bases which are perceived as "soft." As mentioned already, uncertainty gives rise to anxiety, indeed sometimes to deep fear, so it is normal to act in such a way as to try to reduce our uncertainty. This may provide an insight with respect to the statement of van Deth, quoted by Professor Kriesi, that the social science research he was examining could be characterized as "no-risk political science, typified by intellectual laziness and the exchange of substance for technique."[14] While laziness is a possible explanation for the type of research described, it is also possible that the true cause of this approach to research could be an effort to reduce uncertainty, anxiety, and fear.

Professor Kriesi shows how statistics are used to convert uncertainty to apparent certainty, but cites D. McCloskey, who points out that "the statistical criterion of significance cannot do as a replacement of any substantive criterion for evaluating the significance of an empirical result."[15] He adds, "the world does not serve up free intellectual lunches."[16] In short, statistics can tell us something about the reliability of the results that we obtain on the basis of the theory that we have used, but it "does not prevent us from overlooking theoretically relevant alternatives."[17] Yet, McCloskey adds, "practitioners of the discipline [for example of econometrics] let the statistical test decide about the substantive significance of a research finding."[18] This brings to mind the role of ethical analysis and legal doctrines, such as "informed consent," the aims of which are to allow persons, who must decide whether or not to subject themselves to certain interventions, to know the harms, risks, and potential benefits of those interventions as well as their alternatives before they make a decision. Could it be that the aim of our research and research publications should be to inform ourselves and others of a range of alternative approaches and their risks and benefits, rather than seeking to provide apparent certainty through focusing on one theory or outcome? Is there a conflict between, on the one hand, achieving academic recognition and, on the other hand, our ethical obligations to provide the broadest spectrum of knowledge to others (especially to the community which supports our work) to enable them to choose which knowledge will form the basis of their decisions? To the extent that academic recognition depends upon our claim that we are correct and others, who disagree, are wrong; our conviction that we must not display uncertainty; and our disinterest in negative results (they do not win Nobel prizes) there is likely to be such conflict.

Further, we need to consider in the context of this discussion whether we are using the knowledge we develop as a source of control of others through "mystery and mastery"—keeping others under our mastery by ensuring that the knowledge we have, and that they do not, remains a mystery to them. The alternative is to lead others by sharing information. Clearly, while the latter approach is ethically sound, the former is not necessarily. These same distinctions are captured in the concepts of "blind trust" and "earned trust,"[19] which have correlative concepts of "blind authority" (authority claimed on the basis of status, prestige, or knowledge) and "earned authority" (authority given on the basis of earned trust, that is, based on demonstrated trustworthiness, including through shared knowledge).

Professor Kriesi questions where this focus on statistics—"this enticement by methods"—in social sciences comes from and points out that there is a lack of any other agreed upon criteria for evaluating the work of those within the social science disciplines. This brings to mind, again, a situation frequently faced in "applied ethics." When there is no consensus on values (as is often the case in a post-modern, pluralistic, secular society) it is not possible to use substantive principles as the basis for guiding decision making. In their place we have substituted "due process," or right decision-making procedures, hoping that a group of moral actors (for example, an ethics committee) using such process will reach an acceptable decision. In short, we seek to verify and validate our decisions through the use of process in both medical ethics and the social sciences. This is not meant to imply that such process does not perform a legitimate function—it does. The danger is that we tend to rely on process to validate decisions that cannot necessarily be legitimately validated in this way. Most such decisions involve value judgments and usually value conflicts. Further, Professor Kriesi points out that the use of statistics in the social sciences provides persons who are skilled in their use with influence as gatekeepers in the production of research.[20] Likewise, ethics committees and people with skills in ethical analysis perform a similar function in relation to decision making which they undertake or review. Professor

Kriesi proposes that statistics also legitimize the social sciences for the larger public.

Professor Kriesi then discusses the split between theoretical social scientists on the one hand, and statistical, methodological specialists, on the other hand. The latter were the servants of the former, but this status differential and split are rapidly disappearing from the social sciences.[21] He notes, however, that the split continues in the "more prestigious medical science." Again, transdisciplinarity is relevant here, as it would seek to integrate these different facets. Its function is to help to overcome separation when it detracts from rather than promotes knowledge, and to allow integration *without loss of the authenticity of the component parts*. In fact, ideally the aim is to increase this integration, whether the component parts are areas of knowledge, disciplines, methodologies, etc. But in seeking these aims, transdisciplinarity will raise many fundamental questions about reward for academic work: bases for appointment, tenure, and promotion; claims to authorship and prestige; and the allocation of research funding to and within universities; etc. These are dangerous topics, and a dangerous pond in which to dip one's toe. Nothing is more likely to raise united opposition from academics (although often for different reasons) than suggestions for change within structures dealing with recognition, prestige, and the other rewards, especially research funding, they seek.

Professor Kriesi notes that as well as technical errors that can arise because of the ease, even for the uninitiated, of applying sophisticated quantitative methods, there is a syndrome described as "a superstition" that statistics will evaluate the relative merits of different substantive theories.[22] In this respect, statistics may be functioning more or less like a mantra, in that they open up the possibility of access to "knowledge" to which they are not directly related. Statistics may also be functioning as an imprimatur or seal of approval for research "products." Again we need to ask: Why would this have happened? There needs to be some sophisticated research—in particular, historical research—with respect to similar or analogous developments in the "hard" sciences, which might provide insights as to why this is occurring in the social sciences, and how it should be dealt with and judged.

One of the other free association thoughts which came forcefully to mind on reading Professor Kriesi's paper is the necessity for carrying out an assessment of the ethical acceptability of the impact of social science research, in particular when that research is used as the basis for public policy.

Section three of Professor Kriesi's paper is entitled "What to do?" He refers to Feyerabend's advocacy of "methodological permissiveness" and "'anarchistic' methodology" in contrast, it would seem, to scientific methodology. Importantly, Professor Kriesi refers to play, and quotes Phillips who says "[p]lay . . . give[s] free rein to imagination, intuition, and creative urges,"[23] and "suggests that a playful attitude is a necessary precondition for 'experiencing' the world."[24] I strongly endorse this view, and my free association is that we also need to consider the difference between childishness and childlikeness and what the latter has to offer. It would mean that one would be open to different ways of knowing, would be curious, and would count experiential knowledge as being as important as reasoned knowledge. My colleague, Dr. Joan Kahn has identified or generated some "playful" terminology for use in developing transdisciplinary methodologies: "turf terror," "physics envy," "asymmetrical assumptions," and "eureka generator," all have a sense of play. But it would be as much a mistake to focus only on experiential knowledge, or creativity and imagination as generated by play, as it is to focus only on "hard" science methodologies such as statistics. What is needed is not a disjunctive situation, but a conjunctive one. We need both good scientific methodologies, on the one hand, and space for imagination, creativity, and experiential knowledge, on the other hand. It may be fruitful to examine the law with this mind.

The law has a very long-standing and complex set of technical procedures, rules, and methodologies (including a system of precedent, which is used as a system of verification and correction), but it also has large areas of discretion and room for intuitive decision making and interpretation, the latter of which is fundamental. I have suggested elsewhere,[25] that the primary decision-making mechanism in the law is intuitive and is emotionally-based. However, cognitive and rational processes (including reliance on precedent) are an essential secondary verification mechanism that ensures that the primary decision is an acceptable one. In short, we need all of the following: process and substance, and cognitive and "other" ways of knowing.

It may also be that we are coming to a greater realization of the role of and necessity for experiential knowledge in decision making. For instance, it is probably particularly important in relation to societal level decision making regarding such matters as whether we should continue to prohibit or, alternatively, legalize euthanasia. If one takes a purely cognitive, rational approach, at an atomistic or individual level, and particularly in a society that focuses on individual autonomy and individual rights to self-determination, it can be difficult to argue against euthanasia. On the other hand, cognitive and rational analysis of the impact of euthanasia at the societal level, in my view indicates that we should not consider changing our law to legalize it. Furthermore, this view can be supported by our accumulated experiential knowledge (which can be tapped for instance through both "good" death stories and "bad" death stories).[26]

Professor Kriesi then addresses the distinction between proper and improper social science research practice, and notes that some people adopt the dogmatic position that there is only one way to do proper social science research.[27] Again, we return to the phenomenon that the poles are easier to defend than the middle way; that one is more comfortable, more certain, and often can appear more heroic, by standing at a pole and arguing strongly for it rather than for the middle. However, such polar positions are often wrong, which is unfortunate both for the people who hold these views and also for others who are affected by them, including society itself.

Professor Kriesi proposes that objective inference is a counter-productive goal. Social scientists "ought to acknowledge the whimsical character of statistical inference; they ought to admit that subjective opinions play a crucial role in their analyses."[28] We need to ask why we have sought to eliminate the subjective and replace it solely with the objective. At least chronologically the subjective is usually the basis of decision making and cannot be eliminated, although it needs to be safeguarded by the objective. This is the same distinction and connection that has been suggested above in proposing that decision making is, fundamentally, intuitively and emotionally based, but needs to be safeguarded by cognitive and rational processes, which can be regarded as "secondary verification mechanisms."

One of the most important statements in Professor Kriesi's paper is that "curiosity and play . . . are subject to method; to systematic doubt."[29] Professor Kriesi combines playful exploration and a concept of rules: the play is rule-bound; that is, "playful exploration does not imply that one abandons method altogether."[30] An old saying in the law for this type of duality was "freedom within fetters," and, indeed, as law students most of us spent a great deal of time considering how fetters may even be essential to freedom. Certainly we must have fetters in the sense that we take responsibility for what we do in exercising our freedom. In particular, in engaging in our intellectual play, we need to work out what rules (fetters) are needed to achieve two aims. First, we must ensure that we act ethically, and, second, we need to establish and evolve the methodologies and structures through which we can pursue our intellectual play. Our name for this system of rules is transdisciplinarity. This combination of freedom and fetters is also what I have called elsewhere the search for the purple-pink middle—the middle that consists of imagination and creativity, but is neither wild emotionalism nor unfettered and unstructured rambling, and which is guided by ethical sensitivity.[31]

In his conclusion, Professor Kriesi identifies three of the major elements with which social scientists must struggle. The first is the complexity of the large amount of data, which is the indispensable basis for the test of social science theory. The second and third are the elements of variability and chance. They "are inherently present in the non-experimental research designs that dominate in the social sciences."[32] As Professor Kriesi says, it is only the tools of statisticians and computer scientists that allow the social scientist to cope with these three elements. But we need to be careful in using these tools, of what Professor Kriesi calls at the beginning of his text, "overconscientiousness."[33] Again, the law and its standards might provide an interesting model by analogy. The law does not expect that one would always make the best decision possible, but neither will it allow decisions that fall below the standard of reasonably competent practice. Errors of judgment can be either non-negligent or negligent, depending on whether or not, respectively, they are errors that a reasonably competent practitioner could have made in the same circumstance. Perhaps we should follow the same type of approach in the social sciences. We have much to lose, in my view, if we seek always to make the "best" decision (in the sense that we want to avoid being faulted for it) and, in order to achieve this, we focus simply on the cognitive, rational, and logical. This may be what is occurring when there is an overuse, and even more so an exclusive use, of quantitative methods as the source of knowledge in the social sciences. And yet, we need to ensure that, to the greatest extent possible (consistent with allowing creativity, imagination, insight, and wisdom to function) we do have reliable data on which we base our "creative products." In short, this means that we should seek a balance between the use of statistical methodology, for example, and "other ways of knowing."

CONCLUSION

This concludes my free and unfettered associations on the statements made and issues raised in Professor Kriesi's most interesting paper. To summarize, the theme which I see emerging is that of a shift of paradigm, from what could be called a pure science paradigm, to one which will hold knowledge (including that relating to research methodologies) garnered from within both "hard" and "soft" science and the humanities and the arts, and from "other ways of knowing," as well as from cognitive, logical, and rational bases. It may even be that some of the elements from these different sources of knowledge can appear to be in conflict or to constitute "impossible combinations." Even if that is true, we still may need to hold them together in a structure which can accommodate them all and where the tensions between them can play out. Such tensions may well prove to be one of our richest sources of new knowledge and insights. Shakespeare's words spoken through Polonius,[34] which are often colloquially abbreviated to "there is method in his madness," is a better guiding principle than one which conforms to a rule that "there is madness in our method." "Enticement by methods" may come dangerously close to the latter, on occasion.

NOTES AND REFERENCES

1. Kriesi, Hanspeter, "Enticement by methods," p. 223.
2. Greenberg, Jeff/Rosenblatt, Abram/Solomon, Sheldon et al. 1989, "Evidence for Terror Management Theory," in: *Journal of Personality and Social Psychology* 57 (4), 681–690.
3. Kriesi, p. 227.
4. Kriesi, p. 223.
5. Somerville, Margaret A. 1993, "The Song of Death: The Lyrics of Euthanasia," in: *Journal of Contemporary Health Law and Policy* 9, 1–76, 23, 61–62.
6. Somerville, Margaret A. 1992, "New Perceptions, Old Values from Inner and Outer Spaces," in: *Canadian Speeches: Issues of the Day 1992*, 6 (5), 65–68. (Convocation address, University of Windsor, "Spacing-out and Spacing-in: Searching for the Purple-Pink Middle.")
7. Kriesi, p. 224, with reference to Johan Goudsblom.
8. Kriesi, p. 225.
9. Kriesi, p. 225, citing van Deth.
10. It should be noted that I am not, in any way, suggesting that wisdom is limited to highly educated persons. Often the contrary is true. What I am suggesting is that if we are consciously and systematically to pursue the development of wisdom through work in our academic institutions, this search will need to be structured. Wisdom will not just strike us like a bolt of lightning, although the feeling one has on gaining an insight, which is often the starting point for wisdom, can be experienced as being of this nature.
11. When less than 15% of an age cohort attend university, access to such education can be described as "elite"; over 15% and less than 30% represents "mass" university education. See Husen, Torsten 1991, "The Idea of the University: Changing Roles, Current Crisis and Future Challenges," XXI Prospectus, in: *Quarterly Review of Education UNESCO* 78, 171, 175, referring to Trow, Martin 1973, *Problems in the Transition from Elite to Mass Higher Education*, Berkeley, Carnegie Commission of Higher Education 1973.
12. Schulman, D. 1988, "Remembering Who We Are: AIDS and Law in a Time of Madness," in: *AIDS and Public Policy* 3, 75–76.
13. Howe, A. 1986, "Allocation of Resources in the Care of the Aged," in: *Bioethic News*, 5–13.
14. van Deth in Kriesi, p. 225.
15. Kriesi, p. 226.
16. Kriesi, p. 226.

17. Kriesi, p. 226.
18. Kriesi, p. 226.
19. Katz, J. 1984, *The Silent World of Doctor and Patient*, New York, Free Press.
20. Kriesi, p. 227.
21. Kriesi, pp. 229–230.
22. Kriesi, p. 230.
23. Phillips in Kriesi, p. 232.
24. Kriesi, p. 232.
25. Somerville, Margaret A. 1989, "Justice Across the Generations," in: *Social Science and Medicine* 29 (3), 385–394.
26. Somerville 1993, 44–45.
27. Kriesi, p. 233.
28. Kriesi, p. 234.
29. Kriesi, p. 235.
30. Kriesi, p. 235.
31. Somerville 1992.
32. Kriesi, p. 238.
33. Kriesi, p. 223.
34. Polonius: "Though this be madness, yet there is method in it." (on witnessing Hamlet's behavior); cf. "Though this be method, yet there is [query: may be] madness in it." (I am indebted for this insight to Dr. J. Kahn).

Informed Consent in the
Social Sciences:
Agreeing to Being Deceived

HEINZ GUTSCHER

INTRODUCTION

In social science research, lies are employed to discover truth. Especially in social psychological laboratory and field experiments, it has become established practice to withhold the truth about participants' fields of action in order to find truths about their behavior. Participation in such studies is therefore based upon "misinformed consent."

Social scientific research needs to investigate human perception, experience, thought, and behavior. Within the framework of their investigations, scientists seek—for a limited space of time—to establish cooperation with their subjects. Persons faced with the request to cooperate must almost always make their decision to participate in a study without knowledge of the true purposes of the researchers and, very often, on the basis of intentionally misleading information about the project. This is the case despite the fact that their very decision to participate is based upon the assumption of mutual honesty. Trust is the foundation of subjects' decision to take part. Their participation contains an implicit "social contract" between investigators and subjects limited temporally to the duration of the experiment. Research participants rely upon investigators to tell the truth when they assure subjects that participation entails no risks. For their part, investigators assume that subjects will not deliberately deceive them. This expectation of mutual honesty, however, is regularly blatantly ignored by experimenters, in that participants are told only part of the truth of various aspects of experiments, or are deliberately lied to. The extent of this deception varies: almost always the aim of an investigation is not revealed to subjects, a practice which can often be viewed as a harmless form of deception. Very often, however, an elaborate cover story is presented which forms the subjects' basis for deciding to cooperate with the investigator and the basis of their subsequent, observed behavior. The reality of the investigation becomes fiction; it rests upon the investigator's screenplay. The goal of this staging is to hide the purpose of the study as well as to ensure participants' naiveté and lack of bias.

Following evaluation of the data, full debriefing usually takes place: only now are participants told that they were deceived and to what extent; only now are the true purposes of the research revealed. Only at this point do investigators ask participants to be understanding with regard to the deception, and present justifying arguments. A typical sign that such research practices are self-understood and "normal" is the fact that usual debriefing procedures do not include an apology to participants. The thoughtlessness with which researchers respond to objections to these practices and the standard of scientific argumentation employed to support them stand in marked contrast to the professional efforts and expense invested in the construction of the deceiving settings and procedures.

Such research practices break the moral rules of the research participants and contradict—at least in principle—established professional ethical guidelines (American Psychological Association 1973, 1982). The basic requirement of the guidelines, informed consent, cannot be met when researchers withhold information from potential participants or willingly provide them with falsehoods. It must be noted here, however, that the guidelines do already make provision for exceptions: "methodological requirements of a study may make the use of concealment or deception necessary" (American Psychological Association 1982, 6). Appeal to this passage of the guidelines is not the exception but rather the rule in social psychological experimental practice.

The following makes a plea for different treatment of the persons whose behavior we study. From the multitude of ethical dilemmas in social science research, we will discuss only the fundamental problem of deception. First, various types of deception and the justifications used to defend them will be examined. There follows an overview of the possible costs of these practices. Finally, two possible routes to solving the problems are presented.

DECEPTION

Deceptive practices are common in social psychological research. Surveys have shown that in more than 50% of studies published in leading professional journals, deception in some form is involved (Adair/Dushenko/

Lindsay 1985; Gross/Fleming, 1982; McNamara/Woods, 1977; Smith/ Richardson 1983). Adair et al. (1985) show that this trend has not decreased, in spite of the publication of ethical guidelines by various professional organizations (USA, Canada, Germany, Holland, Sweden, Switzerland, etc.; see Schuler 1980, 205). Most of these guidelines do, however, permit that the strict premises of informed consent be waived provided that certain, none too restrictive, conditions pertain. Such qualifications of the informed consent guidelines are as follows:

> (a) The research objective is of great importance and cannot be achieved without the use of deception; (b) on being fully informed later, participants are expected to find the procedures reasonable and to suffer no loss of confidence in the integrity of the investigator or of others involved; (c) research participants are allowed to withdraw from the study at any time, and are free to withdraw their data when the concealment or misrepresentation is revealed; (d) investigators take full responsibility for detecting and removing stressful aftereffects of the experience (American Psychological Association 1982, 41).

The percentage of published studies which are based upon deception increased markedly throughout three decades. "Neither the incidence nor the magnitude of deception reported in social psychological research appears to have decreased since 1973. Thus, the APA guidelines appear to serve an expressive rather than a deterrent function" (Baumrind 1985, 166).

In research practice, different types of deception are employed. Sieber (1978, cited in Geller 1982, 40) identifies three kinds: implicit, technical, and role-related deception. In most cases, there is a combination of these types.

Implicit deception is involved when participants in a study act under false premises—when the real situation and the situation as perceived by participants strongly deviate. This happens when participants are not informed that they are serving as subjects in an investigation (for example, West/Gunn/Chernicky 1975). In technical deception, false information is given about the procedures and apparatus in an experiment (for example, Milgram 1963, 1974). Within the context of role deception, participants are misinformed about the role of others taking part. For example, these others may be presented as fellow subjects when they are in fact confederates of the investigator. A further variant involves participant observation: social scientists investigate human behavior in the field, without revealing their role as observers.

What are the reasons for giving participants incomplete or false information? One main reason is grounded in the fear that information will influence the behavior which is to be studied. The aim is thus to avoid bias. Bias in subjects is probable if information, for example about the goals of a study, places the participants under pressure in terms of certain expectations. It is easy to imagine that a study on prejudice, when the purposes of the investigation are openly revealed at the start, will not yield valid results generalizable to the world outside the experiment. Deception in experiments aims to create a segment of everyday reality. The behavior studied should only be systematically influenced by factors controlled by the experimenters. Expectations, certain strategies of self-presentation, and orientation to norms of social desirability represent undesirable, additional sources of influence which, resulting from disclosure of a study's purposes, affect the behaviors under observation.

Taken together, these fears do seem justified. There are a number of empirical investigations which show that the behavior of participants in a study is in fact strongly influenced by disclosure of a study's aims and procedures. Under conditions of informed consent, some previously reliable and replicated findings could no longer be demonstrated. Gardner (1978) performed an experiment with two groups of subjects treated identically except that one group gave their informed consent while the other did not. Results confirmed that the procedures involving informed consent prevent the emergence of negative aftereffects of noise, possibly because these procedures give the subjects a degree of control over the stressor. The freedom to withdraw from the experiment at any time may play a central role here. Similar phenomena may occur in research on other environmental stressors, in which subjects' perception of control is a critical variable (see also commentary in Trice 1986). Similar conclusions were reached by Dill/Gilden/Hill/Hanselka (1982) as well as Resnick/Schwartz (1973).

COSTS

Deception is often viewed as harmless if experiments do not involve much stress for the participants. In contrast, most critics take the position that—regardless of the amount of stress in experiments—giving false information to participants causes harm on principle (Kelman 1967; Baumrind 1985). Supporters of deceptive procedures usually carry out simple cost-benefit analyses, whereby potential costs are often rashly judged to be low. Neither costs to negatively-affected minorities nor certain long-term costs are seriously taken into consideration.

What types of cost can be distinguished? Baumrind (1985) argues that as a result of deceptive practices within social science research, subjects, the profession, and society come to harm. These three aspects will be examined in the following.

Subjects

Critics of deceptive research practices often present anecdotal evidence of individuals' experience which shows that subjects were deeply harmed by the deception:

> ...I found the experience devastating. I was harmed in an area of my thinking which was central to my personal development at that time. ...I told literally no one about it for eight years because of a vague feeling of shame over having let myself be tricked and duped. It was only when I realized that I was not peculiar but had, on the contrary, had a *typical* experience that I first recounted it publicly. (Baumrind 1985, 168)

Similar experiences are summarized by Geller as follows: "Ethically, it points to the possibly lasting consequences of a deception that mimics a fairly common experience and that was not easily overcome by debriefing" (Geller 1982, 41). It seems that not even extensive, well-meaning debriefing procedures can succeed in every case to make up for the harm done during the course of experiments. In addition to such anecdotal evidence, there is a body of systematic, empirical studies on the question of harm due to deception. Findings are not, however, unequivocal.

It is true that, within the framework of immediate follow-up questionnaires, four out of five participants say that they were glad to have taken part. However, it is logically inconsistent for supporters of deceptive practices to rely on self-reports, which due to their unreliability are themselves often the subject of experimental research. During such questioning at the end of debriefing, participants who in the experiment were shown to be immature, highly influenced, conforming, overly obedient and so on are suddenly to be seen as autonomous and reliable sources of information which can be used to justify investigators' procedures. Furthermore, questions can be raised with regard to the methodological expense and psychometric qualities of such measurements at the end of experiments.

There are reasons to assume that a part of these positive self-reports on being deceived are instead superficial, face-saving statements which do not adequately represent participants' true inner feelings (would subjects feel like speaking openly and honestly about harm experienced when they have only just learned that they have been grossly lied to?). Positive self-reports can also be explained by a variety of social-psychological mechanisms. For example, the mechanism of effort justification may play an important role in the low degree of negative feedback on an experiment just completed. In effort justification, the attractiveness of a task voluntarily performed is rated higher the greater the efforts required by the task; any other rating would impair self-esteem (Aronson 1961; Zimbardo 1965).

In a questionnaire study by Smith & Richardson (1983), participants in a deception experiment rated their experience as more positive than nondeceived participants. In interpreting these findings, however, it was not taken into consideration that deception experiments are probably experienced by the participants as less boring (see Aronson/Ellsworth/Carlsmith/Gonzales 1990, 91). Still, approximately one out of five participants questioned reported experiencing harm, even though this study is often cited by supporters of deception practices (Smith/Richardson 1983, 1079). The majority of such reports was received from persons who had participated in a deception experiment.

Further support to the thesis of harm is lent by an investigation by Walster/Berscheid/Abrahams/Aronson (1967):

> It is disturbing that ... even after a lengthy and thorough debriefing (probably atypical in thoroughness) subjects still behaved to some extent as though the debriefing had not taken place. Subjects behaved in this manner even though they had voiced to the experimenter their understanding that the manipulation was false, their understanding of the true purpose of the experiment, and even though, by their manner and replies, the experimenter had been satisfied that they did indeed understand the nature of the deception. Even more disturbing is the evidence that the aftereffects of debriefing might be complex, unpredictable, and may depend in part upon the personality traits of the subjects. (380)

On the whole, we can assume that participants in experiments involving deception suffer psychological harm in that they can suffer hurt, uncertainty, and humiliation, and lose trust.

A common strategy in dealing with these facts is to assume that in the great majority of cases harm is minimal. But as Baumrind's (1985) arguments against this view state:

> The harm the minority of subjects report they have suffered is not nullified by the majority of subjects who claim to have escaped unscathed, any more than the harm done victims of drunk drivers can be excused by the disproportionate number of pedestrians with sufficient alacrity to avoid being run over by them. (169)

All the same, it must also be considered that, in addition to grave cases, there are also more harmless forms of experimental deception which do not involve the same extent of risk for the participants.

Profession

Harm done by deception also applies to a second group, the investigators themselves. Costs incurred to the profession include endangering the pool of naive and cooperative subjects. To assume that today's undergraduates are naive subjects is itself naive. Studies indicate that a large proportion of the pool of undergraduate subjects expects deception and is not willing, in replies following an experiment, to admit that parts of the experimental design were quite apparent (see Geller 1982, 42; Golding/Lichtenstein 1970; Levy 1967; Orne 1962). Page (1973, cited in Baumrind 1985, 170) showed that the number of participants found to be suspicious depends greatly upon methodological efforts expended: asking subjects fewer than four questions will show only 5% of subjects as suspicious, while extended questionnaires identify up to 40% of participants as mistrustful.

As suspicious subjects no longer behave naively and without bias, they should not, according to the logic of practiced deception, be included in the data. As a result of this, more subjects would have to be included in a study. In spite of the danger that investigators here deceive themselves, the greater efforts which would be required do not provide incentive to increase methodological expenditure in identifying suspicious subjects.

Further costs include a damaging of the profession's reputation. A scientific discipline which invests so much in designing deceptive plans of research and thus routinely injures fundamental rules of everyday ethical conduct puts itself at risk of losing public support. Participants in deception experiments tend to rate psychologists as less trustworthy than nondeceived subjects (Smith/Richardson 1983, 1078). The effects of routinely deceiving subjects upon researchers' handling of truth and upon their ethical sensibilities and integrity can only be surmised; empirical studies on these issues are not available.

Society

The third group having to pay the costs of these research practices is society itself. The main price is the violation and weakening of essential norms and rules of human relations by some elite members of society. Exception may be taken especially to the fact that the violations of rules take place in the service of truth, and that such practices are justified for this reason. "The inherent cost of behaving deceitfully in the research setting is to undermine trust in expert authorities" (Baumrind 1985, 169). In cases where experiments cannot be distinguished from real-life situations, which happens especially in experimentation in the field, there may be additional effects in the form of greater mistrust or decreasing willingness to aid others in unusual public situations.

SOLUTIONS

There are alternatives to continuing to cite only evidence which seems to support the ethics of deceptive research practices and their continued use. I see two possible scenarios. They are not mutually exclusive; their conclusions may be combined.

Alternative Methods without Deception

The first scenario is based upon the assessment that there exist enough viable alternatives to current methods. The element of deception can be dispensed with in research practice.

One of the most important ways to work without deception is to study behavior in its everyday environment. The main problem with this method is the lack of control investigators have on the influencing variables. For this reason, many field studies incorporate experimental control techniques involving deception. Classic examples here are Piliavin and Piliavin's (1972) studies of helping behavior. In these experiments, a confederate of the investigators staged a collapse in a subway, while others covertly observed the intervention behavior of passengers.

For obvious reasons, it is much more difficult, less efficient, and also extremely costly in terms of time to investigate these behaviors in the field without employing deceptive techniques. Use of deception makes it possible to control, upon the background of the manifold interfering factors which can hardly be influenced, at least the most important hypothetical variables. However, the important ethical and legal implications as well as costs to society raised by deception here (Silverman 1975), make it seem advisable to forgo such investigation in the field.

As an alternative, there is the possibility of the combined techniques of observation and intensive interviews during, or following, real-life emergency situations. In other cases, where controlled, experimental techniques do not seem applicable, we must consider, in addition to various quasi-experimental techniques (Campbell/Stanley 1966), the possibilities of time-series investigations. Here the same group of participants are tested a number of times under different, naturally varying conditions. Geller (1982) also discusses techniques of nondeceptive laboratory experiments. A common method of manipulating self-esteem, as an influencing factor in behavior, has consisted in giving subjects false feedback about the quality of their performance. As an alternative, Geller (1982, 46) suggests that we measure the real level of self-esteem following accurate feedback about performance. The influence of self-esteem could then, by means of statistical methods of regression, be related to behaviors assumed to be dependent upon the degree of self-esteem.

The most often cited alternative technique is probably simulation. In the following, we will discuss only interactive simulation, that is, procedures in which real persons are involved (in contrast to pure, non-interactive computer simulation).

Simulations are not deception-free methods per se, but they can be altered to exclude deception at little expense. Geller (1982) distinguishes game simulation, field simulation, and role-playing simulation. In game simulations, participants take on a role in various subject areas such as environment, economics, planning, and the like (Guetzkow 1962). Field simulations take place in a more realistic, temporally longer setting. One of the most well-known studies of this kind is the Stanford prison study (Zimbardo 1973). Here volunteers interacted in a simulated prison. The investigation had to be discontinued after six days, because the realness of the simulation began to exceed set limits. After this short period, the simulation had become for the participants an extremely stressful real situation.

In role-playing simulation, participants are requested to act as if the situation, created more or less realistically by researchers, were real. In this way, experiments can be carried out with fully informed participants. During the course of the simulation, subjects grow into their roles, performing them as if they were real. Geller (1978) demonstrated that, for example, the extent of obedience in the Milgram experiments (Milgram 1963, 1974) can be replicated rather well using this method. Additional successful replications with this method were published by Horowitz/ Rothschild 1970, Mixon 1971, O'Leary/Willis/Tomich 1970, Wahl 1973 and Willis/Willis 1970.

The implementation of simulation methods does not automatically eliminate all ethical risks. Stress to potential subjects of the kind experienced by participants in the Stanford prison study is very difficult to foresee prior to a study. This involves problems requiring difficult solutions if the conditions of informed consent are to be met. It is doubtful that the consequences of simulation can ever be adequately predicted in advance. And, if such knowledge has been gained through previous experiments, there are further issues: Is it enough to give subjects written information in the form of descriptions, or must information be presented more realistically, acoustically and visually in the form of a video film? How can potential participants be protected from over-estimating their ability to bear the effects?

When evaluating these methods, it is important to distinguish between role-playing simulations and forms of role taking (imagining what another person would do in a particular situation). The most vehement criticisms of these procedures are based partly on a misunderstanding. Freedman (1969) tended to oppose role taking; in his objection to this "psychology by consensus," he pointed to the fact that both laymen and experts had falsely predicted the extent of obedience which occurred in the Milgram experiment. An evaluation of role-playing methods in Aronson/Ellsworth/Carlsmith/Gonzales (1990) is also clearly directed towards role taking: ". . . when we ask subjects to predict how they would behave in a given situation, they may well be unable to do so in a veridical fashion" (96).

Other objections concern the danger of distorting demand characteristics (for example, Aronson et al. 1990, 97). Demand characteristics include aspects of instruction, the setting and procedures as well as expectations of the investigator and confederates which have a decisive influence upon subjects' subjective definitions of the situation and their behavior in a study (Orne 1962). However, these problems do not apply only to the alternative approaches described—they also play a crucial role within classical experimental methods.

A central problem area is caused by the emotional engagement of participants which arises in successful simulations. When simulation is experienced as being real, resulting emotional stress in participants presents us with similar ethical problems to those incurred by deception techniques: participants must be shielded from experiencing too much emotional strain. We can expect, however, that in spite of possible similar levels of emotional stress in simulated situations, participants can be debriefed more quickly and reliably. Here participants can be reminded again that the situation was a game. This information during debriefing is not new to participants and is thus not experienced as stressful. In contrast, debriefing about deception often does not represent helpful information. On the contrary, it presents, in addition to the stresses and strains produced by the experimental situation, the subject with yet another experience to be digested.

Agreeing to Being Deceived

The second scenario is based upon the assumption that there do not exist enough viable alternatives to common methods, and that we cannot therefore dispense with them in research practice at the present time.

Within the framework of this scenario, efforts should be undertaken to make deception, as an indispensable part of social scientific methodology, publicly visible.

Potential participants must be informed as to the possibility of incomplete disclosure of information and deception before they decide to take part in an experiment. They should explicitly consent to deception. If researchers are absolutely convinced of the indispensableness of deception as a social scientific research technique, then they should be in a position to explain and justify this to potential participants. If arguments supporting the use of deception in social scientific practice are solid, it should be possible to convince subjects that incomplete information and deception are necessary.

One suggestion, which for example might be used with undergraduate student subject pools, is made by Engelhardt (1986):

> Where the risks from deception are minor, it can usually be presumed that a general disclosure with few details will adequately serve the purpose of respecting the freedom of the would-be subject (e.g., "over the next few weeks you will be subjected to certain minor deceptions in order to study the process of learning"). (330)

The foundation of contractual agreement between researcher and participant is thus the previous presentation of arguments which explain the need for an initially incomplete divulgence of information and possible deception. Participants may also be informed in advance that complete debriefing will follow the investigation.

These precautions make up the fundamental conditions of informed consent. In this way, ethically responsible and fair social contracts can be established between investigators and research participants. "The principle of mutual respect does not require that individuals be protected against deception, but only that they not unwittingly be subjected to deception" (Engelhardt 1986, 297). Under the conditions described, voluntary participation in an experiment is as ethically safe as voluntary participation in a game of poker, where certain forms of deception (but not arbitrary ones) are also part and parcel of the contractual agreement (see Engelhardt 1986, 296).

Naturally, not all problems are thus resolved. Warning participants of possible deception represents a necessary but not sufficient ethical basis for this type of research: participants must further, in an appropriate fashion, be made aware of possible risks or stresses (Kimmel 1988, 68).

Various recommendations have been made with regard to warning potential participants, but they are usually quickly dismissed or only halfheartedly put into practice (see Geller 1982, 43). The fear is widespread that warning subjects about possible deception actually increases mistrust. There is, however, hardly any empirical evidence to support this. It is just as likely that after appropriate and satisfactory information as well as advance notice of debriefing to follow, participants are more relaxed and less apt to make efforts to discover the "real" goals of a study hidden behind the deceiving cover story.

At present, it is not easy to find systematic empirical evidence of the effects of advance information. Because the important professional journals do not have uniform guidelines, very often few or no details on ethical aspects and procedures of empirical studies are reported. Small initial findings supporting the scenario presented here can, however, be found. Gerdes (1979, 107) reports the following: ". . . a general forewarning can be used with volunteers to obtain informed consent for deception, apparently without altering the data." And Holmes & Bennett (1974) conclude that:

> Last, it appears that subjects can be informed that deceptions are sometimes used in experiments without necessarily eliminating the possibility that subjects can be subsequently deceived. However, even if the prior information concerning deceptions were to reduce somewhat the number of subjects deceived (hopefully, these would be identified in the post-experimental debriefing), this would probably be acceptable if it avoided criticism and potential censorship of deception research over the issue of informed consent. Fortunately, it does not appear that even this cost is incurred when using informed consent like that used in the present investigation. (366)

These findings indicate that informing participants about possible deception evidently does not always lead to distortion of the data. Still, too little data is available at present to present conclusive statements on the benefits and risks of the suggested scenario. This is an area which greatly demands further research.

CONCLUSIONS

Two paths towards solving the problem of deception have been examined, both of which amount to largely renouncing the use of deceptive practices in social science research. In each case, deception should become a true exception, which—in contrast to current practice—should pass over the hurdles of the Institutional Review Boards only under very particular and extremely well-founded conditions. Each of the two suggested scenarios requires the courage to give up familiar practices. In the one case, there are risks involved in new methodologies. In the other, the proposal to view research participants as mature partners entails a renunciation of power. More than before, keeping the promise to allow participants free and informed consent forces us to ask for their cooperation by using rational arguments which justify the worth of taking part. Free and informed consent means that potential participants can decide freely. This requires that partners have equal rights, and are not put under the pressure of institutional requirements or their own vital needs, but rather may be convinced to cooperate by means of informative arguments.

We must seriously attempt to put the methods of ethical vandalism, practiced so long and as self-understood, behind us. Upholding the guidelines of free and informed consent could stimulate us to think about the balance between the importance of our scientific efforts and our respect for fellow human beings, whose well-being is supposedly the ultimate object of research. Ethically responsible behavior requires the insight to set limits on our research endeavors and to respect the limits of others.

REFERENCES

Adair, J.G./Dushenko, T.W./Lindsay, R.C. 1985, "Ethical Regulations and Their Impact on Research Practice," in: *American Psychologist* 40 (1), 59–72.

American Psychological Association. Committee for the Protection of Human Participants in Research 1973, *Ethical Principles in the Conduct of Research with Human Participants*, Washington DC, Author.

American Psychological Association. Committee for the Protection of Human Participants in Research 1982, *Ethical Principles in the Conduct of Research with Human Participants* (2nd edtion) Washington DC, Author.

Aronson, E. 1961, "The Effects of Effort on the Attractiveness of Rewarded and Unrewarded Stimuli," in: *Journal of Abnormal and Social Psychology* 63, 375–380.

Aronson, E./Ellsworth, P.C./Carlsmith, J.M./Gonzales, M.H. 1990, *Methods of Research in Social Psychology* (2nd edition), New York, McGraw-Hill.

Baumrind, D. 1985, "Research Using Intentional Deception," in: *American Psychologist* 40 (2), 165–174.

Campbell, D.T./Stanley, J.C. 1966, *Experimental and Quasi-Experimental Designs for Research*, Chicago, Rand McNally.

Dill, C.A./Gilden, E.R./Hill, P.C./Hanselka, L.L. 1982, "Federal Human Subject Regulations: A Methodological Artifact?," in: *Personality and Social Psychology Bulletin* 8, 417–425.

Engelhardt, H.T. 1986, *The Foundations of Bioethics*, New York, Oxford University Press.

Freedman, J.L. 1969, "Role-Playing: Psychology by Consensus," in: *Journal of Personality and Social Psychology* 13, 107–114.

Gardner, G.T. 1978, "Effects of Federal Human Subjects Regulations on Data

Obtained in Environmental Stressor Research," in: *Journal of Personality and Social Psychology* 36, 628–634.

Geller, D.M. 1978, "Involvement in Role-Playing Simulations: A Demonstration with Studies on Obedience," in *Journal of Personality and Social Psychology* 36, 219–235.

———— 1982, "Alternatives to Deception: Why, What, and How?," in: Sieber, J.E. (ed.), *The Ethics of Social Reseach: Surveys and Experiments*, New York, Springer, 39–55.

Gerdes, E.P. 1979, "College Students' Reactions to Social Psychological Experiments Involving Deception," in *Journal of Social Psychology* 107, 99–110.

Golding, S.L./Lichtenstein, E. 1970, "Confession of Awareness and Prior Knowledge of Deception as a Function of Interview Set and Approval Motivation," in: *Journal of Personality and Social Psychology* 14, 213–223.

Gross, A.E./Fleming, I. 1982, "Twenty Years of Deception in Social Psychology," in: *Personality and Social Psychology Bulletin* 8, 402–408.

Guetzkow, M. (ed.) 1962, *Simulation in the Social Sciences*, Englewood Cliffs, N.J., Prentice-Hall.

Holmes, D.S./Bennett, D.H. 1974, "Experiments to Answer Questions Raised by the Use of Deception in Psychological Research: I. Role Playing as an Alternative to Deception; II. Effectiveness of Debriefing After a Deception; III. Effect of Informed Consent on Deception," in: *Journal of Personality and Social Psychology* 29, 358–367.

Horowitz, I.A./Rothschild, B.H. 1970, "Conformity as a Function of Deception and Role Playing," in: *Journal of Personality and Social Psychology* 14, 224–226.

Kelman, H.C. 1967, "Human Use of Human Subjects: The Problem of Deception in Social Psychological Experiments," in: *Psychological Bulletin* 67, 1–11.

Kimmel, A.J. 1988, *Ethics and Values in Applied Social Research*, Newbury Park, Sage.

Levy, L. 1967, "Awareness, Learning, and the Beneficient Subject as Expert Witness," in: *Journal of Personality and Social Psychology* 6, 363–370.

McNamara, J.R./Woods, K.M. 1977, "Ethical Considerations in Psychological Research: A Comparative Review," in: *Behavior Therapy* 8, 703–708.

Milgram, S. 1963, "Behavioral Study of Obedience," in: *Journal of Abnormal and Social Psychology* 67, 371–378.

Milgram, S. 1974, *Obedience to Authority. An Experimental View*, New York, Harper & Row.

Mixon, D. 1971, "Behavior Analysis Treating Subjects as Actors Rather than Organisms," in: *Journal for the Theory of Social Behavior* 1, 19–31.

O'Leary, C./Willis, F./Tomich, E. 1970, "Conformity Under Deceptive and Non-Deceptive Techniques," in: *Sociological Quarterly* 11, 87–93.

Orne, M. 1962, "On the Social Psychology of the Psychological Experiment: With Particular Reference to Demand Characteristics and Their Implications," in: *American Psychologist* 17, 776–783.

Piliavin, J.A./Piliavin, I.M. 1972, "Effect of Blood on Reactions to a Victim," in: *Journal of Personality and Social Psychology* 23, 353–361.

Resnick, J.H./Schwartz, T. 1973, "Ethical Standards as an Independent Variable in Psychological Research," in: *American Psychologist* 28, 134–139.

Silverman, I. 1975, "Nonreactive Methods and the Law," in: *American Psychologist* 30, 764–769.

Smith, S.S./Richardson, D. 1983, "Amelioration of Deception and Harm in Psychological Research: The Important Role of Debriefing," in: *Journal of Personality and Social Psychology* 44, 1075–1082.

Schuler, H. 1980, *Ethische Probleme psychologischer Forschung*, Göttingen, Hogrefe.

Trice, A.D. 1986, "Ethical Variables?," in: *American Psychologist* 41, 482–483.

Wahl, J.M. 1973, "Role Playing vs. Deception: Differences in Experimental Realism as Measured by Subject's Level of Involvement and Level of Suspicion," in: *Dissertation Abstracts International* 33, (98), 44.

Walster, E./Berscheid, E./Abrahams, D./Aronson, V. 1967, "Effectiveness of Debriefing Following Deception Experiments," in: *Journal of Personality and Social Psychology* 6, 371–380.

West, S.G./Gunn, S.P./Chernicky, P. 1975, "Ubiquitous Watergate: An Attributional Analysis," in: *Journal of Personality and Social Psychology* 32, 55–65.

Willis, R./Willis, Y. 1970, "Role-Playing Versus Deception: An Experimental Comparison," in: *Journal of Personality and Social Psychology* 16, 472–477.

Zimbardo, P.G. 1965, "The Effect of Effort and Improvisation on Self-Persuasion Produced by Role-Playing," in: *Journal of Experimental and Social Psychology* 1, 103–120.

Zimbardo, P.G. 1973, "On the Ethics of Intervention in Human Psychological Research: With Special Reference to the Stanford Prison Experiment," in: *Cognition* 2, 243–256.

Social Sciences, Humanities, and Scientific Responsibility
A Comment

PIERRE MOESSINGER

Following Mayntz (1992), the phenomenal difference between humanities and social sciences is a methodological one. To be brief, humanities deal more with interpretive approaches while social sciences are concerned with a systematic confrontation with reality and with integrating knowledge. Of course one could try to object to this distinction by emphasizing systematic approaches in the humanities and/or interpretive approaches in the social sciences. Instead of opposing humanities and social sciences, one could rather oppose two *approaches* found both in humanities and social sciences. Yet, this would not change the fact that research in the social sciences is more systematic than in the humanities, and that interpretation methods are more in use in the humanities than in the social sciences.

Now each of these approaches have their own pitfalls: The problem with humanities—or rather with interpretive approaches—is the tendency to lock themselves into schools of thought. In other words, the danger here is that intersubjective agreement is mainly based on sameness of values. In turn, the two dangers of social sciences have always been extreme empiricism on the one hand, and extreme rationalism on the other. For the extreme empiricist, doing experiments is the alpha and the omega of every research, and for the extreme rationalist, doing science is equivalent to elaborating mathematical models. The former trend leads to theoretical emptiness, the latter to a disjunction between theory and facts.

As Mayntz (1992) observes, the two kinds of approaches (interpretive and systematic) have never operated in watertight compartments.

The history of social sciences and humanities is replete with cases of fruitful interchange and cross-fertilization. On the one hand, interpretive approaches may provide new ideas, or leads, which may become sound hypotheses when integrated into hypothetical systems. On the other hand, systematic approaches provide rigorous methodological procedures that can be used within interpretive approaches. The war between the two approaches is over. Nineteenth century phenomenology, which reduced science to positivism and claimed that only phenomenology could reach essences, is far behind us.

There are attempts to coordinate the two approaches within an integrative methodology. The example of Weber's methodological individualism immediately comes to mind. Piaget's (1927) "clinical method" is another example. By this method, he tried to follow the meandering of the subject's thinking ("les sinuosités de la pensée du sujet"). Surely, Piaget compared subjects, and in this sense his approach was systematic, but he also tried to understand the meaning subjects were giving to the world, particularly the way this meaning is organized. Unlike with phenomenological approaches, the subject's meaning is taken as a fact, yet, making sense of the subject's meaning for the experimenter is an inevitable step of this undertaking. It is obviously difficult here to separate interpretation and systematization, for, on the one hand, the researcher interprets the meaning of the subject's action, and, on the other hand, this interpretation is not merely subjective but is based on comparative observation and integrated into background knowledge.

SCIENCE, NONSCIENCE, AND METAPHYSICS

The demarcation problem can be traced back in this century to logical positivism and to Rudolph Carnap in particular. Disgusted by the gibberish of bad German metaphysics, Carnap (1969) tried to draw a line of demarcation between science and nonscience. Carnap's attempt was a reductionist project. Everything that is scientific (chemistry, biology, psychology, etc.) could ultimately be reduced to the level of physics. Along with this reductionism was the rejection of traditional metaphysical problems and foundational problems as nonscientific and incapable of resolution.

The problem of demarcation was taken up by Popper (1963) who criticized Carnap, arguing that it is impossible to exclude metaphysical claims using Carnap's criteria. For Popper, metaphysical claims are not recognized by their formulation but by the fact that they are not refutable. Popper's solution (or rather creation) of the demarcation problem met little opposition, probably because it looked simple and clear.

Against Popper, Bunge (1983) observes that researchers in their labo-

ratories do not spend much of their time looking for refutable hypotheses, neither do they linger on refuting hypotheses. Very often, they attempt to confirm hypotheses. But more importantly Bunge mentions that some hypotheses, e.g., para-psychological hypotheses, can be refuted, and yet remain outside of science. He thus emphasizes that hypotheses are not made in a vacuum, but within a context of background knowledge. It is today's background knowledge which makes parapsychological claims nonscientific. In other words, Bunge does not make a demarcation between science and metaphysics (for him, they overlap) but between science and nonscience.

PROTOSCIENCE AND PSEUDOSCIENCE

In a recent debate published in *New Ideas in Psychology*, Blitz (1991) takes issue with Bunge (1991), claiming that with Bunge's definition, it is impossible to distinguish pseudoscience from protoscience. Let me first recall that Bunge considers parapsychology as pseudoscience for the following two reasons:

1. This discipline is isolated from the scientific disciplines, admitting such entities as Rhine's PK-energy and paranormal phenomena, which other sciences cannot confirm or discover at all.
2. Parapsychology also falls short on the criterion of repeatable testability, since it involves exceptional individuals.

Now, Blitz mentions the example of phrenology, and more precisely the question of localization of brain functions within the brain. There is here a long tradition of theorizing in this field that can be traced back to Hippocrates and Galen. Localizationism was also quite popular in the sixteenth and seventeenth centuries. Such hypotheses have had a long life before they entered the realm of science. They were thus protoscientific, yet, for Blitz, they sound like pseudoscience. Following Blitz, one cannot exclude that parapsychology will one day be considered a protoscience.

Blitz also mentions that it is sometimes difficult to distinguish a novel and important scientific innovation from a pseudoscientific claim. He mentions the case of Alfred Wegner, who formulated a theory of continental drift in the twenties. Until the mid fifties, this theory was considered as pseudoscience by most geographers, until support was provided by satellites' measurements and the discovery of the underlying mechanism of plate tectonics. In other words, Wegner's ideas are now considered as proto-modern geography, but were considered pseudoscientific earlier. A theory which is viewed as pseudoscientific today may be considered as protoscientific tomorrow. Therefore, it is not prudent, Blitz argues, to categorize parapsychology as a pseudoscience.

Bunge replies that parapsychology explains too much and too cheaply and that it makes no predictions that can be controlled. Conducting experiments is not enough; they have to make sense within a theoretical claim, and this theoretical claim must have some connection with background knowledge. As to phrenology, Bunge distinguishes pseudo from proto aspects of it. For example, the hypothesis that mental functions can be determined from bumps of the skull has never been confirmed and has always been considered as sheer fantasy: it has remained pseudoscientific. In turn, other hypotheses, like Broca's and Wernicke's, could be tested and were soon seen as explaining and predicting. On the whole, Bunge considers phrenology as half protoscience, half pseudoscience. The plate tectonics hypotheses, for Bunge, in their early phase, were unorthodox yet scientific hypotheses. They were soon seen to explain and predict facts that no other theory could account for. The fact that they were seen as unscientific at one stage does not qualify them as nonscientific. Bunge wishes to keep science and truth separate. Science is often wrong, yet it is the best way, he says, to discover falsity and to get deep truths about the world.

This debate also applies to social sciences outside psychology. In sociology, for example, there is a tendency to integrate theories—or rather hypothetical systems—into current background knowledge. What Weber (1958) says on the spirit of capitalism is integrated into historical and sociopolitical knowledge; many plausible psychological and sociopsychological observations were made by Weber that were compatible with his hypotheses. Counter-arguments were discussed. True, Weber's justifications are mainly conceptual, and facts are used to exemplify rather than to prove, but his ideas led to many systematic comparisons, and to a better understanding of economic development. This better understanding, in turn, shed light on some of Weber's ideas.

SCIENTIFIC CREATIVITY

One could object to Bunge that ideas cannot be dissociated from their creation, e.g., that an extravagant hypothesis, even an apparently pseudoscientific one, may be seminal and lead to sound scientific hypotheses. Bunge could argue that this objection deals with scientific creativity—the fact that an individual is led to create a new plausible hypothesis from a pseudoscientific one is a psychological fact, and has nothing to do with the distinction between protoscience and pseudoscience. To follow Bunge's idea, if today's parapsychology leads some creative researchers to new ideas that will be considered tomorrow as the beginnings of a new scientific field, it would not mean that today's parapsychology is a protoscience. Yet, even if one can agree with Bunge's objection, this example suggests that the distinction between pseudoscience and protoscience, which Bunge wishes to be clear-cut, blurs when considering the growth of science in its heuristic aspects. It is difficult to distinguish in advance—at least for some time—a radically new idea that will later be integrated into a well-accepted theory from an idea that will not. Of course, in disciplines built upon a well-established base of knowledge, as in the natural sciences, it is easy to recognize hypotheses which are not integrated in the knowledge base. In the social sciences, not to speak of humanities, such recognition is more difficult, and often does not even make sense. Since these whole fields are less integrated than the natural sciences, it is more difficult to distinguish a hypothesis which is well integrated (into a loosely integrated background knowledge) from one which is not. Due to this lack of systemization, hypotheses are more likely to seem radically new. It is thus more difficult to distinguish science from pseudoscience; or rather, this distinction is of lesser interest.

Such a situation leaves social sciences with a need for heuristic methods, a need which makes room for interpretive approaches. It is a fact that not only in humanities but also in the social sciences, a new hypothesis is sometimes found through a process of interpretation of certain individuals, where the speculating social scientist tries to imagine what these individuals are feeling and thinking. Of course, such interpretation is based on her observations and is intended to be plausible. In other words, the production of hypotheses is often made through a process of systematized interpretation, where subjective ideas are reasoned. In other words, interpretation rarely comes alone.

Thus, novelty in social sciences does not result only from such an attempt to capture personal meaning. The depth of a hypothesis is not proportional to the interpreter's ability to enter into someone else's mind. Meaning is also given by the organization of knowledge itself, via hypothetico-deductive systems. There is a double aspect of meaning, linked to the distinction between *erklären* (explaining) and *verstehen* (comprehending).

EXPLAINING AND COMPREHENDING

Sociologists often believe that in order to understand someone, one has to be able to stand in this someone's shoes. Even more, they maintain that any piece of knowledge that would not be based on this operation of changing shoes would be empty and meaningless. For example, Boudon (1979, 259) claims, following Weber's methodology, that "sociologists deal with a category of phenomena, actions, which cannot be found in the observation field of physicists or chemists. Essentially, the notion of action implies the fundamental phenomenon of *empathy* between observer and observed. Consequently, the work of sociologists has no equivalent in natural sciences" (my translation).

Yet, although this kind of meaning for the sociologist guides his questioning, it cannot by itself justify or corroborate any hypothesis. Following Meyer (1979), the context of discovery has to be distinguished from the context of justification. Discovery requires psychological qualities such as imagination, intuition, flair, possibly empathy, whereas justification asks primarily for rigor and honesty. If indeed we do sometimes make sense of the social world *via* some sort of empathy, this sense-making is linked to the heuristic aspect of knowledge, and remains attached to a rather subjective and egocentric—although possibly reasoned—point of view.

Two points should be made here. First, as we have seen, the context of discovery—or rather of heuristics—does not boil down to empathy. Second, empathy is not the only way, nor is it the most important way, of making sense of the social world. Outside this subjective sense, made out of personal connotations of a social phenomenon, there is also a sense given by its structure, or its internal organization. This sense is brought about by explanation.

As Boudon and many others think, there is indeed something specific to the social sciences and humanities, namely a tendency to produce immediate, non-systematic, interpretation of others' (and ones own's) actions. Interpretations, when they interact, lead to specularity (mirror interpretation)—another feature of social sciences and humanities. Yet, as argued here, such subjective aspects, even if they make social sciences and humanities particularly rich and interesting, do not lead by themselves to well-integrated and well-corroborated hypotheses.

The distinction between heuristic and justificatory aspects of explanations can lead to further separate humanities and social sciences, or else to tie them closer together. They can be separated by emphasizing the importance of subjective heuristics and the lack of justifications within humanities in contrast to social sciences, or the two groups of disciplines can be tied together by insisting on heuristic interchanges between them.

ETHICAL RULES

Insisting on interchanges and on the importance of heuristics, as I have done here, leads to the problem of distinguishing good and bad heuristics—sound and unsound speculation—which is a problem with ethical scope. Whereas justificatory activities request rigor and a good command of methods and procedures, the responsible creation of new hypotheses demands qualities such as curiosity, a deep and insightful understanding of the subject, and possibly an interest in neighboring fields. Yet such qualities can lead to the creation of uninteresting, exceedingly metaphorical, crazy, or even dangerous hypotheses. Some rules must be added to avoid the production of such hypotheses. The only attempt I know to bring such rules into notice is due to Bunge (1983, 267–270). He views his rules as tacit regulative principles guiding the planning and execution of research. They are both ethical and methodological. I will mention just some of them:

- Do not just accumulate data for the sake of increasing the volume of information: Look for patterns.
- Do not just accumulate hypotheses: Try to organize them into theories (hypothetico-deductive systems).
- Do not let the available techniques dictate all of your problems: If necessary try new techniques or even whole new approaches.
- Do not commit yourself before checking: First get to know, then believe—and doubt.
- Do not try to be totally self-reliant in matters of knowledge: Ask others for information, advice, or help—but feel free not to make use of either.
- Shun ideology in basic science but watch for it everywhere, and declare frankly your social values in applied science and technology, particularly in social technology.

Obviously, such rules are not sufficient; they can be considered as factual trends (it is a fact that good researchers do not just accumulate data, etc.), or as advice for young researchers. They suggest how to be a good and honest scientist. If I mention Bunge's attempt here, it is in the hope that its clarity and suggestive power will lead to further work. In particular, similarities and differences between rules for the social sciences and rules for humanities should be further analyzed.

Although Bunge's heuristic rules are not really unexpected, it is interesting to disclose them. It helps to understand how research is rooted in ethics, and, probing deeper, how ethics are rooted in the social world. Ignoring such rules would lead us, at the least, to reinvent them.

REFERENCES

Blitz, D. 1991, "The Line of Demarcation Between Science and Nonscience: The Case of Psychoanalysis and Parapsychology," in: *New Ideas in Psychology*, 9, 163–170.

Boudon, R. 1979, *La logique du social*, Paris, Hachette.

Bunge, M. 1983, *Treatise of Basic Philosophy, Vol. 6: Understanding the World*, Dordrecht, D. Reidel.

Bunge, M. 1991, "A Skeptic's Beliefs and Disbeliefs," in: *New Ideas in Psychology*, 9, 131–149.

Carnap, R. 1969, *The Logical Structure of the World and Pseudoproblems in Philosophy*, Berkeley, University of California Press (Originally published in 1928).

Mayntz, R. 1992, "The Influence of Natural Science Theories on Contemporary Social Science," in: Dierkes, M. & Bievert, B. (eds.), *European Social Science in Transition*, Frankfurt, Campus Verlag.

Meyer, M. 1979, *Découverte et justification en science*, Paris, Kleinsieck.

Moessinger, P. 1996, *Irrationalité individuelle et ordre social*, Genève, Droz.

Piaget, J. 1927, *Le jugement et la pensée chez l'enfant*, Neuchâtel, Delachaux et Niestlé.

Popper, K. 1963, *Conjectures and Refutations: The Growth of Scientific Knowledge*, New York, Harper (Originally published in 1955).

Weber, M. 1958, *The Protestant Ethic and the Spirit of Capitalism*, New York, Scribner.

EPILOGUE

Ethical Responsibility of Academics as Educators and Scientists:
Beating the "Status Quo Machine"

KNUT HAMMARSKJÖLD

Before exploring the above enigmatic subject, I would like to confront you with three unconnected quotes which, however, help me to get into *medias res* without lengthy introduction:

"Air transportation, along with modern communications, has transformed this vast globe, almost in a single generation, into a small world."[1] This was in 1961. Since then "progress", especially in data processed transborder communications—the marriage between computers and telecommunications—has of course been exponential.

"There is nothing more difficult to plan, more doubtful of success, nor more dangerous to manage than the creation of a new system; for the initiator has the enmity of those who would profit by the preservation of the old system and merely lukewarm defenders in those who would gain from the new system."[2]

"Change is a condition for survival." The latest advances of biotechnology allow us to see how bacteria actively build and transmit drug resistance genes as defenses against multiple 'agression' by antibiotics—i.e., a running battle of change and mutation—for survival.

GLOBALIZATION AND FRAGMENTATIONS:
A CONTRADICTORY FACT TO OVERCOME

In this short text, I wish to try to situate some of the dilemmas being faced by academia (and academics) with respect to freedom and responsibility in a larger—in particular, a global—context and reality.

281

In a recent book, Harlan Cleveland[3] coined the expression "status quo machine"[4] for the system(s) of governance put in place by our "leaders" during the present century in order to cope with the situations and problems created by two disastrous world wars. Systems of governance without built-in automatic procedures for review and evolution were a matter of routine *normal* world housekeeping. Over the last forty plus years, as new situations and problems arose, new intergovernmental institutions and agencies were created side by side or partly on top of those already existing—not necessarily coordinated in action or responsibilities—resulting in a maze of such international organizations, now I believe on the order of sixty altogether. They reflect the traditional approaches and structures of governments of nation states and thus lack overall vision or awareness of the global context in which they must operate. They are unavoidably often competing with and duplicating each other.

This, taken together with the notorious petrification, overstaffing, and over-bureaucratization of these large multinational and multicultural organizations accountable to their shareholders—the peoples of the world—only indirectly via their governments, results in an enormous waste of human, financial, and material resources. Regrettably, but perhaps understandably, participation in all facets of international governance is to many of these governments a symbol of statehood and sovereignty, not a duty and service to the peoples of the world. To some of them, this participation is also a means of promoting national policies, even in areas of global interest that clearly should be non-political, such as public health, the battle against endemic diseases, and the promotion of ethics.

The world scenario has been radically affected by the breakdown of political, physical, and conceptual realities of the Communist system in Eastern Europe, the destruction of the Berlin Wall, the uncovering of fundamental social problems previously suppressed, and the unleashing of human aspirations. This led to the political fragmentation of the former Soviet Union, Yugoslavia, and Czechoslovakia. Moreover tendencies toward fragmentation are of course not entirely new—such tendencies even raise their heads in North America and Western Europe—but we have, in our times at least, never experienced them with the force or scope of a political, social, and economic earthquake of this magnitude. We were and still are unprepared. We were prepared for war to the point of overkill; but as the lids blew off the authoritarian pressure cookers, neither we nor they were prepared for the resulting fragmentation of political systems. Nobody was prepared, nationally or internationally, and probably few are now prepared for the (counter) revolution(s) of disappointment that might very well occur as a natural psychological result of this lack of preparedness and historical insight.

Why is this so? There is a clear tendency among many, if not most, of our political, industrial, and business leaders to allow decisions to be dictated by narrow conveniences such as the next election or the next quarter bottom line. Many, including even the most powerful, also seem to be convinced that once their aims have been achieved the world will not continue to change: *vide* Hitler's 1,000-year Reich and Stalin's conviction that by 1975 the industrial production of the USSR would surpass that of the USA. Now this, as we know all too well, is just not the case; the world around us is in a state of constant evolution and that world is now a global scenario.

In this context, it is interesting to note the evolution of units of governance. Since the appearance of humans on earth hundreds of thousands of years ago, we have moved from the family via the village, the tribe, and so on to the nation state and, most recently, to federations or communities of nation states. Now we face the urgent need for a new, broader, more acceptable concept of global governance offering hope of integrative cooperation on major issues while allowing for local diversity and initiative. At the same time we are reaching out into our unknown galactic environment—as if guided by the visionary intuition of Swedish sailor poet Harry Martinsson[5] some sixty years ago, in his epic poem "Aniara" in which he foresaw the need to evacuate "Spaceship Earth" (an expression coined by the renowned economist Dame Barbara Ward) because of over-population and environmental contamination. This is a perspective requiring an even wider dimension of governance; indeed one anticipated to some extent by those who have initiated an approach to an extra-terrestrial legal framework through space law.

It may be useful to try to measure the magnitude of an increasing fragmentation of "empires" and nation states. According to Paul Kennedy[6] almost three times as many states existed in the early 1990s as there had been sixty years earlier. The gradual evolution from family governance to globalization has been made possible and indeed necessary by technological evolution from fire through the sail, the wheel, steam power, and electricity to the achievements of our own generation: in particular, technological advances in transportation and communications. Almost any point on the globe can now be physically reached within a matter of hours and contacted by telecommunications within a matter of seconds. Our global physical framework is like a drop of liquid within which innumerable individual units live their interdependent and independent existences. The surface tension of the drop of liquid is essential to prevent the live content from spilling out and perishing. This surface tension has both physical (e.g., the ozone layer) and conceptual components. Global governance is part of this conceptual surface tension, necessary to maintain the many individual "particles" from perishing or destroying each other, but which is also sensitive to the internal system of complex relationships and builds upon their dynamics.

THE NEED FOR RULES OF GOVERNANCE AT THE "FRAGMENTED LEVEL" AS WELL AS AT THE "WORLD LEVEL"

We are thus faced with the need both for rules and structures of governance at the "fragmented level" which respect and are responsive to persons' cultural, traditional, and survival demands, and for rules and structures of governance at the "world level" to deal with matters of overriding global concern in this increasingly interdependent world. Many of these problems were anticipated and indeed addressed at the conferences in San Francisco, Chicago, Bretton Woods, Havana, *et al.*, during and immediately after World War II, where the powers of the day tried to put together the post-war governance of a world partly in ruin and chaos. They did this on the assumption that the major nation states could be in control and that single-purpose centralized international agencies could exercise that control under the direction of those major players. In fact, as Harlan Cleveland says, "nobody is in control." Passage of time has produced new problems and conflicts with their global consequences and these—as mentioned earlier—have been coped with on a case by case basis as they arose with a patchwork of new institutions and agencies; a costly time and resource-consuming apparatus—a *LEGO* construction—for world governance. Today this system is fighting desperately to cope with urgent and recent surprise situations and problems for which it was neither financed nor structured to cope. Sometimes this status quo machine seems doomed to come to a grinding halt. Like any human being, the post-war grand design is experiencing a mid-life crisis because the premises under which it was conceived and created biased its future toward Harlan Cleveland's status quo machine. Efforts are in hand in several quarters to revitalize, restructure, and reinforce this "machine"—in short, to create a flexible global governance framework responding to the present needs and adaptable to anticipated future requirements. This is a gigantic task, requiring foresight, wisdom, and sacrifices of national sovereignty and, most probably, of personal standards and conveniences. The target date for the new vision and at least the main elements of the new global governance framework should be 1995—the 50th anniversary of San Francisco and the UN Charter.

What are the present and anticipated future areas of a *global* nature that require attention, and whose responsibility go beyond and put into context the traditional United Nations functions of peace-keeping and simply monitoring social and economic development? Some of these issues are clearly manifest today and are being dealt with, somehow. Others are also manifest but are not being properly dealt with for reasons of vested interests, cultural taboos, or political convenience. Still others are just now manifesting themselves or can be intelligently anticipated. Without any pretense of being complete, I limit myself to enumerating four main clusters or areas of concern: the environment; biotechnology; mass- and mini-migration; and cultural conflict and warfare. These clusters are all multi-faceted and complex, and in their turn in one way or another potentially interactive or interdependent. Underneath looms the specter of an exponential population growth for which, since Malthus, the classic and successful remedies have been migration and revolutionary improvements in agricultural production and industrial technology.[7] At the same time the normative superstructure of the fragments in the form of religions or quasi-religions (e.g., some political ideologies)—the human invented "carrot and stick" combination of emotional, intellectual, spiritual, and sometimes physical elements of the "enforcement umbrella"—is giving way to an increasingly secular world. It may not be just coincidence that in an increasing number of disciplines and activities (medicine, law, business, politics to mention just a few) the quest for ethics as one important parameter is making itself felt. Here we can note that ethics is a common element of the traditional religions and also originally of some political ideologies.

Taking all these elements together we could imagine a delicately balanced rhomboid of mutual dependencies, influences, political remedies, and supports. The rhomboid represents important forces and evolutionary factors of our world society. If their mutual equilibrium and balance are not secured, our society will shatter. We remember the comparable balance in Buckminster Fuller's tetrahedron with its dynamic "tensegrity," the essential component of the geodesic dome. The rhomboid might look like this:

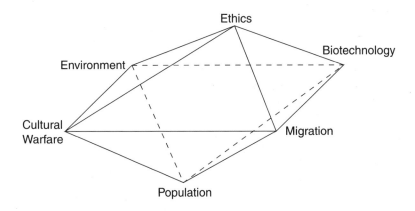

It is interesting to consider some of the traditional peace-monitoring, peace-making, peace-keeping activities of existing global governance structures in light of this constellation of new issues and the words of Samuel Huntington of Harvard University. Huntington recently predicted that the fault lines of conflict in the future will not run along traditional economic or political boundaries but along the dividing or "fault lines" between the "territories" of different cultures and civilizations. These new fault lines are less and less clear and fixed than the traditional boundaries and, furthermore, the cultural, ethnic, and ideologic groups they contain often have multiple loyalties and connections. This, which was long known for a fact in Africa and the Middle East due to the deliberate actions of colonial powers, has now been unveiled with all possible clarity by the political and social earthquakes of recent years in Central and Eastern Europe.

TRANSNATIONAL CORPORATIONS AND NON-GOVERNMENTAL BODIES AS AVANT-GARDE OF GLOBAL POLICY

Before embarking on my final comments with regard to the roles and responsibilities of scientists and other thinkers, I would like to draw your attention to an additional, relatively recent phenomenon which contributes steadily and perhaps quietly to the transformation of the governance evolution: this is the increasing role, power, and responsibility of non-governmental bodies and transnational corporations.

The importance of the transnationals was stressed very recently in a United Nations report highlighting their crucial role in global investment, financing, production, and distribution. This trend can of course be seen as a positive as well as a negative development. It is quite clear however that these organizations are in many respects far ahead of governments in creating rational and well-functioning global structures and networks which simultaneously respect local laws and cultures.

As far as non-governmental bodies of weight and knowledge are concerned, it is obvious that their counsel on and participation in the organization of world affairs is increasingly solicited and welcomed. They often represent forces and opinions of the real world without which governments and intergovernmental organizations could not operate as effectively, a fact that even politicians and bureaucrats are coming to acknowledge and respect.

Indeed it is a fact that non-governmental "experts" who are not acting on behalf of any national governments have taken initiatives and contributed essentially to international cooperation on global problems. Harlan Cleveland mentions as outstanding results of such non-governmental initiatives and contributions the *Stockholm Declaration on the Human Environment* (Aspen Institute) and the *Law of the Sea Treaty* (Law of the Sea Institute, Honolulu, Hawaii). There are and will be many more such nongovernmental initiatives. For instance, the Montréal-based International Institute for Peace through Tourism (IIPT) has developed a national *Code of Ethics and Guidelines for Sustainable Tourism* which has been adopted by the Canadian tourism industry. The Institute is currently working with the United Nations Environment Program (UNEP) with the aim of developing international guidelines for sustainable tourism in collaboration with major international travel and tourism organizations.

"ACADEMIC OF ALL NATIONS" TO SERVE AS SHERPAS

If we look again at our rhomboid, and agree that its delicately balanced elements are—or should be—both dependent and supportive of each other, we may wonder who can and who will take on the responsibility of mastering common sense global governance of such complex situations and problems. Neither the academic nor the bureaucratic worlds are known in general for their openmindedness when it comes to transdisciplinary and transborder problem analysis, solution, or administration. Some are now preaching transdisciplinary, transnational, and transcultural tolerance but are not yet demonstrating this tolerance themselves. This indicates that an essential ingredient and preparation for long-term solutions is education at all levels.

In a recent article entitled "Enlarging the Perspective"[8] Ernest L. Boyer of Princeton University quotes Mark van Doren thirty years ago: "The connectedness of things is what the educator contemplates to the limit of his capacity. No human capacity is great enough to permit a vision of the world as simple, but if the educator does not aim at the vision no one else will, and the consequences are dire when no one does." In the same article, Boyer himself states that, "today, more than at any time in recent memory, researchers find the need to move beyond traditional disciplinary boundaries, communicate with colleagues in other fields, and discover patterns that connect." He also adds that, "today, interdisciplinary and integrative studies, long on the edges of academic life, are moving toward the center, responding both to new intellectual questions and to *pressing human problems*." (Author's emphasis)

Early in his recent book, Harlan Cleveland declares—rightly so in my opinion—that "in the real world, the agenda for action consists mostly of interdisciplinary, interdepartmental, and interprofessional problems. Yet governments are not yet organized that way. Their policy-making tends to be bounded by artificial frontiers that survive from the history of rational thought (physics, biology, economics, anthropology), from the history of governments in simpler times ... and from historical professions (law, medicine, engineering)."[9]

The resulting essentially vertical organization is not viable anymore either nationally or internationally. We need a new concept at all levels: one that is capable of cutting through the barriers that prevent the handling of problems across disciplines and bureaucracies, and that encourages transdisciplinary education, training at all levels, staff work, and decision making. There is also the need for recursiveness among organizations at all levels so that they can communicate meaningfully up and down and horizontally in an interdependent world. In the new world, the leaders should have a 'renaissance' *and* specialized education, with training on how to integrate these, and openness to the multifaceted aspects of their responsibilities.

Academics have enjoyed and still enjoy—at least in what we call the free world—the enviable privilege of largely unfettered latitude both in their work and in their thinking. They should be aware—in whatever discipline they are active—that the world is changing radically and dramatically, requiring their contributions across disciplinary, hierarchical, and other traditional boundaries for the solution of problems which need the participation of persons of good will and intelligence. They should actively help to address these "real-life problems." Traditional academic discussions do not require solutions and can be left open-ended. Real life problems—especially those of the future—require analysis, negotiation, compromise if necessary, and solution.

I would like to end with two illustrations. The first deals with the relativity of science, and is very *apropos* to one of the prime tools that has led to our present one world situation. One hundred years ago, Lord Kelvin, a famous mathematician and physicist and president of the British Royal Society, stated publicly with all the authority of his academic position that: "Heavier-than-air flying machines are impossible."

As a second illustration, I would like to introduce the metaphor of the Sherpas. The Sherpas are Nepalese mountain guides without whose experience, physical and intellectual strength, and stamina, 'earthlings' from other parts of the world who aim for the summits of the Himalayas would not be able to reach their goal. This notion of Sherpas has been transposed to the selected bureaucrats who have the responsibility—individually and in cooperation—of preparing for and, if possible, making a success of, the summit meetings of the G-7 nations. Daring a travesty on a Communist credo, I believe it is the task and the responsibility of academics of all nations to unite as Sherpas, contributing across national and academic boundaries toward the solution of the present and emerging problems of "Spaceship Earth."

POSTSCRIPT ON THE "ÉTHIQUE SUR-NATIONALE"

Only a few days after having sent in the above text to the Academy, I read in my hotel room in Pretoria in the small hours of a sleepless, jet-lagged night the recently published correspondence[10] between then Secretary-General of the UN, Dag Hammarskjöld and French poet Saint-John Perse (a senior French diplomat whose real name was Alexis Léger, winner of the Nobel Prize in Literature, 1960). The expression "éthique sur-nationale" was used by Perse in a letter to Hammarskjöld dated 15 June 1958 and refers to an address entitled "The Walls of Distrust," delivered by Hammarskjöld at Cambridge University on 5 June 1958. In his letter, Perse comments that, "depuis que l'ONU a trouvé sa fin en elle-même, dans l'universalité, il faut bien se dire, avec quelque réalisme, qu'elle ne relève plus en fait du pragmatisme des hommes d'Etat, mais d'une éthique sur-nationale en cours d'élucidation et d'imposition éventuelle." In his preface to the book, Arthur Knodel, Professor of English Literature, Los Angeles, comments: "Ethique que ces deux diplomates rompus au métier savaient d'une réalisation presque impossible, mais, à longue échéance, indispensable à la survie d'un monde civilisé."

We should be grateful that the impossibility was qualified by "presque" because thirty-five years later, our survival is even more tenuous.

NOTES AND REFERENCES

1. *Project Horizon* 1961, *US Government Policy Statement on International Aviation.*
2. Niccolò Machiavelli, 1469–1527.
3. Cleveland, Harlan 1993, *Birth of a New World. An Open Moment for International Leadership*, San Francisco, Jossey-Bass, Inc.
4. In the opposite (too active) sense, but still derogatory, during the North African Crisis General de Gaulle (1958, Tunis-Bizerte) used the expression "le machin about the UN."
5. 1974 Nobel prize in Literature.
6. Kennedy, Paul 1993, *Preparing for the Twenty-first Century*, London, Harper Collins Publishers Ltd., 12.
7. But how much room is left in these directions to cope with a world population of 10 billion by the year 2050 or even earlier?
8. Published in Bulger, Ruth E., Heitman, Elizabeth, Resier, Stanley J. (eds.), *The Ethical Dimensions of the Biological Sciences*, Cambridge-New York, Cambridge University Press 1993.
9. Cleveland 1993, 34.
10. Paris: Gallimard 1993.

Notes on Contributors

REGINALD FRASER AMONOO, D.U.P., is Professor of French Literature at the Department of Modern Languages at the University of Zimbabwe. His research and teaching concentrate on the theater of Pierre Corneille, French Drama from the XVIIth to the XIXth century, French Philosophy (Montaigne, Descartes, Pascal, and Voltaire), translation into and from French, and language problems in Ghana. *Main publications: Language and Nationhood: Reflections on Language Situations with Particular Reference to Ghana*, 1986; "Corneille et les Romantiques," in *Acts of the Rouen Symposium on Corneille*, 1985; "Higher Education in Ghana," in *Encyclopaedia of Higher Education*, Oxford 1992. Other articles focus on aspects of Corneille and on language problems of higher education. *Address*: Department of Modern Languages, University of Zimbabwe, P.O. Box MP 167, Mount Pleasant, Harare, Zimbabwe. *Telephone*: +263–4 303 211. *Fax*: +263–4 333 407/335 249.

GÉRALD BERTHOUD, Ph.D., is Professor of Anthropology at the Institute of Anthropology and Sociology, University of Lausanne. He has been Research Associate at the University of California (Berkeley) and Professor at the University of Montreal. His field research has been mainly in Switzerland, Nigeria, and Niger. His main interests focus on the anthropology and sociology of sciences and techniques, and more generally on social theory. Present research is concentrated on "social links, machines, and technical networks," and "The Gift in a Maussian Perspective: A Theoretical Contribution on Human Sociality." *Main publications: Plaidoyer pour l'Autre. Essais d'anthropologie critique*, Genève 1982; *Vers une anthropologie générale: modernité et altérité*, Genève 1992; *Pratiques sociales et théories: Les discordes des universitaires* (with G. Busino), Genève 1995. He is a frequent contributor to *La revue du M.A.U.S.S.* (Paris) and *Revue européenne des sciences sociales* (Genève). *Address:* Institut d'Anthropologie et de Sociologie, Université de Lausanne, BFSH 2, 1015 Lausanne, Switzerland. *Telephone:* +41–21 692 31 80. *Fax:* +41–21 692 31 85.

THOMAS J. BOLE, III, Ph.D. (philosophy) Ph.D. (classics), is a permanent Fellow at St. Anne Institute, Tulsa, Oklahoma, and is currently visiting in the Department of Philosophy, Brigham Young University, Provo, Utah. His publications are in the areas of: Hegel studies, classics with special emphasis on Neoplatonist commentators of Aristotle, and bioethics. *Main publications: Rights to Health Care* (co-editor), Dordrecht 1991; *Hegel: A Post-Modern Reappraisal*, Dordrecht 1996. *Address:* St. Anne Institute, 550 South Columbia Ave., Tulsa, OK 74101, USA. *Telephone:* (918) 584–7300. *Fax:* (918) 252–2477.

BEAT BÜRGENMEIER, Dr. Oec., has been Professor of Economic Policy at the University of Genève since 1982. He was a Postdoctoral Fellow at M.I.T. in 1978. His research focuses on socio-economics and economic policy. *Main publications: Théorie et pratique des investissements suisses à l'étranger,* Genève 1981; *Fiscalité et investissement privé en Suisse,* Genève 1986; *Socio-economics: An Interdisciplinary Approach. Ethics, Institutions, and Markets,* Boston-Dordrecht-London 1992 (translated from French: 1990; German transl.: 1994); *Analyse et politique économiques,* 1984 (^{4}1992); *La Socio-Economie,* Paris 1994; *Editor: Main d'oeuvre étrangère: Une analyse de l'économie suisse,* Paris 1992; *Economy, Environment, and Technology: A Socioeconomic Approach,* Armon 1994. *Address:* Département d'Economie Politique, FSES, Université de Genève, 102 Blvd. Carl-Vogt, 1211 Genève 4, Switzerland. *Telephone:* +41–22 705 81 11. *Fax:* +41–22 781 41 00.

MAHDI ELMANDJRA graduated from Cornell (USA) and obtained his Ph.D. (economics) from the London School of Economics. He has taught international relations at the University of Rabat since 1958. He was Director General of the Moroccan Broadcasting Service and Counselor of the Moroccan Mission to the United Nations. He performed various functions in the UN System (1961 to 1981), including that of Assistant Director General of UNESCO for Social Sciences, Human Sciences, and Culture, and Coordinator of the Conference on Technical Cooperation between developing countries (UNDP). He was President of the World Future Studies Federation and of Futuribles International (Paris), as well as the Founding President of the Moroccan Association of Future Studies and the Moroccan Organization of Human Rights. He is a member of the African Academy of Sciences and of the Academy of the Kingdom of Morocco. He has published articles in the fields of the human and social sciences. He is a co-author of "No Limits to Learning" (Report to the Club of Rome, 1979), and the author of several books. Main publications: *The United Nations System*, 1973; *Maghreb et Francophonie*, 1988; *Première Guerre Civilisationnelle*, 1991; *Retrospective des Futurs*, 1992; *Nord-Sud: Prélude a l'Ere Postcoloniale*, 1993; *Cultural Diversity: Key to Survival in the Future*, 1995. Professor Elmandjra received the Prix de la Vie Economique 1981 (France) and the Award of World Future Studies Federation in 1995. *Address:* B.P. 53, Rabat, Morocco. *Telephone:* +212-7 774 258. *Fax:* +212–7 757 151.

Hugo Tristram Engelhardt, Jr., Ph.D., M.D., has been Professor in the Department of Medicine, as well as in the Departments of Community Medicine and Obstetrics and Gynecology, at Baylor College of Medicine in Houston since 1983. He is also Professor in the Department of Philosophy, Rice University, and a member of the Center for Medical Ethics and Health Policy at Baylor College of Medicine. He is the author of numerous publications and the editor of over two dozen volumes. His publications are primarily in the fields of biomedical ethics, health care policy, the history of medicine, and moral theory. He is editor of the *Journal of Medicine and Philosophy* and co-editor of *Christian Bioethics*. He is also co-editor of the book series *Philosophy and Medicine* and *Clinical Medical Ethics*. He is editor of the book series *Philosophical Studies in Contemporary Culture*. Main publications: *Mind-Body: A Categorical Relation*, The Hague 1973; *Bioethics and Secular Humanism: The Search for a Common Morality*, London 1991; *The Foundations of Bioethics*, 2nd ed., New York 1996. *Address:* Center for Medical Ethics, Baylor College of Medicine, One Baylor Plaza, Houston, Texas 77030, USA. *Telephone:* (713) 798–3509. *Fax:* (713) 798–5678.

Gabriel Gosselin, Ph.D., is Professor of Sociology at the University of Sciences and Technologies in Lille (France). He is author of numerous publications on tradition, social change, and progress, especially in Africa. His research focuses on interpretation in sociology and new developments of ethics and ethnicity in post-secular multi-cultural societies. *Main publications: Développement et tradition dans les sociétés rurales africaines*, Genève 1970; *Travail et changement social en pays Gbeya*, Paris 1972; *Formation et stratégie de transition en Afrique tropicale*, 2 vols., Lille 1973; *L'Afrique désenchantée*, 2 vols., Paris 1978–1980;

Changer le progrès, Paris 1979; *Une éthique des sciences sociales: la limite et l'urgence*, Paris 1992. He is also editor of numerous publications on anthropology and the social sciences. *Address:* Institut de Sociologie, Université des Sciences et Technologies de Lille, 59655 Villeneuve d'ASCQ Cedex, France. *Telephone:* +33–20 43 45 96. *Fax:* +33–20 43 66 55.

HEINZ GUTSCHER, Ph.D., is Professor of Social Psychology at the University of Zürich. His research includes experimental development of measuring procedures of self-awareness and topics in environmental psychology. He has also written several publications on the health environment and environmental psychology. *Main publications: Status-inkonsistenztheorie: Kritik und Ansatz einer Neuorientierung*, Zürich 1976; "Verhalten unter Belastung—Wege in die Selbst-gefährdung. Eine sozialpsychologische Analyse," in: Braun, H.-J. (ed.) *Selbstzer-störung, Suizid*, Zürich 1985; "Spezifische Probleme und Risiken des Medikationsverhaltens," in: Gutscher, Hornung, May, Schär (eds.), *Medikamentenkonsum und Medikationsrisiken*, Bern 1986; "Medikationsrisiken uns sozialpsychologische Aspekte des Risiko-bewusstseins," in *Sozial- und Präventivmedizin* 31, 1986; "Suicide: Beyond the Regulation of Emotion," in: Möller, Schmidtke, Welz (eds.), *Current Issues in Suicidology*, Berlin 1988; co-author with R. Hornung "Gesundheitspsychologie: Die sozialpsychologische Perspektive," in: Schwenkmezger and Schmidt (eds.), *Lehrbuch der Gesundheits-psychologie*, Stuttgart 1994. *Address:* Institute of Psychology, Department of Social Psychology, University of Zürich, Plattenstrasse 14, 8032 Zürich, Switzerland. *Telephone:* +41–1 257 21 10. *Fax:* +41–1 262 34 49.

KNUT O. HAMMARSKJÖLD, Fil.Kand., has been Chairman/C.E.O. at the Atwater Institute, Montreal, since 1985, is chairman of the Independent Commission for Reform of UNESCO Secretariat, and has served as Ambassador of UNESCO. He entered Foreign Service in 1946, served in Paris, Vienna, Moscow, Bucharest, Kabul, and Sofia from 1947 to 1955. From 1955 to 1957 he was First Secretary of the Foreign Office, and from 1957 to 1959 Head of the Foreign Relations Department of the Royal Board of Civil Aviation, Stockholm. Deputy Head of the Swedish Delegation to OEEC, Paris, (1959–1960), Deputy Secretary General of EFTA (1960–1966), he was Minister Plenipotentiary and Director general of IATA in Montreal and Geneva between 1966 and 1984, and from 1981 to 1984 was Chairman of the Executive Committee. His research focuses mainly on evolution of international governance, the national and international changes connected with the transition from an industrial to an information society, and the enhanced role of non-governmental elements and interests in society. *Publications:* articles on political, economic, and aviation topics. *Address:* Atwater Institute, 1625 de Maisonneuve Blvd. West, Suite PH-210, Montréal, Québec, Canada H3H 2N4. *Telephone:* (514) 931– 2319. *Fax:* (514) 931–3165.

HANSPETER KRIESI, Ph.D., is Professor of Political Science at the University of Genève. His research and teaching are in the fields of Swiss and comparative politics, new social movements in Western Europe, and collective political action. *Main publications: Entscheidungsstrukturen und Entscheidungsprozesse in der Schweizer Politik*, Frankfurt/M.-New York 1980; *Politische Aktivierung in der Schweiz 1945–1978*, Diessenhofen 1981; editor of *Bewegung in der Schweizer Politik*, Frankfurt/M. 1985; *Political Mobilization and Social Change: The Dutch Case in Comparative Perspective*, Aldershot 1993; *Les démocraties occidentales: une approche comparée*, Paris 1994; *Le systeme politique suisse*, Paris 1995; co-author with R. Koopmaus, J.W. Duyvendak, and M.G. Giugni of *New Social Movements in Western Europe*, Minneapolis 1995. *Address:* Département de Science Politique, FSES, Université de Genève, 102 Blvd. Carl-Vogt, 1211 Genève 4, Switzerland. *Telephone:* +41–22 705 8381. *Fax:* +41–22 781 8364.

RUDOLF PRINZ ZUR LIPPE, Ph.D., Dipl.rer.pol., disciple of Karlfried Graf Dürckheim since 1960, is Professor of social philosophy and aesthetics at the University of Oldenburg. In 1969 he started his philosophical investigation into the modern history of the human body with Theodor W. Adorno. A former fellow of the Wissenschaftskolleg in Berlin, he is the spiritus rector of the Karl Jaspers Lectures on "Matters of Our Time." In 1982 he founded the Institute for Practical Anthropology through which he staged a scientific exposition on "Geometrising Man." The exposition has been shown in numerous countries all over the world. His work mainly concerns social philosophy, aesthetics, applied cultural anthropology, philosophy of the body, and education. *Main publications: Naturbeherrschung am Menschen*, 2nd ed. Frankfurt /M. 1981; *Am eigenen Leibe: Zur Oekonomie des Lebens*, 3rd ed. Frankfurt/M. 1983; *Entfaltung der Sinne: Ein Erfahrungsfeld*, 15th ed. Frankfurt/M. 1995 (with H. Kükelhaus); *Sinnesbewusstsein: Grundlegung einer anthropologischen Aesthetik*, 1987; *Freiheit die wir meinen*, 1991. Further articles concerning the subject in discussion: *Anthropologie für wen?*, 1976; *Einige anthropologische Prämissen und ihre Konsequenzen in politischen Theorien*, 1984; *Praxis und Bewusstsein in der Neuzeit*, 1985. *Address:* Fachbereich Philosophie (5), Universität Oldenburg, Ammerländer

Heerstrasse 67–99, Postfach 2503, 26129 Oldenburg, Germany. *Telephone:* +49–44 177 71 92. *Fax:* +49–44 1 51 68.

CAROLA MEIER-SEETHALER, Ph.D., Philosophy and Psychology, is working as a psychotherapist in Bern. *Main publication: Ursprünge und Befreiungen: Eine dissidente Kulturtheorie,* Zürich 1988. *Address:* Moserstrasse 42, 3014 Bern, Switzerland. *Telephone/Fax:* +41–31 331 08 47.

PIERRE MOESSINGER is Professor at the Department of Sociology of the University of Genève. Former collaborator of Piaget at the Geneva Center of Epistemology, founder and first editor of *New Ideas in Psychology,* his main interests deal with the foundations of social sciences. *Recent books: La psychologie morale,* Paris 1989; *Les fondements de l'organisation,* Paris 1991; *Irrationalité individuelle et ordre social,* Genève 1996. *Address:* Rue des Maraîchers 46, 1205 Genève, Switzerland. *Telephone:* +41–22 328 85 91.

GRACIELA ARROYO PICHARDO, Ph.D., is Professor of Political Sciences, specializing in International Relations, at the Centro de Relaciones Internacionales, Universidad Nacional Autónoma de México. Her research and teaching mainly concern the methodology of international relations studies, East-European studies, and regional studies in general. She is working on: "Cultural Worlds, Global Processes, and International Relations." *Main publications: El estúdio científico de las relaciones internacionales,* 1978; *La evolución de las relaciones entre México y Rumania en el contexto internacional del siglo XX,* 1981; *Alfonso García Robles: Una biografía,* 1993. Her other articles deal with the disciplinary study of International Relations and with former socialist countries in Europe. Graciela Arroyo Pichardo is a member of the editorial staff of the monthly "Mexico Internacional." *Address:* Centro de Relaciones Internacionales, Facultad de Ciencias Políticas y Sociales, Universidad Nacional Autónoma de México, Ciudad Universitaria, C.P. 04510, México, D.F. *Telephone:* +52–5 622 94 13. *Fax:* +52–5 666 83 34.

PETER SALADIN, Dr.Jur., is Professor of Constitutional, Administrative, and Church Law and Director of the Seminar of Public Law at the University of Bern. He was Secretary General and Vice-President of the Swiss Council of Science and was a member of several Federal Expert Commissions, among which is the Commission for the Revision of the Swiss Federal Constitution. His research includes work on the theory of State and Law, human rights, federalism, democracy, and law of environmental protection. *Main publications: Der Widerruf von Verwaltungsakten,*

Basel 1960; *Grundrechte im Wandel,* 3rd ed., Bern 1982; *Das Verwaltungsverfahrensrecht des Bundes,* Bern 1979; *Verantwortung als Staatsprinzip,* Bern 1984; (with Christoph Zenger) *Rechte künftiger Generationen,* Basel-Stuttgart 1988; "Wozu noch Staaten? Zu den Funktionen eines modernen demokratischen Rechtsstaats in einer zunehmend überstaatlichten Welt," Bern/Müchen/Wien 1995. *Address:* Seminar für öffentliches Recht, Hochschulstrasse 4, 3012 Bern, Switzerland. *Telephone:* +41–31 631 88 96. *Fax:* +41–31 631 38 83.

MARTIN SCHAFFNER, Ph.D., is Professor of Modern European and Swiss History at the University of Basel (Switzerland). His research concerns mainly microhistorical approaches in history (historical anthropology), the mentally ill in the second half of the nineteenth century, and rural Ireland during the Great Famine. *Main publications: Die Basler Arbeiterbewegung im 19. Jahrhundert: Beiträge zur Geschichte ihrer Lebensformen,* Basel-Stuttgart 1972; *Die demokratische Bewegung der 1860er Jahre: Beschreibung und Erklärung der Zürcher Volksbewegung von 1867,* Basel-Stuttgart 1982; "Expertenbefragung: Der Landarbeiter Michael Sullivan vor der Kommission von Lord Devon, 10. September 1844," in: Degen et al. (eds.) *Fenster zur Geschichte,* Basel-Frankfurt/M. 1992; editor of *Brot, Brei und was dazugehört: Über sozialen Sinn und physiologischen Wert der Nahrung,* Zürich 1992. *Address:* Department of History, University of Basel, Hirschgässlein 21, 4051 Basel, Switzerland. *Telephone:* +41–61 271 08 35. *Fax:* +41–61 271 08 60.

BEAT SITTER-LIVER, Ph.D., is Secretary General of the Swiss Academy of Humanities and Social Sciences and of the Conference of the Swiss Scientific Academies. From 1975 through 1986 he was a member of the Swiss Science Council, and is today its permanent guest. He serves on several councils of foundations, among them the Swiss National Science Foundation. Visiting Professor at Munich University in 1986/87, he is currently teaching at the University of Fribourg. His research is mainly concerned with ethics, natural law theory, philosophy of nature, and philosophy of the humanities. *Main publications: Dasein und Ethik,* Fribourg-München 1975; *Die Geisteswissenschaften und ihre Bedeutung für unsere Zukunft,* Bern 1977. Among the books he edited are: *Scientists and their Responsibilities,* Canton MA 1989; *Widerstand im Rechtsstaat,* Fribourg 1988; *Wissenschaft in der Verantwortung,* Bern 1985; *Menschliches Verhalten,* Fribourg 1976. *Other recent publications: Wie lässt sich ökologische Gerechtigkeit denken?,* 1987; *Kulturwissenschaften für unsere Zukunft,* Lenzburg 1993; *Einheit aus der Viefalt,* Luzern 1994; *Skepsis als Praxis,* 1994. *Address:* Swiss Academy of Humanities and Social Sciences,

Hirschengraben 11, P.O. Box 8160, 3001 Bern, Switzerland. *Telephone:* +41–31 311 33 76. *Fax:* +41–31 311 91 64.

MARGARET A. SOMERVILLE holds professorships in both the Faculty of Law and the Faculty of Medicine at McGill University, Montreal. She is Gale Professor of Law (as such, she is the first woman in Canada to hold a named Chair in Law) and the Founding Director of the McGill Centre for Medicine, Ethics and Law. She has a background in science (pharmacy) as well as in law. Professor Somerville received the Order of Australia in 1989 and was elected a Fellow of the Royal Society of Canada in 1991. She has an extensive publishing and speaking record, and has consulted to governments and non-governmental bodies, in particular, to the Global Programme on AIDS of the World Health Organization, the United Nations Human Rights Secretariat in Geneva, and law reform commissions in Canada and Australia. She is currently the Chairperson of the National Research Council of Canada Ethics Committee, a member of the Board of Directors of the Canadian Centre for Drug-Free Sport, and a member of the American Society of Law, Medicine, and Ethics. Her work includes research on euthanasia, pain relief, reproductive technology, biotechnology, genetics, aging populations, quality of life, human rights in medicine and health care, the pharmaceutical industry, public health, health care systems, medical malpractice, human medical research, AIDS, abortion, and the allocation of medical resources. *Main publications: Consent to Medical Care,* Ottawa 1979; "Pain and Suffering at Interfaces of Medicine and Law," in *University of Toronto Law Journal* XXXVI, 1986; "The Song of Death: The Lyrics of Euthanasia," in *Journal of Contemporary Health Law Policy* 9, 1993. *Address:* McGill Centre for Medicine, Ethics and Law, 3690 Peel Street, Montréal, Québec, Canada H3A 1W9. *Telephone:* (514) 398–7401. *Fax:* (514) 398–4668.

DOMINIQUE SPRUMONT is Deputy Director of the Institute of Health Law, University of Neuchâtel, and Legal Advisor to the Intercantonal Office for the Control of Medicines, Bern. His main fields of interest are the ethics and regulation of biomedical research involving human subjects, the rights of patients, and the relation of law and ethics in regulating biomedical progress (organ transplant, human genetic analysis, and medically assisted procreation). *Main publications: La protection des sujets de recherche, notamment dans le domaine biomédical,* Bern 1993; *Le consentement éclairé du patient: comment briser le mur du silence?,* Sion 1994; *La transplantation d'organes: repères pour une législation fédérale,* Fribourg 1995; "De l'éthique au droit: la réglementation des recherches sur l'être humain dans l'ordre juridique suisse," in *Les cahiers médico-sociaux, 39, 1995. Address:* Institute of Health Law, University of Neuchâtel, Faubourg de l'Hôpital 106, 2000 Neuchâtel, Switzerland. *Telephone:* +41–38 21 16 50.

NEALE W. WATSON is President of Watson Publishing International and Science History Publications/USA. *Address:* Box 1390, Nantucket, MA 02554-1390, USA. *Telephone:* (508) 228–5490. *Fax:* (508) 228–7541.

CHARLES WIDMER, Ph.D., is Lecturer in anthropological ethics at the University of Lausanne. He also teaches philosophy at the Collège de Genève (Collège Rousseau and Collège pour Adultes). His research concentrates on ethics, particularly human rights, considered in an anthropological perspective. *Main publications: Dépossession,* Turin 1988; *Droits de l'Homme et Sciences de l'Homme, pour une éthique anthropologique,* Genève 1992. *Address:* 38, Ave. William-Favre, 1207 Genève, Switzerland. *Telephone:* +41-22 700 50 62.

Index of Names